FULL MARKS

CBSE

SCIENCE

(As per the latest CBSE Syllabus)

Jasvinder Kaur Randhawa
M.Sc, B.Ed
MIT's Vishwashanti Gurukul, Pune

Full Circle Education Pvt Ltd
(Progressive Educational Publishers)
Formerly
Full Marks Pvt Ltd
New Delhi-110002

Published by:

Full Circle Education Pvt Ltd

4238 A, 1-Ansari Road, Daryaganj, New Delhi-110002
Phone: 40556600 (100 Lines)
Fax: 40556688
Website: www.fullcircleeducation.in
E-mail: info@fcepl.in

Branches:

• Ahmedabad • Bengaluru • Chennai • Dehradun • Guwahati • Hyderabad • Jaipur • Kochi • Kolkata • Lucknow • Mumbai • Ranchi

NEW EDITION

Printed at:

Note from the Publishers

FULL MARKS Science-9 has been thoroughly revised and updated in view of recent examination reforms propounded by the CBSE.

The revised edition of this book is a complete support book based on NCERT textbook. This provides all sorts of study-cum-practice material and thus builds up strong confidence in the students. It is an up-to-date, dependable and friendly resource as per the guidelines of the CBSE.

Salient features of the book:

- Chapterwise important points have been given under the heading **Facts that Matter**.
- All **In-text Questions** have also been solved for better understanding.
- All NCERT textual Exercise questions have been solved.
- Plenty of additional questions have been given with solutions.
- At the end of each chapter, some questions have been given under the heading **Test Your Skills** to test the students what they have learnt.

The support website **www.fullcircleeducation.in** is an added benefit for the users where one can get much more and also an opportunity to share one's academic complexities.

SYLLABUS

Marks : 80

Unit No.	Unit	Marks
I	Matter - Its Nature and Behaviour	23
II	Organisation in the Living World	20
III	Motion, Force and Work	27
IV	Our Environment	06
V	Food; Food Production	04
	Total	80
	Internal assessment	20
	Grand Total	100

Note : Above weightage includes the weightage of questions based on practical skills.

THEME : MATERIALS

Unit I : Matter-Nature and Behaviour **(50 Periods)**

Definition of matter; solid, liquid and gas; characteristics - shape, volume, density; change of state-melting (absorption of heat), freezing, evaporation (cooling by evaporation), condensation, sublimation.

Nature of matter : Elements, compounds and mixtures. Heterogeneous and homogenous mixtures, colloids and suspensions.

Particle nature, basic units : Atoms and molecules, Law of constant proportions, Atomic and molecular masses. Mole concept : Relationship of mole to mass of the particles and numbers.

Structure of atoms : Electrons, protons and neutrons, valency, chemical formula of common compounds. Isotopes and Isobars.

THEME : THE WORLD OF THE LIVING

Unit II : Organization in the Living World **(45 Periods)**

Cell - Basic Unit of life : Cell as a basic unit of life; prokaryotic and eukaryotic cells, multicellular organisms; cell membrane and cell wall, cell organelles and cell inclusions; chloroplast, mitochondria, vacuoles, endoplasmic reticulum, Golgi apparatus; nucleus, chromosomes - basic structure, number.

Tissues, Organs, Organ System, Organism : Structure and functions of animal and plant tissues (only four types of tissues in animals; Meristematic and Permanent tissues in plants).

Biological Diversity : Diversity of plants and animals - basic issues in scientific naming, basis of classification. Hierarchy of categories / groups, Major groups of plants (salient features) (Bacteria, Thallophyta, Bryophyta, Pteridophyta, Gymnosperms and Angiosperms). Major groups of animals (salient features) (Non-chordates upto phyla and chordates upto classes).

Health and Diseases : Health and its failure. Infectious and Non-infectious diseases, their causes and manifestation. Diseases caused by microbes (Virus, Bacteria and Protozoans) and their prevention; Principles of treatment and prevention. Pulse Polio programmes.

THEME : MOVING THINGS, PEOPLE AND IDEAS

Unit III : Motion, Force and Work (60 Periods)

Motion : Distance and displacement, velocity; uniform and non-uniform motion along a straight line; acceleration, distance-time and velocity-time graphs for uniform motion and uniformly accelerated motion, derivation of equations of motion by graphical method; elementary idea of uniform circular motion.

Force and Newton's laws : Force and Motion, Newton's Laws of Motion, Action and reaction forces, Inertia of a body, Inertia and mass, Momentum, Force and Acceleration. Elementary idea of conservation of Momentum.

Gravitation : Gravitation; Universal Law of Gravitation, Force of Gravitation of the earth (gravity), Acceleration due to Gravity; Mass and Weight; Free fall.

Floatation : Thrust and Pressure. Archimedes' Principle; Buoyancy; Elementary Idea of Relative Density.

Work, energy and power : Work done by a Force, Energy, Power; Kinetic and Potential energy; Law of conservation of energy.

Sound : Nature of sound and its propagation in various media, speed of sound, range of hearing in humans; ultrasound; reflection of sound; echo and SONAR.

Structure of the Human Ear (Auditory aspect only).

THEME : NATURAL RESOURCES : BALANCE IN NATURE

Unit IV : Our Environment (15 Periods)

Physical resources : Air, Water, Soil. Air for respiration, for combustion, for moderating temperatures; movements of air and its role in bringing rains across India.

Air, Water and Soil pollution (brief introduction). Holes in ozone layer and the probable damages.

Bio-geo chemical cycles in nature : Water, Oxygen, Carbon and Nitrogen.

THEME : FOOD

Unit V : Food Production (10 Periods)

Plant and animal breeding and selection for quality improvement and management; Use of fertilizers and manures; Protection from pests and diseases; Organic farming.

QUESTION PAPER DESIGN FOR SCIENCE (CODE NO. 086)

Time : 3 Hours **Max. Marks : 80**

S.No.	Typography of Questions	Very Short Answer (VSA) 1 Mark	Short Answer-I (SAI) 2 Marks	Short Answer-II (SAII) 3 Marks	Long Answer (LA) 5 Marks	Total Marks	% Weight age
1.	Remembering (Knowledge based simple recall questions, to know specific facts, terms, concepts, principles, or theories, Identify, define or recite, information)	2	–	1	1	10	15%
2.	Understanding (Comprehension - to be familiar with meaning and to understand conceptually, interpret, compare, contrast, explain, paraphrase, or interpret information)	–	1	4	2	24	35%
3.	Application (Use abstract information in concrete situation, to apply knowledge to new situations, use given content to interpret a situation, provide an example or solve a problem)	–	1	2	2	18	26%
4.	High Order Thinking Skills (Analysis & Synthesis - Classify, compare, contrast or differentiate between different pieces of information, organize and / or integrate unique pieces of information from a variety of sources)	–	–	1	1	8	12%
5.	Inferential and Evaluative (Appraise, judge and / or justify the value or worth of a decision or outcome, or to predict outcomes based on values)	–	1	2	–	8	12%
	Total (Theory Based Questions)	2×1=2	3×2=6	10×3=30	6×5=30	68(21)	100%
	Practice Based Questions (PBQs)		6×2=12	–	–	12(6)	
	Total	2×1=2	9×2=18	10×3=30	6×5=30	80(27)	

1. Question paper will consist of 27 questions.
2. All questions would be compulsory. However, an internal choice will be provided in two questions of 3 marks each and one question of five marks each and one question (for assessing the practical skills) of 2 marks.

CONTENTS

1 Matter in Our Surroundings

Syllabus

Solids, Liquids, Gases, Melting Point, Boiling Point, Evaporation

Facts that Matter

Introduction

- Everything in this universe is made of materials which scientist has named 'matter'.
- **Matter** is made up of very small tiny particles.
- **Matter** is anything that occupies space and has mass.
- Particles of matter have space between them and are continuously moving.
- Particles of matter attract each other.
- **States of Matter:** It has three states.

Solids	***Liquids***	***Gases***
Strong intermolecular force.	Weak intermolecular force.	Very weak intermolecular force.
Very less intermolecular space.	Large intermolecular space.	Very large intermolecular space.
Have definite shape and volume.	No definite shape but definite volume.	No definite shape and volume.
High density, melting point and boiling point.	Density is lower, low melting and boiling point.	Density is very low.
Solids cannot be compressed.	Liquids can be compressed.	Gases are highly compressible.
Solids cannot flow.	Liquids can flow.	Gases can flow.
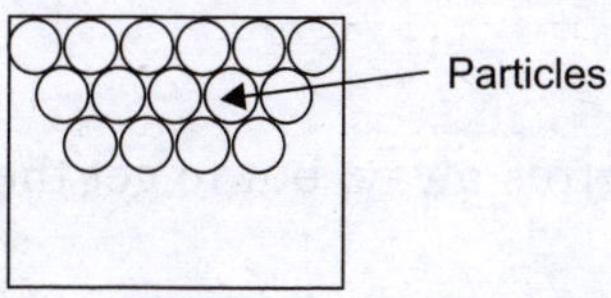 Solid	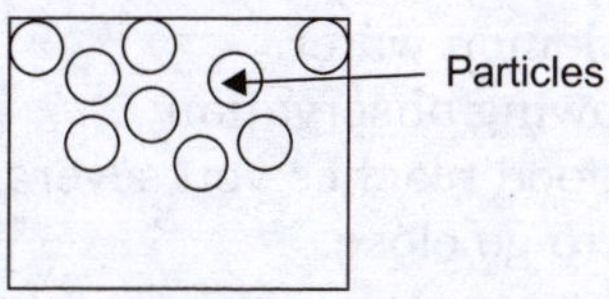 Liquid	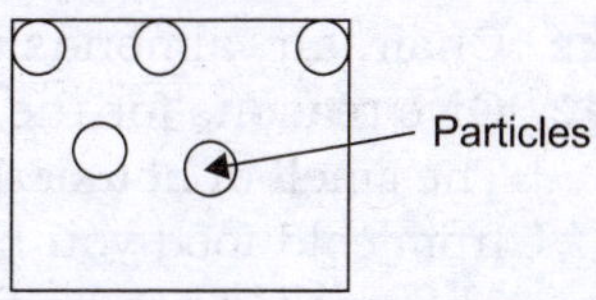 Gas

- Matter can change its state from solid to liquid and from liquid to gas and vice-versa.

$$\text{Solid} \underset{\text{freeze}}{\overset{\text{heat}}{\rightleftharpoons}} \text{liquid} \underset{\text{cool}}{\overset{\text{heat}}{\rightleftharpoons}} \text{gas}$$

- **Effect of temperature:** On increasing the temperature, the particles gain energy and start vibrating with greater energy. Due to increased kinetic energy the particles overcome the force of attraction and a new state is obtained.
- **Melting point:** The minimum temperature at which a solid melts to become a liquid at the atmospheric pressure is called its melting point.
- **Boiling point:** The temperature at which a liquid starts boiling at the atmospheric pressure is known as its boiling point. Boiling is a bulk phenomena.

- **Latent heat of fusion:** The amount of heat energy required to change 1 kg of a solid into liquid at its melting point is called the latent heat of fusion of the solid.
- **Latent heat of vapourization:** The amount of heat energy required to change 1 kg of a liquid to vapour at atmospheric pressure, at its boiling point is called the latent heat of vapourization of the liquid.
- **Sublimation:** A change of state directly from solid to gas without changing to liquid state is called sublimation.
- **Effect of change of pressure on matter:** On applying pressure, the particles of matter can be brought close together and the state of matter can be changed. For example, CO_2 gas can be solidified by applying pressure and lowering temperature.
- **Evaporation:** The phenomenon of changing of a liquid into its vapour state at any temperature below its boiling point is called evaporation. Evaporation is a surface phenomena.
- **Factors affecting evaporation.**
  - An increase in surface area increases evaporation.
  - An increase in temperature increases the rate of evaporation.
  - A decrease in humidity increases the rate of evaporation.
  - An increase in wind speed increases the rate of evaporation.
- Evaporation causes cooling effect.

Some measurable quantities and their units

Quantity	*Unit*	*Symbol*
Temperature	Kelvin	K
Length	Metre	m
Mass	Kilogram	Kg
Weight	Newton	N
Volume	Cubic metre	m^3
Density	Kilogram per cubic metre	Kg/m^3
Pressure	Pascal	Pa

NCERT IN-TEXT QUESTIONS SOLVED

Q1. Which of the following are matters?
Chair, air, love, smell, hate, almonds, thought, cold, lemon water, smell of perfume.

Ans. Chair, air, almonds and lemon water.

Q2. Give reasons for the following observation:
The smell of hot sizzling food reaches you several metres away, but to get the smell from cold food you have to go close.

Ans. The smell of hot sizzling food reaches several metres away, as the particles of hot food have more kinetic energy due to higher temperature and hence the rate of diffusion is more than the particles of cold food.

Q3. A diver is able to cut through water in a swimming pool. Which property of matter does this observation show?

Ans. A diver is able to cut through water in a swimming pool. as the particles of water have large intermolecular space and less force of attraction.

Q4. What are the characteristics of the particles of matter?

Ans. The characteristics of the particles of matter are:
(1) Particles have intermolecular space between them.
(2) Particles inhibits intermolecular force.
(3) Particles of matter are in continuous motion.

Q5. The mass per unit volume of a substance is called density. (density = mass/volume).

Arrange the following in order of increasing density: air, exhaust from chimneys, honey, water, chalk, cotton and iron.

Ans. Increasing density:

air < exhaust from chimneys < cotton < water < honey < chalk < iron.

Q6. (*a*) Tabulate the differences in the characteristics of states of matter.

(*b*) Comment upon the following:
rigidity, compressibility, fluidity, filling a gas container, shape, kinetic energy and density.

Ans. (*a*) Difference in the characteristics of three states of matter.

Characteristics	***Solid***	***Liquid***	***Gas***
1. Shape	fixed shape	no fixed shape	no fixed shape
2. Volume	fixed volume	fixed volume	no fixed volume
3. Rigidity/fluidity	are rigid, cannot flow	can flow, not rigid	can flow, not rigid
4. Intermolecular force	maximum	less than solids	negligible
5. Intermolecular space	very less	more than solids and less than gases	maximum
6. Compressibility	negligible	compressible	highly compressible

(*b*) **Comment on:**

(*i*) **Rigidity:** The tendency of a substance to retain/maintain its shape when subjected to outside force.

(*ii*) **Compressibility:** The matter has intermolecular space between its particles. The external force applied on the matter can bring these particles closer. This property is called compressibility. Gases and liquids are compressible.

(*iii*) **Fluidity:** The tendency of particles to flow is called fluidity. Liquids and gases flow.

(*iv*) **Filling of a gas container:** Gases have particles which vibrate randomly in all the directions due to negligible intermolecular force between them. Therefore the gas can fill the container.

(*v*) **Shape:** Solids have maximum intermolecular force and definite shape. Whereas liquids and gases takes the shape of container in which they are filled or poured.

(*vi*) **Kinetic energy:** The energy possessed by particles due to their motion is called kinetic energy. Molecules of gases vibrate randomly so they have maximum kinetic energy.

(*vii*) **Density:** It is defined as mass per unit volume, the solids have highest density.

Q7. Give reasons

(*a*) A gas fills completely the vessel in which it is kept.

(*b*) A gas exerts pressure on the walls of the container.

(*c*) A wooden table should be called a solid.

(*d*) We can easily move our hand in air but to do the same through a solid block of wood we need a karate expert.

Ans. (*a*) The molecules of gas have high kinetic energy due to which they keep moving in all directions and hence fill the vessel completely in which they are kept.

(b) A gas exerts pressure on the walls of the container because the molecules of the gas are in constant random motion due to high kinetic energy. These molecules constantly vibrate, move and hit the walls of the container thereby exerting pressure on it.

(c) The molecules/particles of wooden table are tightly packed with each other, there is no intermolecular space, it cannot be compressed, it cannot flow, all these characteristics are of solid. So wooden table should be called a solid.

(d) We can easily move our hand in air but to do the same through a solid block of wood we need a karate expert. It is because the molecules of air have less force of attraction between them and a very small external force can separate them and pass through it. But in case of solids, the molecules have maximum force of attraction, the particles are tightly bound due to this force. Hence large amount of external force is required to pass through solid.

Q8. Liquids generally have lower density as compared to solids. But you must have observed that ice floats on water. Find out why.

Ans. Ice is a solid but its density is lower than water due to its structure. The molecules in ice make a cage like structure with lot of vacant spaces, this makes ice float on water.

Q9. Convert the following temperature to celsius scale:

(a) 300 K (b) 573 K

Ans. (a) 300 − 273 = 27°C (b) 573 − 273 = 300°C

Q10. What is the physical state of water at:

(a) 250°C (b) 100°C

Ans. (a) 250°C = gas (b) 100°C liquid as well as gas

Q11. For any substance, why does the temperature remain constant during the change of state?

Ans. During the change of state of any matter heat is supplied to the substance. The molecules of matter observe heat to overcome the force of attraction between the particles, at this period of time, temperature remains constant. This extra heat is acquired by the molecules in the form of hidden heat called latent heat to change from one state of matter to the other state.

Q12. Suggest a method to liquefy atmospheric gases?

Ans. The atmospheric gases are taken in a cylinder with piston fitted on it. By cooling and applying pressure on them, the gases can be liquefied.

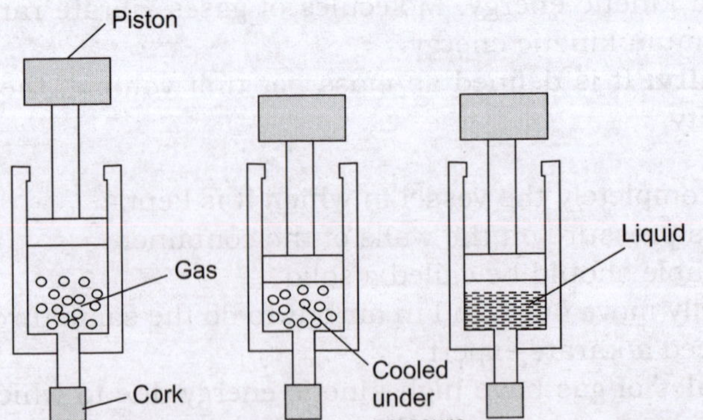

Q13. Why does a desert cooler cool better on a hot dry day?

Ans. The outer walls of the cooler get sprinkled by water constantly. This water evaporates due to hot dry weather. Evaporation causes cooling of inside air of the cooler. This cool air is sent in the room by the fan.

Q14. How does the water kept in an earthen pot (matka) become cool during summer?

Ans. The earthen pot is porous with lot of pores on it, the water oozes out through these pores and the water gets evaporated at the surface of the pot thereby causing cooling effect. This makes the pot cold and the water inside the pot cools by this process.

Q15. Why does our palm feel cold when we put some acetone or petrol or perfume on it?

Ans. Acetone, petrol or perfume evaporate when they come into contact with air or our palm. Their particles gain energy from our palm or surrounding and evaporate. The evaporation causes cooling sensation in our hands.

Q16. Why are we able to sip hot tea or milk faster from a saucer rather than a cup?

Ans. Tea in a saucer has larger surface area than in a cup. The rate of evaporation is faster with increased surface area. The cooling of tea in saucer takes place sooner than in a cup. Hence we are able to sip hot tea or milk faster from a saucer rather than a cup.

Q17. What type of clothes should we wear in summer?

Ans. We should wear light coloured cotton clothes in summer.

Light colour reflects heat and cotton clothes has pores in it, which absorbs sweat and allows the sweat to evaporate faster thereby giving cooling effect.

NCERT TEXTUAL QUESTIONS SOLVED

Q1. Convert the following temperatures to the celsius scale.

(*a*) 293 K (*b*) 470 K.

Ans. (*a*) 293 K into °C (°C + 273 = K)

293 − 273 = 20°C

(*b*) 470 K into °C

470 − 273 = 197°C

Q2. Convert the following temperatures to the Kelvin scale.

(*a*) 25°C (*b*) 373°C.

Ans. (*a*) 25°C into K

25 + 273 = 298 K

(*b*) 373°C into K

373 + 273 = 646 K

Q3. Give reason for the following observations.

(a) Naphthalene balls disappear with time without leaving any solid.

(*b*) We can get the smell of perfume sitting several metres away.

Ans. (*a*) Naphthalene balls disappear with time without leaving any solid, because naphthalene balls sublime and directly changes into vapour state without leaving any solid.

(*b*) We can get the smell of perfume sitting several metres away because perfume contains volatile solvent i.e. gaseous particles, which have high speed and large space between them and diffuse faster and can reach people sitting several metres away.

Q4. Arrange the following substances in increasing order of forces of attraction between the particles—water, sugar, oxygen.

Ans. Oxygen → water → sugar.

Q5. What is the physical state of water at—
(*a*) 25°C (*b*) 0°C (*c*) 100°C
Ans. (*a*) 25°C is liquid (*b*) 0°C is solid or liquid
(*c*) 100°C is liquid and gas
Q6. Give two reasons to justify—
(*a*) water at room temperature is a liquid.
(*b*) an iron almirah is a solid at room temperature.
Ans. (a) Water at room temperature is a liquid because its freezing point is 0°C and boiling point is 100°C.
(*b*) An iron almirah is a solid at room temperature because melting point of iron is higher than the room temperature.
Q7. Why is ice at 273 K more effective in cooling than water at the same temperature?
Ans. Ice at 273 K will absorb heat energy or latent heat from the medium to overcome the heat of fusion to become water. Hence the cooling effect of ice is more than the water at same temperature because water does not absorb this extra heat from the medium.
Q8. What produces more severe burns, boiling water or steam?
Ans. Steam at 100°C will produce more severe burns as extra heat is hidden in it called latent heat whereas the boiling water does not have this hidden heat.
Q9. Name A, B, C, D, E and F in the following diagram showing change in its state

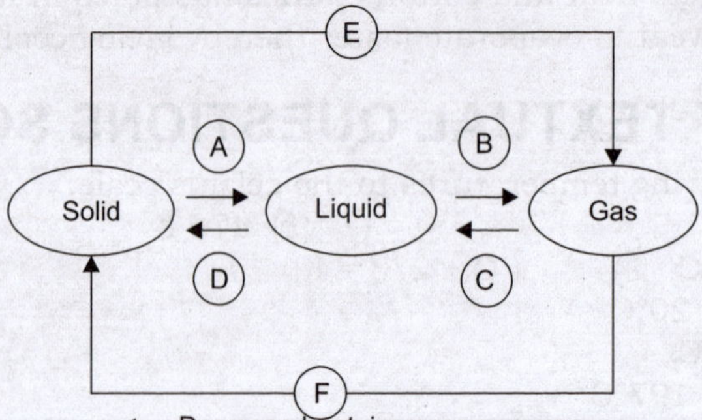

Ans. A → Liquefication/melting/fusion B → Vapourisation/evaporation
C → Condensation D → Solidification
E → Sublimation F → Sublimation

ADDITIONAL QUESTIONS SOLVED

I. Multiple Choice Questions

Choose the correct option:

1. Evaporation of a liquid occurs at
(*a*) boiling point (*b*) a fixed temperature
(*c*) temperature lower than boiling point
(*d*) all temperatures

2. The conversion of gas into liquid is called
(*a*) freezing (*b*) condensation
(*c*) sublimation (*d*) fusion

3. The fusion is the process in which
(*a*) liquid changes into solid (*b*) solid changes into liquid
(*c*) solid changes into gas (*d*) gas changes into solid

4. The ice floats on water because
(a) its density is more than water (b) its density is less than water
(c) it has less intermolecular space (d) none of the above

5. Ice at 0°C is more effective in cooling than water at the same temperature because
(a) it holds latent heat
(b) the molecules use the heat to overcome the force of attraction
(c) both (a) and (b)
(d) none of the above

6. The density of water is maximum at
(a) 0°C (b) 100°C
(c) 4°C (d) 273 *K*

7. Solids and gases mix/dissolve in water
(a) because water is a good solvent
(b) because water has intermolecular space
(c) diffusion is faster in water
(d) all of the above

8. Choose the correct statement from the following:
(a) the volume of gas expands on heating
(b) two gases cannot diffuse into each other
(c) gas is converted into solid, it is called condensation
(d) gases cannot diffuse in solids

9. As the pressure of air decreases, the boiling point of the liquid
(a) decreases (b) increases
(c) does not changes (d) none of these

10. Which among the following can exist in vapour state?
(a) oxygen (b) hydrogen
(c) carbon dioxide (d) water

11. At normal pressure (1atmospheric pressure) the boiling point of water is
(a) 98°C (b) 100°C
(c) 110°C (d) 90°C

12. The pressure of air is measured in atmosphere and pascal. 1 atmospheric pressure is equal to
(a) 1.01325×10^5 Pa (b) 1.01325×10^4 Pa
(c) 10.1325×10^5 Pa (d) 10.1325×10^6 Pa

13. Cooking of rice at higher altitudes is difficult because
(a) water boils at 100°C (b)water boils at <100°C
(c) boiling point of water is constant (d) none of the above

Ans. 1—(c), 2—(b), 3—(b), 4—(b), 5—(c), 6—(c), 7—(d), 8—(a), 9—(a), 10—(d), 11—(b), 12—(a), 13—(b).

II. Very Short Answer Type Questions

Q1. Define matter.

Ans. Anything that occupies space and has mass is called matter.

Q2. State different states of matter with an example.

Ans. Matter has three different states

$$\underset{\text{ice}}{\text{Solid}} \longrightarrow \underset{\text{water}}{\text{liquid}} \longrightarrow \underset{\text{steam}}{\text{gas}}$$

Q3. What is diffusion?

Ans. The intermingling of molecules of one substance with that of the other is called diffusion.

Q4. What happen to the rate of diffusion if the temperature is increased?

Ans. With increased temperature, the rate of diffusion also increases as the particles gain energy and vibrate more.

Q5. Name the state of matter that have the tendency to maintain their shape when subjected to outside force.

Ans. Solid.

Q6. Define melting point.

Ans. The minimum temperature at which a solid melts to become a liquid at the atmospheric pressure is called its melting point.

Q7. Define boiling point.

Ans. The temperature at which a liquid starts boiling at the atmospheric pressure is known as its boiling point.

Q8. Define latent heat of vaporization.

Ans. Latent heat of vaporization is the heat energy required to change 1 kg of a liquid to gas at atmospheric pressure at its boiling point.

Q9. Define latent heat of fusion.

Ans. Latent heat of fusion is the amount of heat energy required to change 1 kg of solid into liquid at atmospheric pressure at its melting point.

Q10. Define sublimation.

Ans. Sublimation is the change of gaseous state directly to solid state without going through liquid state.

Q11. What is dry ice?

Ans. Solid carbon dioxide obtained by cooling and applying pressure on carbon dioxide gas. It does not melt so it is called dry ice.

Q12. What is humidity?

Ans. The air holds water vapour, this air with water is called humid air and the amount of water vapour present in air is called humidity.

Q13. Give two properties of solid.

Ans. (1) Solids have fixed shape and are rigid. (2) Solids cannot be compressed.

Q14. What will happen if the pressure is reduced on solid carbon dioxide (dry ice)?

Ans. If the pressure is reduced on solid carbon dioxide it will directly change into gaseous state without melting.

Q15. Name any three substances that show sublimation.

Ans. Ammonium chloride, camphor and naphthalene balls.

Q16. Sponge is solid, but we can still compress it. Why?

Ans. Sponge is a solid with minute pores in it. When we press the sponge the air present in these pores is released out and hence we are able to compress it.

Q17. What is normal atmospheric pressure?

Ans. The atmospheric pressure at sea level is 1 atmosphere and taken as the normal atmospheric pressure.

Q18. What is Kelvin?

Ans. Kelvin is the SI unit of temperature (0°C = 273 K).

Q19. Give two examples of diffusion.

Ans. Milk drops dissolved in water and perfume sprayed in a room.

Q20. Give the temperature at which water exists in two different phases/states.

Ans. At 0°C water can be in solid or in liquid state.
At 100°C water can be in liquid or in gaseous state.

III. Short Answer Type questions

Q1. Why do we see water droplets collected on the outer surface of a glass container, containing ice?

Ans. The water vapour present in air, comes in contact with the cold outer surface of the container thereby condensing it to form water droplets.

Q2. Explain why solids have fixed shape but liquids and gases do not have fixed shape.

Ans. Solids have fixed shape due to strong intermolecular force of attraction between them. The liquids and gases have molecules with less intermolecular force of attraction and hence they can flow and take shape of the container.

Q3. Liquids and gases can be compressed but it is difficult to compress solids. Why?

Ans. Liquids and gases have intermolecular space, on applying pressure externally on them the molecules can come closer thereby minimizing the space between them. But in case of solids there is no intermolecular space to do so.

Q4. A balloon when kept in sun, bursts after some time. Why?

Ans. The balloon has air filled in it. The balloon when kept in sun gets heated and the air inside it also gets heated. The molecules of air get energy, and vibrate faster thereby exerting large force on the walls of the balloon. Due to this expansion of gases the balloon bursts.

Q5. Why do people perspire a lot on a hot humid day?

Ans. On a hot humid day, due to the heat our body starts sweating for the cooling mechanism *i.e.,* by evaporation and gets cooling effect. But the air cannot hold any more water on a humid day and therefore the sweat or perspiration is seen.

Q6. Distinguish between evaporation and boiling.

Ans.

Evaporation	*Boiling*
1. Evaporation is a surface phenomenon.	Boiling is a bulk phenomenon.
2. It is a slow process.	It is a fast process.
3. It takes place at all temperatures.	It takes place at a definite temperature.

Q7. Why is it advisable to use pressure cooker at higher altitudes?

Ans. At higher altitudes, the atmospheric pressure is low and the water boils very fast and evaporates at faster rate therefore the pressure is required to increase the cooking process and this is done by using pressure cooker which increases the pressure inside the container and cooks food faster.

Q8. What are fluids?

Ans. The states of matter that can flow due to less intermolecular force of attraction liquid and gases are fluids are called as fluids.

Q9. One kg cotton and one kg sand, which is more denser? Why?

Ans. One kg sand is more denser than 1 kg cotton.
The volume required by cotton is more than the sand and density and volume are inversely proportional. Density = mass/volume.

Q10. Why is water liquid at room temperature?

Ans. The room temperature cannot provide sufficient heat to the molecules of water to overcome their force of attraction and therefore it remains in liquid phase.

Q11. State the differences between solid, liquid and gas.

Ans.

Solid	***Liquid***	***Gas***
1. Have strong inter-molecular force.	Weak intermolecular force.	Very weak intermolecular force.
2. Very less intermolecular space.	Large intermolecular force.	Very large intermolecular space.
3. Have definite shape and volume.	Do not have definite shape but have definite volume.	No definite shape and volume.
4. Have high density.	Density is low.	Very low density.
5. Solids cannot be compressed.	Liquids can be compressed.	Gases are highly compressed.

Q12. Cotton is solid but it floats on water. Why?

Ans. Cotton has large number of pores, in which air is trapped. Hence reducing its density and increasing the volume. Therefore cotton floats on water. But when these pores get filled with water it starts sinking.

Q13. Why are solids generally denser than liquids and gases?

Ans. Density of a substance is given by a formula

$$\text{Density} = \frac{\text{Mass}}{\text{Volume}}$$

In case of solids the molecules are tightly packed and hence large mass is concentrated in very small volume. Hence their density is more. But in case of liquids and gases, their molecules have intermolecular space and hence they don't have large mass concentrated in small volume. So the density of solids is generally more than that of the liquids and gases.

Q14. On a hot sunny day, why do people sprinkle water on the roof or open ground?

Ans. During hot sunny day, the surface of roof or ground absorbs large amount of heat and remains hot, on sprinkling water on these surfaces, the water absorbs large amount of heat from the surface due to its large latent heat of vaporisation and evaporates thereby allowing the hot surface to cool.

Q15. The temperature at which liquids change into vapours is very high, for example, water vaporises at 100°C then how is it possible for water to evaporate at room temperature or at any other temperature?

Ans. The molecules of water present on the surface of the exposed area which are in very small fraction, gains the energy from the surrounding. With this higher kinetic energy they are able to break the force of attraction between them and hence get converted into vapour state.

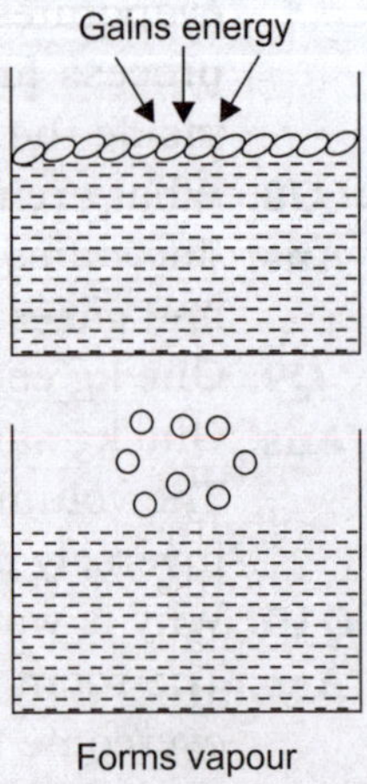

This phenomenon of change of a liquid into vapours that takes place at any temperature below its boiling point is called evaporation.

Q16. On a hot sunny day why do we feel pleasant sitting under a tree?

Ans. Tree has lot of leaves which constantly show transpiration. Transpiration is loss of water through small tiny pores of leaves called stomata. When this water comes on the surface of leaf the water evaporates thereby causing cooling effect. Therefore we feel pleasant sitting under the tree on a hot sunny day.

Q17. Name the factors that affect evaporation.

Ans. The rate of evaporation will increase with
(1) an increase of surface area,
(2) an increase of temperature,
(3) a decrease in humidity,
(4) an increase in wind speed.

Q18. The melting point of ice is 273.16 K. What does this mean? Explain in detail.

Ans. Ice is solid at 0°C *i.e.,* 273° K. The molecules of ice are tightly packed. These molecules have to overcome the force of attraction with which they are held and hence they gain this heat from the surrounding but the temperature remains the same as their energy is used to overcome the force of attraction between the particles. The particles of ice start vibrating freely and a stage reaches when the solid ice melts and is converted to liquid state at the same temperature *i.e.,* 273 K.

Q19. How is the high compressibility property of gas useful to us?

Ans. The gases have high compressibility. This property is used in the following situation:
(1) LPG (liquefied petroleum gas) is a fuel which is made up of petroleum gas. On compressing this petroleum gas it forms liquid.
(2) Oxygen cylinders in the hospitals have compressed gas filled in it.
(3) CNG (compressed natural gas) is a natural gas, methane, which is compressed and used as a fuel in vehicles and at home.

Q20. With the help of an example, explain how diffusion of gases in water is essential?

Ans. The gases from the atmosphere diffuse and dissolve in water. Gases like oxygen and carbon dioxide diffuse in water, are essential for the survival of aquatic animals and plants.
Animals breathe in this oxygen dissolved in water for their survival and plants can use carbon dioxide dissolved in water for photosynthesis.

Q21. On adding impurity to a substance what happens to its Boiling point/ Melting point?

Ans. Its boiling point and the melting point changes. It does not remain fixed. The boiling point is elevated and the melting point is decreased.

Q22. How will you separate miscible and immiscible liquids?

Ans. To separate the miscible liquids we can used distillation or fractional distillation.
To separate two immiscible liquids we can use separating funnel as the densities of the two liquids is different .

Q23. Pure ethanol boils at 78.4°C and freezes at –114.3°C. You have a sample of ethanol which boils between 79.1°C and 79.9°C
(*a*) What can you say about its purity?
(*b*) What will you expect to find, when you measure its freezing point?

Ans. (*a*) The sample is not pure as it is not boiling at the fixed point rather it boils at the range of temperature.
(*b*) Its freezing point will also not remain fixed rather over a range of temperature it will freeze and the range will be lower than the freezing point.

Q24. It is important that some substances are pure. Give two examples.

Ans. The pure substances are important for our life as some impurities may affect its nature or our health. For *e.g.,* if we eat food which is not pure like suppose oil is adulterated with some impurities, it may cause heart problems. Similarly, medicines should be in purest form impurities in it may cause complications and death.

Q25. Explain: solute and solvent.

Ans. **Solute:** Any substance that dissolves in the solvent.
Solvent: Any substance in which the solute can dissolve.

Q26. State the difference between condensation and sublimation.

Ans. **Condensation:** The cooling of the gaseous vapours when it comes in contact with the low temperature.

Sublimation: The conversion of solid substance directly into vapours without attaining the liquid state.

Q27. Suppose you are given a solution of salt and water. Suggest how would you separate this mixture to obtain:

(*a*) Pure salt and (*b*) pure water

Ans. (*a*) To obtain pure salt I shall evaporate the water by controlled heating or keeping it in sun.

(*b*) To obtain pure water, I shall use the process of simple distillation in which the water shall evaporate and pass through the condenser to liquefy.

Q28. When a metal like copper is heated it expands. Explain what happens to the metals particles as the solid metal expands

Ans. The particles of metal in solid state are tightly packed and close to each other. On heating this metal the particles gain energy and they start vibrating randomly to move away from each other and hence expansion of metal is seen.

Q29. Explain why diffusion is faster in gases than in liquids?

Ans. Diffusion is dependent on two factors one is the mass of the particles and the other is the temperature. The particles in gaseous state are at higher temperature and has more energy hence the diffusion in gas is faster than in liquid state.

Q30. How is the movement and arrangement of the molecules in a crystal of nitrogen different from those seen in the gaseous state of nitrogen?

Ans. The molecules in the crystal of nitrogen are closely packed and vibrate at its mean position. The molecules in the gaseous state of nitrogen are in random motion and free to move.

Q31. A sealed container contains helium gas and the pressure of the gas is increased if the temperature of the gas inside is increased by heating it. Explain.

Ans. The particles of helium gas exert pressure on the walls due to its random motion and striking the walls of the container. On heating these particles gain more energy and its vibration increases thereby causing more bombardment and strikes on the wall of the container. This increases the pressure of the gas.

Q32. The diagram shows a heating curve for a sample of compound X.

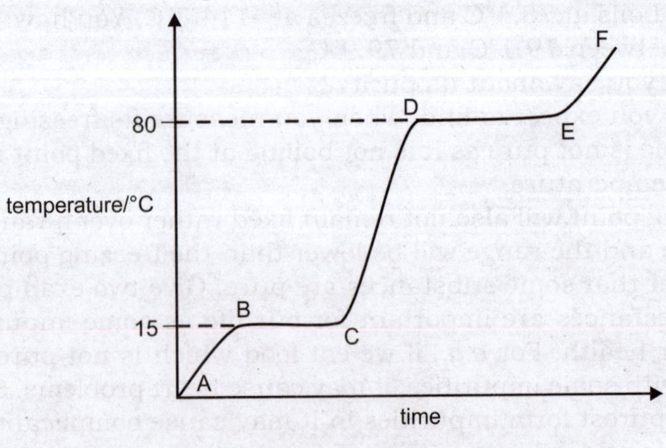

(*a*) Is X a solid, a liquid or a gas at room temperature, 20°C?

(*b*) Name the change of state which occurs in region DE.

(*c*) Explain how the curve shows that a pure sample of compound X was used?

Ans. (*a*) The solid melts at around 15 degrees and hence it is a liquid at room temperature.
(*b*) The change is from liquid to gas.
(*c*) As the curves are sharp the sample is pure as it is having fixed melting and boiling point.

IV. Long Answer Type questions

Q1. Pressure and temperature determine the state of a substance. Explain this in detail.

Ans. (1) Any matter *i.e.*, solid, liquid or gas when experiences an increase in temperature they change their state.

Example: $\underset{\text{Ice}}{\text{Solid}} \xrightarrow{\text{heat}} \underset{\text{Water}}{\text{Liquid}} \xrightarrow{\textit{heat}} \underset{\text{Steam}}{\text{Gas}}$

Take ice cubes in a beaker or heat them slowly, the temperature increases and the ice melts to form liquid. Heat this liquid further it will become steam.

(2) On lowering down the temperature of any matter, show change in their state.

Example: $\underset{\text{Steam}}{\text{Gas}} \xrightarrow{\text{cool}} \underset{\text{Water}}{\text{Liquid}} \xrightarrow{\textit{heat}} \underset{\text{Ice}}{\text{Solid}}$

Take the steam that is coming out of a boiling water and allow it to cool down, it condenses to form water and on further cooling of this water we get ice.

(3) On applying pressure and reducing temperature we can liquefy gases or change them into solid.

Example: Take carbon-dioxide gas, reduce its temperature and apply lot of pressure on it so that it changes into solid carbon dioxide, called dry ice, which is used as refrigerant for cooling.

If the pressure on it is further decreased it directly changes into gas.

In LPG cylinders, the petroleum gas is first cooled and further lot of pressure change is applied to it into liquid state.

While using this LPG, we release the pressure exerted on it and hence it comes out in the form of gas.

Q2. Explain giving examples the various factors on which rate of evaporation depends.

Ans. The rate of evaporation depends on the following factors:

(1) **Surface area:** If the surface area is increased the rate of evaporation also increases.
(*a*) To dry the clothes we spread them to dry faster.
(*b*) Tea in saucer cools faster than in a cup.

(2) **Temperature:** If the temperature is increased the rate of evaporation also increases. Due to increase in temperature the particles gain more kinetic energy and change their phase from liquid to gaseous. Water will evaporate faster in sun than in shade.

(3) **Humidity:** It is the amount of water vapour present in air. The air can hold definite amount of water vapour, at a given temperature. If the amount of water vapour is high in the air then the rate of evaporation decreases.
On hot and humid day, desert coolers are not effective as the air cannot hold anymore moisture to get the cooling effect.

(4) **Wind speed:** With the increase in wind speed, the rate of evaporation increases. The particles of water vapour move away with the wind, decreasing the amount of water vapour in the surrounding.

Q3. Cooking gas is often stored and delivered in steel bottles. Over a period of time pressure of the gas in the steel bottles does not change.

Air and helium are gases that are often used to fill rubber balloons. Over a period of time balloons gradually shrink. Explain these observations.

Ans. The molecules of gas exert pressure on the walls of the container. The steel containers have a wall strong enough to withstand the pressure of the gas but the walls of the balloon are not that rigid and hence shrinks.

Q4. The observations given below determine whether the changes described are likely to involve the formation of new combinations of matter, or are physical changes. Analyse.

	Observation	Chemical or Physical	Scientifically Supported Judgements
1.	Edge of towel hanging in a wet bath draws up water.		
2.	A fire cracker explodes. Producing noise, smell and smoke		
3.	Pink colored copper tap becomes green over a period of time.		
4.	Glass of car windscreen gets all water droplets on inner surface.		

Ans.

	Observation	Chemical or Physical	Scientifically Supported Judgements
1.	Edge of towel hanging in a wet bath draws up water.	Physical	No new substance formed
2.	A fire cracker explodes. Producing noise, smell and smoke	Chemical	Heat involved and new product formed
3.	Pink colored copper tap becomes green over a period of time.	Chemical	New compound formed
4.	Glass of car windscreen gets all water droplets on inner surface.	Physical	No new substance formed

V. Activity-Based Questions

1.
- Take 2-3 crystals of potassium permanganate and dissolve them in 100 ml of water.
- Take out approximately 10 ml of this solution and put in into another 90 ml of clear water.
- Take out 10 ml of this solution and put it into another 90 ml of clear water.
- Keep diluting the solution like this 5 to 8 times.
- Is the water still coloured?

Observation:

Yes, the water is still coloured but its colour has faded in each dilution. This experiment shows that just a few crystals of potassium permanganate can colour a large volume of water. This is because potassium permanganate (matter) is made up of millions of tiny particles.

2. • Take a 100 ml beaker.
• Fill half the beaker with water and mark the level of water.
• Dissolve some salt/sugar with the help of a glass rod.
• What do you think has happened to the salt?
• Where does it disappear?
• Does the level of water change?

Observations:
• The salt get dissolved in water.
• The particles of salt get into the spaces between particles of water.
• The level of water does not change as the salt particles occupy the intermolecular space between the water molecules.

3. • Put an unlit incense stick in a corner of your class. How close do you have to go so as to get its smell?
• Now light the incense stick. What happens? Do you get the smell sitting at a distance?
• Record your observation.

Observation:
• To smell the unlit incense stick one has to go very close to sense its smell.
• In case of lit incense stick, even if you are sitting at a distance, you get the smell. This is because the particles of matter on gaining heat energy start moving faster and vibrate, diffuse in all possible directions due to increased kinetic energy.

4. • Take two glasses/beakers filled with water.
• Put a drop of blue or red ink slowly and carefully along the sides of the first beaker and honey in the same way in the second beaker.
• Leave them undisturbed in your house or in a corner in the class.
• Record your observation.
• What do you observe immediately after adding the ink drop?
• What do you observe immediately after adding a drop of honey?
• How many hours or days does it take for the colour of ink to spread evenly throughout the water?

Observation:
• The beaker in which ink drops are added, the ink diffuses completely in the water within 5–10 minutes.
• The beaker in which honey is added in water, takes longer time for diffusion.
• This activity shows that viscous or dense liquids take longer time for diffusion as compared to the liquids which are not viscous.

5. • Drop a crystal of copper sulphate or potassium permanganate into a glass of hot water and another containing cold water. Do not stir the solution. Allow the crystals to settle at the bottom.

- What do you observe just above the solid crystals in the glass?
- What happens as time passes?
- What does this suggest about the particles of solid and liquid?
- Does the rate of mixing change with temperature? Why and how?

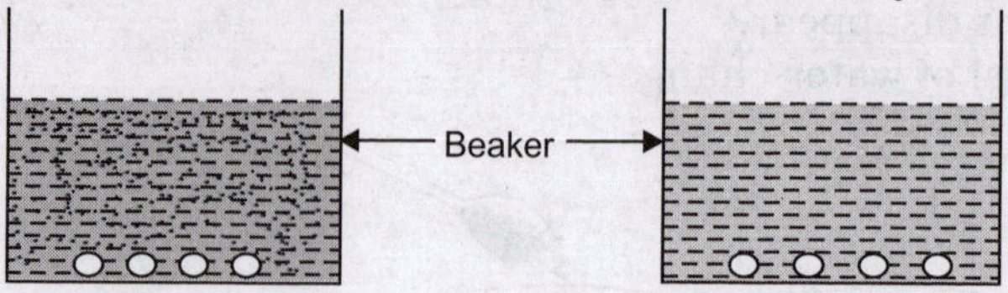

Hot water with copper sulphate crystals

Cold water with copper sulphate crystals

Observation:

- In the hot water just above the crystals, the blue colour appears to be intermingling at very fast rate and gets diffused in the water. Within minutes the copper sulphate dissolves in it.
- In the cold water, just above the crystal, the intermingling of copper sulphate is not visible and the rate of diffusion is very slow in it.
- This shows that with the increase in temperature the rate of diffusion increases.

6. - Take an iron nail, a piece of chalk and a rubber band.
   - Try breaking them by hammering, cutting or stretching.
   - In which of the above three substances do you think the particles are held together with greater force?

Observation:

- It is very easy to cut the rubber band.
- The chalk piece also breaks into 2 pieces with hand.
- The iron nail is difficult to be broken into two pieces.
- This shows that the iron particles are held together tightly and need extra effort to break them. The particles of chalk and rubber band are not that tightly held and hence, it can be broken easily.

7. - Take some water in a container, try cutting the surface of water with your fingers.
   - Were you able to cut the surface of water?
   - What could be the reason behind the surface of water remaining together?

Observation:

One cannot cut the surface of water because the molecules of water are held by force of attraction and hand cannot spread or cut or break this force of attraction between the molecules.

8. - Collect the following articles—a pen, a book, a needle and a piece of wooden stick.
   - Sketch the shape of the above articles in your notebook by moving a pencil around them.
   - Do all these have a definite shape, distinct boundaries and a fixed volume?
   - What happens if they are hammered, pulled or dropped?
   - Are they capable of diffusing into each other?
   - Try compressing them by applying force. Are you able to compress them?

Observation:

- All the articles given *i.e.*, a pen, a book, a needle, and a piece of wooden stick have definite shape, distinct boundaries and a fixed volume.
- Above articles may break under external force but it is difficult to change their shape.
- These objects cannot diffuse in each other, nor can they be compressed.
- All the articles have characteristics of solid.

9. Collect the following:

(*a*) Water, cooking oil, milk, juice and cold drink.

(*b*) Take containers of different shapes. Put a 50 ml mark on these containers using a measuring cylinder from the laboratory.

- What will happen if these liquids are spilt on the floor?
- Measure 50 ml of any one liquid and transfer it into different containers one by one. Does the volume remain the same?
- Does the shape of the liquid remain the same?
- When you pour the liquid from one container into another, does it flow easily?

Observation:

- If these liquids are spilled over on the floor, these liquids will flow.
- Let us put in any container, it takes the shape of the container but the volume remains the same.
- On pouring liquid from one container to another, the liquids flow easily.

10.
- Take three 100 ml syringes and close their nozzles by rubber corks.
- Remove the pistons from all the syringes.
- Leaving one syringe untouched, fill water in the second and pieces of chalk in the third.
- Insert the pistons back into the syringes. You may apply some vaseline on the pistons before inserting them into the syringes for their smooth movement.
- Now try to compress the content by pushing the piston in each syringe.
- What do you observe? In which case was the piston easily pushed in?
- What do you infer from your observation?

Observation:

- The piston is pushed in easily in the syringe containing air.
- The piston is pushed with very difficulty in the syringe containing chalk pieces.

Inference:

Gases are highly compressible followed by liquids but solids are non-compressible.

11.
- Take about 150 g of ice in a beaker and suspend a laboratory thermometer so that its bulb is in contact with the ice, as shown in the figure.

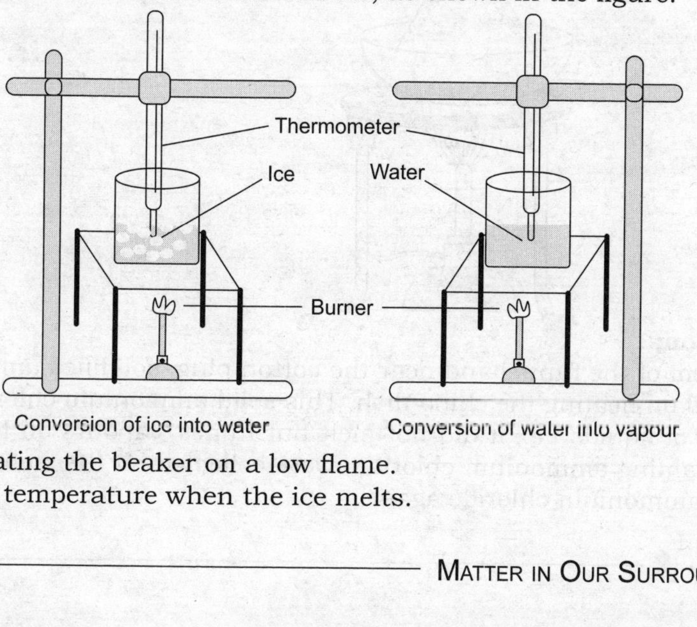

Convorsion of icc into water

Conversion of water into vapour

- Start heating the beaker on a low flame.
- Note the temperature when the ice melts.

- Note the temperature when all the ice has converted into water.
- Record your observations for this conversion of solid to liquid state.
- Now, put a glass rod in the beaker and heat while stirring till the water starts boiling.
- Keep a careful eye on the thermometer reading till most of the water has vaporised.
- Record your observations for the conversion of water in the liquid state to the gaseous state.

Observation:

- The ice starts melting at 0°C when the temperature increases slowly, the entire ice melts and the water is formed in the beaker.
- Water is heated continuously and at 100°C the water starts boiling and changes into gaseous state. On further heating for few more minutes, the temperature remains the same, but water boils and gets converted into steam.

Inference:

- The temperature at which solid changes into liquid is called its **melting point**.
- The temperature at which liquid changes into vapour or gaseous form is called its **boiling point**.
- The extra heat supplied to liquid even when it had attained its boiling point, this extra heat remains hidden in the gaseous state and is called **latent heat of vaporisation**.

  The temperature of water therefore does not change inspite of supplying it extra heat.

12.
- Take some camphor or ammonium chloride. Crush it and put it in a China dish.
- Put an inverted funnel over the China dish.
- Put a cotton plug on the stem of the funnel as shown in the figure.
- Now heat slowly and observe.
- What do you infer from the above activity.

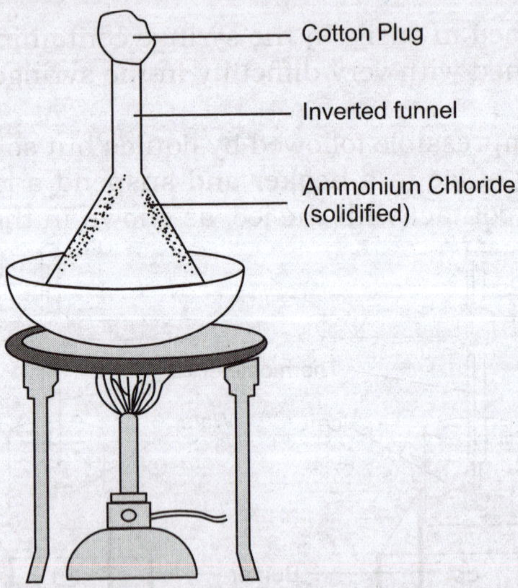

Observation:

On the stem of the funnel and near the cotton plug, solidified ammonium chloride is collected on heating the china dish. This solid ammonium chloride did not enter the phase of liquids *i.e.,* it did not melt but fumes/vapours on heating the china dish, containing ammonium chloride, were collected on the stem of the funnel as solidified ammonium chloride again.

Inference:

A solid on heating changed into a gas without changing into liquid state. This process is called sublimation.

VI. Value-Based Questions

Q1. Adil parked his bicycle on a sunny day in a parking stand of his school campus. When the school got over Adil saw his burst cycle tyre. Thereafter he kept less air in his cycle tyres and did not inflate them fully.

(*a*) Why did the tyre burst?

(*b*) Why is air compressible?

(*c*) What value of Adil is reflected in the above act?

Ans. (a) The tyre burst because the air inside the tyre got heated and therefore exerted greater pressure on the walls of the tyre.

(*b*) Air is compressible because it has large intermolecular space.

(*c*) Adil showed the value of intelligence, awareness and self responsibility.

Q2. Akshay's friend visited his house in Mumbai and he was surprised to see air conditioners installed in all of his rooms. His friend advised Akshay to use water-coolers and save electricity. On this Akshay told him that the water-cooler is not at all effective in coastal areas.

(*a*) Why are water-cooler not effective in coastal areas?

(*b*) What are the other two factors on which evaporation of water depends?

(*c*) What value of Akshay's friend is seen in this act?

Ans. (*a*) Water coolers are not effective in coastal areas due to high humidity.

(*b*) The other two factors on which evaporation of water depends are temperature and surface area.

(*c*) Akshay's friend showed the value of concerned citizen, morally responsible and friendly in nature.

Q3. Sita lived in a village and could not afford refrigerator in her house. She knew how to keep water cold and preserve all perishable items in her house. She kept wet cloth surrounding the earthen pot to keep water cool, she also kept vegetables fresh by keeping them in wet gunny bag and timely sprinkled water over it.

(*a*) Why did Sita keep wet cloth surrounding the earthen pot?

(*b*) Suggest one more method of keeping the house cool in summer.

(*c*) What value of Sita is reflected in the above case?

Ans. (*a*) The wet cloth gave the cooling effect to the pot, as the water in the cloth evaporated and evaporation causes cooling effect.

(*b*) By sprinkling some water on the lawn/veranda of the house can keep the house cool.

(*c*) Sita showed the value of responsible behaviour.

Q4. Shreya commutes in a CNG fitted van to school every day along with many other students. She told the van driver to get the CNG connection certified and timely checked it for any leakage or loose connection of pipes. She told the driver to be more careful during summers.

(*a*) What is CNG?

(*b*) Why should one be more careful with CNG cylinders during summer?

(*c*) What value of Shreya is seen in the above act?

Ans. (*a*) CNG is Compressed Natural Gas used as fuel.

(*b*) During summers, the CNG connections and cylinder need to be checked because the gas expands due to heat and if there would be any leakage then it would cause fire in the vehicle.

(*c*) Shreya showed the value of concerned citizen and morally responsible behaviour.

VII. Practical Based Questions (Solved)

Q1. How many grams of magnesium bromide are needed to make 1.0 L of a 4.0 M magnesium bromide solution?

Ans. $$1.0\,L\,MgBr_2 \times \frac{4.0\,mole\,MgBr_2}{1\,L\,MgBr_2} \times \frac{184.3\,g\,MgBr_2}{1\,mole\,MgBr_2} = 737.2\,g\,MgBr_2$$

Q2. What are the three different types of mixtures? Define each one.

Ans. Suspensions, Colloids, and Solutions.

Suspensions: A suspension is a heterogeneous mixture containing particles that are distinct from the surrounding medium.

Colloids: A colloid is a suspension in which a solute-like phase is dispersed throughout a solvent-like phase.

Solutions: A solution is a liquid mixture in which the minor component (the solute) is uniformly distributed within the major component (the solvent).

Q3. How is a solution different from the other two types of mixtures?

Ans. A solution is different from the other types of mixtures as it is homogeneous. While a suspension is made up of different phases and a colloid is made up of two distinct, different phases. A solution is made up of a solute and a solvent and solution cannot be separated easily into its components.

Q4. Describe (in detail) the three steps involved in solution formation.

Ans. **Step 1:** Take a required amount of solvent in a beaker

Step 2: Add the required amount of solute into it.

Step 3: Stir the solute into the solvent till it gets completely dissolved in it, if needed you may heat it for fast dissolution.

Q5. Use the solubility graph below to answer the following questions.

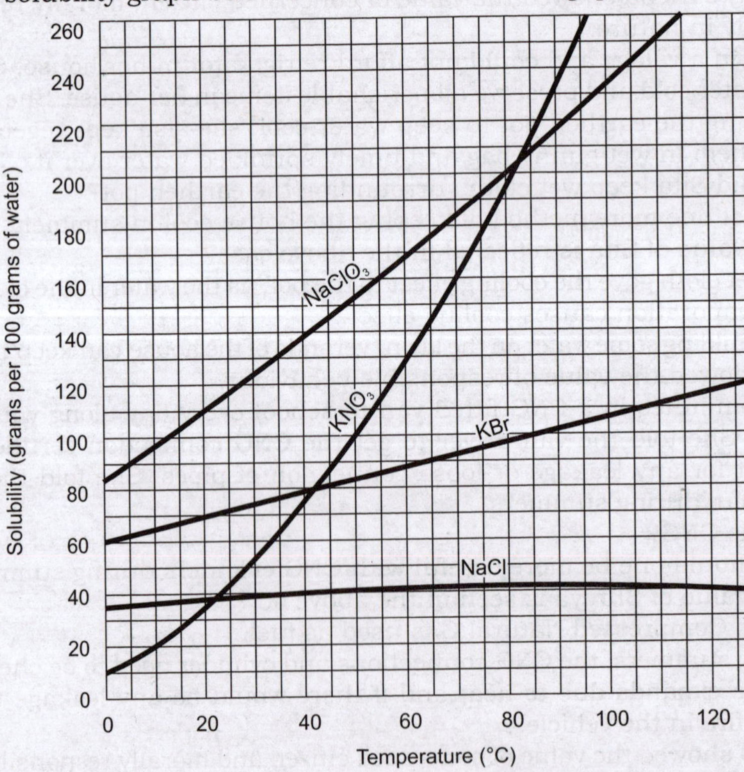

(*a*) Which salt is least soluble at 20°C?

(*b*) How many grams of KBr can be dissolved in 100g of water at 60°C?

(*c*) How many grams of NaCl can be dissolved in 100 g of water at 100°C?

(*d*) Classify the type of solution: At 40°C, 180g of $NaClO_3$ is dissolved in 100g of water.

(*e*) Classify the type of solution: At 70°C, 70g of KBr is dissolved in 100g of water.

Ans. (*a*) KNO_3 (*b*) 80-90g (*c*) 40g (*d*) It is supersaturated

(*e*) unsaturated

Q6. Not all solutions of solids are dissolved in liquids. Provide two examples of other types of solutions other than this.

Ans. (*a*) Gas dissolved in liquid: CO_2 in H_2O (carbonated beverage).

(*b*) Solid dissolved in solid: Alloys like steel solution of carbon atoms in iron atoms

Q7. How could you tell by looking at a solution that it was saturated?

Ans. If the additional solute is added and it remains undissolved the solution can be considered as saturated.

Q8. What is the Tyndall Effect? Cite a common example of this effect.

Ans. The Tyndall Effect occurs when light is scattered by particles in a colloid or particles in a fine suspension. For example—The sky appears blue due to the scattering of light by dust particles suspended in it.

Q9. Given an unknown mixture consisting of two substances, explain how a scientist could use lab techniques to determine whether the mixture is a true solution, a colloid, or a suspension.

Ans. If the unknown mixture can be separated by filtration then it is a suspension. If the scattering of light by the particles is observed then it is a colloid. Otherwise all others are true solutions.

TEST YOUR SKILLS

Q1. What is dry ice?

Q2. What is normal atmospheric pressure?

Q3. Give two examples of diffusion.

Q4. At what temperature is the density of water maximum?

Q5. Name the factors that affect evaporation.

Q6. With the help of an example, explain how diffusion of gases in water is essential?

Q7. How is the high compressibility property of gas useful to us?

Q8. Liquids and gases can be compressed but it is difficult to compress solids. Why?

Q9. State the differences between solid, liquid and gas.

Q10. Pressure and temperature determine the state of a substance. Explain.

Q11. Give reasons for the following:

(*a*) Water kept in earthen pots become cool during summer.

(*b*) Naphthalene balls disappear with time without leaving any solid.

(*c*) A gas fills completely the vessel in which it is kept.

❑❑❑

2 Is Matter Around Us Pure

Syllabus

Elements, Molecules, Compounds, Mixture, Suspension, Colloids, Solution

Facts that Matter

Matter

- **Pure substances**
  - **Elements**: cannot be broken into simpler substances. *E.g.*, copper, oxygen, hydrogen,
  - **Compounds**: have fixed composition can be broken down into elements by chemical or electrochemical reactions. *E.g.*, water, sugar, salt, etc.
- **Impure substances (Mixtures)**
  - **Homogeneous**: uniform composition. *E.g.*, sugar + H_2O, water + alcohol
  - **Heterogeneous**: non-uniform composition. *E.g.*, sand + sugar, water + oil,

Elements

It is a pure substance which cannot be split into two or more simpler substances.

- **Metals**: malleable, ductile, good conductors of heat. *E.g.*, copper, gold, iron
- **Metalloids**: shows some properties of metals and some of non-metals. *E.g.*, silicon, boron, arsenic
- **Non-metals**: non-malleable, non-ductile bad conductors of heat. *E.g.*, sulphur, oxygen

• Compounds

Compound is a pure substance made up of two or more elements combined chemically in a definite ratio.

Characteristics:

1. The properties of compound differ from those of its constituents.
2. Compound has fixed melting point and boiling point.
3. Compound is a homogeneous substance.
4. Constituent elements can be separated by chemical process.

• Mixtures

It is made up of two or more elements or compounds mixed in any ratio/proportion.

Properties:

- It may be homogeneous or heterogeneous.
- The properties of constituent substances are retained.
- No new compound is formed.
- Constituents of a mixture can be separated by simple physical processes.
- It does not have fixed melting and boiling point.

Separation of Mixtures:

Type of Mixture	*Separation method*
1. Two immiscible liquids. Example, oil + water	By using separating funnel
2. Ammonium chloride + sand	Sublimation
3. Dyes in black ink. (One solvent; different constituents)	Chromatography
4. Two miscible liquids. (Acetone + water)	Distillation
5. Solid particles insoluble from (solvent) liquid. (Milk + Cream)	Centrifugation

Physical and Chemical Change

Physical Change	*Chemical Change*
• No new substance is formed.	A new substance is formed.
• Properties of constituent elements/ substance is retained.	Properties of constituent elements/substance changes.
• Change does not involve loss or gain of heat.	Loss or gain of heat may be involved in this reaction.
• This change is generally reversible.	This change is generally irreversible (can be reversible also).

• Solution

It is a homogeneous mixture of two or more substances.

Solute	*Solvent*
A substance which is dissolved in a solvent. *E.g.,* salt, sugar.	Liquid part of solution in which a substance is dissolved. *E.g.,* water.
Solute can be solid, liquid or gas.	Solvent can be liquid, solid or gas.

TYPES OF SOLUTION

Aqueous solution
A solution in which water is a solvent. E.g., salt + water

Non-aqueous solution
A solution in which water is not a solvent. E.g., sulphur + carbon disulphide.

True solution
Solute particles completely dissolve in solvent and are not visible. E.g., sugar + water

Solution can be dilute or concentrated
(Depending on the amount of solute dissolving in solvent).

Saturated solution
A solution in which no more solute can dissolve at given temperature.

Unsaturated solution
A solution in which more solute can dissolve at a given temperature.

- Concentration of solution = $\frac{\text{Amount of solute}}{\text{Amount of solution}}$ or $\frac{\text{Amount of solute}}{\text{Amount of solvent}} \times 100$
- Mass by mass percentage of a solution

$$= \frac{\text{Mass of solute}}{\text{Mass of solvent}} \times 100$$

- Mass by volume percentage of a solution

$$= \frac{\text{Mass of solute}}{\text{Volume of solvent}} \times 100$$

- Volume by volume percentage of a solution

$$= \frac{\text{Volume of solute}}{\text{Volume of solution}} \times 100$$

Suspension	***Colloidal Solution***
• Size of solute particles are visible with naked eyes	Size of solute particles are not visible with naked eyes.
• Shows tyndall effect	Shows tyndall effect
• Translucent or opaque	Translucent
• Solute particles settle down	Colloidal particles do not settle down

- **Different Types of Colloids**

Dispersed Phase	***Dispersing Medium***	***Type***	***Example***
Liquid	Gas	Aerosol	Fog, clouds, mist
Solid	Gas	Aerosol	Smoke, automobile exhaust
Gas	Liquid	Foam	Shaving cream
Liquid	Liquid	Emulsion	Milk, face cream
Solid	Liquid	Solution	Milk of magnesia, mud
Gas	Solid	Foam	Sponge, pumice
Liquid	Solid	Gel	Jelly, cheese, butter
Solid	Solid	Solid sol	Coloured gemstone, milky glass

NCERT IN-TEXT QUESTIONS SOLVED

Q1. What is meant by a substance?

Ans. A pure substance consists of a single type of particles. A substance is a pure single form of matter.

Q2. List the points of differences between homogeneous and heterogeneous mixtures.

Ans.

Homogeneous mixtures	***Heterogeneous mixtures***
• It has uniform composition.	It does not have a uniform composition.
• No visible boundaries of separation.	Shows visible boundaries of separation.
• They consist of only one phase. Example: sugar + water → sugar solution.	They consist of more than one phase. Example: sugar + sand

Q3. Differentiate between homogeneous and heterogeneous mixtures with examples.

Ans. Same as Q2 above.

Q4. How are sol, solution and suspension different from each other?

Ans.

Sol. (colloid)	***Solution***	***Suspension***
1. Size of solute particles between 1 nm to 100 nm.	Size of solute particles less than 1 nm (10^{-9} m)	Size of solute particles is more than 100 nm.
2. It is stable.	Stable.	Unstable.
3. It scatters a beam of light.	It does not scatter light.	It scatters a beam of light.
4. Solute particles pass through filter paper.	Solute particles pass through filter paper.	Solute particles do not pass through filter paper.

Q5. To make a saturated solution, 36 g of sodium chloride is dissolved in 100 g of water at 293 K. Find its concentration at this temperature.

Ans. Mass of solute (sodium chloride) = 36 g

Mass of solvent (water) = 100 g

∴ Mass of solution = Mass of solute + Mass of solvent

= 36 g + 100 g = 136 g

$$\text{Concentration} = \frac{\text{Mass of solute}}{\text{Mass of solution}} \times 100$$

$$= \frac{36}{136} \times 100 = 26.47\%$$

Q6. How will you separate a mixture containing kerosene and petrol (difference in their boiling points is more than 25°C), which are miscible with each other?

Ans. A mixture of kerosene and petrol which are miscible with each other can be separated by distillation.

Method

- Take the mixture in a distillation flask.
- Fit it with a thermometer.
- Arrange the apparatus as shown in the figure.
- Heat the mixture slowly.
- Petrol vaporises first as it has lower boiling point. It condenses in the condenser and is collected from the condenser outlet.
- Kerosene is left behind in the distillation flask.

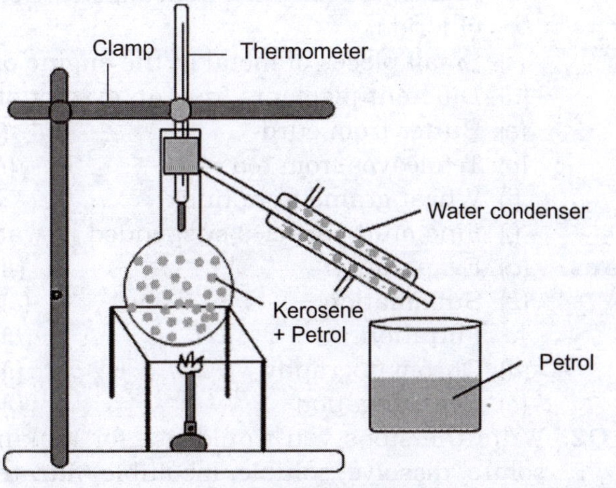

Distillation process

Q7. Name the technique to separate

(*i*) butter from curd,

(5) salt from sea-water,

(*iii*) camphor from salt.

Ans. (*i*) Centrifugation,

(*ii*) Evaporation,

(*iii*) Sublimation.

Q8. What type of mixtures are separated by the technique of crystallisation?

Ans. Crystallisation technique is used to purify solid with some impurities in it. Example: Salt from sea-water.

Q9. Classify the following as chemical or physical changes:

- cutting of trees,
- melting of butter in a pan,
- rusting of almirah,
- boiling of water to form steam,
- passing of electric current, through water and the water breaking down into hydrogen and oxygen gas,
- dissolving common salt in water,
- making a fruit salad with raw fruits and
- burning of paper and wood.

Ans.

Physical Change	***Chemical Change***
• cutting of trees	• rusting of almirah
• melting of butter in a pan	• passing of electric current through water and then breaking down into hydrogen and oxygen gas
• boiling of water to form steam	• burning of paper and wood
• dissolving common salt in water	
• making a fruit salad with raw fruits	

Q10. Try segregating the things around you as pure substances or mixtures.

Ans. **Pure substances**—Water, bread, sugar and gold.

Mixtures—Steel, plastic, paper, talc, milk and air.

NCERT TEXTUAL QUESTIONS SOLVED

Q1. Which separation techniques will you apply for the separation of the following?

(*a*) Sodium chloride from its solution in water.

(*b*) Ammonium chloride from a mixture containing sodium chloride and ammonium chloride.

(*c*) Small pieces of metal in the engine oil of a car.

(*d*) Different pigments from an extract of flower petals.

(*e*) Butter from curd.

(*f*) Oil from water.

(*g*) Tea leaves from tea.

(*h*) Iron pins from sand.

(i) Wheat grains from husk.

(*j*) Fine mud particles suspended in water.

Ans. (*a*) Evaporation

(*b*) Sublimation

(*c*) Filtration

(*d*) Chromatography

(*e*) Centrifugation

(*f*) Separating funnel

(*g*) Filtration

(*h*) Magnetic separation

(*i*) Winnowing/sedimentation

(*j*) Decantation and filtration

Q2. Write the steps you would use for making tea. Use the words, solution, solvent, solute, dissolve, soluble, insoluble, filtrate and residue.

Ans.

1. Take a cup of water in a container as solvent and heat it.
2. Add sugar in it which is solute. Heat it till all sugar dissolves.
3. You get a solution of water and sugar.
4. Sugar is soluble in water completely.
5. Add half a tea-spoon of tea-leaves, it is insoluble in water.
6. Boil the content, add milk which is also soluble in water, boil again.
7. Filter the tea with the help of strainer, the tea collected in cup is filtrate and the tea leaves collected on the strainer is residue.

Q3. Pragya tested the solubility of three different substances at different temperatures and collected the data as given below (results are given in the following table, as grams of substance dissolved in 100 grams of water to form a saturated solution).

Substance Dissolved	***Temperature in K and Solubility***				
	283	293	313	333	353
Potassium nitrate	21	32	62	106	167
Sodium chloride	36	36	36	37	37
Potassium chloride	35	35	40	46	54
Ammonium chloride	24	37	41	55	66

(*a*) What mass of potassium nitrate would be needed to produce a saturated solution of potassium nitrate in 50 grams of water at 313 K?

(*b*) Pragya makes a saturated solution of potassium chloride in water at 353 K and leaves the solution to cool at room temperature. What would she observe as the solution cools? Explain.

(*c*) Find the solubility of each salt at 293 K. Which salt has the highest solubility at this temperature?

(*d*) What is the effect of change of temperature on the solubility of a salt?

Ans. (*a*) Mass of KNO_3 needed to produce a saturated solution of KNO_3 in 100 grams of water at 313 K = 62 g

$\therefore$ Mass of KNO_3 needed in 50 grams of water at 313 K = $= \frac{62.0 \times 50}{100} = \mathbf{31.0\ g}$

(*b*) Crystals of potassium chloride will be obtained on cooling the saturated solution.

(*c*) Solubility of each salt at 293 K is

(*i*) Potassium nitrate → 32 g
(*ii*) Sodium chloride → 36 g
(*iii*) Potassium chloride → 35 g
(*iv*) Ammonium chloride → 37 g

Ammonium chloride has the highest solubility at this temperature.

(*d*) On increasing the temperature, solubility of a salt increases.

Q4. Explain the following giving examples:

(*a*) Saturated solution (*b*) Pure substance
(*c*) Colloid (*d*) Suspension

Ans. (*a*) **Saturated solution:** In a given solvent when no more solute can dissolve further at a given temperature is called saturated solution.

(*b*) **Pure substance:** A pure substance consists of a single type of particles. E.g., gold, silver.

(*c*) **Colloid:** A colloid is a solution in which the size of solute particles are bigger than that of true solution. These particles cannot be seen with our naked eyes, they are stable. e.g., ink, blood.

(*d*) **Suspension:** It is a heterogeneous mixture in which the solute particles are big enough to settle down. e.g., chalk-water, paints, etc.

Q5. Classify each of the following as a homogeneous or heterogeneous mixture: soda water, wood, air, soil, vinegar, filtered tea.

Ans. Homogeneous: Soda water, vinegar, filtered tea, air.
Heterogeneous: Wood, soil.

Q6. How would you confirm that a colourless liquid given to you is pure water?

Ans. By finding the boiling point of a given colourless liquid. If the liquid boils at 100°C at atmospheric pressure, then it is pure water. This is because pure substances have fixed melting and boiling point.

Q7. Which of the following materials fall in the category of a "pure substance"?

(*a*) Ice (*b*) Milk (*c*) Iron
(*d*) Hydrochloric acid (*e*) Calcium oxide (*f*) Mercury
(*g*) Brick (*h*) Wood (*i*) Air.

Ans. Pure substances are: Ice, iron, hydrochloric acid, calcium oxide and mercury.

Q8. Identify the solutions among the following mixtures.

(*a*) Soil (*b*) Sea water (*c*) Air
(*d*) Coal (*e*) Soda water.

Ans. Solutions are: Sea water, soda water and air.

Q9. Which of the following will show "Tyndall effect"?

(*a*) Salt solution (*b*) Milk
(*c*) Copper sulphate solution (*d*) Starch solution.

Ans. Milk and starch solution.

Q10. Classify the following into elements, compounds and mixtures.

(*a*) Sodium (*b*) Soil (*c*) Sugar solution
(*d*) Silver (*e*) Calcium carbonate (*f*) Tin
(*g*) Silicon (*h*) Coal (*i*) Air
(*j*) Soap (*k*) Methane (*l*) Carbon dioxide
(*m*) Blood

Ans.

Elements	**Compounds**	**Mixtures**
Sodium	Calcium carbonate	Sugar solution
Silver	Methane	Soil
Tin	Carbon dioxide	Coal
Silicon	Soap	Air
		Blood

Q11. Which of the following are chemical changes?

(*a*) Growth of a plant (*b*) Rusting of iron
(*c*) Mixing of iron filings and sand (*d*) Cooking of food
(*e*) Digestion of food (*f*) Freezing of water
(*g*) Burning of a candle.

Ans. Chemical changes are:

(*a*) Growth of a plant (*b*) Rusting of iron
(*c*) Cooking of food (*d*) Digestion of food
(*e*) Burning of a candle

ADDITIONAL QUESTIONS SOLVED

I. Multiple Choice Questions

Choose the correct option:

1. Fog, clouds are an example of

(*a*) aerosol (*b*) colloid
(*c*) suspension (*d*) emulsion

2. Sponge can be compressed, it is a

(*a*) solid (*b*) liquid
(*c*) gas (*d*) foam

3. An impure sample of potash alum can be purified by

(*a*) evaporation (*b*) crystallisation
(*c*) centrifugation (*d*) filtration

4. Chalk dissolved in water is an example of
   (*a*) true solution (*b*) colloid
   (*c*) suspension (*d*) saturated solution
5. 50 gm sugar is dissolved in a glass of water at 30°C. On heating this solution it will
   (*a*) crystallise (*b*) evaporate
   (*c*) become unsaturated (*d*) sugar will char
6. Which of the following shows tyndall effects?
   (*a*) salt solution (*b*) sugar solution
   (*c*) starch solution (*d*) copper sulphate solution
7. Pick up the odd one out.
   (*a*) brass (*b*) air
   (*c*) sand (*d*) graphite
8. Which of the following is liquid-liquid solution?
   (*a*) face-cream (*b*) emulsion
   (*c*) milk (*d*) all of these
9. To separate two miscible liquids by fractional distillation, it should have one of the following condition
   (*a*) should be miscible (*b*) should be immiscible
   (*c*) difference in the boiling point should be less than 25 K
   (*d*) none of these
10. To obtain toned and double toned milk from full-cream milk we can
   (*a*) filtrate it (*b*) sediment it
   (*c*) distillate it (*d*) centrifuge it
11. The separation technique which involves the difference in their densities is
   (*a*) sublimation (*b*) separation by separating funnel
   (*c*) centrifugation (*d*) both (*b*) and (*c*)

Ans. 1—(*a*), 2—(*d*) or (*a*), 3—(*b*), 4—(*c*), 5—(*c*), 6—(*c*), 7—(*d*), 8—(*d*), 9—(*c*), 10—(*d*), 11—(*d*).

II. Very Short Answer Type Questions

Q1. Define solvent.

Ans. The component of the solution that dissolves the other component in it is called the solvent.

Q2. Define solute.

Ans. The component of the solution that is dissolved in the solvent is called solute.

Q3. What is 'tincture of iodine'?

Ans. A solution of iodine in alcohol is known as tincture of iodine. It has iodine (solid) as the solute and alcohol (liquid) as the solvent.

Q4. What are alloys?

Ans. The homogeneous mixture of two or more metals or a metal and non-metal is called an alloy. E.g., steel is an alloy of iron and carbon.

Q5. Give one example of gas in liquid solution.

Ans. Cold-drinks, carbon dioxide gas as solute is mixed with water as a solvent.

Q6. How can a solution be dilute or concentrated?

Ans. The amount of solute dissolved in a solvent decides whether the solution is dilute or concentrated.

Q7. What is "concentration of a solution"?

Ans. The concentration of a solution is the amount of solute present in a given amount of solution or the amount of solute dissolved in a given mass or volume of solvent.

Q8. State the difference between aqueous and non-aqueous solution.

Ans. Aqueous solutions have water as solvent and non-aqueous solutions do not have water as solvent.

Q9. What is "solubility" of a solute?

Ans. The amount of the solute present in the saturated solution at the given temperature is called its solubility.

Q10. What is saturated solution?

Ans. The maximum amount of solute that can be dissolved in a solvent at given temperature is called saturated solution, where no more solute can dissolve further.

Q11. What is unsaturated solution?

Ans. If the amount of solute contained in a solution is less than the saturation level, it is called an unsaturated solution.

Q12. How can you convert saturated solution into unsaturated or vice-versa?

Ans. Saturated solution on heating becomes unsaturated and unsaturated solution on cooling becomes saturated.

Q13. Why water is called universal solvent?

Ans. Water can dissolve large number of substances in it.

Q14. What is Tyndall effect?

Ans. The scattering of light by colloidal particles is known as Tyndall effect.

Q15. How can we separate colloidal mixtures?

Ans. By centrifugation, in a centrifuge machine the colloidal solution is kept in a test tube, rotated very fast and due to centrifugal force the colloidal particles are separated.

Q16. What is emulsion?

Ans. When both the dispersed phase and dispersing medium is liquid, it is called emulsion. E.g., milk, face cream.

Q17. What is aerosol?

Ans. When the solid or liquid is dispersed in a gas it is called aerosol. E.g., smoke, fog.

Q18. What is the principle for separation of immiscible liquids?

Ans. The principle of separating immiscible liquids into layers depends on their densities. The less denser liquid collects at the top and more denser liquid at the bottom.

Q19. What is chromatography?

Ans. Chromatography is the technique used for separation of those solutes that dissolve in the same solvent.

Q20. What is distillation?

Ans. Distillation is the separation technique of two miscible liquids that boils without decomposition and have sufficient difference in their boiling points.

Q21. How can you separate two liquids that have less than 25 K difference of boiling points?

Ans. To separate a mixture of two or more miscible liquids for which the difference in boiling points is less than 25 K, is fractional distillation.

Q22. What is condenser?

Ans. It is an apparatus used to convert gas into liquid by cooling it.

Q23. What is crystallisation?

Ans. When a saturated solution is heated and allowed to cool slowly, crystal of the solute dissolved in the saturated solution are separated from it. It is used to purify solids.

Q24. How will you separate miscible and immiscible liquids?

Ans. Miscible liquid can be separated by distillation and immiscible liquids can be separated by using separating funnel.

III. Short Answer Type questions

Q1. Why is mixture called impure substance?

Ans. Mixture consists of different components which retain their properties and can be easily separated by physical processes, hence it is called as impure substance.

Q2. Give the differences between mixture and compound.

Ans.

Mixture	***Compound***
1. Constituents combine in any ratio to form mixture.	1. Constituents combine in fixed ratio to form a compound.
2. Constituents retain their properties.	2. Constituents do not retain their properties as a new substance is formed.
3. Constituents can be separated by physical processes.	3. Constituents cannot be separated by physical processes.

Q3. Distinguish between a physical change and chemical change.

Ans.

Physical Change	***Chemical Change***
1. No new substance is formed.	1. New substance is formed.
2. It is a reversible change.	2. It is irreversible change.
3. The properties of constituents are retained.	3. The properties of constituents are not retained.
4. No new substance is formed.	4. Completely new substance is formed.

Q4. State the properties of a solution.

Ans. **Properties of a solution are:**

1. A solution is a homogeneous mixture.
2. Particles of a solution are smaller than 1 nm and cannot be seen by naked eyes.
3. Do not scatter beam of light.
4. Solute particles cannot be separated from the mixture by the process of filtration and thus, solution is stable.

Q5. State the properties of a suspension.

Ans. Properties of a suspension

- Suspension is a heterogeneous mixture having particle size greater than 100 nm.
- The particles of a suspension can be seen by naked eyes.
- Particles can scatter a beam of light.
- It is unstable.

Q6. What is a colloidal solution?

Ans. It is a heterogeneous solution which appears to be homogeneous, particles size is very small and so cannot be seen with naked eyes but it is stable. E.g., milk and blood.

Q7. State the properties of colloidal solution.

Ans. **Properties of colloidal solution.**

- It is a heterogeneous mixture having particle size between 1 nm to 100 nm.
- Size of particles is very small, cannot be seen with naked eyes.
- It scatters a beam of light.
- They are stable as the particles do not settle when left undisturbed.

Q8. Give the applications of centrifugation.

Ans. **Application of centrifugation are:**

1. Used in diagnostic laboratories for blood and urine test.
2. Used in dairies and home to separate butter from cream.
3. Used in washing machines as a spinner to squeeze out water from wet clothes.

Q9. Give the applications of chromatography.

Ans. **Applications of chromatography are**

1. To separate colours in a dye.
2. To separate pigments from natural colours.
3. To separate drugs from blood.

Q10. Why is crystallisation better than evaporation?

Ans. Crystallisation is a process that separates a pure solid in the form of its crystals from a solution.

Crystallisation is better than evaporation because during evaporation

- Some solids decompose or some, like sugar may get charred on heating to dryness.
- Some impurities may remain dissolved in the solution even after filtration which on evaporation contaminates the solid.

Q11. How will you separate a mixture of oil and water?

Ans. To separate a mixture of oil and water, we need a separating funnel as both are immiscible liquids.

Pour the mixture in separating funnel and let the funnel stand undisturbed for sometime. So that separate layer of oil and water are formed. Open the stopcock of the separating funnel and pour out the lower layer of water carefully.

Q12. A student is given a mixture of naphthalene ball's powder and common salt. He need to separate this mixture. How will he do this?

Ans. The properties of both naphthalene and common salt should be known, before we choose the separation technique.

Naphthalene is a sublimate which on heating changes to gaseous state directly. Hence to separate a volatile compound (sublimate) from a non-volatile compound (non-sublimate), the sublimation process is used.

In a China dish the mixture is kept, and is placed on a stand. An inverted funnel is kept over the mixture in China dish with plugged stem. The sublimate on heating gets collected on the funnel and common salt remains in the China dish.

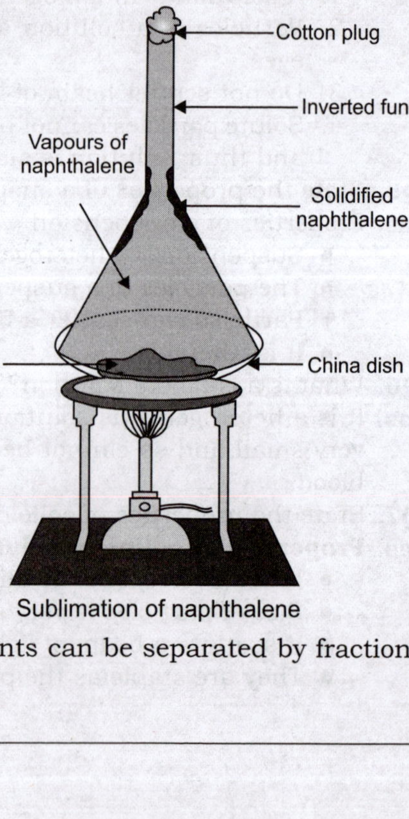

Sublimation of naphthalene

Q13. How can we obtain different gases from air?

Ans. Air is a homogeneous mixture and its components can be separated by fractional distillation.

The flow diagram shows the steps involved in the process.

Air

↓

Compressed and cooled by increasing pressure and decreasing temperature.

↓

Liquid Air

↓

Allow to warm up slowly in fractional distillation column.

↓

Gases get separated at different heights.

↓

	Oxygen	Argon	Nitrogen
Boiling Point (°C)	– 183	– 186	– 196
% Air by volume	20.9	0.9	78.1

Q14. Draw a flow diagram to show how the water purification system in water works.

Ans.

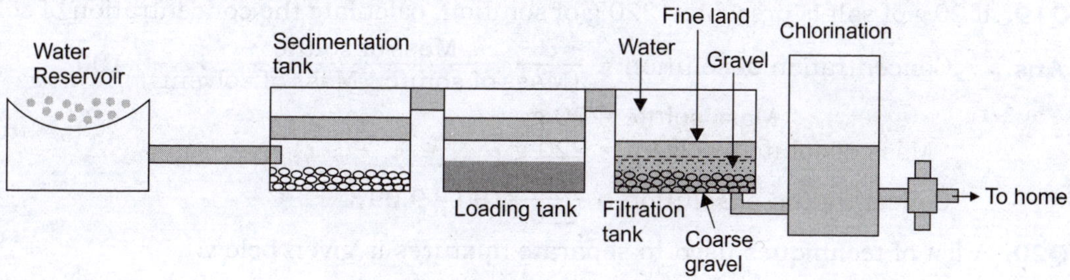

Water purification system in water works

Water is collected in the reservoir → The water is sent to sedimentation tank to allow solids to settle →

It is then passed to 2nd tank i.e., loading tank, so that the suspended impurities are loaded to settle down as sediment. → Then water reaches the filtration tank

In **filtration tank** water passes through different layers of sand and gravel as shown in the above figure. This is for adsorption of impurities.

The clear water reaches a chlorinated tank where water is mixed with bleaching powder/chlorine to kill bacteria and then supplied to houses.

Q15. Why is air considered as a mixture and not compound?

Ans. Air is considered as a mixture because it exhibits following properties:

1. Each component present in air retains its properties.
2. Each component can be separated by simple physical processes.
3. The components do not have any fixed proportion. All gases are present in different amount. Example, in greener area—more oxygen and water vapour is present; near industrial area—air consists of lot of impurities and smoke suspended in it.

Q16. How can you prove that water is a compound?

Ans. When electricity is passed through water at two different electrodes, we get two different gases i.e., oxygen and hydrogen during electrolysis of water are produced. The ratio of oxygen: hydrogen is 1:2 by number of molecules.

- The properties of oxygen and hydrogen gases are entirely different from that of liquid water.
- The ratio of oxygen: hydrogen combination is always constant i.e., 1: 2 by volume.
- To separate the components of water, we need electrolytic cell, and it is not a simple process.
- This proves that water is a compound.

Q17. How can we convert saturated solution into unsaturated by heating?

Ans. Saturated solution is said to be saturated at a given temperature when there is no more scope of solute particles to dissolve/dissociate into water. It is because the solute particle has taken all the intermolecular space present in the solvent.

On heating, the molecules of solvent gain kinetic energy, start vibrating and try to move away from each other thereby accommodating some more solute particle in this space and hence it becomes an unsaturated solution.

Q18. What is the difference in fog and smoke?

Ans. Fog is a colloidal solution with liquid dispersed in gas.

Smoke is a colloidal solution with solid dispersed in gas.

Q19. If 20 g of salt is present is 220 g of solution, calculate the concentration of solution.

Ans. $$\text{Concentration of solution} = \frac{\text{Mass of solute}}{(\text{Mass of solute} + \text{Mass of solvent})} \times 100$$

$$\text{Mass solute} = 20 \text{ g}$$

$$\text{Mass of solute + solvent} = 220 \text{ g}$$

$$\therefore \text{ Concentration of solution} = \frac{20}{220} \times 100 = 9.09\%$$

Q20. A list of techniques used to separate mixtures is given below.

fractional distillation **simple distillation** **crystallisation** **filtration** **diffusion**

From the list choose the most suitable technique to separate the following:

(*a*) Water from aqueous copper (II) sulphate ....

(*b*) Helium from a mixture of helium and argon ....

(*c*) Copper (II) sulphate from aqueous copper (II) sulphate ....

(*d*) Ethanol from aqueous ethanol ....

(*e*) Barium sulphate from a mixture of water and barium sulphate ....

Ans. (*a*) simple distillation (*b*) fractional distillation

(*c*) crystallisation (*d*) diffusion

(*e*) filtration

Q21. In Chromatography: Sometimes a spot will remain on the base line, where sample was first applied:

(*a*) Suggest what affinity this substance would have for solvent.

(*b*) Suggest the value for Rf of this substance.

(*c*) Outline how you could determine whether these materials are pure or a mixture?

Ans. (*a*) The spot on the base line is not soluble in the solvent.

(*b*) Its Rf value is 0.

(*c*) The solvent can be changed, only such solvent should be used in which the given sample can travel. The pure substances always have rf value less than 1.

Q22. Some students proposed measuring the position of each spot from the top, others proposed from the center. Explain which method is better?

Ans. To measure the distance travelled by the spot it is always advisable to measure the distance from the base line. The measurement from the center will not give the correct value of Rf.

Q23. Distinguish between the pure and impure substances.

Ans. Pure substance have fixed boiling and melting point and the impure substances boil or melt over the range of the temperature.

Q24. On adding impurity to a substance what happens to its Boiling point/ Melting point?

Ans. The boiling point and the melting point does not remain fixed. The boiling point increases on addition of impurity.

Q25. Pure ethanol boils at 78.4° C and freezes at –114.3° C. You have a sample of ethanol which boils between 79.1° C and 79.9° C

(*a*) What can you say about its purity?

(*b*) What will you expect to find, when you measure its freezing point?

Ans. (*a*) The sample is impure as it is boiling over a range of temperature.

(*b*) The freezing point will lower.

Q26. It is important that some substances are pure. Give two examples.

Ans. Pure substances are required for several things in life like medicine and food should be pure if impurities are added into it can become fatal.

IV. Long Answer Type questions

Q1. Give the difference between true solution, colloidal solution and suspension.

Ans. The difference between true solution, colloidal solution and suspension

Property	***True Solution***	***Colloidal Solution***	***Suspension***
1. Particle size	less than 1nm.	between 1nm and 100 nm.	more than 100 nm.
2. State	Stable	Stable	Unstable
3. Tyndall effect (Scattering of light)	No	Yes	Yes
4. Separation by filtration	Not possible	Not possible	Is possible
5.Nature	Transparent	Translucent	Translucent/ opaque

Q2. State the different types of colloids with examples.

Ans. Different colloids are formed due to different dispersed phase and dispersing medium.

Dispersed Phase	***Dispersing Medium***	***Type***	***Example***
Liquid	Gas	Aerosol	Fog, clouds, mist
Solid	Gas	Aerosol	Smoke, automobile exhaust
Gas	Liquid	Foam	Shaving cream
Liquid	Liquid	Emulsion	Milk, face cream
Solid	Liquid	Solution	Milk of magnesia, mud
Gas	Solid	Foam	Sponge, pumice
Liquid	Solid	Gel	Jelly, cheese, butter
Solid	Solid	Solid sol	Coloured gemstone, milky glass

Q3. (*a*) Define solution.

(*b*) Give different types of solutions with one example each.

Ans. (*a*) **Solution:** It is a homogeneous mixture of two or more substances. It consists of solute and solvent.

(*b*) **Different types of solution:**

(*i*) Based on solvent—Aqueous and non-aqueous
Aqueous solution has water as solvent (sugar + water)
Non-aqueous solution has some other solvent but not water. Example, (sulphur + carbon disulphide)

(*ii*) Depending on the amount of solute dissolved in solvent—Dilute solution and concentrated solution
Dilute solution—Less amount of solute particles are present in a solvent.
Concentrated solution—Amount of solute present in its maximum capacity in a solvent.

(*iii*) Amount of solute present in its maximum capacity at a given temperature—Saturated and unsaturated solution.
Saturated solution—It is a solution in which no more solute can further dissolve in a given solvent at a given temperature.
Unsaturated solution—It is a solution in which some more solute can dissolve in a solvent at a given temperature.

(*iv*) Depending on the size of solute particles

True solution	**Suspension**	**Colloid**
Size is very small and particles cannot be seen through naked eyes	Size is very big and can be seen through naked eyes	Size is intermediate between true solution and suspension

Q4. How can you separate the following mixtures?

(*a*) Sand + iron
(*b*) Cream from milk
(*c*) Salt + water
(*d*) Ammonium chloride + NaCl
(*e*) Copper sulphate + water
(*f*) Rice and dal (uncooked)
(*g*) Gases from air
(*h*) Petrol and diesel from crude oil
(*i*) Drugs from blood
(*j*) Acetone from water

Ans.
(*a*) Sand + iron – magnetic separation
(*b*) Cream from milk – centrifugation
(*c*) Salt + water – evaporation
(*d*) Ammonium chloride + NaCl – sublimation
(*e*) Copper sulphate + water – crystallisation
(*f*) Rice and dal (uncooked) – hand picking
(*g*) Gases from air – fractional distillation
(*h*) Petrol and diesel from crude oil – fractional distillation
(*i*) Drugs from blood – chromatography
(*j*) Acetone from water – distillation

Q5. The R*f* value of a sample = $\frac{\text{distance travelled by sample}}{\text{distance travelled by solvent front}}$

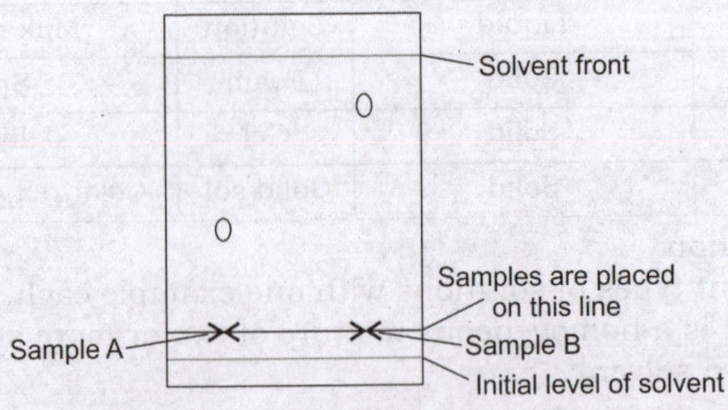

The R*f* value of the mixture used in chromatogram is:

A = 0.4, B = 0.5, C = 0.7, D = 0.9

(*a*) Calculate the Rf value of the two chromatograms shown in the figure.

(*b*) Name one solvent used in chromatography.

(*c*) Why is the line used for spotting drawn with pencil?

(*d*) If the chromatograms are colorless how can you locate them on the paper?

Ans. (*a*) Use scale to find the solvent front and find the Rf value by using the above formula.

(*b*) Water and alcohol.

(*c*) The pencil will not interfere in the chromatography.

(*d*) By using the locating agent like ninhydrin the colorless spots can be detected.

Q6. A metal coin is dissolved in acid. Chromatography is used to test the solution formed. The diagram given shows the chromatogram obtained.

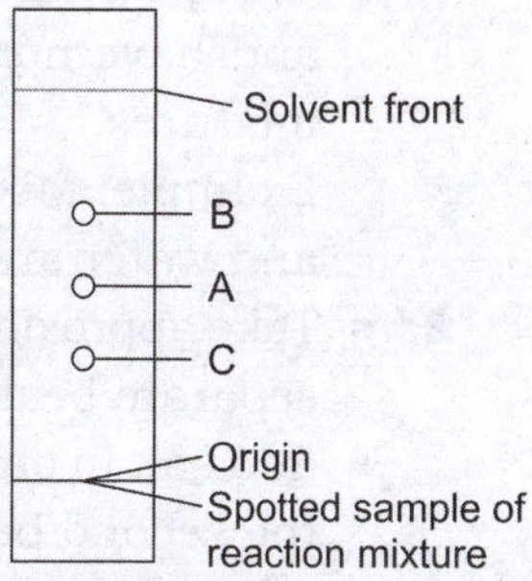

(*a*) Describe how the chromatogram would be set up in the laboratory.

(*b*) What can you say about the composition of the coin?

(*c*) Which of the spots (A, B or C) is more soluble in the solvent that was used in the chromatography?

Ans. (*a*) To set up the chromatogram use the solvent, take chromatography paper and draw the base line with pencil, place the spot of the chromatogram on this line and dip it in the solvent such that the base line of the paper stays above the solvent line.

(*b*) The coin consists of three different materials as the chromatogram shows three spots.

(*c*) The spot B is more soluble in the solvent as it travelled the maximum distance.

Q7. Compare the simple distillation and fractional distillation.

Ans. **Simple distillation:** The distillation flask is used to separate two substances having the difference in their boiling point more than 23 degrees.

Fractional distillation: The fractionating column in the set up helps in the separation of the fractions which may have very low difference in their boiling point. The fractionating column is a long chamber which controls the separation of one fraction at a time starting from the one with the lowest boiling point.

V. Activity-Based Questions

1. Let us divide the class into groups A, B, C and D.

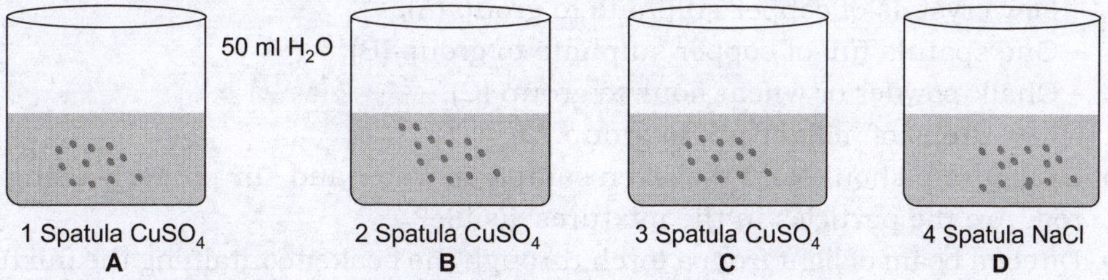

- Group A takes a beaker containing 50 ml of water and one spatula full of copper sulphate powder. Group B takes 50 ml of water and two spatula full of copper sulphate powder in a beaker.
- Groups C and D can take different amounts of copper sulphate and potassium permanganate or common salt (sodium chloride) and mix the given components to form a mixture.
- Report the observations on the uniformity in colour and texture.

Observations:

- Groups A and B have obtained a uniform composition throughout. Such mixtures are called homogeneous mixtures or solutions.
  Some other examples of mixtures are:
  (*i*) salt dissolved in water. (*ii*) sugar dissolved in water.
- Comparing the colour of the solutions of the two groups. Though both the groups have obtained copper sulphate solution but the intensity of colour of the solutions is different. This shows that a homogeneous mixtures can have a variable composition.
- Groups C and D have obtained mixtures, which contain physically distinct parts and have non-uniform compositions. Such mixtures are called heterogeneous mixtures.
  Example: Mixture of sodium chloride and iron fillings, salt and sulphur; and oil and water are examples of heterogeneous mixtures.

2. - Take approximately 50 ml of water each in two separate beakers.
   - Add salt in one beaker and barium chloride in the second beaker with continuous stirring.
   - When no more solute can be dissolved, heat the contents of the beaker to raise the temperature by about 5°C.
   - Start adding the solute again.
   - Is the amount of salt and sugar or barium chloride, that can be dissolved in water at a given temperature, the same?

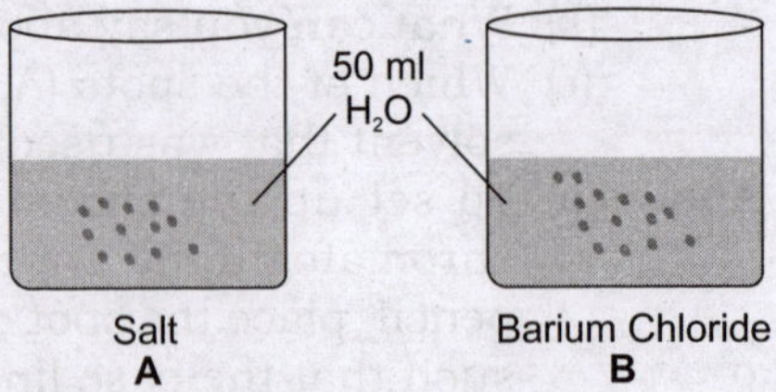

Answers:

- Beakers (A) and (B) are saturated solutions. On heating the beakers, the solution becomes unsaturated. Some more solute can be dissolved in it.
- No, different substances in a given solvent have different solubilities at the same temperature.

3. - Let us again divide the class into four groups—A, B, C and D.
   - Distribute the following samples to each groups:
     – Few crystals of copper sulphate to group (A).
     – One spatula full of copper sulphate to group (B).
     – Chalk powder or wheat flour to group (C).
     – Few drops of milk or ink to group (D).
   - Each group should add the given sample in water and stir properly using a glass rod. Are the particles in the mixtures visible?
   - Direct a beam of light from a torch through the beaker containing the mixture and observe from the front. Was the path of the beam of light visible?
   - Leave the mixtures undisturbed for a few minutes (and set up the filtration apparatus in the meantime).
     Is the mixture stable or do the particles begin to settle after sometime?
   - Filter the mixture. Is there any residue on the filter paper?
   - Discuss the results and form an opinion.

Observations:

Group	*A*	*B*	*C*	*D*
1. Mixture crystals	H_2O + $CuSO_4$ crystals	H_2O + $CuSO_4$ powder	Water + Chalk powder	Water + Milk
2. Visibility of particles in water.	No	No	Yes	No
3. Light beam scattering	No	No	Yes	Yes
4. Stability of particles	Stable	Stable	Unstable	Stable
5. Residue obtained on filtration	No	No	Yes	No
6. Inference	Solution	Solution	Suspension	Colloidal

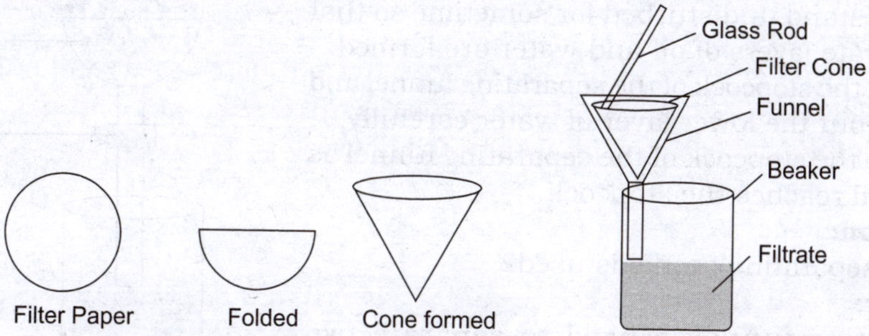

Filtration

4. • Fill half a beaker with water.
   • Put a watch glass on the mouth of the beaker, as shown in the figure given on next page.
   • Put few drops of ink on the watch glass.
   • Now start heating the beaker. We do not want to heat the ink directly. You will see that evaporation is taking place from the watch glass.
   • Continue heating as the evaporation goes on and stop heating when you do not see any further change on the watch glass.
   • Observe carefully and record your observations.

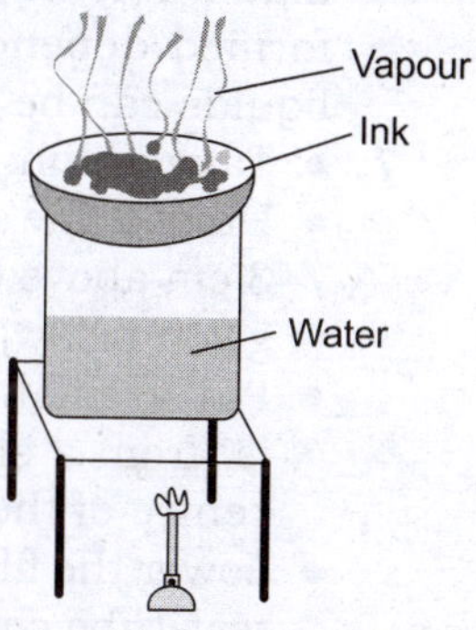

Evaporation

Questions:

- What do you think has got evaporated from the watch glass?
- Is there a residue on the watch glass?
- What is your interpretation? Is ink a single substance (pure) or is it a mixture?

Answers:

- Water and volatile substances get evaporated from the watch glass.
- Yes, residue is obtained on the watch glass.
- Ink is a mixture of a dye in water.

5. • Take some full-cream milk in a test tube.
   • Centrifuge it by using centrifuging machine for two minutes. If a centrifuging machine is not available in the school, you can do this activity at home by using a milk churner, used in the kitchen.
   • If you have a milk dairy nearby, visit it and ask
     (*i*) how they separate cream from milk.
     (*ii*) how they make cheese (paneer) from milk.

Questions:

- What do you observe on churning the milk?
- Explain how the separation of cream from milk takes place.

Answers:

- On churning of the milk, denser solid particles in the test tube remain at the bottom and the lighter particles stay at the top.
- Separation of cream from milk takes place by centrifugation due to the differences in the densities of the particles present in a mixture.

6. • Let us try to separate kerosene oil from water using a separating funnel.

- Pour the mixture of kerosene oil and water in a separating funnel.
- Let it stand undisturbed for sometime so that separate layers of oil and water are formed.
- Open the stopcock of the separating funnel and pour out the lower layer of water carefully.
- Close the stopcock of the separating funnel as the oil reaches the stopcock.

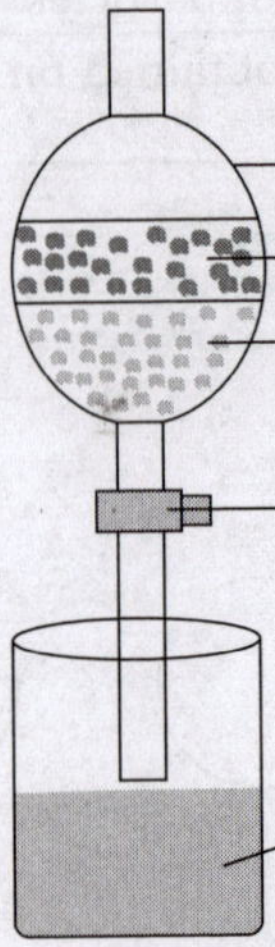

Separation of immiscible liquids

Question:

Why a separating funnel is used?

Answer:

Separating funnel is used to separate two immiscible liquids, because the two layers are formed depending on their densities and the liquids can be separated.

7. • Take a thin strip of filter paper.

- Draw a line on it using a pencil, approximately 3 cm above the lower edge (as shown in figure given below).
- Put a small drop of ink (water soluble, that is, from a sketch pen or fountain pen) at the centre of the line. Let it dry.
- Lower the filter paper into a jar/glass/beaker/test-tube containing water so that the drop of ink on the paper is just above the water level, as shown in the figure above and leave it undisturbed.
- Watch carefully, as the water rises up on the filter paper. Record your observations.

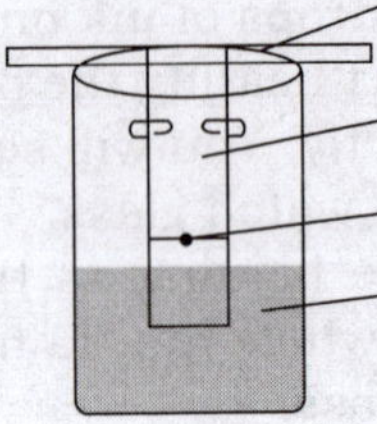

Chromatography

Questions:

- What do you observe on the filter paper as the water rises on it?
- Do you obtain different colours on the filter paper strip?
- What according to you, can be the reason for the rise of the coloured spot on the paper strip?

Answers:

- As the water rises up, the ink particles (dye) also rises along with it.
- Different colours are obtained on the filter paper strip as ink contains dye–mixture of two or more colour.
- The rise of the coloured spot on the paper strip shows the solubility of coloured components of ink in water. Those which rise faster are more soluble and get separated from the mixture.

8. • Let us try to separate acetone and water from their mixture.
• Take the mixture in a distillation flask. Fit it with a thermometer.
• Arrange the apparatus as shown in the figure below.
• Heat the mixture slowly keeping a close watch at the thermometer.
• The acetone vaporises, condenses in the condenser and can be collected from the condenser outlet.

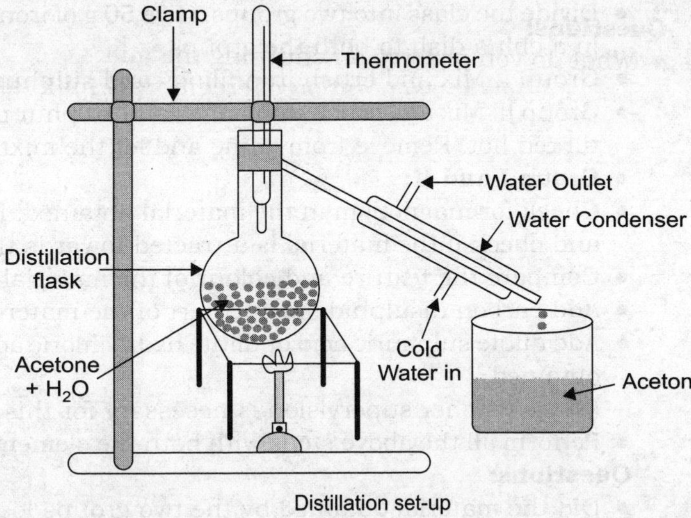

Distillation set-up

• Water is left behind in the distillation flask.

Questions:

• What do you observe as you start heating the mixture?
• At what temperature does the thermometer reading become constant for some time?
• What is the boiling point of acetone?
• Why do the two components separate?

Answers:

• On heating the mixture, the vapours of more volatile liquid i.e., acetone start rising in the flask.
• Thermometer reading became constant at 56.6°C.
• Boiling point of acetone is 56.6°C.
• The two components separate due to difference in their boiling point and these substances do not decompose on heating. The difference in the boiling point of acetone and water is large.

9. • Take some (approximately 5 g) impure sample of copper sulphate in a china dish.
• Dissolve it in minimum amount of water.
• Filter the impurities out.
• Evaporate water from the copper sulphate solution so as to get a saturated solution.
• Cover the solution with a filter paper and leave it undisturbed at room temperature to cool slowly for a day.
• You will obtain the crystals of copper sulphate in the china dish.
• This process is called crystallisation.

Questions:

• What do you observe in the china dish?
• Do the crystals look alike?
• How will you separate the crystals from the liquid in the china dish?

Answers:

• The crystals of copper sulphate are obtained in the china dish.
• The crystals look alike to some extent.
• To separate crystals from the liquid in the china dish, we will use filter paper. The crystals will be spread on the filter paper so that water is absorbed by the paper and crystals are dried.

10. • Divide the class into two groups. Give 50 g of iron filings and 3 g of sulphur powder in a china dish to both the groups.
- Group I: Mix and crush iron filings and sulphur powder.
- Group II: Mix and crush iron filings and sulphur powder. Heat this mixture strongly till red hot. Remove from flame and let the mixture cool.
- **Group I and II:**
- Check for magnetism in the material obtained. Bring a magnet near the material and check if the material is attracted towards the magnet.
- Compare the texture and colour of the material obtained by the groups.
- Add carbon disulphide to one part of the material obtained. Stir well and filter.
- Add dilute sulphuric acid or dilute hydrochloric acid to the other part of the material obtained.
  (Note: Teacher supervision is necessary for this activity.)
- Perform all the above steps with both the elements. (iron and sulphur separately).

Questions:
- Did the material obtained by the two groups look the same?
- Which group has obtained a material with magnetic properties?
- Can we separate the components of the material obtained?
- On adding dilute sulphuric acid or dilute hydrochloric acid, did both the groups obtain a gas? Did the gas in both the cases smell the same or different?

Answers:
- The material obtained after the activity by the two groups looked different.
- Group I obtained a material with magnetic properties.
- The components of the material can be separated only in the case of Group I.
- Yes, both the groups obtained a gas, on adding dilute sulphuric acid or dilute hydrochloric acid.
  The smell of the gas in both the cases is different.
  The gas obtained by group I is hydrogen. It is colourless and odourless.
  The gas obtained by group II is hydrogen sulphide. It is a colourless gas but smells like rotten egg.

VI. Value-Based Questions

Q1. Anil's sister accidentally added some water into the bottle containing olive oil and she was afraid of the scolding. Anil helped his sister and separated the water from olive oil using bottle as separating funnel.

(*a*) What is the principle of using and working of separating funnel?
(*b*) Suggest two separation techniques used to separate liquid mixtures.
(*c*) What value of Anil is seen in the above case?

Ans. (*a*) The principle of separating funnel is difference in the densities of two liquids.
(*b*) Liquid mixtures can be separated by distillation and fractional distillation.
(*c*) Anil showed the value of helping, caring and responsible behaviour.

Q2. Preeti saw a labour entering into the sewage manhole immediately after removing the lid. She promptly stopped the labour from entering into the manhole and told him to wait for some time before he enters into it.

(*a*) What will happen if the labour immediately enters into the manhole (for cleaning) after removing the lid?
(*b*) Name main gases that are released from the manhole.
(*c*) What value of Preeti is seen in the above act?

Ans. (*a*) If the labour immediately enters the manhole on removing its lid he would die due to suffocation and inhalation of poisonous gases which are compressed and released by sewage.

(*b*) Gases released from the sewage manhole are methane, carbon dioxide and hydrogen sulphide.

(*c*) Preeti shows the value of moral responsible behaviour and aware citizen.

Q3. Prasanna wanted to buy a deodorant from the shop. While buying a bottle he felt that it was slightly heavier than usual deodorant bottle that he purchased everytime. He read the weight mentioned on the bottle and told the shopkeeper to weigh the same. He found the bottle was heavy and on opening the deodorant bottle he found it half-filled with water. He complained the matter to the consumer authority.

(*a*) Define density.

(*b*) Apart from water what is the other substance that some shopkeepers add into the deodorant.

(*c*) What value of Prasanna is reflected in this act?

Ans. (*a*) Density of any substance is defined to be the mass of the substance per unit volume.

(*b*) One can add some cheap gases or compressed air in the deodorant bottles.

(*c*) Prasanna showed the value of being having leadership quality, rightful, aware and responsible citizen.

Q4. Rita's father always got his vehicle checked for pollution control. He got it tested for the aerosol if released by his car. He also uses unleaded petrol and makes use of public transport wherever possible. He sparingly use his car.

(*a*) What is aerosol?

(*b*) What happens when smoke released from vehicle mixes with fog?

(*c*) What are the values of Rita's father is reflected here?

Ans. (*a*) When the solid or liquid is dispersed in a gas it is called aerosol e.g. smoke.

(*b*) When smoke mixes with fog it forms smog.

(*c*) Rita's father is an aware citizen, environmentally concerned and dutiful.

VII. Practical Based Questions (Solved)

Q1. A student was given a mixture containing copper oxide (insoluble) and copper sulfate (soluble) and asked to separate them. Firstly, she stirred the mixture into water, then filtered it. Next, she evaporated the filtrate.

(*a*) What substance was the residue in the filtration?

(*b*) Describe what the filtrate was.

(*c*) What difference in properties allows substances to be separated by filtration?

(*d*) What substance was collected by evaporation?

Ans. (*a*) copper oxide (*b*) A solution of copper sulphate

(*c*) Particle size (*d*) Solid copper sulphate

Q2. Sandy is learning to cook. He accidentally mixed the icing sugar with the corn flour and spilled some raw rice grains into it as well. (Icing sugar and cornflour are both fine powders. Icing sugar is soluble, cornflour is not.) To separate this mess, he firstly sieved it. What went through the sieve he stirred into water, and let it stand overnight? In the morning a sediment had formed. He carefully poured the clear liquid into a tray and put it into the warm oven to evaporate.

(*a*) What was caught by the sieve?

(*b*) What difference in properties allows substances to be separated by sieving?

(*c*) What was the sediment?

(*d*) What solid will be in the oven tray when dry?
(*e*) What other method might Sandy have used to collect the substance which was a sediment?

Ans. (*a*) Rice (*b*) Particle size
(*c*) Corn flour (*d*) Icing sugar (or just sugar)
(*e*) Filtration

Q3. Name the technique(s) which are suitable for separating the following mixtures:

	Situation	Separation Technique
(*a*)	To obtain drinking water from muddy water.	
(*b*)	To separate petrol from crude oil.	
(*c*)	To remove leaves from a swimming pool.	
(*d*)	To obtain pure sugar from a solution.	
(*e*)	To determine whether the colouring in a fruit juice is a single substance or a mixture of coloured substance.	
(*f*)	Obtain gasoline from crude oil.	
(*g*)	Purifying rain water for drinking.	
(*h*)	Obtain drinking water from sea water.	

Ans.

	Situation	Separation Technique
(*a*)	To obtain drinking water from muddy water.	Filtration
(*b*)	To separate petrol from crude oil.	Fractional distillation
(*c*)	To remove leaves from a swimming pool.	Handpicking
(*d*)	To obtain pure sugar from a solution.	Evaporation
(*e*)	To determine whether the colouring in a fruit juice is a single substance or a mixture of coloured substance.	Chromatography
(*f*)	Obtain gasoline from crude oil.	Fractional distillation
(*g*)	Purifying rain water for drinking.	Sedimentation, filtration and chlorination
(*h*)	Obtain drinking water from sea water.	Evaporation

Q4. The following diagram shows a set-up of a simple distillation.

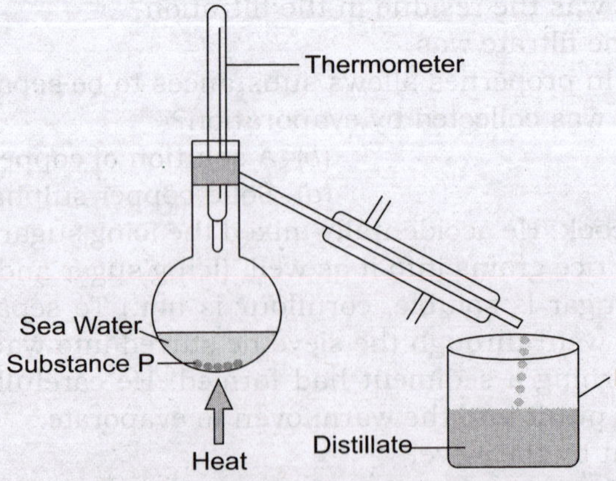

Identify the distillate collected in the receiver. How would you determine that the distillate collected is a pure substance?

Ans. On boiling sea water the water boils and turns into gas and then condensed as the distillate. A pure substance boils at a fixed temperature and the same can be noted on the thermometer in the apparatus.

Q5. A mixture of pebbles, fine sand and salt was sieved. What passed through the sieve was mixed with water and allowed to stand? A sediment formed. The clear liquid was poured off and evaporated. The sediment was also dried. Use a flowchart to show the procedure and what was collected.

Ans.

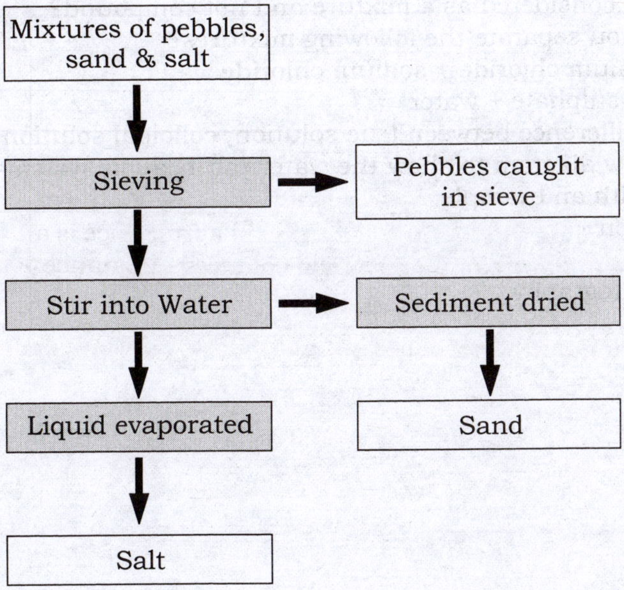

Q6. A mixture of salt, water and chalk dust (insoluble) was filtered. The residue was dried. The filtrate was divided into two parts. One part was evaporated, the other part was distilled. Construct a flowchart and show what was collected at each step.

Ans.

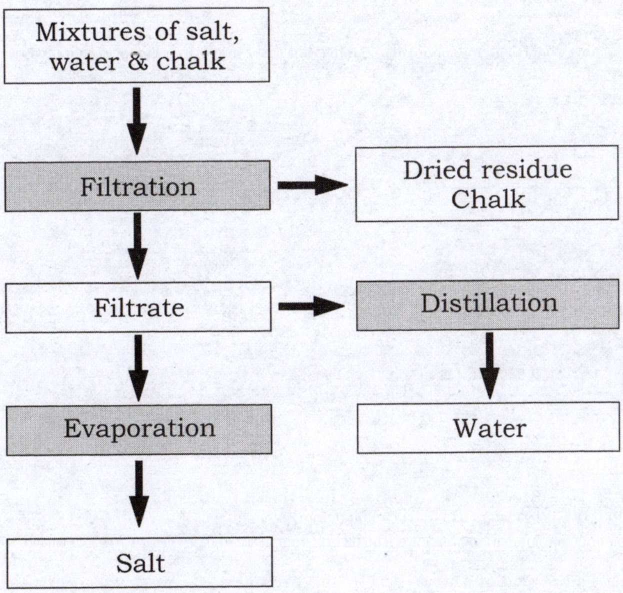

TEST YOUR SKILLS

Q1. How will you separate two immiscible liquids?

Q2. You are given a saturated solution, how can you make it unsaturated solution?

Q3. If you have a dilute solution, how will you make it a concentrated solution?

Q4. Why is water called a universal solvent?

Q5. Give one example of gas in liquid solution.

Q6. Give two applications of centrifugation.

Q7. Why is air considered as a mixture and not compound?

Q8. How can you separate the following mixtures?

(*a*) ammonium chloride + sodium chloride

(*b*) copper sulphate + water

Q9. Give the difference between true solution, colloidal solution and suspension.

Q10. Draw a flow diagram to show the water purification system in water works.

Q11. Explain with an example:

(*a*) emulsion

(*b*) aerosol

(*c*) chromatography

❑❑❑

3 Atoms and Molecules

Syllabus

Particle nature, Basic units, Atoms and molecules, Law of constant proportions, Atomic and molecular masses.

Facts that Matter

• Law of Chemical Combination

Given by Lavoisier and Joseph L. Proust as follows:

(*i*) **Law of conservation of mass:** Mass can neither be created nor destroyed in a chemical reaction.

e.g., $A + B \rightarrow C + D$

Reactants → Products

Mass of reactants = Mass of products

(*ii*) **Law of constant proportion:** In a chemical substance the elements are always present in definite proportions by mass.

E.g., in water, the ratio of the mass of hydrogen to the mass of oxygen is always 1 : 8 respectively.

These laws lacked explanation. Hence, John Dalton gave his theory about the nature of matter. He said that the smallest particles of matter is called 'atom'.

• Dalton's Atomic Theory

1. Every matter is made up of very small or tiny particles called atoms.
2. Atoms are not divisible and cannot be created or destroyed in a chemical reaction.
3. All atoms of a given element are same in size, mass and chemical properties.
4. Atoms of different elements are different in size, mass and chemical properties.
5. Atoms combine in the ratio of small whole numbers to form compounds.
6. The relative number and kinds of atoms are constant in a given compound.

• Atom

Atoms are the smallest particles of an element which can take part in a chemical reaction.

Size of an atom: Atomic radius is measured in nanometres.

$$1\text{nm} = \frac{1}{10^9}\text{ m}$$

$$\therefore \quad 1\text{m} = 10^9\text{ nm}$$

Atomic radii of hydrogen atom = 1×10^{-10} m.

Symbols of atoms:

(*a*) Symbols for some elements as proposed by Dalton:

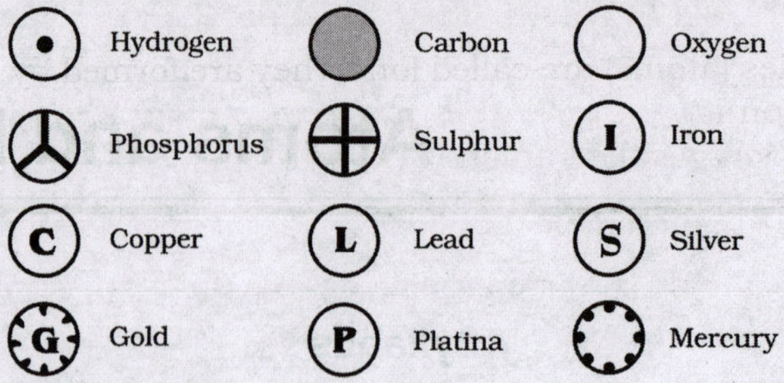

(*b*) Symbols of some common elements:

Name of the element	Latin name	Symbol
Hydrogen	–	H
Helium	–	He
Carbon	–	C
Copper	Cuprum	Cu
Cobalt		Co
Chlorine		Cl
Cadmium		Cd
Boron		B
Barium		Ba
Bromine		Br
Bismuth		Bi
Sodium	Natrium	Na
Potassium	Kalium	K
Iron	Ferrum	Fe
Gold	Aurum	Au
Silver	Argentum	Ag
Mercury	Hydragyrum	Hg

• Molecule

It is the smallest particle of an element or a compound which can exist independently.

- Molecules of an element constitutes same type of atoms.
- Molecules may be monoatomic, di-atomic or polyatomic.
- In molecules of compounds atoms of different elements join together in definite proportions and constitutes different type of atoms.

• Atomicity

The number of atoms constituting a molecule is known as its atomicity.

Name of the element	Atomicity	Molecules formula
Helium	Monoatomic	He
Neon	,,	Ne
Argon	,,	Ar
Sodium	,,	Na
Iron	,,	Fe
Aluminium	,,	Al
Hydrogen	Di-atomic	H_2
Oxygen	,,	O_2
Chlorine	,,	Cl_2
Nitrogen	,,	N_2
Phosphorus	Polyatomic (Tetra)	P_4
Sulphur	Polyatomic (Octa)	S_8

- **Ions**

The charged particles (atoms) are called ions, they are formed by attaining positive charge or negative charge on it.
Negatively charged ion is called anion (Cl^-).
Positively charge ion is called cation (Na^+).

- **Valency**

The combining capacity of an element is known as its valency. Valency is used to find out how atom of an element will combine with the atom of another element to form a chemical compound.
(Every atom wants to become stable, to do so it may loose, gain or share electrons.)

(*i*) If an atom consists of 1, 2 or 3 electrons in its valence shell then its valency is 1, 2 or 3 respectively,

(*ii*) If an atom consists of 5, 6 or 7 electrons in the outermost shell, then it will gain 3, 2 or 1 electron respectively and its valency will be 3, 2 or 1 respectively.

(*iii*) If an atom has 4 electrons in the outermost shell than it will share these electrons and hence its valency will be 4.

(*iv*) If an atom has 8 electrons in the outermost shell then its valency is 0.

Name of the Element	**Symbol**	**Valency**	**Ion.**
Hydrogen	H	1	H^+/H^-
Helium	He	0	–
Lithium	Li	1	Li^+
Beryllium	Be	2	Be^{2+}
Boron	B	3	B^{3+}
Carbon	C	4 (Shares electrons)	–
Nitrogen	N	3	N^{3-}
Oxygen	O	2	O^{2-}
Fluorine	F	1	F^-
Neon	Ne	0	–
Sodium	Na	1	Na^+
Magnesium	Mg	2	Mg^{2+}
Aluminium	Al	3	Al^{3+}

- Some elements show more than one valency hence, termed as **variable valency.**

e.g., Iron shows valency II – Fe^{2+}
and valency III – Fe^{3+}
Copper shows valency I – Cu^+
and valency II – Cu^{2+}

- **Chemical Formulae**

The chemical formula of a compound is a symbolic representation of its composition.

Rules: (*i*) The valencies or charges on the ion must balance.

(*ii*) A metal and non-metal compound should show the name or symbol of the metal first.

e.g., $Na^+ Cl^- \longrightarrow NaCl$

(*iii*) If a compound consist of polyatomic ions. The number of ions present in the compound is indicated by enclosing the formula of ion in a bracket and writing the number of ions outside the bracket.

e.g., $(OH)^- \longrightarrow$ polyatomic radical
$Mg^{2+} \longrightarrow Mg(OH)_2$

Chemical formula of some simple compounds

(*a*) Calcium hydroxide

Symbol → Ca OH

Valency → +2 −1

Criss-cross.

Formula → $Ca(OH)_2$

(*b*) Aluminium oxide

Symbol → Al O

Valency → +3 −2

Formula → Al_2O_3

• Molecular Mass

It is the sum of the atomic masses of all the atoms in a molecule of the substance. It is expressed in atomic mass unit (u).

e.g., $H_2 + \frac{1}{2}O_2 \rightarrow H_2O$ [H = 1, O = 16]

$1 \times 2 + 16 = 18$ u

• Formula Unit Mass

It is the sum of the atomic masses of all atoms in a formula unit of a compound. The constituent particles are ions.

e.g., $Na^+ + Cl^- \rightarrow NaCl$

$1 \times 23 + 1 \times 35.5 = 58.5$ u

• Mole Concept

Definition of mole: It is defined as one mole of any species (atoms, molecules, ions or particles) is that quantity in number having a mass equal to its atomic or molecular mass in grams.

1 mole = 6.022×10^{23} in number

Molar mass = mass of 1 mole → is always expressed in grams, and is also known as gram atomic mass.

1u of hydrogen has → 1 atom of hydrogen

1g of hydrogen has → 1 mole of hydrogen

= 6.022×10^{23} atoms of hydrogen

NCERT IN-TEXT QUESTIONS SOLVED

Q1. In a reaction 5.3 g of sodium carbonate reacted with 6 g of acetic acid. The products were 2.2 g of carbon dioxide, 0.9 g water and 8.2 g of sodium acetate. Show that these observations are in agreement with the law of conservation of mass carbonate.

Sodium carbonate + Acetic acid → Sodium acetate + Carbon dioxide + Water

Ans. Sodium carbonate + Acetic acid → Sodium acetate + Carbon dioxide + Water

5.3 g + 6 g → 8.2 g + 2.2 g + 0.9 g

LHS RHS

∴ 11.3 g = 11.3 g

(Mass of reactant) = (Mass of product)

This shows that during a chemical reaction mass of reactant = mass of product.

Q2. Hydrogen and oxygen combine in the ratio of 1 : 8 by mass to form water. What mass of oxygen gas would be required to react completely with 3 g of hydrogen gas?

Ans. Ratio of H : O by mass in water is:

Hydrogen : Oxygen $\rightarrow$ H_2O

$$1 : 8 = 3 : x$$

$$\therefore \quad x = 8 \times 3$$

$$x = 24 \text{ g}$$

$\therefore$ 24 g of oxygen gas would be required to react completely with 3 g of hydrogen gas.

Q3. Which postulate of Dalton's atomic theory is the result of the law of conservation of mass?

Ans. The postulate of Dalton's atomic theory that is the result of the law of conservation of mass is—the relative number and kinds of atoms are constant in a given compound. Atoms cannot be created nor destroyed in a chemical reaction.

Q4. Which postulate of Dalton's atomic theory can explain the law of definite proportions?

Ans. The relative number and kinds of atoms are constant in a given compound.

Q5. Define the atomic mass unit.

Ans. One atomic mass unit is equal to exactly one-twelfth (1/12th) the mass of one atom of carbon-12. The relative atomic masses of all elements have been found with respect to an atom of carbon-12.

Q6. *Why is it not possible to see an atom with naked eyes?*

Ans. Atom is too small to be seen with naked eyes. It is measured in nanometres.

$$1 \text{ m} = 10^9 \text{ nm}$$

Q7. Write down the formulae of

(*i*) Sodium oxide (*ii*) Aluminium chloride

(*iii*) Sodium sulphide (*iv*) Magnesium hydroxide

Ans. The formulae are

(*i*) Formula of Sodium Oxide

Symbol $\rightarrow$ Na O

Charge $\rightarrow$ +1 –2

Formula $\rightarrow$ Na_2O

(*ii*) Formula of aluminium chloride

Symbol $\rightarrow$ Al Cl

Charge $\rightarrow$ +3 –1

Formula $\rightarrow$ $AlCl_3$

(*iii*) Formula of Sodium Sulphide

Symbol $\rightarrow$ Na S

Charge $\rightarrow$ +1 –2

Formula $\rightarrow$ Na_2S

(*iv*) Formula of magnesium hydroxide

Symbol $\rightarrow$ Mg OH

Charge $\rightarrow$ +2 1

Formula $\rightarrow$ $Mg(OH)_2$

Q8. Write down the names of compounds represented by the following formulae:

(*i*) $Al_2(SO_4)_3$ (*ii*) $CaCl_2$ (*iii*) K_2SO_4

(*iv*) KNO_3 (*v*) $CaCO_3$.

Ans.

(*i*) $Al_2(SO_4)_3$ $\rightarrow$ Aluminium sulphate

(*ii*) $CaCl_2$ $\rightarrow$ Calcium chloride

(*iii*) K_2SO_4 $\rightarrow$ Potassium sulphate

(*iv*) KNO_3 $\rightarrow$ Potassium nitrate

(*v*) $CaCO_3$ $\rightarrow$ Calcium carbonate

Q9. What is meant by the term chemical formula?

Ans. The chemical formula of the compound is a symbolic representation of its composition, *e.g.*, chemical formula of sodium chloride is NaCl.

Q10. How many atoms are present in a

(i) H_2S molecule and (ii) PO_4^{3-} ion?

Ans. (i) $H_2S \rightarrow$ 3 atoms are present, 2 atoms of hydrogen and 1 atom of sulphur

(ii) $PO_4^{3-} \rightarrow$ 5 atoms are present, 1 atom of phosphorus and 4 atoms of oxygen.

Q11. Calculate the molecular masses of H_2, O_2, Cl_2, CO_2, CH_4, C_2H_6, C_2H_4, NH_3, CH_3OH.

Ans. The molecular masses are:

$$H_2 \Rightarrow 1 \times 2 \rightarrow 2 \text{ u}$$
$$O_2 \Rightarrow 16 \times 2 \rightarrow 32 \text{ u}$$
$$Cl_2 \Rightarrow 35.5 \times 2 \rightarrow 71 \text{ u}$$
$$CO_2 \Rightarrow 1 \times 12 + 2 \times 16 = 12 + 32 = 44 \text{ u}$$
$$CH_4 \Rightarrow 1 \times 12 + 4 \times 1 = 16 \text{ u}$$
$$C_2H_6 \Rightarrow 2 \times 12 + 6 \times 1 = 30 \text{ u}$$
$$C_2H_4 \Rightarrow (2 \times 12) + (4 \times 1) = 28 \text{ u}$$
$$NH_3 \Rightarrow (1 \times 14) + (3 \times 1) = 17 \text{ u}$$
$$CH_3OH \Rightarrow 12 + (3 \times 1) + 16 + 1 = 32 \text{ u}$$

Q12. Calculate the formula unit masses of ZnO, Na_2O, K_2CO_3, given atomic masses of Zn = 65 u, Na = 23 u, K = 39 u, C = 12 u, and O = 16 u.

Ans. The formula unit mass of

(i) $ZnO = 65 \text{ u} + 16 \text{ u} = 81 \text{ u}$

(ii) $Na_2O = (23 \text{ u} \times 2) + 16 \text{ u} = 46 \text{ u} + 16 \text{ u} = 62 \text{ u}$

(iii) $K_2CO_3 = (39 \text{ u} \times 2) + 12 \text{ u} + (16 \text{ u} \times 3) = 78 \text{ u} + 12 \text{ u} + 48 \text{ u} = 138 \text{ u}$

Q13. If one mole of carbon atoms weigh 12 grams, what is the mass (in grams) of 1 atom of carbon?

Ans. 1 mole of carbon atoms = 6.022×10^{23} atoms = 12 g

Mass of 1 atom = ?

$\therefore$ Mass of 1 atom of carbon = $\dfrac{12}{6.022 \times 10^{23}} = 1.99 \times 10^{-23}$ g

Q14. Which has more number of atoms, 100 grams of sodium or 100 grams of iron (given atomic mass of Na = 23 u, Fe = 56 u)?

Ans. 23 g of Na = 6.022×10^{23} atoms (1 mole).

$\therefore$ 100 g of Na = ?

$$= \frac{100 \times 6.022 \times 10^{23}}{23} = \frac{6022}{23} \times 10^{23}$$
$$= 26.182 \times 10^{23} = 2.6182 \times 10^{24} \text{ atoms}$$

56 g of Fe = 6.022×10^{23} atoms

100 g of Fe = ?

$$= \frac{100 \times 6.022 \times 10^{23}}{56} = \frac{6022}{56} \times 10^{23}$$
$$= 10.753 \times 10^{23} = 1.075 \times 10^{24} \text{ atoms}$$

100 g of Na contain→ 2.618×10^{24} atoms
100 g of Fe contain→ 1.075×10^{24} atoms
∴ 100 g of Na contains more atoms.

NCERT TEXTUAL QUESTIONS SOLVED

Q1. A 0.24 g sample of compound of oxygen and boron was found by analysis to contain 0.096 g of boron and 0.144 g of oxygen. Calculate the percentage composition of the compound by weight.

Ans. Boron and oxygen compound → Boron + Oxygen
0.24 g → 0.096 g + 0.144 g

Percentage composition of the compound

For boron:
0.24 g → 0.096 g
100 g → ?
$$\frac{100 \times 0.096}{0.24} = 40\%$$

For oxygen:
0.24 g → 0.144 g of oxygen
100 g → ?
$$= \frac{100 \times 0.144}{0.24} = 60\%$$

Q2. When 3.0 g of carbon is burnt in 8.00 g oxygen, 11.00 g of carbon dioxide is produced. What mass of carbon dioxide will be formed when 3.00 g of carbon is burnt in 50.00 g of oxygen? Which law of chemical combination will govern your answer?

Ans. The reaction of burning of carbon in oxygen may be written as:

$$\underset{\text{1 mole carbon 12 g}}{C} + \underset{\text{oxygen 1 mole 32 g}}{O_2} \longrightarrow \underset{\text{carbon dioxide 44 g}}{CO_2}$$

It shows that 12 g of carbon burns in 32 g oxygen to form 44 g of carbon dioxide. Therefore 3 g of carbon reacts with 8 g of oxygen to form 11 g of carbon dioxide. It is given that 3.0 g of carbon is burnt with 8 g of oxygen to produce 11.0 g of CO_2. Consequently 11.0 g of carbon dioxide will be formed when 3.0 g of C is burnt in 50 g of oxygen consuming 8 g of oxygen, leaving behind 50 – 8 = 42 g of O_2. The answer governs the law of constant proportion.

Q3. What are polyatomic ions? Give examples.

Ans. The ions which contain more than one atoms (same kind or may be of different kind) and behave as a single unit are called polyatomic ions *e.g.*, OH^-, SO_4^{2-}, CO_3^{2-}.

Q4. Write the chemical formulae of the following:
(*a*) Magnesium chloride (b) Calcium oxide
(c) Copper nitrate (d) Aluminium chloride
(e) Calcium carbonate.

Ans. (*a*) Magnesium chloride
Symbol → Mg Cl
Change → +2 –1
Formula → $MgCl_2$

(*b*) Calcium oxide
Symbol → Ca O
Charge → +2 –2
Formula → CaO

(*c*) Copper nitrate
Symbol → Cu NO_3
Change → +2 –1
Formula → $Cu(NO_3)_2$

(*d*) Aluminium chloride
Symbol → Al Cl
Change → +3 –1
Formula → $AlCl_3$

(*e*) Calcium carbonate
Symbol → Ca CO_3
Change → +2 –2
Formula → $CaCO_3$

Q5. Give the names of the elements present in the following compounds:

(*a*) Quick lime (*b*) Hydrogen bromide
(*c*) Baking powder (*d*) Potassium sulphate.

Ans. (*a*) Quick lime → Calcium oxide
Elements → Calcium and oxygen

(*b*) Hydrogen bromide
Elements → Hydrogen and bromine

(*c*) Baking powder → Sodium hydrogen carbonate
Elements → Sodium, hydrogen, carbon and oxygen

(*d*) Potassium sulphate
Elements → Potassium, sulphur and oxygen

Q6. Calculate the molar mass of the following substances.

(*a*) Ethyne, C_2H_2 (*b*) Sulphur molecule, S_8
(*c*) Phosphorus molecule, P_4 (Atomic mass of phosphorus = 31)
(*d*) Hydrochloric acid, HCl (*e*) Nitric acid, HNO_3

Ans. The molar mass of the following: [Unit is '*g*']

(*a*) Ethyne, $C_2H_2 = (2 \times 12) + (2 \times 1)$
$= 24 + 2 = 26$ g

(*b*) Sulphur molecule, $S_8 = 8 \times 32 = 256$ g

(*c*) Phosphorus molecule, $P_4 = 4 \times 31 = 124$ g

(*d*) Hydrochloric acid, HCl $= (1 \times 1) + (1 \times 35.5) = 1 + 35.5 = 36.5$ g

(*e*) Nitric acid, $HNO_3 = (1 \times 1) + (1 \times 14) + (3 \times 16) = 1 + 14 + 48 = 63$ g

Q7. What is the mass of

(*a*) 1 mole of nitrogen atoms?
(*b*) 4 moles of aluminium atoms (Atomic mass of aluminium = 27)?
(*c*) 10 moles of sodium sulphite (Na_2SO_3)?

Ans. (*a*) Mass of 1 mole of nitrogen atoms = 14 g

(*b*) 4 moles of aluminium atoms
Mass of 1 mole of aluminium atoms = 27 g
∴ Mass of 4 moles of aluminium atoms = 27 × 4 = 108 g

(*c*) 10 moles of sodium sulphite (Na_2SO_3)
Mass of 1 mole of $Na_2SO_3 = (2 \times 23) + 32 + (3 \times 16)$
$= 46 + 32 + 48 = 126$ g
∴ Mass of 10 moles of $Na_2SO_3 = 126 \times 10$
$= 1260$ g

Q8. Convert into mole.

(a) 12 g of oxygen gas (b) 20 g of water (c) 22 g of Carbon dioxide.

Ans. (*a*) Given mass of oxygen gas = 12 g
Molar mass of oxygen gas (O_2) = 32 g

∴ Mole of oxygen gas = $\frac{12}{32}$ =0.375 mole

(*b*) Given mass of water = 20 g
Molar mass of water (H_2O) = $(2 \times 1) + 16 = 18$ g

∴ Mole of water = $\frac{20}{18}$ = 1.11 mole

(*c*) Given mass of Carbon dioxide = 22 g
Molar mass of carbon dioxide (CO_2) = $(1 \times 12) + (2 \times 16) = 12 + 32 = 44$g

∴ Mole of carbon dioxide = $\frac{22}{44}$ = 0.5 mole

Q9. What is the mass of:

(*a*) 0.2 mole of oxygen atoms? (*b*) 0.5 mole of water molecules?

Ans. (*a*) Mole of Oxygen atoms = 0.2 mole

Molar mass of oxygen atoms = 16 g

∴ Mass of oxygen atoms = 16 × 0.2 = 3.2 g

(*b*) Mole of water molecule = 0.5 mole

Molar mass of water molecules = (2 × 1) + 16 = 18 g

∴ Mass of H_2O = 18 × 0.5 = 9 g

Q10. Calculate the number of molecules of sulphur (S_8) present in 16 g of solid sulphur.

Ans. Molar mass of S_8 sulphur = 256 g = 6.022 × 10^{23} molecules

Given mass of sulphur = 16 g

$$\text{Molecules of sulphur} = \frac{16 \times 6.022 \times 10^{23}}{256} = \frac{96.35 \times 10^{23}}{256}$$

$$= 0.376 \times 10^{23}$$

$$= 3.76 \times 10^{22} \text{ molecules}$$

Q11. Calculate the number of aluminium ions present in 0.051 g of aluminium oxide. (***Hint:*** The mass of an ion is the same as that of an atom of the same element. Atomic mass of Al = 27 u)

Ans. Molar mass of aluminium oxide Al_2O_3

$$= (2 \times 27) + (3 \times 16)$$

$$= 54 + 48 = 102 \text{ g.}$$

∴ 102 g of Al_2O_3 contains = 2 × 6.022 × 10^{23} aluminium ions

∴ 0.051 g of Al_2O_3 contains $= \frac{2 \times 6.022 \times 10^{23}}{102} \times 0.051$

$$= \frac{12.044 \times 10^{23} \times 0.051}{102} = \frac{0.614 \times 10^{23}}{102}$$

$$= 0.006022 \times 10^{23}$$

$$= 6.022 \times 10^{20} \ Al^{3+} \text{ ions}$$

ADDITIONAL QUESTIONS SOLVED

I. Multiple Choice Questions

Choose the correct option:

1. The atomicity of $K_2Cr_2O_7$ is

(*a*) 9 (*b*) 11 (*c*) 10 (*d*) 12

2. The formula for quick lime is

(*a*) $CaCl_2$ (*b*) $CaCO_3$ (*c*) $Ca(OH)_2$ (*d*) CaO

3. The symbol of cadmium is

(*a*) Ca (*b*) Cu (*c*) Cm (*d*) Cd

4. All noble gas molecules are

(*a*) monoatomic (*b*) diatomic (*c*) triatomic (*d*) both (*a*) and (*b*)

5. The valency of nitrogen in NH_3 is

(*a*) 1 (*b*) 3 (*c*) 4 (*d*) 5

6. The formula of ethanol is C_2H_5—OH. Its molecular mass is

(*a*) 46 u (*b*) 34 u (*c*) 34 g (*d*) 46 g

7. How many moles are present in 28g of nitrogen atoms?

(*a*) 1 mole (*b*) 2.3 moles (*c*) 0.5 mole (*d*) 2 moles

8. The molecular mass of x is 106. x among the following is
(a) $CaCO_3$ (b) SO_3 (c) Na_2CO_3 (d) NaCl

9. Which among the following is not a postulate of Dalton's atomic theory?
(a) Atoms cannot be created or destroyed.
(b) Atoms of different elements have different sizes, masses and chemical properties.
(c) Atoms of same elements can combine in only one ratio to produce more than one compound.
(d) Atoms are very tiny particles which cannot be divided further.

10. Pick up the wrong pairs/combination
(a) 6.022×10^{23} molecules of oxygen = 32 g of oxygen
(b) 6.022×10^{23} ions of sodium = 23 g of Na
(c) 6.022×10^{23} atoms of C = 24 g of carbon
(d) 6.022×10^{23} atoms of H = 1 g of H atoms

Ans. 1—(b), 2—(d), 3—(d), 4—(a), 5—(b), 6—(a), 7—(d), 8—(c), 9—(c), 10—(c).

II. Very Short Answer Type Questions

Q1. Define law of conservation of mass.
Ans. In a chemical reaction mass can neither be created nor destroyed.
E.g.,
$$2Na + Cl_2 \longrightarrow 2NaCl$$
$$2 \times 23 + 2 \times 35.5 \longrightarrow 2(23 + 35.5)$$

Q2. Explain law of constant proportion.
Ans. In a chemical substance the elements are always present in definite proportions by mass.
E.g., In water, the ratio of the mass of hydrogen to the mass of oxygen H : O is always 1 : 8

Q3. Who coined the term atom?
Ans. John Dalton coined the term atom.

Q4. Define atom.
Ans. The smallest particle of matter, which can take part in a chemical reaction is called atom.

Q5. Define molecule.
Ans. The smallest particle of an element or compound which can exist independently is called molecule.

Q6. Define atomicity.
Ans. The number of atoms constituting a molecule is known as its atomicity.

Q7. What is atomic mass unit?
Ans. The sum of the atomic masses of all the atoms in a molecule of the substance is expressed in atomic mass unit.
E.g., $H_2O = (1 \times 2) + 16 = 18$ amu

Q8. How do atoms exist?
Ans. Atoms exist in the form of atom, molecule or ions.

Q9. Give the atomicity of phosphorous and nitrogen.
Ans. The atomicity of phosphorus is P_4 *i.e.,* 4.
The atomicity of nitrogen is N_2 *i.e.,* 2.

Q10. What is an ion?
Ans. Charged atom is called as an ion. The ion can be positively charged called cation or negatively charged called anion.

Q11. Give one example of cation and anion.
Ans. Cation ⇒ Na^+
Anion ⇒ Cl^-

Q12. Give one difference between cation and anion.

Ans. Cations are positively charged ion.
Anions are negatively charged ion.

Q13. Give the chemical formula for ammonium sulphate.

Ans. Ammonium sulphate
NH_4^+ SO_4^{2-}
Chemical formula → $(NH_4)_2SO_4$.

Q14. What is Avogadro's constant?

Ans. The Avogadro's constant (6.022×10^{23}) is defined as the number of atoms that are present in exactly 12 g of carbon–12.

Q15. Find the molecular mass of H_2O.

Ans. Molecular mass of $H_2O = (2 \times 1) + (16) = 2 + 16 = 18$ u

III. Short Answer Type Questions

Q1. Give the unit to measure size of atom and give size of hydrogen atom.

Ans. The unit to measure size of atom is nanometer, size of hydrogen atom is 10^{-10}m.

Q2. What is IUPAC, give its one function?

Ans. IUPAC stands for International Union of Pure and Applied Chemistry. It approves the names of elements.

Q3. Give the Latin name for sodium, potassium, gold and mercury.

Ans. Sodium → Natrium, Gold → Aurum
Potassium → Kalium, Mercury → Hydrargyrum

Q4. What is the ratio by mass of combining elements in H_2O, CO_2 and NH_3?

Ans. H_2O ratio by mass of combining elements 2 : 16 → 1 : 8 (H : O)
CO_2 ratio by mass of combining elements 12 : 32 → 3 : 8 (C : O)
NH_3 ratio by mass of combining elements 14 : 3 → 14 : 3 (N : H)

Q5. Define valency and give the valency for the following elements:
Magnesium, Aluminium, Chlorine and Copper.

Ans. Valency: The combining capacity of an element is called its valency.
Valency of the following elements:

Magnesium – 2
Aluminium – 3
Chlorine – 1
Copper – 2

Q6. What is polyatomic ion? Give one example.

Ans. A group of atoms carrying a charge is known as a polyatomic ion.
E.g., Ammonium – NH_4^+
Nitrate – NO_3^-

Q7. *Write down the formula for:*
Copper nitrate, calcium sulphate and aluminium hydroxide.

Ans. Chemical formula:

Copper nitrate → $Cu(NO_3)$
Calcium sulphate → $CaSO_4$
Aluminium hydroxide → $Al(OH)_3$

Q8. What is formula unit mass? How is it different from molecular mass?

Ans. The formula unit mass of a substance is a sum of the atomic masses of all atoms in a formula unit of a compound. The constituent particles of formula unit mass are ions and the constituent particles of molecular mass are atoms.

Q9. Find the number of moles in the following:

(i) 50 g of H_2O (ii) 7 g of Na

Ans. Number of moles in

(i) Molar mass of H_2O = 18 g

Given mass of H_2O = 50 g

$\therefore$ No. of moles in 50 g of H_2O = $\frac{50}{18}$ = 2.78 moles.

(ii) Molar mass of Na = 23 g

Given mass of Na = 7 g

$\therefore$ No. of moles in 7 g of Na = $\frac{7}{23}$ = 0.304 moles.

Q10. Find the number of atoms in the following:

(i) 0.5 mole of C atom

(ii) 2 mole of N atom

Ans. (i) 0.5 mole of C atom:

Number of atoms in 1 mole of C atom = 6.022×10^{23} atoms

Number of atoms in 0.5 mole of C atom = $6.022 \times 10^{23} \times 0.5$

= 3.011×10^{23} atoms

(ii) 2 mole of N atom:

Number of atoms in 1 mole of N atom = 6.022×10^{23} atoms

$\therefore$ Number of atoms in 2 mole of N atom = $6.022 \times 2 \times 10^{23}$

= 1.2044×10^{24} atoms

Q11. Find the mass of the following:

(i) 6.022×10^{23} number of O_2 molecules

(ii) 1.5 mole of CO_2 molecule

Ans. (i) 6.022×10^{23} number of O_2 molecules:

Mass of 1 mole of O_2 molecule = 6.022×10^{23} molecules = 32 g

(ii) 1.5 mole of CO_2 molecule:

Mass of 1 mole of CO_2 molecule = 6.022×10^{23} molecules = 44 g

Mass of 1.5 mole CO_2 molecule = 44 × 1.5 = 66 g

Q12. Show the relationship between mole, Avogadro number and mass.

Ans.

Avogadro number	Mole Mole	Mass
6.022×10^{23} atoms ←	1 mole	→ Molar mass in (g)

1 mole of carbon atoms

6.022×10^{23} atoms of carbon — 12 g of carbon atoms

1 mole of any particle [atoms, molecules, ions]

6.022×10^{23} number of that particle — Relative mass of those particles in grams

1 mole of molecules

6.022×10^{23} number of molecules | Molecular mass in grams

Q13. What are the rules for writing the symbol of an element?

Ans. IUPAC → International Union of Pure and Applied Chemistry approves name of elements.

Symbols are the first one or two letters of the element's name in English. The first letter of a symbol is always written as a capital letter (upper case) and the second letter as a small letter (lower case).

e.g., Hydrogen → H
Helium → He

Some symbols are taken from the names of elements in Latin, German or Greek.

e.g., Symbol of iron is Fe, its Latin name is Ferrum.
Symbol of sodium is Na, its Latin name is Natrium.

Q14. *Explain relative atomic mass and relative molecular mass.*

Ans. **Relative atomic mass:** It can be defined as the number of times one atom of given element is heavier than $\frac{1}{12}$th of the mass of an atom of carbon-12.

Relative Molecular Mass: It is defined as the number of times one molecule of a substance or given element is heavier than $\frac{1}{12}$th of the mass of one atom of carbon-12.

Q15. The formula of carbon-dioxide is CO_2. What information do you get from this formula?

Ans. (*i*) CO_2 represents carbon-dioxide.

(*ii*) CO_2 is one molecule of carbon-dioxide.

(*iii*) CO_2 is one mole of carbon-dioxide *i.e.,* it contains 6.022×10^{23} molecules of carbon dioxide.

(*iv*) CO_2 contains 1 atom of carbon and two atoms of oxygen.

(*v*) CO_2 represents 44 g of molar mass.

Q16. State 3 points of difference between an atom and an ion.

Ans.

Atom	*Ion*
1. An atom has no charge.	An ion has either positive or negative charge.
2. Number of electrons = number of protons.	Number of electrons ≠ number of protons.
3. Atom is reactive.	Ion is stable.

Q17. Calculate the formula unit mass of NaCl and $CaCl_2$.
(Na = 23, Cl = 35.5, Ca = 40)

Ans. Formula unit mass of NaCl = 23 + 35.5
= 58.5 u

Formula unit mass of $CaCl_2$ = 40 + (2 × 35.5)
= 40 + 71
= 111 u

Q18. Write down the chemical formula for the following compounds:

(*a*) Aluminium carbonate
(*b*) Calcium sulphide
(*c*) Zinc carbonate
(*d*) Copper phosphate
(*e*) Magnesium bicarbonate
(*f*) Aluminium hydroxide.

Ans. The chemical formula are:

(*a*) Aluminium carbonate
Al^{3+} CO_3^{2-}
Formula → $Al_2(CO_3)_3$

(*b*) Calcium sulphide
Ca^{2+} S^{2-}
CaS

(*c*) Zinc carbonate
Zn^{2+} CO_3^{2-}
$ZnCO_3$

(*d*) Copper phosphate
Cu^{2+} PO_4^{3-}
$Cu_3(PO_4)_2$

(*e*) Magnesium bicarbonate
Mg^{2+} HCO_3^-
$Mg(HCO_3)_2$

(*f*) Aluminium hydroxide
Al^{3+} OH^-
$Al(OH)_3$

Q19. The ratio by mass for hydrogen and oxygen in water is given as 1 : 8 respectively. Calculate the ratio by number of atoms for a water molecule.

Ans. The ratio by number of atoms for a water molecule are:

Element	*Ratio by mass*	*Atomic mass*	*Mass ratio / Atomic mass*	*Simplest ratio*
H	1	1	$\frac{1}{1} = 1$	2
O	8	16	$\frac{8}{16} = \frac{1}{2}$	1

Thus, the ratio by number of atoms for water is H : O = 2 : 1.

Q20. Give the atomicity of the following compounds:

(*a*) $Ca(OH)_2$
(*b*) $Mg(HCO_3)_2$
(*c*) Cu_2O.
(*d*) H_2SO_4
(*e*) $Al_2(SO_4)_3$
(*f*) $MgCl_2$

Ans. The atomicity of the molecules are:

(*a*) $Ca(OH)_2$ → 05
(*b*) $Mg(HCO_3)_2$ → 11
(*c*) Cu_2O → 03
(*d*) H_2SO_4 → 07
(*e*) $Al_2(SO_4)_3$ → 17
(*f*) $MgCl_2$ → 03

Q21. Explain the difference between 2O, O_2 and O_3.

Ans. 2O → It represents 2 atoms of oxygen (cannot exist independently).

O_2 → It represents one molecule of oxygen (made up of 2 atom) can exist freely.

O_3 → It represents one molecule of ozone (made up of 3 atoms) it can exist independently.

Q22. 1.50 g sample of barium hydroxide was dissolved in water. The total volume of the solution was 100 cm^3.

A 25.0 cm^3 portion of the barium hydroxide solution was titrated against hydrochloric acid. The volume of hydrochloric acid required was 18.75 cm^3.

$$Ba(OH)_2 + 2HCl \longrightarrow BaCl_2 + 2H_2O$$

(*i*) Calculate how many moles of barium hydroxide were in the 25.0 cm3 portion used in the titration.

(*ii*) Calculate the concentration of the hydrochloric acid used.

Ans. (*i*) Moles of barium hydroxide = 0.00219 mol.

(*ii*) Moles of HCl = 2 × 0.00219 = 0.00438.

Q23. Analysis of a certain compound showed that 39.348 grams of it contained 0.883 grams of hydrogen, 10.497 grams of Carbon, and 27.968 grams of Oxygen. Calculate the empirical formula of the compound.

Ans.
- First divide the amount by the atomic mass to get the number of moles of each kind of atom in the formula

$$\text{Hydrogen,} \quad H = \frac{0.883\text{ g}}{1.01\text{ g mol}^{-1}} = 0.874\text{ mol}$$

$$\text{Carbon,} \quad C = \frac{10.497\text{ g}}{12.01\text{ g mol}^{-1}} = 0.874\text{ mol}$$

$$\text{Oxygen,} \quad O = \frac{27.968\text{ g}}{16.00\text{ g mol}^{-1}} = 1.748\text{ mol}$$

- Analysis of the ratio shows that the first two are identical and that the third is twice the other two. Therefore the ratio of H to C to O is 1 to 1 to 2. The empirical formula is HCO_2.

Q24. If the molecular mass of the above compound HCO_2 is 90.0. Calculate the molecular formula.

Ans.
- The empirical formula mass of HCO_2 is

H :	1 × 1.0	=	1.0
C :	1 × 12.0	=	12.0
O :	2 × 16.0	=	32.0
			45.0

- Note that 45 is exactly half of the molecular mass of 90. So the formula mass of HCO_2 is exactly half of the molecular mass. Hence the molecular formula is double that of the empirical formula *i.e.*, $H_2C_2O_4$.

Q25. $2K_3PO_4 + 3BaCl_2 \longrightarrow Ba_3(PO_4)_2 + 6KCl$

Calculate the mass of $BaCl_2$ that is required to react with 21.2 grams of K_3PO_4 in the above reaction.

Ans. Given molar mass of K_3PO_4 = 3(39.1) + (31.0) + 4(16.0) = 212.1 g mol^{-1}

Required molar mass of $BaCl_2$ = 137.3 + 2(35.5) = 208.3 g mol^{-1}

= (21.2 g K_3PO_4)(3 mol $BaCl_2$)(208.3 g mol^{-1} $BaCl_2$) = 31.2 g $BaCl_2$.

Q26. Zinc reacts with copper sulfate in a single replacement reaction as follows

$$Zn\ (s) + CuSO_4\ (aq) \longrightarrow ZnSO_4\ (aq) + Cu\ (s)$$

50.00 grams of zinc metal was added to excess copper sulphate dissolved in a water solution. 42.50 grams of copper was recovered. Calculate the theoretical yield of copper in this experiment

(*i*) Solve the mass-mass Stoichiometry problem to find the theoretical yield.

(*ii*) Find the percent yield.

Ans. (*i*) $\text{Mass Cu} = \frac{50.00\text{ g Zn}}{65.38\text{ gmol}^{-1}\text{ Zn}} \times \frac{1\text{ mol Cu}}{1\text{ mol Zn}} \times 63.55\text{ g mol}^{-1}\text{ Cu} = 48.60\text{ g Cu}$

(*ii*) Percent Yield of Cu = $\frac{42.50 \text{ g Cu}}{48.60 \text{ g Cu}} \times 100 = 87.44\%$

Q27. Silver can be produced by reacting silver nitrate with magnesium in the following reaction

$$Mg(s) + 2AgNO_3\ (aq) \longrightarrow Mg(NO_3)_2\ (aq) + 2Ag\ (s)$$

How much Silver can be recovered by reacting a silver nitrate solution with 50.00 grams of powdered magnesium? Assume that 95% of the silver can be recovered.

(*i*) Solve the mass-mass Stoichiometry problem to find the theoretical yield.

(*ii*) Find the percent yield.

Ans. (*i*) Mass Ag = $\frac{50.00 \text{ g Mg}}{24.31 \text{ g mol}^{-1} \text{ Mg}} \times \frac{2 \text{ mol Ag}}{1 \text{ mol Mg}} \times 107.88 \text{ g mol}^{-1} \text{ Mg} = 443.77 \text{ g Ag}$

(*ii*) Percent yield of Ag = 443.77 g Ag × 0.95 = 421.58 g

Q28. Compound X has the following percentage composition by mass: C = 26.7%, O = 71.1% and H = 2.2%. Calculate the empirical formula of compound B.

Ans.

	C	H	O
%	26.7	2.2	71.1
Mr	12.01	1.01	16.00
Moles	2.22	2.2	4.44
Simplest R	2.2 1	2.2 1	2.2 2

Empirical formula: CHO_2.

Q29. Work out the molecular formula for each of the following given the empirical formula and the relative molecular mass:

(*a*) CH_2, Mr = 70 (*b*) OH, Mr = 34 (*c*) C_2H_5O, Mr = 90

Ans. (*a*) CH_2, Mr = 70(12.01) + (2 × 1.01) = 14.03

70 ÷ 14.03 = 5

$CH_2 \times 5 = C_5H_{10}$

(*b*) OH, Mr = 34 (16.00) + (1.01) = 17.01

34 ÷ 17.01 = 2

$OH \times 2 = H_2O_2$

(*c*) C_2H_5O, Mr = 90 (2 × 12.01) + (5 × 1.01) + (16.00) = 45.07

90 ÷ 45.07 = 2

$C_2H_5O \times 2 = C_4H_{10}O_2$

IV. Long Answer Type Questions

Q1. (*a*) How do atoms exist?

(*b*) What is atomicity?

(*c*) What are polyatomic ions?

Ans. (*a*) Atoms of some elements are not able to exist independently. For such elements atoms form molecules and ions. In case of metals and inert gases atoms can exist independently.

Atoms of metals and inert gases: *E.g.,* $\underset{\text{Metals}}{\underline{\text{Na, Mg, Al}}}$ $\underset{\text{Inert gases}}{\underline{\text{He, Ne, Ar}}}$

Non-metals: *E.g.,* H_2, Cl_2, P_4, S_8

Exceptional non-metal C

(*b*) The number of atoms constituting a molecule is known as its atomicity.

E.g., $O_3 \rightarrow$ atomicity is 3

$O_2 \rightarrow$ atomicity is 2

(c) Polyatomic ions: When more than two atoms combine together and act like an atom with a charge on it is called polyatomic ion.

E.g., OH^-, NO_3^-, NH_4^+

Q2. Calculate

(a) the mass of one atom of oxygen

(b) the mass of one molecule of oxygen

(c) the mass of one mole of oxygen gas

(d) the mass of one ion of oxygen

(e) the number of atoms in 1 mole of oxygen molecule

Ans. (a) Mass of one atom of oxygen

1 mole of oxygen atom = 16gm = 6.022×10^{23} atoms.

$$\therefore \text{Mass of one atom of oxygen} = \frac{16}{6.022 \times 10^{23}} = 2.65 \times 10^{-23}$$

(b) Mass of one molecule of oxygen

1 molecule of oxygen = O_2

= 2×16

= 32 u

(c) Mass of one mole of oxygen gas

1 mole of oxygen gas is O_2 = 32 u or 32 g

(d) Mass of one ion of oxygen

One mole of oxygen = 6.022×10^{23} atoms = 16g.

$$\text{Mass of one ion of oxygen} = \frac{16}{6.022 \times 10^{23}} = 2.65 \times 10^{-23}$$

(e) Number of atoms in one mole of oxygen molecule

1 mole of oxygen molecule *i.e.,*

O_2 = 6.022×10^{23} molecules.

1 molecule of O_2 = 2 atoms.

$\therefore$ Number of atoms in 1 mole of oxygen molecule = $6.022 \times 10^{23} \times 2$ atoms

= 1.2044×10^{24} atoms

Q3. What is meant by atomic mass, gram atomic mass of an element? Why is the mass have different expressions i.e., 'u' and 'g'?

Ans. The atoms are very tiny and their individual mass cannot be calculated as it is negligible. Hence the mass of atoms is expressed in units with respect to a fixed standard. Initially hydrogen atom with mass 1 was taken as standard unit by Dalton. Later, it was replaced by oxygen atom (O=16). But due to the isotopes the masses were found in fractions instead of whole number. Hence, carbon (C=12) isotope was taken as standard unit and was universally accepted.

The atomic mass unit is equal to one twelfth $\left(\frac{1}{12}\right)$ the mass of an atom of carbon-12, its unit is u.

Gram atomic mass: When the atomic mass of an element is expressed in grams, it is called the gram atomic mass of the element.

The mass of atoms, molecules is expressed in 'u' and the mass of moles *i.e.,* molar mass is expressed in g.

Q4. Define a mole. Give the significance of the mole.

Ans. **Mole**–One mole of any species (atoms, molecules, ions or particles) is that quantity or number having a mass equal to its atomic or molecular mass in grams.

1 mole = 6.022×10^{23} in number (atoms, molecules, ions or particles)

Significance of the mole

1. A mole gives the number of entities present *i.e*, 6.022×10^{23} particles of the substance.
2. Mass of 1 mole is expressed as M grams.
3. Mass of 1 mole = mass of 6.022×10^{23} atoms of the element.

E.g.,

$$1 \text{ mole of } O_2 = 6.022 \times 10^{23} \text{ atoms}$$
$$1 \text{ mole of } O_2 = 2 \times 16 = 32\,g$$
$$6.022 \times 2 \times 10^{23} = 1.2044 \times 10^{4} \text{ atoms}$$
$$1 \text{ mole of (compound) HCl} = 6.022 \times 10^{23} \text{ atoms of H and Cl atoms}$$
$$(1 + 35.5 = 36.5\text{ g}) \qquad (6.022 \times 10^{23} \text{ molecules of HCl})$$

Q5. Barium carbonate decomposes when heated

$BaCO_3\,(s) \longrightarrow BaO(s) + CO_2(g)$

(*a*) A student heated a 10.0 g sample of barium carbonate until it was fully decomposed.

(*i*) Calculate the number of moles of barium carbonate the student used.

(*ii*) Calculate the volume of carbon dioxide gas produced at room temperature and pressure. Give your answer in dm^3.

(*b*) The student added 2.00 g of the barium oxide produced to water.

$BaO + H_2O \longrightarrow Ba(OH)_2$

Calculate the mass of barium hydroxide that can be made from 2.00 g of barium oxide. The molecular mass of $Ba(OH)_2$ is 171.

Ans. (*a*) (*i*) Relative formula mass $BaCO_3$ = 197,

moles of barium carbonate = (10.0/197 = 0.0508 mol.

(*ii*) Volume of carbon dioxide = 1.22 dm^3

(*b*) Mass of barium hydroxide = 2.24 g

Q6. Magnesium sulphate crystals are hydrated. A student heated some hydrated magnesium sulphate crystals in a crucible and obtained the following results.

Mass of hydrated magnesium sulfate crystals = 4.92 g

Mass of water removed = 2.52 g

(*i*) Calculate the number of moles of water removed.

(*ii*) Calculate the number of moles of anhydrous magnesium sulfate remaining in the crucible. The molecular mass of anhydrous magnesium sulfate is 120.

(*iii*) Calculate the ratio of moles of anhydrous magnesium sulfate : moles of water.

Ans. (*i*) Moles of water = 2.52/18 = 0.14. moles.

(*ii*) Moles of anhydrous magnesium sulfate = 0.02 moles.

(*iii*) Ratio = 0.02/0.02 : 0.14/0.02 = ratio in whole numbers is 1 : 7.

Q7. Calculate the mass of each element in potassium carbonate, K_2CO_3.

Ans.

- First calculate the formula mass for K_2CO_3. Find the atomic mass of each element from the periodic table. Multiply it by the number of times it appears in the formula and add up the total

2 Potassium atoms	K	= 2 × 39.10 =	78.20
1 carbon atom	C	= 1 × 12.01 =	12.01
3 Oxygen atoms	O	= 3 × 16.00 =	48.00
			138.21

- To find the percent of each element divide the part of the formula mass that pertains to that element with the total formula mass

Percent of Potassium $K = \dfrac{78.20}{138.21} \times 100 = 56.58\%$

Percent of Carbon $C = \frac{12.01}{138.21} \times 100 = 8.69\%$

Percent of Oxygen $O = \frac{48.00}{138.21} \times 100 = 34.73\%$

Q8. For each of the following calculate the empirical formula:

(*a*) When 2.20 g of a hydrocarbon, D, is burnt in excess oxygen, 6.90 g of CO_2 and 2.83 g of water are produced.

(*b*) When 1.52 g of compound E, which contains carbon, hydrogen and oxygen only, is burnt in excess oxygen, 3.04 g CO_2 and 1.24 g H_2O are produced.

Ans. (*a*) Moles of CO_2 = 6.90 ÷ 44.01 = 0.157 mol

Moles of H_2O = 2.83 ÷ 18.02 = 0.157 mol

Moles of C = 0.157 mol moles of H = 2 ÷ 0.157 = 0.304 mol

Empirical formula = CH_2

(*b*) Mass of C in CO_2 = 12.01 ÷ 44.01

3.04 = 0.830 g

Mass of H in H_2O = 2.02 ÷ 18.02

1.24 = 0.139 g

Mass of O = 1.52 – (0.830 + 0.139) = 0.551 g

Ratio of moles C : H : O = 0.0691 : 0.139 : 0.0344

Whole number ratio = 2.01 : 4.04 : 1

Empirical formula: C_2H_4O

V. Activity-Based Questions

- Take one of the following sets X and Y of chemicals—

	X	Y
(*i*)	Copper sulphate	Sodium carbonate
(*ii*)	Barium chloride	Sodium sulphate
(*iii*)	Lead nitrate	Sodium chloride

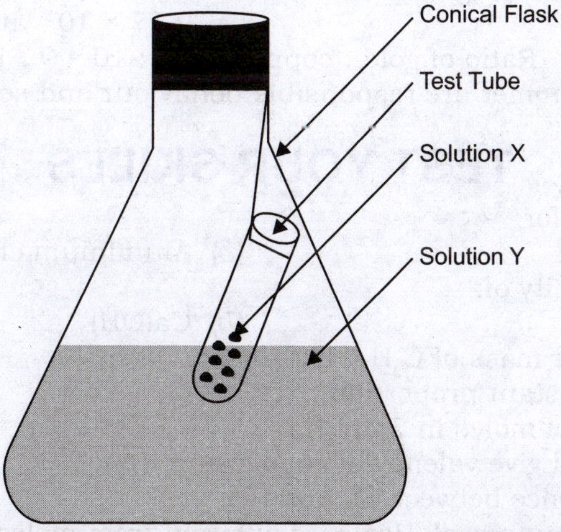

Fig *Ignition tube containing solution of X, dipped in a conical flask containing solution of Y.*

- Prepare separately 95% solution of any one pair of substances listed under X and Y in water.
- Take little amount of solution of Y in a conical flask and some solution of X in an ignition tube.
- Hang the ignition tube in the flask carefully; see that the solutions do not get mixed. Put a cork on the flask as shown in the figure.

- Weigh the flask with its contents carefully.
- Now tilt and swirl the flask, so that the solutions X and Y get mixed.
- Weigh again.
- What happens in the reaction flask?
- Do you think that a chemical reaction has taken place?
- Why should we put a cork on the mouth of the flask?
- Does the mass of the flask and its contents change?

Ans.
- In the reaction flask both the reactants combined to give new products.
- Yes a chemical reaction has taken place.
- We should put a cork on the mouth of the flask so that no other gases in the air combine or get added into the reaction, neither any gas formed in the reaction should escape.
- No. The mass of the flask before and after reaction do not change.

VI. Value-Based Questions

Q1. A customer buys a gold jewellery, he is told that the jewellery has 90% gold and the rest copper. He is given a bill which amounts 100% charges of gold. The customer refuses to pay the bill for 100% gold but brings it to 90% gold amount and settles the bill.

(*a*) How many atoms of gold are present in 1 gram of gold?
(*b*) What is the ratio of gold and copper in the jewellery?
(*c*) What value of customer is reflected in the above statement?

Ans. (*a*) 1 gram of gold will contain $\frac{90}{100} = 0.9$g of gold.

$$\therefore \quad \text{Number of moles of gold} = \frac{\text{Mass of gold}}{\text{Atomic mass of gold}} = \frac{0.9}{197}$$

$$= 0.0046$$

$$\therefore \quad 0.0046 \text{ mole of gold will contain} = 0.0046 \times 6.022 \times 10^{23}$$

$$= 2.77 \times 10^{21} \text{ atoms}$$

(*b*) Ratio of gold : copper = 90 : 10 = 9 : 1.

(*c*) Values of customer are responsible behaviour and self awareness.

TEST YOUR SKILLS

Q1. Write the formula for:
(*a*) Sodium oxide (*b*) Aluminium chloride

Q2. What is the atomicity of:
(*a*) $K_2Cr_2O_7$ (*b*) $Ca(OH)_2$

Q3. Find the molecular mass of C_2H_5OH.

Q4. Explain law of constant proportion.

Q5. Find the number of moles in 7 g of Na.

Q6. Define valency and give valency of copper and iron.

Q7. Explain the difference between O_2 and 2O.

Q8. What is formula unit mass? How is it different from molecular mass?

Q9. State the difference between sodium atom and sodium ion.

Q10. Calculate:
(*a*) the mass of one atom of chlorine
(*b*) the mass of one molecule of chlorine
(*c*) the mass of one mole of chlorine gas

Q11. With the help of an activity prove the law of conservation of mass. ❑❑❑

4 Structure of the Atom

Syllabus

Electrons, Protons and neutrons; Isotopes and isobars.

Facts that Matter

- John Dalton assumed that atom is indivisible.
- In 1866 E. Goldstein discovered the presence of new radiations in a gas discharge tube and called them canal rays. These rays were positively charged radiations which led to the discovery of sub-atomic particle called proton.
- In 1897 J.J. Thomson discovered the sub-atomic particle—the electron with negative charge.
- Difference in electron and proton

Negatively charged (e^-)	**Positively charged (p^+)**
Its mass is negligible.	Its mass is 1 unit.
Charge is – 1	Charge is + 1
J.J Thomson discovered it.	E. Goldstein discovered it.

- The neutron was discovered by **Chadwick.** Neutrons have no charge.

• Structure of an Atom

1. Thomson's model of an atom

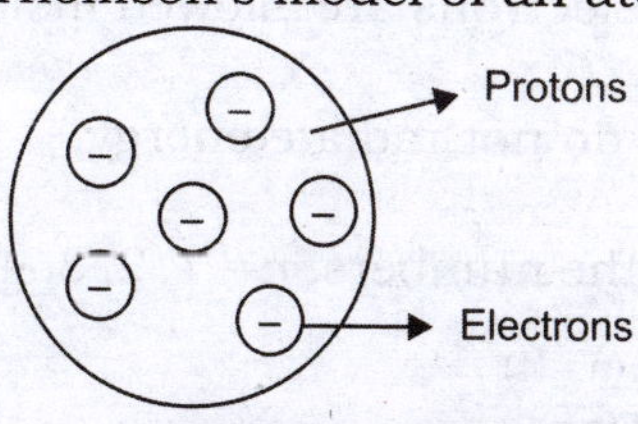

Thomson's Model

- In sphere of protons electrons are distributed
- +ve charge = –ve Charge
- Atom is electrically neutral.

2. Rutherford's Model of an Atom

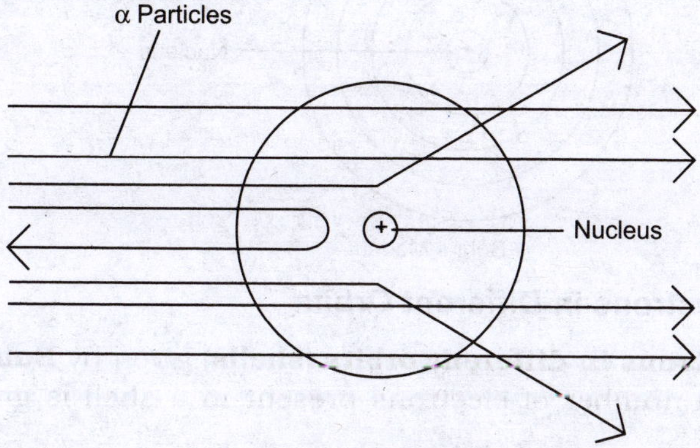

Rutherford's Model

- **α-Particles:** (+2 charge and 4 mass) when fast moving α-particles are bombarded on very thin gold foil, following observations were made:
  - (*i*) Most of the α-particles passed straight through the gold foil.
  - (*ii*) Some of the α-particles were deflected by the foil by small angles.
  - (*iii*) One out of 12000 particles appeared to rebound.
- **Conclusions made by Rutherford based on his observations:**
  - (*i*) Most of the space inside the atom is empty because most of the α-particles passed through the gold foil.
  - (*ii*) Very few particles were deflected from their path because +ve charge of the atom occupies a very little space.
  - (*iii*) A very small fraction of α-particles were rebounded back, shows all +ve charge and mass of the gold atoms were concentrated in a very small volume within atom.
- Radius of nucleus calculated was 10^5 times less than the radius of the atom.

• Nuclear Model of an Atom given by Rutherford

- (*i*) Centre → +ve charge → called nucleus. All mass resides in nucleus.
- (*ii*) Electrons → revolve around the nucleus in orbits.
- (*iii*) Size of nucleus is very small as compared to the size of the atoms.

- **Drawbacks of Rutherford's model of the atom:** When an electron undergoes acceleration, it radiates energy. Thus revolving electron would lose energy and finally fall into the nucleus. Due to this atom should be highly unstable and hence matter would not exist in the form that we know.
  But we know that atoms are quite stable.

• Bohr's Model of Atom

Postulates of Neil Bohr

- (*i*) Only special orbits known as discrete orbits of electrons are allowed inside the atom.
- (*ii*) While revolving in discrete orbits the electrons do not radiate energy.
  These orbits are called energy levels.
  Orbits or shells are represented by K, L, M, N or the numbers, $n = 1, 2, 3, 4, \ldots\ldots$

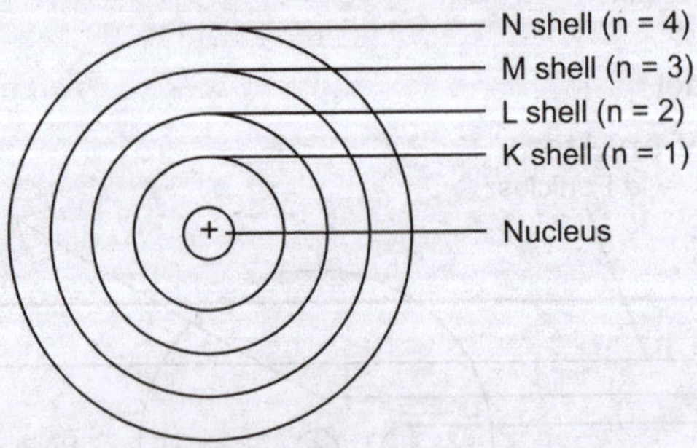

Bohr's Model

• Distribution of Electrons in Different Orbits

Distribution of electrons in different orbits (shells) given by **Bohr and Bury:**

Rules: (*i*) Maximum number of electrons present in a shell is given by $2n^2$ (n = shell number)

E.g., $n = 1$ (K shell) $2(1)^2 = 2$ electron

(*ii*) The maximum number of electrons that can be accommodated in the outermost orbit is 8.

(*iii*) Electrons are not accommodated in a given shell, unless the inner shells are completely filled.

• Definitions

(*i*) **Valency:** The combining capacity of an atom is called its valency.

(*ii*) **Atomic number:** It is equal to number of **protons.**

(*iii*) **Mass number:** It is equal to sum of protons and neutrons.

Mass number A ↘

X → Element symbol → *E.g.,* $^{12}_{6}C$, $^{14}_{7}N$

Atomic number Z ↗

(*iv*) **Isotopes:** Atoms of same element with same atomic number but different mass number, are called isotopes.

Chemical properties → same

but Physical properties → different

E.g., $^{12}_{6}C$, $^{14}_{6}C$

– **Applications of Isotopes:**

(*a*) An isotope of Uranium is used as fuel in nuclear reactors.

(*b*) An isotope of Cobalt is used in treatment of cancer.

(*c*) An isotope of Iodine is used in treatment of goitre.

(*v*) **Isobars:** Atoms of different elements with same mass number but different atomic numbers are called isobars.

E.g., $^{40}_{20}Ca$, $^{40}_{18}Ar$

NCERT IN-TEXT QUESTIONS SOLVED

Q1. What are canal rays?

Ans. Canal rays are positively charged radiations which led to the discovery of positively charged sub-atomic particle called proton.

Q2. If an atom contains one electron and one proton, will it carry any charge or not?

Ans. The atom will be electrically neutral as one –ve charge balances one +ve charge.

Q3. On the basis of Thomson's model of an atom, explain how the atom is neutral as a whole.

Ans. According to Thomson's model of an atom

(*i*) An atom consists of a positively charged sphere and the electrons are embedded in it.

(*ii*) The negative and positive charges are equal in magnitude. So the atom is electrically neutral.

Q4. On the basis of Rutherford's model of an atom, which sub atomic particle is present in the nucleus of an atom?

Ans. As per Rutherford's model of an atom, the protons which are positively charged are present in the nucleus of an atom.

Q5. Draw a sketch of Bohr's model of an atom with three shells.

Ans.

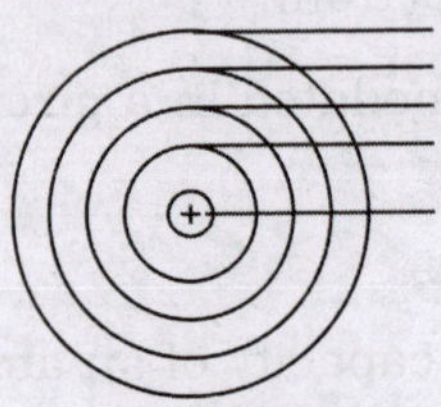

Bohr's Model

Q6. What do you think would be the observation if the α-particle scattering experiment is carried out using a foil of a metal other than gold?

Ans. On using any metal foil, the observations of the α-particle scattering experiment would remain the same as all atoms would have same structure.

Q7. Name the three sub-atomic particles of an atom.

Ans. The sub-atomic particles of an atom are

Protons → Positively charged

Electrons → Negatively charged

Neutrons → No charge

Q8. Helium atom has an atomic mass of 4 u and two protons in its nucleus. How many neutrons does it have?

Ans. Atomic mass of He = 4u.

Atomic mass = No. of protons + No. of neutrons

∴ 4 = 2 + no. of neutrons.

∴ No. of neutrons = 4 − 2 = 2

Helium atom has 2 neutrons.

Q9. Write the distribution of electrons in carbon and sodium atoms.

Ans. **Carbon** Atomic number = 6

∴ No. of protons = 6

and Number of protons = Number of electrons

∴ Distribution of electrons = K L

2 4

Sodium Atomic number = 11

∴ No. of protons = 11 = No. of electrons

∴ Distribution of electrons = K L M

2 8 1

Q10. If K and L shells of an atom are full, then what would be the total number of electrons in the atom?

Ans. K shell can hold 2 electrons and L shell can hold 8 electrons.

When both the shells are full, there will be (8 + 2) 10 electrons in the atom.

Q11. How will you find the valency of chlorine, sulphur and magnesium?

Ans. Valency is the combining capacity of an atom of an element.

Chlorine, Atomic Number = 17

∴ Protons = 17, Electrons = 17

∴ Distribution of electrons = K L M

2 8 7

Chlorine needs 1 electron to complete its outermost orbit/shell.

∴ Its valency is −1 (gains 1 electron).

Sulphur, Atomic number = 16

∴ Protons = 16, Electrons = 16

∴ Distribution of electrons = K L M

2 8 6

Sulphur needs 2 electrons to complete its outermost shell.

∴ Its valency is −2 (gains 2 electrons)

Magnesium, Atomic number = 12

∴ Protons = 12, electrons = 12

∴ Distribution of electrons = K L M

2 8 2

Magnesium needs to donate 2 electrons from its outermost shell to become stable.

∴ Its valency is +2 (donates 2 electrons).

Q12. If number of electrons in an atom is 8 and number of protons is also 8, then

(*i*) What is the atomic number of the atom? and

(*ii*) What is the charge on the atom?

Ans. No. of electrons = 8

No. of protons = 8

(*i*) Atomic number = no. of protons = 8

(*ii*) As Electrons = Protons

⊕ = ⊖

∴ Atom is electrically neutral (No charge)

Q13. With the help of given Table 4.1, find out the mass number of oxygen and sulphur atom.

Table 4.1 : Composition of Atoms of the First Eighteen Elements with Electron Distribution in Various Shells

Name of Element	*Symbol*	*Atomic Number*	*Number of Protons*	*Number of Neutrons*	*Number of Electrons*	*Distribution of Electrons* K	L	M	N	*Valency*
Hydrogen	H	1	1	-	1	1	-	-	-	1
Helium	He	2	2	2	2	2	-	-	-	0
Lithium	Li	3	3	4	3	2	1	-	-	1
Beryllium	Be	4	4	5	4	2	2	-	-	2
Boron	B	5	5	6	5	2	3	-	-	3
Carbon	C	6	6	6	6	2	4	-	-	4
Nitrogen	N	7	7	7	7	2	5	-	-	3
Oxygen	O	8	8	8	8	2	6	-	-	2
Fluorine	F	9	9	10	9	2	7	-	-	1
Neon	Ne	10	10	10	10	2	8	-	-	0
Sodium	Na	11	11	12	11	2	8	1	-	1
Magnesium	Mg	12	12	12	12	2	8	2	-	2
Aluminium	Al	13	13	14	13	2	8	3	-	3
Silicon	Si	14	14	14	14	2	8	4	-	4
Phosphorus	P	15	15	16	15	2	8	5	-	3, 5
Sulphur	S	16	16	16	16	2	8	6	-	2
Chlorine	Cl	17	17	18	17	2	8	7	-	1
Argon	Ar	18	18	22	18	2	8	8		0

Ans. **Oxygen,** No. of protons = 8

∴ No. of neutrons = 8

∴ Atomic number = 8

∴ Atomic mass number = P + N = 8 + 8 = 16

Sulphur, No. of protons = 16

∴ Atomic number = 16

No. of neutrons = 16

∴ Atomic mass number = P + N = 16 + 16 = 32

Q14. For the symbol H, D and T tabulate three sub-atomic particles found in each of them.

Ans. (Protium) H → (^1_1H) Atomic number = 1, Mass number = 1

∴ No. of protons = 1

No. of electrons = 1

No. of neutrons = Nil

D → (^2_1H) (Deuterium) ∴ Atomic number = 1, Mass number = 2

No. of protons = 1

No. of electrons = 1

No. of neutrons = 1

T→ (^2_1H) (Tritium) ∴ Atomic number = 1, Mass number = 3

No. of protons = 1

No. of electrons = 1

No. of neutrons = 2

Q15. Write the electronic configuration of any one pair of isotopes and isobar.

Ans. **Isotopes:** Atoms of same element having same atomic number but different mass number.

∴ Electronic configuration of isotopes remain the same.

E.g., $^{12}_{6}C$ $^{14}_{6}C$

Electronic configuration

K	L
2	4

K	L
2	4

Isobars: Atoms of different elements with different atomic number but same mass number.

E.g., $^{40}_{20}Ca$ $^{40}_{18}Ar$

Electronic configuration

K	L	M	N
2	8	8	2

K	L	M
2	8	8

NCERT TEXTUAL QUESTIONS SOLVED

Q1. Compare the properties of electrons, protons and neutrons.

Ans.

Electrons	*Protons*	*Neutrons*
1. Negatively charged.	Positively charged	No charge
2. Mass is negligible $\left(\frac{1}{1800} \text{ times of protons}\right)$.	Mass is 1 a.m.u.	Mass is 1 a.m.u.

3. Get attracted towards +ve charge.	Get attracted towards –ve charge.	Do not get attracted, as they are neutral
4. Present outside the nucleus	Present in the nucleus	Present in the nucleus of an atom

Q2. What are the limitations of J.J. Thomson's model of the atom?

Ans. According to J.J. Thomson's model of an atom, the electrons are embedded all over in the positively charged spheres. But experiments done by other scientists showed that protons are present only in the centre of the atom and electrons are distributed around it.

Q3. What are the limitations of Rutherford's model of the atom?

Ans. According to Rutherford's model of an atom the electrons are revolving in a circular orbit around the nucleus. Any charged particle that revolves would undergo acceleration and radiate energy. The revolving electron would lose its energy and finally fall into the nucleus, thus the atom would be highly unstable.
But we know that atoms are quite stable.

Q4. Describe Bohr's model of the atom.

Ans. Bohr's model of the atom

(1) Atom has nucleus in the centre.
(2) Electrons revolve around the nucleus.
(3) Certain special orbits known as discrete orbits of electrons, are allowed inside the atom.
(4) While revolving in discrete orbits the electrons do not radiate energy.
(5) These orbits or shells are called energy levels.
(6) These orbits or shells are represented by the letters K, L, M, N or the numbers $n = 1, 2, 3, 4$

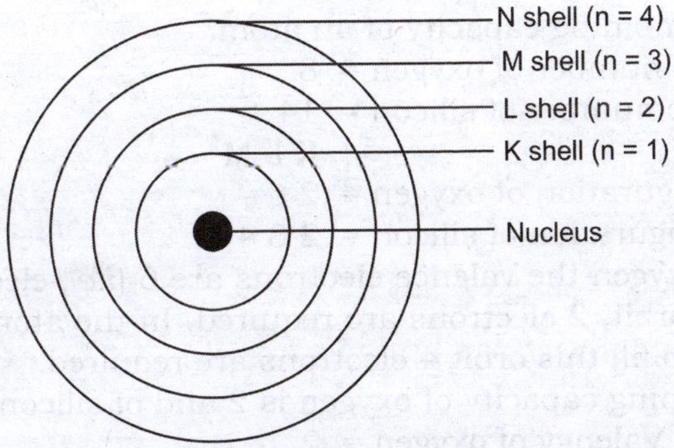

Q5. Compare all the proposed models of an atom given in this chapter.

Ans.

Thomson	*Rutherford*	*Bohr*
• Sphere of positive charge	• Sphere of positive charge in centre called nucleus. All mass of an atom resides in the nucleus	• Positive charge in centre called nucleus.
• Electrons are spread randomly all over in the sphere	• Electrons revolve around the nucleus in well defined orbits.	• Electrons revolve in discrete orbits and do not radiate energy.

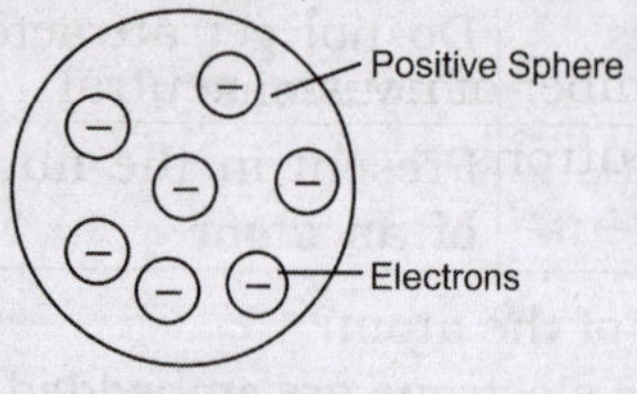

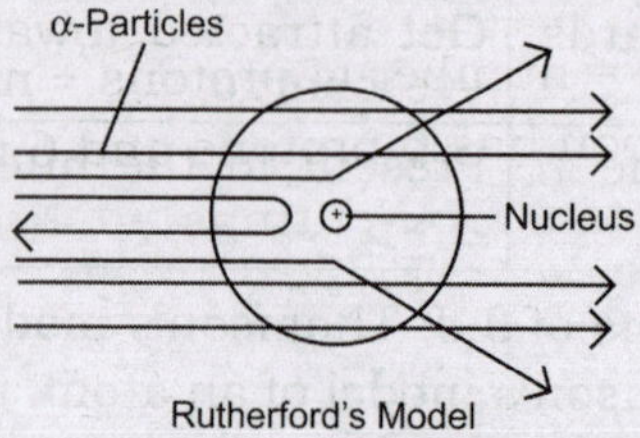

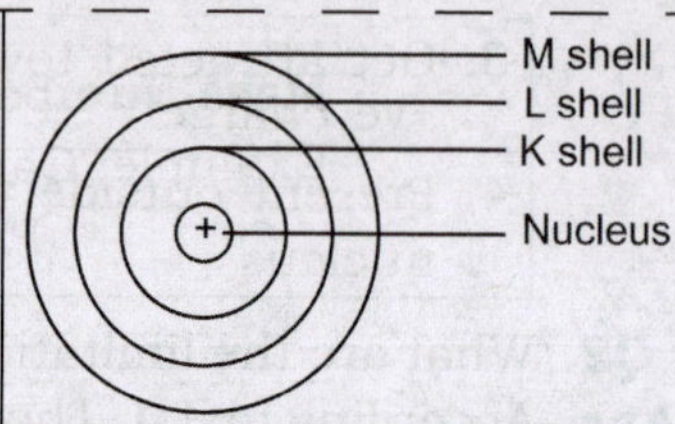

Thomson's Model	Rutherford's Model	Bohr's Model
• Positive charge = Negative charge. • Atom is electrically neutral.	• Size of nucleus is very small as compared to size of atom.	• The orbits were termed as energy shells labelled as K, L, M, N or $n = 1, 2, 3, 4$ (numbered)

Q6. Summarise the rules for writing of distribution of electrons in various shells for the first eighteen elements.

Ans. The rules for writing of distribution of electrons in various shells for the first eighteen elements are:

(*i*) The maximum number of electrons present in a shell is given by the formula–$2n^2$

$\because$ n = orbit number *i.e.*, 1, 2, 3

$\therefore$ Maximum number of electrons in different shells are:

K shell	$n = 1$	$2n^2$	$\Rightarrow$	$2(1)^2 = 2$
L shell	$n = 2$	$2n^2$	$\Rightarrow$	$2(2)^2 = 8$
M shell	$n = 3$	$2n^2$	$\Rightarrow$	$2(3)^2 = 18$
N shell	$n = 4$	$2n^2$	$\Rightarrow$	$2(4)^2 = 32$

(*ii*) The maximum number of electrons that can be accommodated in the outermost orbit is 8.

(*iii*) Electrons are not accommodated in a given shell unless the inner shells are filled. (Shells are filled step-wise).

Q7. Define valency by taking examples of silicon and oxygen.

Ans. Valency is the combining capacity of an atom.

Atomic number of oxygen = 8

Atomic number of silicon = 14

	K L M
Electronic configuration of oxygen =	2 6 –
Electronic configuration of silicon =	2 8 4

In the atoms of oxygen the valence electrons are 6 (*i.e.*, electrons in the outermost shell). To fill the orbit, 2 electrons are required. In the atom of silicon, the valence electrons are 4. To fill this orbit 4 electrons are required.

Hence, the combining capacity of oxygen is 2 and of silicon is 4.

i.e., Valency of oxygen = 2

Valency of silicon = 4

Q8. Explain with examples:

(*i*) Atomic number (*ii*) Mass number,

(*iii*) Isotopes and (*iv*) Isobars.

Give any two uses of isotopes.

Ans. (*i*) **Atomic number:** The atomic number of an element is equal to the number of protons in the nucleus of its atom.

e.g., Oxygen has 6 protons hence atomic no. = 6.

(*ii*) **Mass number:** The mass number of an atom is equal to the number of protons and neutrons in its nucleus.

Mass Number = number of protons + number of neutrons

Example: Carbon has 6 protons and 6 neutrons.

Protons + Neutrons = Nucleus = Mass number

6 + 6 = 12

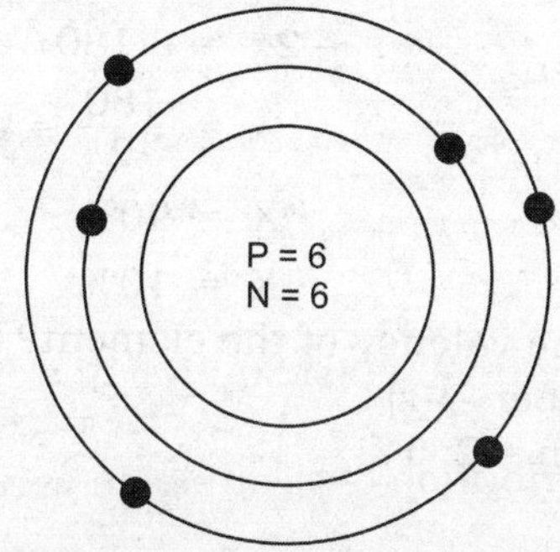

(*iii*) **Isotopes:** Isotopes are atoms of the same element which have different mass number but same atomic number.

E.g., ${}^{1}_{1}H$, ${}^{2}_{1}H$, ${}^{3}_{1}H$

(*iv*) **Isobars:** Isobars are atoms having the same mass number but different atomic numbers.

E.g., ${}^{40}_{20}Ca$, ${}^{40}_{18}Ar$

Both calcium and argon have same mass number but different atomic number.

Two uses of isotopes are:

(*a*) An isotope of iodine is used in the treatment of goitre.

(*b*) An isotope of uranium is used as a fuel in nuclear reactors.

Q9. Na^+ has completely filled K and L shells. Explain.

Ans. Sodium atom (Na), has atomic number = 11

Number of protons = 11

Number of electrons = 11

∴ Electronic configuration of Na = K L M
2 8 1

Sodium atom (Na) loses 1 electron to become stable and form Na^+ ion. Hence it has completely filled K and L shells.

Q10. If bromine atom is available in the form of, say, two isotopes ${}^{79}_{35}Br$ (49.7%) and ${}^{81}_{35}Br$ (50.3%), calculate the average atomic mass of bromine atom.

Ans. The average atomic mass of bromine atom

$$= \left(79 \times \frac{49.7}{100}\right) + \left(81 \times \frac{50.3}{100}\right)$$

$$= 39.263 + 40.743$$

$$= 80.006 \text{ u}$$

Q11. The average atomic mass of a sample of an element X is 16.2 u. What are the percentages of isotopes ${}^{16}_{8}X$ and ${}^{18}_{8}X$ in the sample?

Ans. Let the percentage of ${}^{16}_{8}X$ be x and the percentage of ${}^{18}_{8}X$ be $100 - x$.

$$\therefore \quad \left(16 \times \frac{x}{100}\right) + \left(\frac{18(100 - x)}{100}\right) = 16.2$$

$$\frac{16x}{100} + \frac{1800 - 18x}{100} = 16.2$$

$$\therefore \quad \frac{16x - 18x + 1800}{100} = 16.2$$

$$\therefore \quad -2x + 1800 = 16.2 \times 100$$

$$\therefore \quad -2x = 1620 - 1800$$

$$\therefore \quad -2x = -180$$

$$\therefore \quad x = \frac{180}{2} = 90$$

$$\therefore \quad {}^{16}_{8}X = 90\%$$

and $${}^{18}_{8}X = 10\%$$

Q12. If Z = 3, what would be the valency of the element? Also, name the element.

Ans. Z = 3, (*i.e.*, atomic number → z)

∴ Electronic configuration = 2, 1

Valency = 1

Name of the element is lithium.

Q13. Composition of the nuclei of two atomic species X and Y are given as under

	X	Y
Protons	= 6	6
Neutrons	= 6	8

Give the mass number of X and Y. What is the relation between the two species?

Ans. Mass number of X = Protons + Neutrons

= 6 + 6

= 12

Mass number of Y = Protons + Neutrons

= 6 + 8 = 14

As the atomic number is same *i.e.*, = 6.

[atomic number = number of protons].

Both X and Y are isotopes of same element.

Q14. For the following statements, write T for True and F for False.

(*a*) J.J. Thomson proposed that the nucleus of an atom contains only nucleons.

(*b*) A neutron is formed by an electron and a proton combining together. Therefore, it is neutral.

(*c*) The mass of an electron is about 1/2000 times that of proton.

(*d*) An isotope of iodine is used for making tincture iodine, which is used as a medicine.

Ans. (*a*) False (*b*) False (*c*) True (*d*) False

Put tick (✓) against correct choice and cross (×) against wrong choice in questions 15, 16 and 17.

Q15. Rutherford's alpha-particle scattering experiment was responsible for the discovery of

(*a*) Atomic nucleus (*b*) Electron (*c*) Proton (*d*) Neutron

Ans. (*a*) Atomic nucleus

Q16. Isotopes of an element have

(*a*) the same physical properties (*b*) different chemical properties

(*c*) different number of neutrons (*d*) different atomic numbers.

Ans. (*c*) different number of neutrons

Q17. Number of valence electrons in Cl^- ion are :

(*a*) 16 (*b*) 8 (*c*) 17 (*d*) 18

Ans. (*b*) 8

Q18. Which one of the following is a correct electronic configuration of sodium?

(*a*) 2, 8 (*b*) 8, 2, 1 (*c*) 2, 1, 8 (*d*) 2, 8, 1

Ans. (*d*) 2, 8, 1

Q19. Complete the following table.

Atomic Number	Mass Number	Number of Numbers	Number of Protons	Number of Electrons	Name of the Atomic Species
9	–	10	–	–	–
16	32	–	–	–	Sulphur
–	24	–	12	–	–
–	2	–	1	–	–
–	1	0	1	0	–

Ans.

Atomic Number	Mass Number	Number of Numbers	Number of Protons	Number of Electrons	Name of the Atomic Species
9	19	10	9	9	Fluorine
16	32	16	16	16	Sulphur
12	24	12	12	12	Magnesium
1	2	1	1	1	Hydrogen Deuterium
1	1	0	1	0	Hydrogen

ADDITIONAL QUESTIONS SOLVED

I. Multiple Choice Questions

Choose the correct option:

1. The nucleons are

(*a*) protons and electrons (*b*) neutrons and electrons
(*c*) protons and neutrons (*d*) none of these

2. The isotope deuterium of hydrogen has

(*a*) no neutrons and one proton (*b*) one neutron and two protons
(*c*) one electron and two neutron (*d*) one proton and one neutron

3. The electrons present in the outermost shell are called

(*a*) valency electrons (*b*) octate electrons
(*c*) duplet electrons (*d*) valence electrons

4. An α-particle contains

(*a*) 4 positive charge and 2 mass unit (*b*) 2 positive charge and 4 mass unit
(*c*) 2 positive charge and 2 mass unit (*d*) 4 positive charge and 4 mass unit

5. The atomic number of sodium is 11 and its mass number is 23. It has

(*a*) 11 neutrons and 12 protons (*b*) 12 protons and 11 electrons
(*c*) 11 electrons and 12 neutrons (*d*) 12 electrons and 11 neutrons

6. The electronic configuration of chlorine is

(*a*) 2, 7 (*b*) 2, 8, 8, 7 (*c*) 2, 8, 7 (*d*) 2, 7, 8

7. The isotope used to remove the brain tumours and treatment of cancer is

(*a*) U-235 (*b*) Na 24 (*c*) Iodine (*d*) Co-60

8. The isobars among the following is

(*a*) $^{40}_{20}Ca$ $^{23}_{11}Na$ (*b*) $^{20}_{18}Ar$ $^{20}_{19}K$ (*c*) $^{16}_{8}O$ $^{18}_{8}O$ (*d*) $^{19}_{7}X$ $^{13}_{7}Y$

9. The elements with same valence electrons and form same type of ions

(a) $^{16}_{8}O$ $^{23}_{11}Na$ (b) $^{20}_{18}Ar$ $^{20}_{19}K$ (c) $^{14}_{5}N$ $^{27}_{13}Al$ (d) $^{23}_{11}Na$ $^{20}_{19}K$

10. In the α-scattering experiment, few α-particles rebounded because

(a) Most of the space in the atom is occupied.

(b) Positive charge of the atom occupies very little space.

(c) The mass of the atom is concentrated in the centre.

(d) all positive charge and mass of the atom is concentrated in small volume.

Ans. 1—(c), 2—(d), 3—(d), 4—(b), 5—(c), 6—(c), 7—(d), 8—(b), 9—(d), 10—(d).

II. Very Short Answer Type Questions

Q1. Draw the atomic structure of hydrogen atom.

Ans.

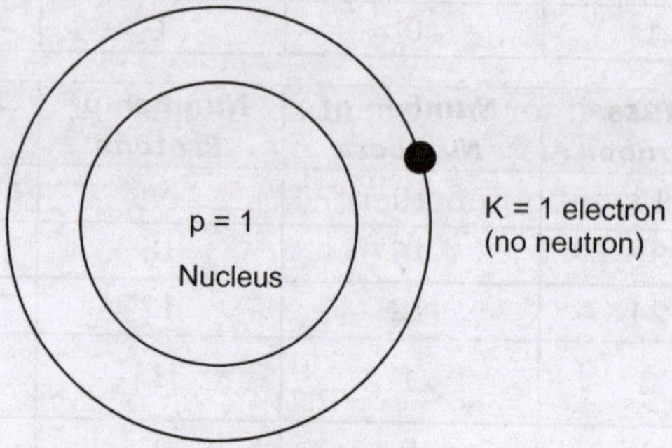

Hydrogen atom

Q2. Why are some elements chemically inert?

Ans. Because their outermost shell is completely filled.

Q3. Why is atom electrically neutral?

Ans. It has same number of protons and electrons, (⊕ charge = ⊖ charge).

Q4. What is the charge and mass of α-particles?

Ans. Charge is + 2

Mass is 4 a.m.u.

Q5. What are valence electrons?

Ans. Electrons present in the outermost shell of an atom are called valence electrons.

Q6. An atom has atomic number 12, what is its valency and name the element?

Ans. Atomic number = 12

∴ Protons = Electrons = 12

Electronic Configuration = K L M

2 8 2

∴ Valency = 2

Element is magnesium.

Q7. Find the number of neutrons in $^{27}_{13}X$.

Ans. Mass number = 27

∴ p + n = 27 p = 13, (Atomic No. = Number of protons)

∴ 13 + n = 27

∴ n = 14

∴ Neutrons = 14

Q8. Where is the mass of an atom concentrated?

Ans. Mass of an atom is concentrated in nucleus.

Q9. Name two elements with same number of protons and neutrons?

Ans. Carbon (Protons = Neutrons = 6)

Oxygen (Protons = Neutrons = 8)

Q10. Draw the atomic structure of sodium atom.

Ans.

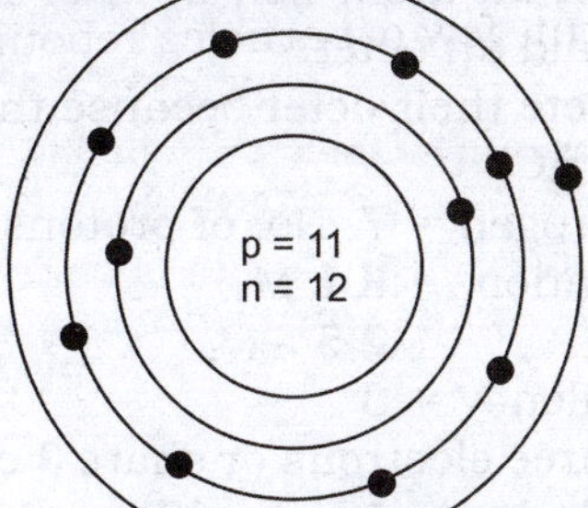

Na atom

Q11. Name the isotope used for treatment of cancer?

Ans. Isotope of cobalt, Co—60.

Q12. $^{A}_{Z}X$ What does this symbol represent?

Ans. X → Symbol of element

A → Mass number

Z → Atomic number

Q13. Can the value of 'Z' be same for two different atoms?

Ans. No, (Z = atomic number), two different atoms cannot have same atomic number.

Q14. Can the value of 'A' be same for two different atom?

Ans. Yes, it can be e.g. Ca and Ar has A–40 (*i.e.*, mass number) are called isobars.

III. Short Answer Type Questions

Q1. Name the scientist who discovered protons and neutrons in an atom.

Ans. Protons were discovered by E. Goldstein in 1866 and neutrons were discovered by J. Chadwick in 1932.

Q2. What is the contribution of Bohr and Bury together in the structure of atom's explanation?

Ans. Both Bohr and Bury gave the distribution of electrons into different atoms by giving the formula $2n^2$, where n = shell number.

Q3. Draw the atomic structure of (*i*) an atom with same number of sub-atomic particles, (*ii*) an atom with the same number of electrons in L and M shell.

Ans. (*i*) An atom with same number of sub-atomic particles is $^{4}_{2}He$

No. of protons = 2

No. of electrons = 2

No. of neutrons = 2

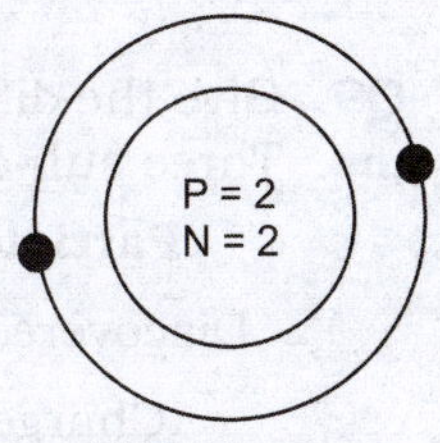

Helium atom

(*ii*) An atom with L and M shell filled → K L M

2 8 8

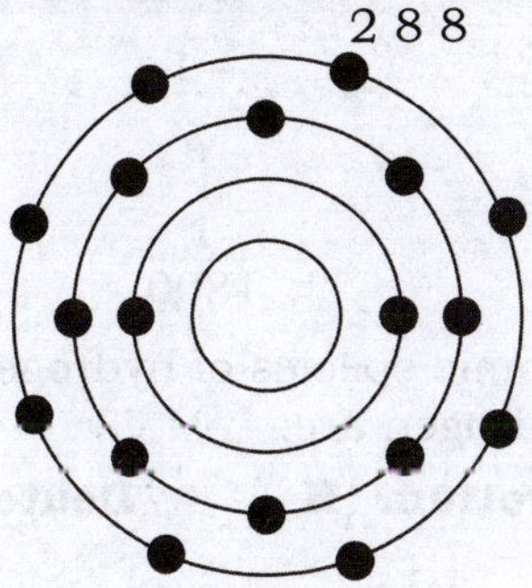

Argon

Q4. What is an octet? Why would atoms want to complete their octet?

Ans. When the outermost shell of an atom i.e., L, M or N are completely filled with 8 electrons in the shell, it is said an octet.

Atoms would want to complete their octet because they want to become stable.

Q5. Find the valency of $^{14}_{7}N$ and $^{35}_{17}Cl$.

Ans. The atomic number of nitrogen = 7, No. of protons = 7, No. of electrons = 7

∴ Electronic configuration = K L M
2 5 –

∴ Valency = 3

Because either it will gain three electrons or share 3 electrons to complete its octet.

The atomic number of chlorine = 17, p = 17, e = 17

∴ Electronic configuration = K L M
2 8 7

∴ Valency = 1

Because it will gain 1 electron to complete its octet.

Q6. Pick up the isotopes among the following and state reason.

$^{17}_{7}X$ $^{35}_{17}X$ $^{24}_{14}X$ $^{37}_{17}X$

Ans. The isotopes are $^{35}_{17}X$ and $^{37}_{17}X$ as both the atoms show same atomic number but different mass number.

Q7. Pick up atoms which have same number of neutrons from the following:

$^{23}_{11}Y$ $^{28}_{14}Y$ $^{24}_{12}Y$ $^{27}_{13}Y$

Ans. $^{23}_{11}Y$ and $^{24}_{12}Y$ – have same number of neutrons, 12 in each.

$^{28}_{14}Y$ and $^{27}_{13}Y$ – have same number of neutrons, 14 in each.

Q8. What are nucleons? What is the name given to those atoms which have the same number of nucleons in it?

Ans. Protons and neutrons present in the nucleus are called nucleons. Isobaric elements have the same number of nucleons in it.

E.g.,

Element	Protons	Neutrons	(Protons + Neutrons)
Argon	18	22	40
Calcium	20	20	40
Potassium	19	21	40

Q9. Give the difference between three sub-atomic particles.

Ans. Three sub-atomic particles are electron, proton and neutron.

Particle	⇒	Electron	Proton	Neutron
Discovered by	⇒	J.J. Thomson	E. Goldstein	J. Chadwick
Charge	⇒	–1	+1	0
Symbol	⇒	*e*	P	*n*
Mass	⇒	$\frac{1}{1800}$	1	1

Q10. Give the names of three atomic species of hydrogen.

Ans. Three atomic species of hydrogen are:

Name	Protium $^{1}_{1}H$	Deuterium $^{2}_{1}H$	Tritium $^{3}_{1}H$
Symbol	$^{1}_{1}H$	$^{2}_{1}H$	$^{3}_{1}H$

Protons	1	1	1
Atomic no.	1	1	1
Neutrons	0	1	2

Q11. Atomic mass exists as whole number, why do we write the atomic mass of chlorine as 35.5u.

Ans. Chlorine has two isotopes and the mass of an atom is taken as the average mass of all the naturally occurring isotopes of that element.

This is obtained by knowing the percentage of each isotopic form and then the average mass is calculated Cl = 35 × 75% and Cl = 37 × 25%

$$\therefore \quad \left(35 \times \frac{75}{100}\right) + \left(37 \times \frac{25}{100}\right)$$

$$\frac{105}{4} + \frac{37}{4} = \frac{142}{4} = 35.5 \text{ u}$$

Q12. Give difference between isotopes and isobars.

Ans.

Isotopes	*Isobars*
• Atoms of same element	Atoms of different element
• Have same atomic number	Have different atomic number
• Have different mass number	Have same mass number
• Number of protons and electrons are same in these atoms.	Number of protons and electrons are not same in these atoms.

Q13. Number of protons and electrons are same in an atom. Then why is it wrong to say that atomic number of an atom is equal to its number of electrons. (V. Imp)

Ans. Atomic number ≠ Number of electrons, although number of protons = number of electrons because the electron's number can change in an atom by loss, or gain of it. But the proton's number remain constant (as it does not take part in loss or gain).

Q14. An atom is electrically neutral, on loss or gain of electrons. Why does it become charged?

Ans. An atom is electrically neutral because of the same number of protons and electrons. But it becomes charged, to become stable atom, loses or gains electrons. Hence, Number of protons ≠ Number of electrons

If it loses electrons p > e; hence +ve charge is obtained.

If it gains electrons e > p; hence –ve charge is obtained.

Q15. *What is valency? Explain different types of valencies.*

Ans. The combining capacity of an atom is called its valency.

There are 2 types of valencies.

Covalency	*Electrovalency*
When an atom share electrons have combining capacity.	When an atom loses or gains electrons have combining capacity.

Some atoms also show zero valency when there outermost shell is completely filled.

Q16. With the help of an activity in daily life, how can you prove that atoms are divisible.

Ans. Activity

- Take a scale, rub it on hair, try to attract a small bit of paper.
- Now divide the bit of paper further into smaller pieces.
- Again bring the charged scale near to this pieces of papers.
- You will observe that the bits of paper still get attracted.

Conclusion: This activity shows that atom contains charges and these charges are opposite in nature which shows the attraction. Here both scale and paper are oppositely charged and hence attract each other. Also, every atom has at least one sub-atomic particle.

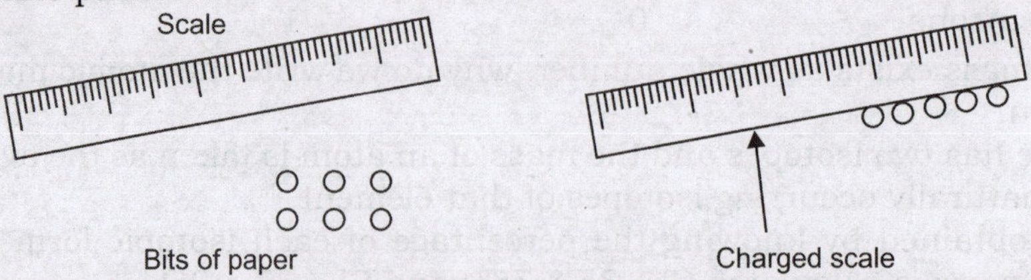

Q17. In the structure of an atom why are protons present in the centre and are not pulled outside by the electrons as both are oppositely charged with same unit of charge?

Ans. Protons are heavy with mass 1 unit and hence are concentrated in the centre of the atom. The mass of electrons is negligible *i.e.* $\frac{1}{1800}$ times less than that of protons. Hence are not able to attract the protons and pull them out of the nucleus, although their charge is of same value.

Q18. According to you, among the structure of atom studied which model is correct and why?

Ans. Bohr's model of an atom is the best model and is correct because it gives the explanation of nucleons (protons and neutrons) in the centre and how electrons revolve around the nucleon in their discrete, special orbits, so electrons don't loose/radiate energy and remain bonded in their shell.

Q19. Neon has two main isotopes that can be represented as ^{20}Ne and ^{22}Ne.

(*i*) Explain, with reference to sub-atomic particles, what is meant by the term isotopes?

(*ii*) The relative atomic mass of neon is 20.2. How does this information support the fact that a sample of neon contains more ^{20}Ne and ^{22}Ne?

Ans. (*i*) The increased number of neutrons in the atom of the same element having same atomic number.

(*ii*) The two Neon isotopes are Ne^{20} and Ne^{22}. The relative atomic mass of Neon is 20.2 which shows that the Neon with the atomic mass 20 is more.

Q20. The diagram shows a section of the Periodic Table and the symbols for the first 20 elements.

H																	He
Li	Be											B	C	N	O	F	Ne
Na	Mg											Al	Si	P	S	Cl	Ar
K	Ca																

(*a*) (*i*) What name is given to a horizontal row of element such as Na to Ar?

(*ii*) Name two metals in the row Na to Ar.

(*iii*) Which is the least reactive element in the row Na to Ar? Explain your answer.

Ans. (*a*) (*i*) The horizontal row is called a period.

(*ii*) Mg and Al.

(*iii*) The least reactive element is Ar as it is a noble gas.

Q21. An atom has atomic number 8 and mass number 18. How many protons, neutrons and electrons does this atom contain?

Ans. The number of protons and electrons are the same and is equal to the atomic number i.e. 8. The number of neutrons are 18 – 8 = 10.

Q22. The diagram shows the electronic configuration of an element X.

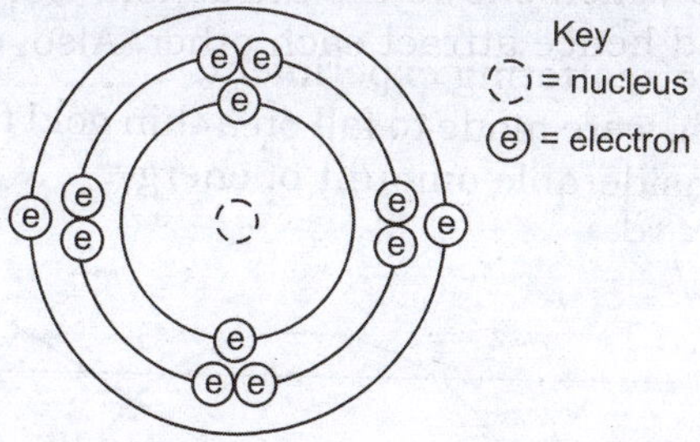

How many protons does the nucleus of the atom contain?

Ans. The atom contains same number of protons and electrons. As the structure shows 12 electrons therefore, the number of protons are also 12.

Q23. What period are the following elements in?

(*a*) He (*b*) Ge (*c*) Rb (*d*) I

Ans. (*a*) 1 (*b*) 4 (*c*) 5 (*d*) 5

Q24. What group are the following elements

(*a*) Sulfur (*b*) Ca (*c*) Iodine (*d*) Fe

Ans. (*a*) 16 (*b*) 2 (*c*) 17 (*d*) 8

IV. Long Answer Type Questions

Q1. Give an activity to understand the implications of Rutherford's α scattering experiment by a gold foil.

Ans. To understand the implications of Rutherford's α-particle scattering experiment:

Activity: Let a child stand in front of a wall with his eyes closed. Let him throw stones at the wall from a distance. He will hear sound for each strike of stone on the wall. This is like a nucleus of the atom. But if a blind-folded child has to throw stones at a barbed-wire fence, most of the stones would not hit the fencing and no sound would be heard.

This is because there are lots of gap in the fence which allows the stone to pass through them. This is like empty space in an atom through which α-particles will pass through. Based on the above activity and similar reasoning Rutherford concluded the α-particle scattering experiment as:

(1) Most of the space inside the atom is empty as α-particles passed through the foil.

(2) Very few particles deflected from their path, this show that positive charge occupies less space.

(3) A very small fraction of α-particles are deflected by 180°, this shows that all the positive charge and mass of the gold atom were concentrated in a very small volume within the atom.

Q2. What are isotopes? State its characteristics, give uses of isotopes?

Ans. Atoms of same element with same atomic number but different mass number are called isotopes.

Characteristics:

(1) Physical properties of the isotopes are different e.g. mass, density.

(2) Chemical properties of the isotopes are same due to same number of electrons.

Uses:

(1) Uranium isotope is used as a fuel in nuclear reactor (U-235).

(2) Cobalt isotope is used for treatment of cancer (Co-60).

(3) Iodine isotope is used in the treatment of goitre.

Q3. Explain Rutherford's α-particle scattering experiment and give its observation and conclusion drawn.

Ans. Rutherford's α-particle scattering experiment:
Fast moving α-particles were made to fall on a thin gold foil. Particles have +2 charge and 4u mass, and considerable amount of energy.

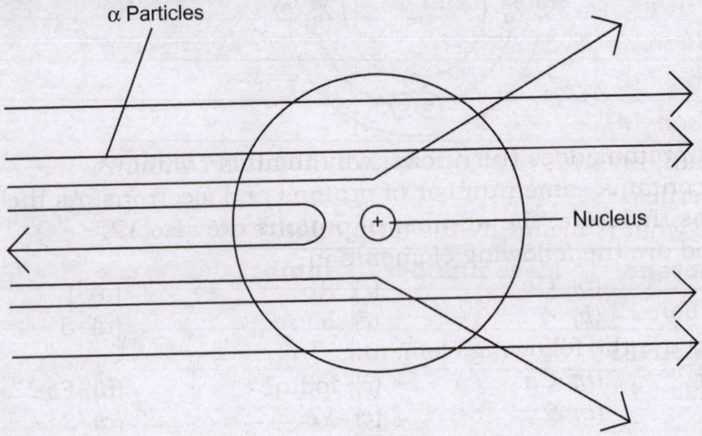

Observations:
(1) **Most** of the α-particles **passed straight** through the foil.
(2) **Some** of the α-particles **were deflected** by small angles by the foil.
(3) One out of every 12000 particles rebounded.

Conclusion from observation:
(1) **Most** of the **space** inside the foil is **empty.**
(2) Positive charge of atom occupies very less space.
(3) Mass of the atom is concentrated in the centre with all positive charge concentrated in small volume within the atom.

Q4. Establish the relationship between atomic number, mass number, isotopes, isobars and valency of an atom.

Ans. **Atomic number** — Gives the number of protons (Z)
Mass number — Gives the number of protons and neutrons (A)
Isotopes — When atoms of same element have same number of protons (Z) but different number of a neutrons (s) such atoms are called isotopes.
Isobars — When atoms of different element have same mass number (A) but different atomic number (Z) such atoms are called isobars.
Valency — It is the combining capacity of an atom.

E.g., $^{12}_{6}C$	$^{14}_{6}C$		
Z = 6	Z = 6	→	(Protons = Z)
A = 12	A = 14	→	(Protons + Neutrons = A)
Valency = 4	Valency = 4	→	Combining capacity

↘ ↙

Isotopes of C

$^{40}_{20}Ca$ $^{40}_{18}Ar$

↘ ↙

Isobars → same mass number but different atomic number.

Q5. The element carbon has three common isotopes. These are Carbon-12, Carbon-13 and Carbon-14.

(*a*) Complete the table to show the number of protons and neutrons in each isotope of carbon.

Isotope	Mass number	Number of protons	Number of electrons
Carbon-12	12	6	6
Carbon-13	13		
Carbon-14	14		

(*b*) Explain, in terms of electrons, why the three isotopes have the same chemical properties.

(*c*) State what is meant by the term relative atomic mass, A.

Ans. (*a*)

Isotope	Mass number	Number of protons	Number of electrons
Carbon-12	12	6	6
Carbon-13	13	6	7
Carbon-14	14	6	8

(*b*) The number of electrons are same in the three isotopes and hence the chemical properties of the three are the same.

(*c*) The relative atomic mass of Ar is the ratio of the average mass of atoms of an element (in a given sample) to one unified atomic mass unit. The unified atomic mass unit, symbol u, is defined being 1/12 of the mass of a carbon-12 atom.

Q6. Fill in the following chart.

Symbol	Atomic No.	Mass No.	Protons	Electrons	Neutrons
Hg	80	201			
Mo	42	96			
	29			29	35
C		14			
	15	31			
Pb		208	82		
Na	11				13

Ans.

Symbol	Atomic No.	Mass No.	Protons	Electrons	Neutrons
Hg	80	201	80	80	121
Mo	42	96	42	42	54
Cu	29	64	29	29	35
C	6	14	6	6	8
P	15	31	15	15	16
Pb	82	208	82	82	126
Na	11	23	11	11	13

Q7. Give an atom with the following characteristics.

(*a*) Halogen (*b*) Non metal (*c*) Alkali metal (*d*) Metalloid

(*e*) Lanthanide series (*f*) Alkaline Earth metal

(*g*) Transition Metal (*h*) Nobel gas

Ans. (*a*) F, Cl, Br, I, or At (*b*) C (*c*) Li, Na, K, Rb, Cs or Fr
(*d*) B (*e*) Eu (*f*) Be, Mg, Ca, Sc, Ba or Ra
(*g*) Cr (*h*) He, Ne, Ar, Kr, Xe or Rn

V. Value-Based Questions

Q1. Aryan could not solve the following question in the group; his groupmate explained him and solved his difficulty. The question was as follows:
What information do you get from the given figure about the atomic number, mass number and valency of the given atom 'X'.

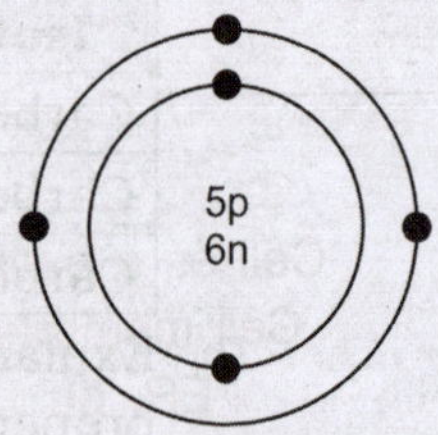

(*a*) What is the answer for the above question?
(*b*) Name the element 'X'.
(*c*) What value of Aryan's friend is reflected in this behaviour?

Ans. (*a*) The atomic number is 5.
The mass number is 11.
The valency is 3.
(*b*) The element 'X' is boron.
(*c*) Aryan's friend showed the value of helping and caring nature.

TEST YOUR SKILLS

Q1. What are nucleons?
Q2. Give the electronic configuration of Cl^- ion.
Q3. Draw the atomic structure of helium atom.
Q4. What are isobars?
Q5. What is mass number of an atom?
Q6. Find the valency of ${}^{4}_{2}He$ and ${}^{14}_{7}N$.
Q7. What are isotopes? Give its two applications.
Q8. An atom is electrically neutral. How can it become charged?
Q9. Explain Rutherford's α-particle scattering experiment and give its observation and conclusion drawn.
Q10. Give the difference between three sub-atomic particles.
Q11. Give the names of three atomic species of hydrogen.

❑❑❑

5 The Fundamental Unit of Life

Syllabus

Cell as a basic unit of life, Prokaryotic and eukaryotic cells, Multicellular organisms, Cell membrane and cell wall, Cell organelles: chloroplast, mitochondria, vacuoles, ER, golgi apparatus, nucleus and chromosomes (basic structure, number)

Facts that Matter

- The smallest functional unit of life is cell, discovered by Robert Hooke in 1665. A cell can independently perform all necessary activities to sustain life. Hence cell is the basic unit of life.

There are two types of cells → plant cell and animal cell. The different cell organelles and their functions are as follows:

1. **Plasma/Cell membrane:** This is the outermost covering of the cell that separates the contents of the cell from its external environment. The plasma membrane allows or permits the entry and exit of some materials in and out of the cell so the cell membrane is called as selectively permeable membrane.

Some gases like CO_2 or O_2 can move across the cell membrane by a process called **diffusion.** The movement of water molecules **(liquid)** through such a selectively permeable membrane is called **osmosis.** Osmosis is the passage of water from a region of higher water concentration through a semi-permeable membrane to a region of lower water concentration.

If the medium surrounding the cell has a higher water concentration than the cell, the cell will gain water by osmosis. Such a solution is known as a *hypotonic* solution.

If the medium has exactly the same water concentration as the cell, there will be no net movement of water across the cell membrane. Such a solution is known as an *isotonic* solution.

If the medium has a lower water concentration than the cell, it will lose water by osmosis. Such a solution is known as *hypertonic* solution.

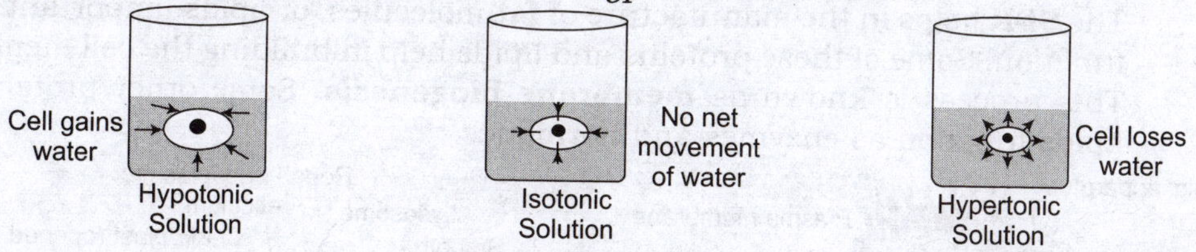

Types of different solution

The plasma membrane is flexible and is made up of organic molecules called **lipids** and **proteins**. The flexibility of cell membrane also enables the cell to engulf in food and other material from its external environment. Such process is known as **endocytosis.** It is observed in *Amoeba*.

2. **Cell wall (Protective wall):** Plants cells, in addition to the plasma membrane have another rigid outer covering called cell wall. The cell wall lies outside the plasma membrane. The plant cell wall is mainly composed of cellulose. It is a complex substance and provides structural strength to plant cells. When a living plant loses

water through osmosis there is shrinkage or contraction of contents of the cell away from cell wall. This phenomenon is known as **plasmolysis.**

3. **Nucleus (Brain of a cell):** The nucleus has a double-layered covering called nuclear membrane. The nuclear membrane has pores which allow the transfer of material from inside the nucleus to its outside, *i.e.,* to the cytoplasm.
The nucleus contains chromosomes, which are visible as rod-shaped structures only when the cell is about to divide. Chromosomes contain information for inheritance of features from parents to next generation in form of **DNA** [Deoxyribo Nucleic Acid) molecules. Chromosomes are composed of DNA and protein. Functional segments of DNA are called genes. The nucleus plays a central role in cellular reproduction.

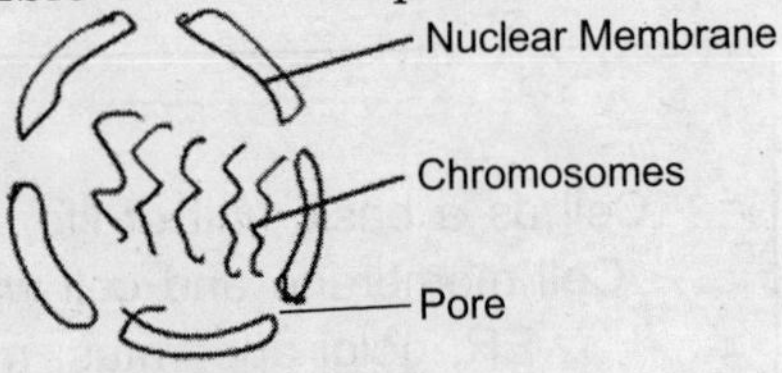

Nucleus

Prokaryotic Cells: In some organisms like bacteria, the nuclear material is not enclosed by nuclear membrane and membrane bound cell organelle are absent. Such nucleus is called nucleoid and such cells are known as prokaryotic cell. Such cells have single chromosome.
Eukaryotic Cells: Cells having well defined nucleus and having membrane bound cell organelles is termed as eukaryotic cell. Such cells have more than one chromosomes.

4. **Cytoplasm:** The cytoplasm is the fluid content inside the plasma membrane. It also contains many specialised cell organelles. Each of these organelles performs a specific function for the cell.
5. **Cell Organelles:** Every cell has a membrane around it to keep its content separate from the external environment. The different components of cell perform different functions and these components are called cell organelles.
   (*i*) **Endoplasmic Reticulum (ER) (Channels, Network for transport):** The ER is a large network of membrane-bound tubes and sheets. It looks like long tubules or round or oblong bags.
   There are two types of ER–*Rough endoplasmic reticulum* [*RER*] and *smooth endoplasmic reticulum* [*SER*]. RER has particles called ribosomes attached to its surface. The ribosomes are the sites of protein manufacturing.
   The **SER** helps in the manufacture of **fat** molecules, or lipids, important for cell function. Some of these proteins and lipids help in building the cell membrane. This process is known as **membrane biogenesis.** Some other proteins and lipids function as enzymes and hormones.

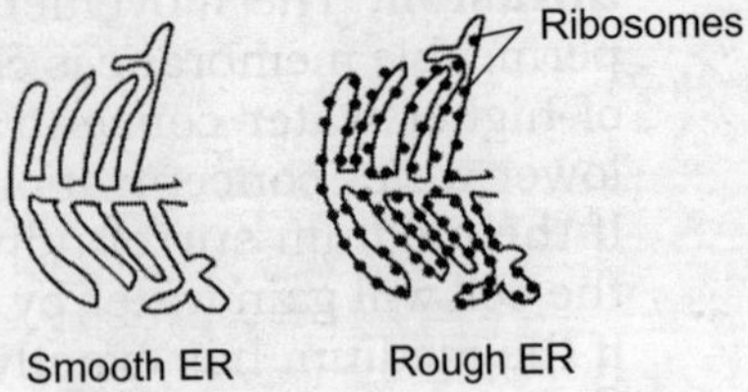

Endoplasmic Reticulum

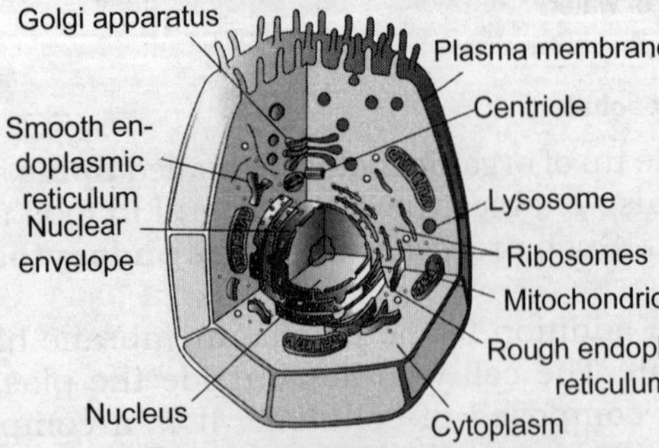

Animal Cell

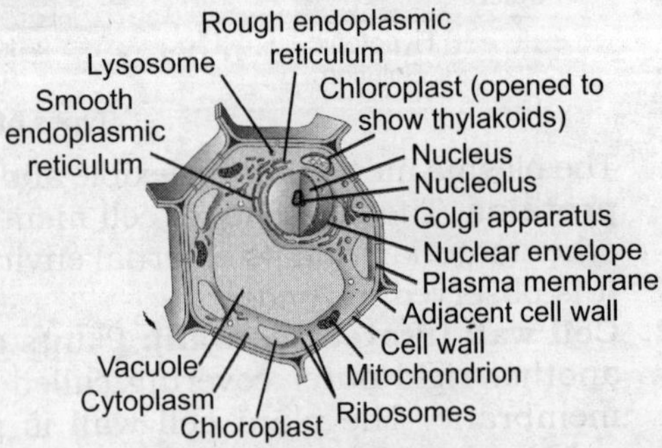

Plant Cell

The one function of ER is to serve as channels for the transport of materials between various regions of the cytoplasm or between the cytoplasm and the nucleus. The ER also functions as a cytoplasmic framework providing a surface for some of the biochemical activities of the cell.

(*ii*) **Golgi Apparatus (Packaging)**: The Golgi apparatus, first described by Camillo Golgi, consists of a system of membrane-bound vesicles (flattened sacs) arranged approximately. parallel to each other in stacks called **cisterns.**
The material synthesised near the ER is **packaged** and dispatched to various targets inside and outside the cell through the Golgi apparatus. Its function include the storage, modification and packages of products in vesicles. In some cases complex sugar may be made from simple sugars in the Golgi apparatus. It is also involved in the formation of lysosomes.

(*iii*) **Lysosomes [Suicide bags] (Cleanliness of cell)**: Lysosomes are a kind of waste dispatch and disposal system of the cell. Lysosomes help to keep the cell clean by digesting any foreign material as well as worn-out cell organelles. Foreign materials entering the cells such as bacteria or food, as well as old organelles, end up in the lysosomes, which break them up into small pieces. They are able to do this because they contain powerful digestive enzymes capable of breaking down all organic material. Under abnormal condition, when the cell gets damaged, lysosomes may burst and the enzymes digest their own cell. Therefore, they are also known as "suicide bags".

(*iv*) **Mitochondria (Powerhouse, Energy provider):** Mitochondria are known as powerhouses of the cell. The energy required for various chemical activities needed for life is released by mitochondria in the form of ATP [Adenosine triphosphate] molecules. ATP is known as energy currency of the cell. Mitochondria have two membrane coverings instead of just one. The outer membrane is very porous while the inner membrane is deeply folded. They are able to make some of their own protein.

(*v*) **Plastids:** Plastids are present only in **plant cells**. There are two types of plastids—chromoplasts and leucoplasts. Chromoplasts are the coloured plastids present in leaves, flowers and fruits. Plastids containing the pigment chlorophyll are known as chloroplasts. They are important for photosynthesis in plants. Chloroplasts also contain various yellow or orange pigments in addition to chlorophyll. **Leucoplasts** are found primarily in organelles in which materials such as starch, oils and protein granules are stored.
The internal organisation of the plastids consists of numerous membrane layers embedded in a material called stroma. Plastids are similar to mitochondria in external structure. Plastids have their own DNA and ribosomes.

(*vi*) **Vacuoles (Storage)**: Vacuoles are storage sacs for solid or liquid contents. Vacuoles are small-sized in animal cells while plant cells have very large vacuoles [50% to 90% cell volume].
In plant cells, vacuoles are full of cell sap and provide turgidity and rigidity to the cell. In *Amoeba*, the food vacuole contains the food items that is consumed by it and contractile vacuoles expel excess water and some wastes from the cell.

NCERT IN-TEXT QUESTIONS SOLVED

Q1. Who discovered cells, and how?

Ans. Robert Hooke discovered cells in 1665 while examining a thin slice of cork through a self-designed microscope. He saw that the cork resembled the structure of a honey comb consisting of many little compartments. He called these small boxes as cells.

Q2. Why the cell is called the structural and functional unit of life?

Ans. A cell is capable of independently carrying out all necessary activities of life. So, they are called basic or functional unit of life.

Q3. How do substances like CO_2 and water move in and out of the cell? Discuss.

Ans. CO_2 moves by diffusion and H_2O move by osmosis through cell membrane.

Q4. Why is the plasma membrane called a selectively permeable membrane?

Ans. It is called selectively permeable membrane because it allows the entry and exit of some substances, only and not all.

Q5. Fill in the gaps in the following table illustrating differences between prokaryotic and eukaryotic cells.

Ans.

Prokaryotic Cell	***Eukaryotic Cell***
1. **Size:** Generally small (1–10 μm) (1μm = 10^{-6} m)	1. **Size:** Generally large (5–100 μm)
2. Nuclear region is poorly defined due to absence of a nuclear membrane and known as nucleoid.	2. Nuclear region is well defined and surrounded by a nuclear membrane.
3. There is a single chromosome.	3. There are more than one chromosomes.
4. Membrane-bound cell organelles absent.	4. Membrane-bound cell organelles present.

Q6. Can you name the two organelles we have studied that contain their own genetic material?

Ans. The two organelles which have their own genetic material are:

1. Mitochondria 2. Plastids

Q7. If the organisation of a cell is destroyed due to some physical or chemical influence, what will happen?

Ans. The cell will not be able to survive and lysosomes will digest it.

Q8. Why are lysosomes known as suicide bags?

Ans. When the cell gets damaged, lysosomes may burst, and the enzymes digest their own cell. Therefore lysosomes are known as suicide bags.

Q9. Where are proteins synthesised inside the cell?

Ans. The proteins are synthesised in the ribosomes. They are also known as protein factories.

NCERT TEXTUAL QUESTIONS SOLVED

Q1. Make a comparison and write down ways in which plant cells are also different from animal cells.

Ans.

Plant Cell	***Animal Cell***
1. Plant cells have cell wall.	1. Animal cells don't have a cell wall.
2. They contain chloroplast.	2. They don't have chloroplasts.
3. They do not have centriole.	3. Centriole is present in them.

4. Vacuole is large and present in centre of the cell.	4. Vacuole is small.
5. Nucleus is present in the side of the plant cell.	5. Nucleus is present in the centre of the animal cell.

Q2. How is prokaryotic cell different from a eukaryotic cell?

Ans. Prokaryotic cell is generally smaller in size (1-10 µm), nuclear region is poorly defined, the cell organelles are not membrane-bound and has a single chromosome.
Eukaryotic cell is generally larger in size (5-100 µm), nuclear region is well defined with nuclear membrane. Membrane-bound cell organelles are present and has more than one chromosome.

Q3. What would happen if the plasma membrane ruptures or breaks down?

Ans. If plasma membrane ruptures or breaks down then molecules of some substances will freely move in and out of the cell.

Q4. What would happen to the life of a cell if there was no Golgi apparatus?

Ans. Golgi apparatus has the function of storage, modification and packaging of the products in vesicles. If there were no Golgi bodies, packaging and dispatching of materials synthesised by the cell will be stocked.

Q5. Which organelle is known as the powerhouse of the cell? Why?

Ans. Mitochondria is known as powerhouse of the cell because it releases the energy required for different activities of life.

Q6. Where do the lipids and proteins constituting the cell membrane get synthesised?

Ans. Lipids and proteins are synthesised in Endoplasmic Reticulum (ER).

Q7. How does Amoeba obtain it's food?

Ans. *Amoeba* take it's food by the cell membrane which forms the food vacuole.

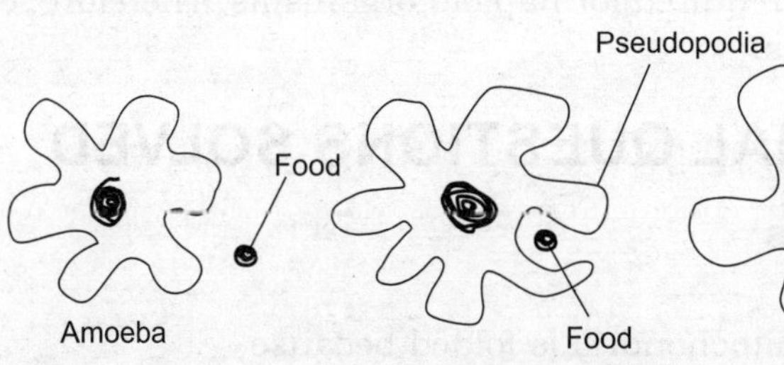

Endocytosis in *Amoeba*

Q8. What is osmosis?

Ans. Osmosis is the process of movement of water molecules from a region of higher water concentration through a semi-permeable membrane to a region of lower water concentration.

Q9. Carry out the following osmosis experiment:
Take four peeled potato halves and scoop each one out to make potato cups, one of these potato cups should be made from a boiled potato. Put each potato cup in a trough containing water.
Now,

(*a*) Keep cup A empty
(*b*) Put one teaspoon sugar in cup B
(*c*) Put one teaspoon salt in cup C
(*d*) Put one teaspoon sugar in the boiled potato cup D

Keep these for two hours. Then observe the four potato cups and answer the following:

(*i*) Explain why water gathers in the hollowed portion of B and C.

(*ii*) Why is potato A necessary for this experiment?

(*iii*) Explain why water does not gather in the hollowed out portions of A and D.

Ans.

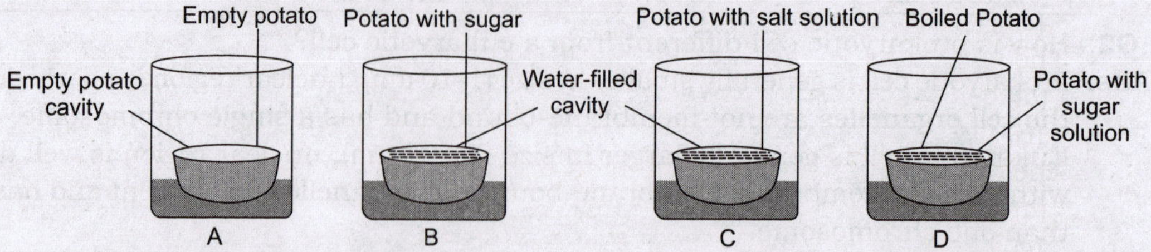

(*i*) Water gathers in B and C because in both the situations there is difference in the concentration of water in the trough and water in the cup of Potato. Hence, osmosis takes place as the potato cells act as a semi-permeable membrane.

(*ii*) Potato A is necessary for this experiment for comparison, it acts as a point of control.

(*iii*) Water does not gather in the hollowed out portions of A and D. As cup of A does not have any solution for concentration difference inside the potato. For osmosis to occur one of the concentration should be higher than the other. In cup D, the cells are dead and hence the semi-permeable membrane does not exists for the flow of water and no osmosis takes place.

Q10. Which type of cell division is required for growth and repair of body and which type is involved in formation of gametes?

Ans. Mitosis is required for growth and repair of body. Meiosis is required for diploid organisms and mitosis is required for haploid organisms. Therefore, cell division is not same for all organisms.

ADDITIONAL QUESTIONS SOLVED

I. Multiple Choice Questions

Choose the correct option:

1. The inner membrane of mitochondria is folded because

(*a*) it has no space inside (*b*) it helps in transportation of material

(*c*) it increases the surface area (*d*) it stores more food

2. Proteins are formed in

(*a*) Golgi bodies (*b*) nucleus

(*c*) plastids (*d*) ribosomes

3. The organelle that helps in the membrane biogenesis is

(*a*) lysosome (*b*) Golgi bodies

(*c*) endoplasmic reticulum (*d*) ribosome

4. The solution in which a cell will gain water by osmosis is termed as

(*a*) isotonic solution (*b*) hypertonic

(*c*) hypotonic solution (*d*) both (*a*) and (*b*)

5. The root hair absorbs water by the process called

(*a*) diffusion (*b*) osmosis

(*c*) endocytosis (*d*) plasmolysis

6. The animal cell which does not possess nucleus is
   (a) egg of hen (b) white blood cell
   (c) red blood cell (d) nerve cell
7. The nucleus of the cell was discovered by
   (a) Robert Hooke (b) Leeuwenhoek
   (c) Robert Brown (d) Purkinje
8. The plant cells are more rigid than the animal cell due to
   (a) cell wall (b) vacuoles
   (c) plastids (d) both (a) and (b)
9. The opening and closing of stomata is due to
   (a) sunlight (b) osmosis
   (c) plasmolysis (d) endocytosis
10. The cells with no membrane bound organelles, and the chromosomes are composed of only nucleic acids are
   (a) plant cells (b) animal cells
   (c) prokaryotic cells (d) eukaryotic cells

Ans. 1—(c), 2—(d), 3—(c), 4—(c), 5—(b), 6—(c), 7—(c), 8—(d), 9—(b), 10—(c).

II. Very Short Answer Type Questions

Q1. What are plastids? Name the different types of plastids found in plant cell.

Ans. Plastids are organelles found only in plants. They are:
(a) **Chloroplast**–Containing chlorophyll
(b) **Chromoplast**–Containing carotenoids and xanthophyll (coloured plastids)
(c) **Leucoplast**–White or colourless plastids

Q2. What is plasma membrane made up of?

Ans. Plasma membrane is made up of proteins and lipids.

Q3. What did Robert Hooke observed first in cork cell?

Ans. Robert Hooke observed that cork consists of box like compartments which formed a honeycomb structure.

Q4. Name the autonomous organelles in the cell.

Ans. Chloroplasts and mitochondria are the autonomous organelles in the cells.

Q5. What does protoplasm refer to?

Ans. Protoplasm refer to cytoplasm and nucleus.

Q6. Name two cells which keep changing their shape.

Ans. Amoeba and white blood cells.

Q7. Name the smallest cell and the longest cell in human body.

Ans. The smallest cell is the red blood cell or sperm cell in male. Longest cell is the nerve cell.

Q8. Name 3 features seen/present in almost every cell.

Ans. Plasma membrane, nucleus and cytoplasm.

Q9. What is diffusion?

Ans. The movement of particles or molecules from a region of higher concentration to a region of lower concentration is called diffusion. For example diffusion of CO_2 and O_2, across the cell membrane.

Q10. What is osmosis?

Ans. The movement of water molecules through a selectively permeable membrane is called osmosis. This takes place from high water concentration to low water concentration.

Q11. What is the full form of DNA?

Ans. DNA → Deoxyribo Nucleic Acid.

Q12. What is the function of chromosome?

Ans. Chromosomes contain information for the inheritance of features from parents to next generation in the form of DNA molecules.

Q13. Name the organelles present in liver of animals for detoxifying many poisons and drugs.

Ans. Smooth endoplasmic reticulum helps in detoxifying many poisons and drugs in the liver of animal cells

Q14. What is the energy currency of the cell?

Ans. ATP—Adenosine Triphosphate.

Q15. What is the function of ribosome?

Ans. Ribosomes help in protein synthesis.

Q16. Where are genes located in the cell?

Ans. Genes are located in the chromosomes which are present in the nucleus of the cell.

Q17. Name the cell organelles that helps in packaging?

Ans. Golgi apparatus.

Q18. Name the cell organelle which helps in the transportation of material.

Ans. Endoplasmic reticulum.

Q19. Name the cell organelle due to which leaves, flowers and fruits get their colour.

Ans. Chromoplast.

Q20. Name the cell organelle which helps in the formation of lysosome.

Ans. Golgi apparatus.

Q21. Name the cleansing organelle in the cell.

Ans. Lysosomes.

Q22. Name two cells with cell wall.

Ans. Onion cell (plant cell) and fungi.

Q23. Why does mitochondria have largely folded inner membrane?

Ans. Mitochondria is the site for cellular respiration and provides energy to the cell. The largely folded inner membrane provides the increased surface area for ATP-generating chemical reactions.

Q24. Which organelle makes the digestive enzyme of lysosome?

Ans. Rough endoplasmic reticulum makes the digestive enzyme of lysosomes.

Q25. What are cisterns?

Ans. The Golgi bodies consist of a system of membrane-bound vesicles arranged in stacks called cisterns.

III. Short Answer Type Questions

Q1. State two conditions required for osmosis.

Ans. (*i*) The difference in the concentration of water in and outside the cell, one should have higher concentration than the other.

(*ii*) Presence of semi-permeable membrane through which water will flow.

Q2. What is plasmolysis?

Ans. When a living plant cell loses water through osmosis there is shrinkage or contraction of the contents of the cell away from the cell wall. This phenomenon is known as plasmolysis.

Q3. How does fungi and bacteria can withstand much greater changes in the surrounding medium than animal cells?

Ans. The cell wall present in fungi and bacteria permits these cells to withstand very dilute external medium without bursting.

The cells take up water by osmosis, swells, and builds the pressure against the cell wall. The wall exerts an equal pressure against the swollen cell. It is because of the cell wall, such cells can withstand much greater changes in the surrounding medium than animal cells.

Q4. Give the function of nuclear membrane.

Ans. The nuclear membrane present as outer covering in the nucleus allows the transfer of material inside and out of the nucleus to cytoplasm.

Q5. Name the cell-organelles that have their own DNA and ribosomes.

Ans. The cell organelles with their own DNA and ribosomes are mitochondria and plastids.

Q6. State the difference between smooth endoplasmic reticulum and rough endoplasmic reticulum.

Ans.

Smooth Endoplasmic Reticulum	*Rough Endoplasmic Reticulum*
1. It looks smooth.	1. It looks rough.
2. SER helps in the manufacture of fat molecules or lipids.	2. Ribosomes are attached to RER which synthesise proteins.

Q7. What is endocytosis?

Ans. The cell membranes flexibility allows the cell to engulf in food and other material from its external environment. This process is known as endocytosis. E.g., *Amoeba* acquires its food through such processes.

Q8. What is the function of vacuoles?

Ans. Vacuoles are storage sacs for solid or liquid content. In plant cells it provides turgidity and rigidity to the cell. In single-celled organisms vacuoles store food, *e.g., Amoeba.*

Q9. When we put raisins in water, why do they swell?

Ans. Raisins are dry with less water inside, when they are kept in water, osmosis takes place, water flows in through the cell membrane of the raisins and therefore it swells.

Q10. Why are lysosomes called suicidal bags?

Ans. Lysosomes contain digestive enzymes in it and helps in the cleaning of cell by digesting any foreign materials entering the cell, such as bacteria, food and old cell organelles.

When the lysosomes burst, the digestive enzyme digest its own cell. Hence it is called as suicidal bag.

Q11. Label the figure and answer the questions:

(*i*) A – It is the packaging organelle
(*ii*) B – Provides energy
(*iii*) C – helps in the transport of material
(*iv*) D – Carries the information.

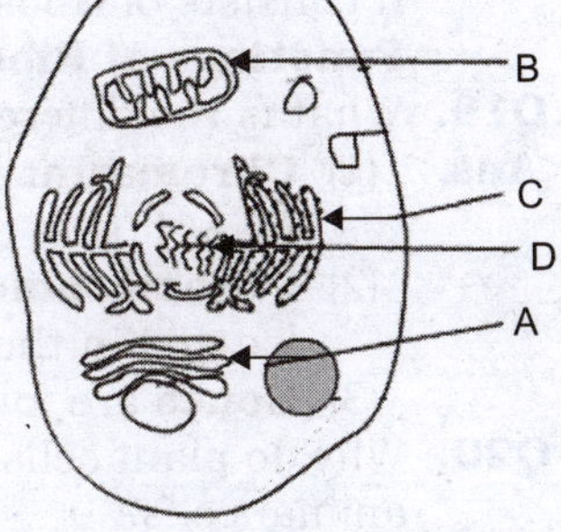

Animal Cell

Ans. (*i*) A – Golgi body
(*ii*) B – Mitochondria
(*iii*) C – Endoplasmic reticulum
(*iv*) D – Chromosomes

Q12. What is the role of cell organelles in the cell?

Ans. Each kind of cell organelles performs a specific function such as making new material, clearing of the waste, transporting material, etc.

Q13. What is nucleoid?

Ans. The nuclear region in some cells are poorly defined due to the absence of a nuclear membrane, it contains only nucleic acid. This undefined nuclear region with nucleic acid in it is called nucleoid.

Q14. What is the function of nucleus in a cell?

Ans. The nucleus plays a very important role in the reproduction of cells. It also helps the single cell to divide and form two new daughter cells.

It also plays an important role in determining how the cell will develop and what form it will exhibit at maturity, by directing the chemical activities of the cell.

Q15. What is the function of plastids?

Ans. Plastids are present only in plant cells. There are two types of plastids chromoplasts (coloured plastids) and leucoplasts (white or colourless)

Chromoplast—Consists of coloured pigments and gives different colours to flowers, fruits and leaves. The green colour pigment present in leaf is called chlorophyll which helps in the photosynthesis and a plastid with chlorophyll is called **chloroplast.**

Leucoplast—It stores starch, oil and protein granules in it.

Q16. Do vacuoles store some material? If yes, name them.

Ans. Yes, vacuoles also store some important substances required in life of the plant cell. These are amino acids, sugars, various organic acids and some proteins. In some unicellular organisms, e.g. *Amoeba*, vacuoles also store food.

Q17. Explain the structure and function of Golgi bodies.

Ans. **Structures:** Golgi bodies consist of a system of membrane-bound vesicles arranged in stacks parallel to each other called cisterns. These membranes have connections with the membrane of endoplasmic reticulum (ER).

Functions:

(1) The material synthesised near the ER is packaged and dispatched to various target inside and outside the cell through Golgi apparatus.

(2) It also stores, modifies and helps in the packaging of products in vesicles.

(3) In some cases, complex sugars may be made from simple sugars in it.

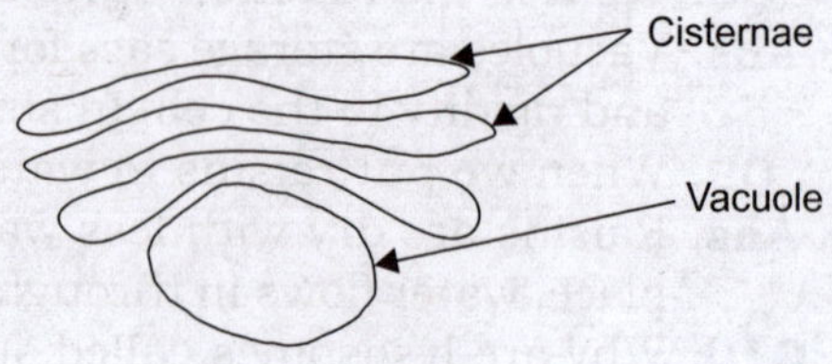

Golgi Body

(4) It also helps in the formation of lysosomes.

Q18. What are ribosomes? Where are they located in the cell? What is their function?

Ans. Ribosomes are spherical organelles present in the cell which are either freely distributed in the cytoplasm or may be attached to the endoplasmic reticulum. It consists of ribosomal RNA (Ribonucleic acid) and proteins.

Functions of Ribosomes: It helps in the synthesis of proteins.

Q19. What is the difference in chromatin, chromosomes and gene?

Ans. (1) **Chromatin:** It is a fine network of thread-like structure made up of DNA or RNA. It gets condense to form chromosomes.

(2) **Chromosome:** The chromosomes are made from chromatin material and are located in the cell, inside the nucleus.

(3) **Genes** are found in chromosomes.

Q20. Why do plant cells have more in number and big-sized vacuoles as compared to the animal cells?

Ans. Plant cells attain turgidity and rigidity due to the more number of vacuoles as well as large-sized vacuoles help the plant cells to withstand the wear and tear, external environmental conditions.

They also help in the storage of essential material required by plants for their growth like amino acids, sugar and various organic substances.

Q21. Explain the following terms:

(*a*) Plasma membrane (*b*) Cytoplasm

(*c*) Nucleus.

Ans. (*a*) **Plasma membrane:** It is a thin membrane which controls the passage of materials in and out of the cell. It is also called as selectively permeable membrane. It makes the outer boundary of the cell and is made up of lipo protein,

(*b*) **Cytoplasm:** It is transparent jelly-like thick substance present in the cell outside nucleus. It makes the ground of the cell in which all the cell organelles are suspended.

(*c*) **Nucleus:** It is a double-layered membrane structure which contains chromosomes required for the inheritance of characteristics from one generation to the other.

Q22. What is membrane biogenesis?

Ans. The endoplasmic reticulum helps in the manufacture of proteins and fat molecules or lipids which are important for the cell function. The building of the cell membrane with the help of proteins and lipids is known as membrane biogenesis.

Q23. Which organelle is known as powerhouse of the cell?

Ans. Mitochondria is known as powerhouse of the cell because it store energy in the form of ATP. [Adenosine Triphosphate]

Q24. What are genes?

Ans. Genes are the heredity unit of a cell which pass from one generation to another generation. Gene is a composed of DNA. They are located on chromosomes in linear fashions. One gene may perform one or more function. They are carrier of genetic codes.

Q25. Draw various cells of human body.

Ans.

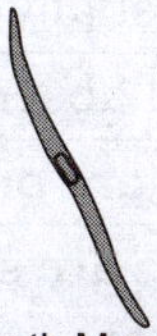
Smooth Muscle Cell

Sperm Cell

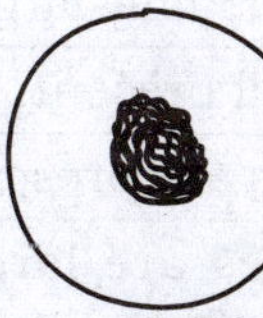
Egg Cell

Smooth Muscle Cell

Bone Cell

Blood Cells

Q26. State four adaptations seen in RBC.

Ans. (*i*) They have a biconcave disc shape that gives it a large surface area to carry more oxygen.

(*ii*) They contain a chemical called haemoglobin that combines with oxygen and carbon dioxide.

(*iii*) They have no nucleus to carry more oxygen and CO_2.

(*iv*) They are tiny enough to squeeze through capillaries.

Q27. Explain Osmosis.

Ans. Osmosis is the diffusion of water molecules from a region of their higher concentration to a region of their lower concentration, through a partially permeable membrane. Osmosis is a special form of diffusion and always involves the movement of water across a membrane.

Osmosis is the movement of water molecules across a selectively permeable membrane down a water potential gradient.

Q28. What is the role of cell membrane in osmosis?

Ans. Partially permeable membrane (let some substances pass through, but not others) separate two solutions, *i.e.*, cytoplasm and solution around the cell. If the solutions are of different concentrations, osmosis will occur.

Q29. When a plant cell and an animal cells are placed in water, what is the effect of osmosis on both?

Ans. Concentration of water outside the cell is higher than inside it. Cells will take in water by osmosis: plant cells become turgid (swollen) but do not burst (have tough cell wall which is fully permeable) and animal cells will burst (no cell wall).

Q30. When a plant cell and an animal cell are placed in sugar or salt solution, what is the effect of osmosis on both?

Ans. When both cells are placed in concentrated sugar or salt solutions. Water gets out of the cells by osmosis as concentration of water inside the cell is higher than outside it. Plant cells become flaccid (soft and limp), cytoplasm is no longer pressed against the cell wall. The plant loses it firmness and begin to wilt and animal cells shrink.

IV. Long Answer Type Questions

Q1. Give five points of differences between plant cell and animal cell.

Ans.

Plant Cell	***Animal Cell***
1. Size is usually larger than animal cell.	1. Size is usually smaller than plant cell.
2. Cell wall present.	2. Cell wall absent.
3. Plastids are present.	3. Plastids are present.
4. Vacuoles are large in number and bigger in size.	4. Vacuoles are small in size and less in number.
5. Centriole absent.	5. Centriole present.

Q2. Give five points of differences between prokaryotic cell and eukaryotic cell.

Ans.

Characters	***Prokaryotic Cell***	***Eukaryotic Cell***
1. Size	Diameter 1–10 μm.	Diameter 5–100 μm.
2. Nucleus	No true nucleus, single chromosome, nuclear membrane absent.	True nucleus, nuclear membrane is present, more than one chromosome is present.
3. Organelles	Membrane-bound organelles are absent.	Membrane-bound organelles are present.
4. Ribosomes	Ribosomes are 70S and randomly scattered.	Ribosomes are 80S, can be free or attached to ER.
5. Cell division	Cell divides by simple fission.	Cell divides by mitosis or by meiosis.

Q3. Draw a neat labelled diagram of plant cell and label its parts.

Ans.

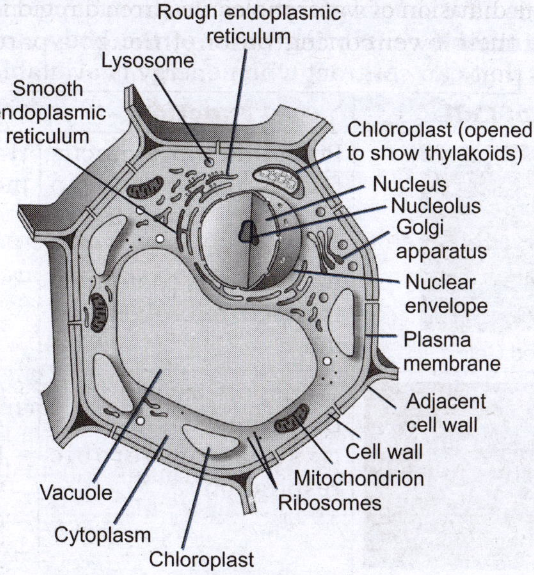

A plant cell

Q4. Draw a neat labelled diagram of animal cell.

Ans.

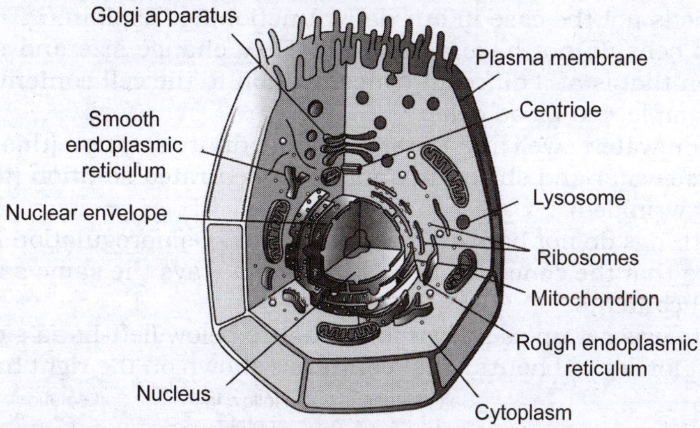

An animal cell

Q5. Name the cell organelle for the following:

(*a*) Present only in plant cell, provides strength and rigidity to the cell.
(*b*) It is the site for lipids synthesis and helps in detoxification of drugs.
(*c*) The inner membrane is folded to form cristae, it has its own DNA and proteins.
(*d*) It helps in the formation of lysosomes.
(*e*) It imparts colour to the fruit and flowers.

Ans. (*a*) Cell wall
(*b*) Smooth endoplasmic reticulum
(*c*) Mitochondria
(*d*) Golgi apparatus
(*e*) Chromoplast

Q6. What are specialised cells? Give few examples.

Ans. Specialised cells have special structures that are adapted for their specialised function. For example, muscle cells bring parts of the body closer together. They contain protein fibres that can contract when energy is available, making the cells shorter.

Type of Cell	***Function***	***Adaptations***
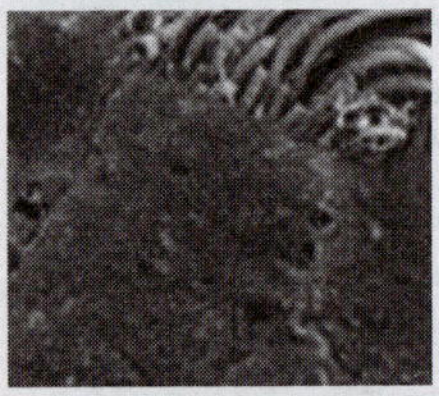 Ciliated Cell	Push and move mucus from one place to another. The cilia in the respiratory tract move mucus containing trapped microbes and dust.	Has a thin layer of tiny moving 'hairs' called cilia.
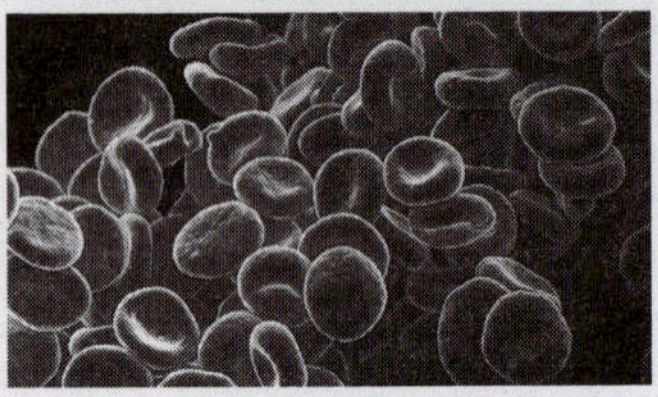 Red Blood Cell	Transport oxygen from the lungs to the body tissues for aerobic respiration.	– Contains haemoglobin, a pigment that carries oxygen. – Does not contain a nucleus, which increases the volume of haemoglobin in the cell. – Very flexible so it can move through narrow blood vessels.

Q7. Animal cells do not have cell wall and it is very easy for the movement of substances in and out of the cells like RBC etc which can change the overall nature of the cell. But this is not the case in our daily functioning. Explain.

Ans. Animal cells do not have a cell wall. They change size and shape when put into solution that is at a different concentration to the cell contents.

For example, red blood cells:

- gain water, swell and burst in a more dilute solution (this is called haemolysis)
- lose water and shrink in a more concentrated solution (they become crenated or wrinkled)

These things do not happen inside the body. Osmoregulation involving the kidneys ensures that the concentration of the blood stays the same as the concentration of the cell contents.

Q8. A potato was set up as shown in the figure below (left-hand side). The investigation was left for several hours. The results are shown on the right hand side of the figure.

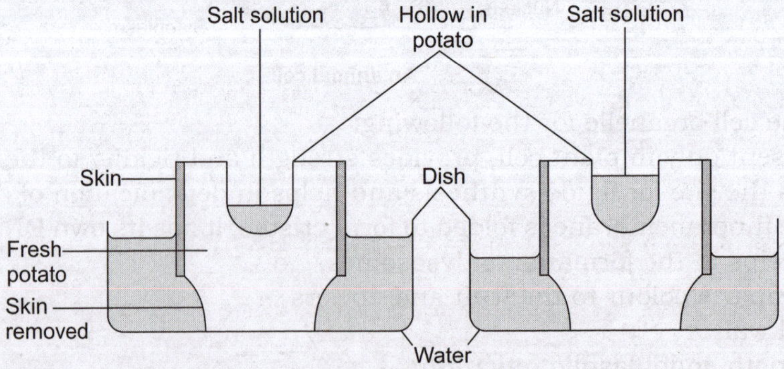

(*i*) Describe what happened to:

(*a*) the water in the disk

(*b*) the salt solution in the hollow in the potato.

(*ii*) (*a*) Name the process that is responsible for the changes that have occurred.

(b) Explain why these changes have occurred.
(c) Where does this process occur in a plant?
(d) What is the importance to the plant of this process?

Ans. (i) (a) The volume of water in the dish decreases.
(b) The volume of salt solution in the potato increases.

(ii) (a) Osmosis
(b) There was a higher concentration of water in the dish than inside the potato - so water moved into the potato. - from a high concentration of water to a lower concentration of water - by osmosis.
(c) Root hairs, or in the roots.
(d) Osmosis enables the plant to absorb water to maintain cell turgidity (or to replace water lost by transpiration).

Q9. Discuss in detail the chromosome, its structure and function.

Ans. Chromosomes are organized structure of DNA and proteins found in cells. They are thread-like structures located inside the nucleus of animal and plant cells. Chromosomes are made up of proteins and a molecule of deoxyribonucleic acid (DNA). Chromosomes are passed on from parents to offspring. The term chromosome is derived from a Greek word 'chroma' which means 'color' and 'soma' which means 'body'. The chromosomes are named so because they are cellular structures or cellular bodies and they are strongly stained by some dyes used in research. Chromosomes play an important role and ensures that DNA is copied and distributed accurately in the process of cell division. In most of the organisms chromosomes are arranged in pairs in the nucleus of the cell. We have 23 pairs of chromosomes.

V. Activity-Based Questions

1. To prepare a temporary mount of onion peel.

Method: Take out a small piece of onion peel, with the help of a pair of forceps. Keep it in a watch glass containing water.

Take a glass slide, put a drop of water on it at the centre, transfer a small piece of peel on the slide from the watch glass. The peel should be flat. Add a drop of **iodine** solution on this peel and slowly cover the peel with the help of a cover-slip. Avoid air bubbles. Now focus the slide under compound microscope.

Observation: Small compartments, structures all alike are observed called as cells.

Diagram:

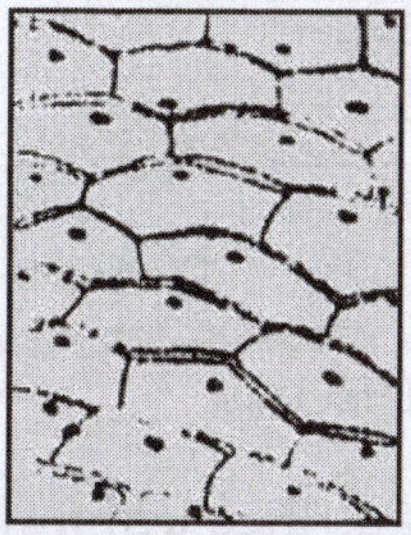

Slide of onion peel

2. As given in above Activity, a temporary mounts of leaf peel, tips of roots of onion or even peels of onion of different sizes can also be prepared.

Questions:
(a) Do all cells look alike in terms of size and shape?
(b) Do all cells look alike in structure?
(c) Could we find differences among cells from different parts of a plant body?
(d) What similarities are found in all the cells?

Answers:

(*a*) The shape and size of cells are different for different parts of the plant.

(*b*) The only similarity in all the cells is, they all have cell wall and nucleus.

(*c*) Yes, the cells are different in shape, size, colour and function.

(*d*) The similarities in all these cells is, they all have cell wall and have prominent nucleus in it, they have vacuoles in large number.

3. **Osmosis with an egg.**

(*a*) Remove the shell of an egg by dissolving it in dilute hydrochloric acid. The shell is mostly calcium carbonate. A thin outer skin now encloses the egg. Put the egg in pure water and observe after 5 minutes. Record your Observation.
The egg swells because water enters into it by osmosis.

(*b*) Place a similar de-shelled egg in a concentrated salt solution and observe for 5 minutes.

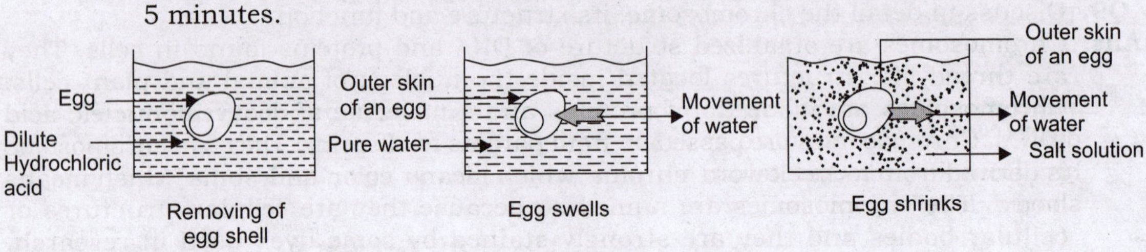

Osmosis in an egg

Observation: Water passes out of the egg solution through semi-permeable shell membrane into the salt solution because the salt solution is more concentrated. Water flow from the region of high water concentration to the region of low water concentration.

4. • Put dried raisins or apricots in plain water and leave them for some time. Then place them into a concentrated solution of sugar or salt. Record your observation.

Observation:

(*a*) Each raisin/apricot gains water and swells when placed in pure water.

(*b*) But, when placed in the concentrated solution, it loses water and shrinks.

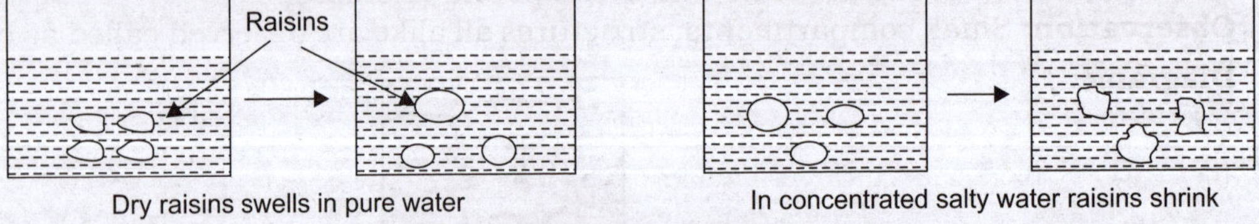

Osmosis in raisins

5. Find out about the electron microscope from resources in the school library or through the internet. Discuss.

Ans. Do it yourself.

6. (*a*) Mount the peel of a Rheo leaf in water on a slide and examine cells under the high power of a microscope. Note the small green granules called chloroplasts. They contain a green substance called chlorophyll. Put a strong solution of sugar or salt on the mounted leaf on the slide.
Record your observation.

(*b*) Now place some Rheo leaves in boiling water for few minutes. This kills the cells. Then mount one leaf on a slide and observe it under a microscope. Put a strong solution of sugar or salt on the mounted leaf on the slide. Wait and record your observation.

Observation:

(*a*) In this case water from the cells move out by osmosis thereby shrinking the cells and this process is called plasmolysis.

(*b*) On boiling the leaves, the cells die and the osmosis does not take place in these leaves.

7. Take a glass slide with a drop of water on it. Using an ice-cream stick gently scrape the inside surface of the cheek.
With the help of a needle transfer this material and spread it evenly on the glass slide kept ready for this. To colour the material put a drop of methylene blue solution on it. Put a cover-slip on it.
Observe the slide under the microscope.
Observation: The cells are seen in the slide with no cell wall but prominent nucleus. The cells are slightly round/oval in shape. They are cheek cells.

VI. Value-Based Questions

Q1. Vasu was helping his mother in laying the table when they had some guest for dinner. Vasu was about to sprinkle salt on salad for dressing. His mother stopped him from doing so and told him that it is too early to sprinkle salt on the salad, he should do so only when they are seated for having the dinner.

(*a*) What would happen if salt is sprinkled on the salad?

(*b*) Which property of cells is seen in adding salt to it?

(*c*) What value of Vasu is seen?

Ans. (*a*) On sprinkling of some salt on the salad, the salad will release water.

(*b*) The salt outside the salad acts as hypertonic solution as it has less water concentration and therefore the cell looses water by osmosis.

(*c*) Vasu showed the value of being very helpful, caring and responsible.

Q2. Anu is a five year old girl who joined the swimming classes. After the first class she was worried when she saw her wrinkled fingers. She asked her elder sister about the wrinkling and shrinking of her fingers. Her sister explained Anu why it was so.

(*a*) Why did the fingers wrinkle after swimming?

(*b*) What caused the shrinking/wrinkling of fingers?

(*c*) What value of Anu is seen in the above case?

Ans. (*a*) Fingers wrinkled because the cells of the skin lost some water.

(*b*) This happened because of the difference in the concentration of water in the skin cells and swimming pool's water.

(*c*) Anu showed the value of aware citizen and a good learner who clarifies the doubts.

Q3. Two sailors got marooned on the island, both of them were very thirsty and one of the sailors tried to drink sea water. The other sailor immediately stopped him from drinking the salty water of sea and suggested to wait for some help, stay calm and patient.

(*a*) What would happen if the sailor drinks salty water?

(*b*) What is osmosis?

(*c*) What value of sailors is reflected in the above act?

Ans. (*a*) On drinking salty water, osmosis in the intestine will cause dehydration and vomiting.

(*b*) The movement of water molecules through a permeable membrane from a region of higher concentration to a region of lower concentration is called osmosis.

(*c*) Sailors showed the value of being patient, composed, empathtic and determinant.

Q4. Sachin's mother wanted to use some eggs for incubation. Sachin helped his mother in separating rotten and spoilt eggs from the good ones. He took a bucket of water to separate them.

(*a*) How can one separate the rotten eggs from the good ones using water?

(*b*) What is the shell of egg made up of?

(*c*) What value of Sachin is seen in this act?

Ans. (*a*) We can separate the rotten eggs by dipping them in water. The eggs that will float in water are rotten eggs and the one that sinks are good one.

(*b*) Egg shell is made up of calcium carbonate.

(*c*) Sachin showed the value of being helpful and responsible behaviour.

VII. Practical Based Questions (Solved)

Q1. A student observes two slide in the lab under the microscope. The slide A and slide B. The diagrams of the same are shown below:

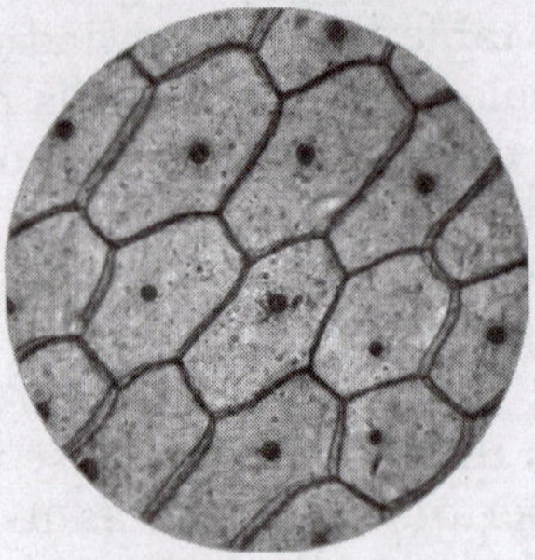

A

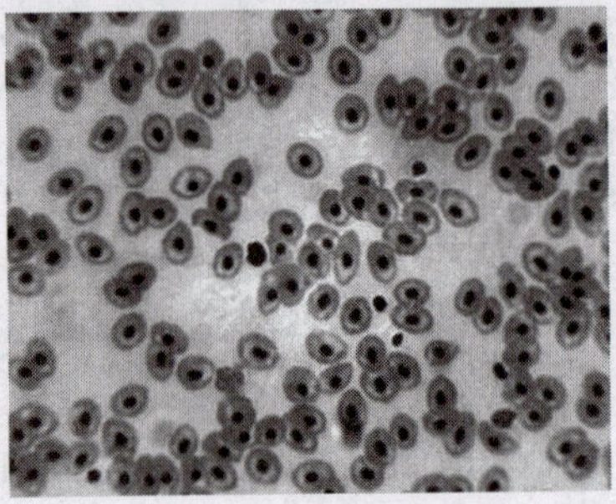

B

(*i*) Which slide contained the plant cell?

(*ii*) How were you able to distinguish the difference?

(*iii*) Draw an example of the plant cell you see under the microscope, and label as many parts as you can distinguish.

Ans. (*i*) The slide A shows plant cell

(*ii*) The plant cells have a cell wall and the shape the cells is in proper geometry.

(*iii*)

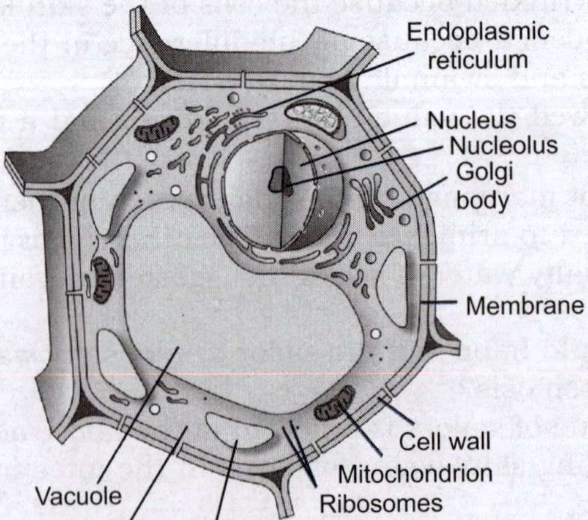

Plant Cell

Q2. A person wants to view the permanent slide under the microscope.

(*i*) Why might a person have trouble viewing their cells with the microscope?

(*ii*) What does it mean to draw a cell "to scale?"

(*iii*) Name two organelles found in the animal cell that could not be seen in your cheek cells.

(*iv*) Keeping in mind that the mouth is the first site of chemical digestion in humans. Your saliva starts the process of breaking down the food you eat. Keeping this in mind, what organelle do you think would be most numerous inside the cells of your mouth? (**Hint:** In your muscle cells, the mitochondria are the most numerous.)

Ans. (*i*) The person must be viewing the slide under the low resolution and then under the high resolution without making any coarse adjustments.

(*ii*) The cell in actual is very small when we have to draw it. The components of the cell should be in the proportion.

(*iii*) Chloroplast and vacuole.

(*iv*) Lysosomes

Q3. A student checks the onion cell and the leaf cell in the lab under the microscope to study. Answer the following questions based on the observation of the slide.

(*i*) Describe the shape and the location of chloroplasts.

(*ii*) Why were no chloroplasts found in the onion cells?

(*iii*) Which type of cell was smaller - the onion cells or the leaf cell? How do you know?

Ans. (*i*) The chloroplast is an oval structure seen in the cell. It is present outside the vacuole more in leaf cells.

(*ii*) Onion cells have no chloroplast because onions grow underground.

(*iii*) The onion cells looked bigger when viewed under the microscope.

TEST YOUR SKILLS

Q1. Name two cell organelles we have studied that contain their own genetic material.

Q2. Name the smallest cell and longest cell in human body.

Q3. What is the function of chromosome?

Q4. Name the cleansing organelle in the cell.

Q5. What is the full form of DNA?

Q6. Give the difference between prokaryotic and eukaryotic cell.

Q7. How do substances like CO_2 and water move in and out of the cell?

Q8. Why is plasma membrane called a selectively permeable membrane?

Q9. Draw a neat labelled diagram of animal cell.

Q10. What is the function of nucleus in a cell?

Q11. Give the difference between plant cell and animal cell.

❑❑❑

6 Tissues

Syllabus

Tissues, Organs, Organ systems, Organism

Facts that Matter

Tissues

A group of cells having a common origin and performing similar function are termed as tissues.

A. Plant tissues: On the basis of the dividing capacity, plant tissues are of two types:

1. Meristematic tissues
2. Permanent tissues

1. Meristematic tissues: Consist of actively-dividing cells. Meristematic tissues are of three types:

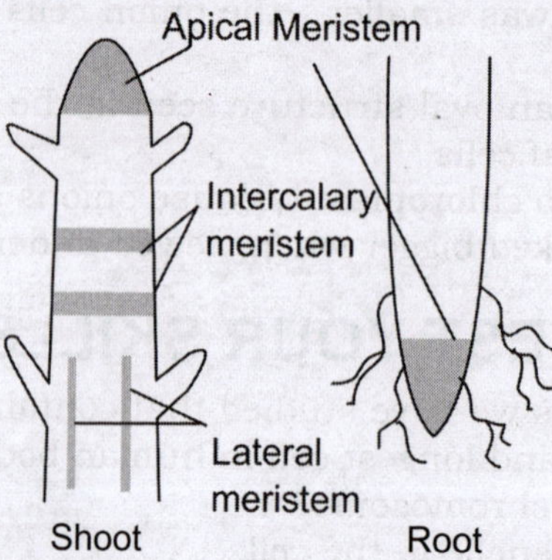

(*i*) **Apical meristem:** Present at the growing tips of stems and roots.
Important function: To increase the length of stems and roots.

(*ii*) **Intercalary meristem:** Present at the base of leaves or near the nodes.
Important function: For the longitudinal growth of plants.

(*iii*) **Lateral meristem:** Present on the lateral sides of the stems and roots.
Important function: To increase the thickness of stems and roots.

2. Permanent tissues: Formed from meristematic tissues, the cells in the tissue loose the ability to divide. Permanent tissues are divided into two categories:

(*i*) **Simple permanent tissue:** Consist of only one type of cells.
Types of simple permanent tissues:

(*a*) **Parenchyma:** Composed of unspecialised cells with relatively thin cell walls, large intercellular space, present in soft parts of the plant. Their main function is storage.

(*b*) **Collenchyma:** Composed of living and elongated cells with cell walls and irregularly thickened at the corners. Very little intercellular space. It provides mechanical support and elasticity to plant. It helps in bending of leaves and stems.

(c) **Sclerenchyma:** Composed of long, narrow, and thick-walled cells. This tissue is made up of dead cells and there are no intercellular spaces. Sclerenchyma cells are dead, present in seeds, nuts, husk of coconut, fibres of jute, etc.

(ii) **Complex permanent tissue:** Made up of more than one type of cells (Conducting tissues).

Types of complex permanent tissues:

(a) **Xylem:** Conducts water and minerals from the roots to the different parts of the plant.
Composed of four different types of cells—tracheids, vessels, xylem parenchyma and xylem fibres.

(b) **Phloem:** Conducts food material from the leaves to the different parts of the plant.
Composed of four different types of cells—sieve tubes, companion cells, phloem parenchyma and phloem fibres.

Protective tissue: It is made of a single layer of cells. E.g., epidermis. Epidermis of the leaf bears stomata.

B. Animal tissues: Animal tissues are classified into four types based on the functions they perform:

(i) Epithelial (ii) Connective (iii) Muscular (iv) Nervous

(i) **Epithelial tissues:** Form the covering of the external surfaces, internal cavities and organs of the animal body. Various types of epithelial tissues are:

(a) **Simple squamous epithelium:** Single layer of flat cells.
Location in the human body: Lining of the mouth, oesophagus, lung, alveoli, etc.

(b) **Cuboidal epithelium:** Consists of cube like cells.
Location in the human body: Lining of the kidney tubules and ducts of the salivary glands. It's function is secretion and absorption. It provides mechanical support.

(c) **Columnar epithelium:** Consists of elongated or column-like cells.
Location in the human body: Inner lining of the intestine and gut. Its function is of secretion and absorption.

(ii) **Connective tissues:** Specialised to connect various body organs. Various types of connective tissues are:

(a) **Areolar tissue:** Found between the skin and muscles, around the blood vessels and nerves, etc.

(b) **Adipose tissue:** Acts as the storage site of fats; found between the internal organs and below the skin; acts as an insulator for the body.

(c) **Dense regular connective tissue:** Main components are tendons and ligaments; tendons connect muscles to bones, while ligaments connect two bones together.

(d) **Skeletal tissue:** Main components of skeletal tissues are cartilage and bone.

(e) **Fluid tissue:** Blood is the vascular tissue present in animals.

(iii) **Muscular tissues:** Main function of muscular tissues is to provide movement to the body. Muscular tissues are of three types:

(a) **Striated muscles or skeletal muscles or voluntary muscles:** Cells are cylindrical, unbranched and multinucleated.

(b) **Smooth muscles or involuntary muscles:** Cells are long, spindle-shaped and possess a single nucleus.

(c) **Cardiac muscles or involuntary muscles:** Cells are cylindrical, branched and uninucleated.

(iv) **Nervous tissues:** Present in the brain, spinal cord and nerves.

(a) Neuron: Cells of the nervous tissue.

(b) A neuron consists of a cell body, an axon and a dendrite.

NCERT IN-TEXT QUESTIONS SOLVED

Q1. What is a tissue?

Ans. A group of cells that are similar in structure and work together to do a peculiar function is called a tissue.

Q2. What is the utility of tissues in multicellular organisms?

Ans. Tissues provide structural and mechanical strength and show division of labour.

Q3. Name the types of simple tissues.

Ans. The types of simple tissues are parenchyma, collenchyma and sclerenchyma.

Q4. Where is apical meristem found?

Ans. Apical meristem is found at the tip of root or shoot of the plant.

Q5. Which tissue makes up the husk of coconut?

Ans. The husk of coconut is made of sclerenchymatous tissue.

Q6. What are the constituents of phloem?

Ans. Phloem is made up of four types of elements: sieve tubes, companion cells, phloem fibres and phloem parenchyma.

Q7. Name the tissue responsible for movement in our body.

Ans. 1. Muscular tissue, 2. Nervous tissue, combination of both the tissues are responsible for the movement in our body.

Q8. What does a neuron look like?

Ans. A neuron consists of a cell body with a nucleus and cytoplasm, from which long thin hair like parts arise. Each neuron has a single long part called the axon, and many small, short branched parts called dendrite.

An individual nerve cell is called neuron, it may be upto a metre long.

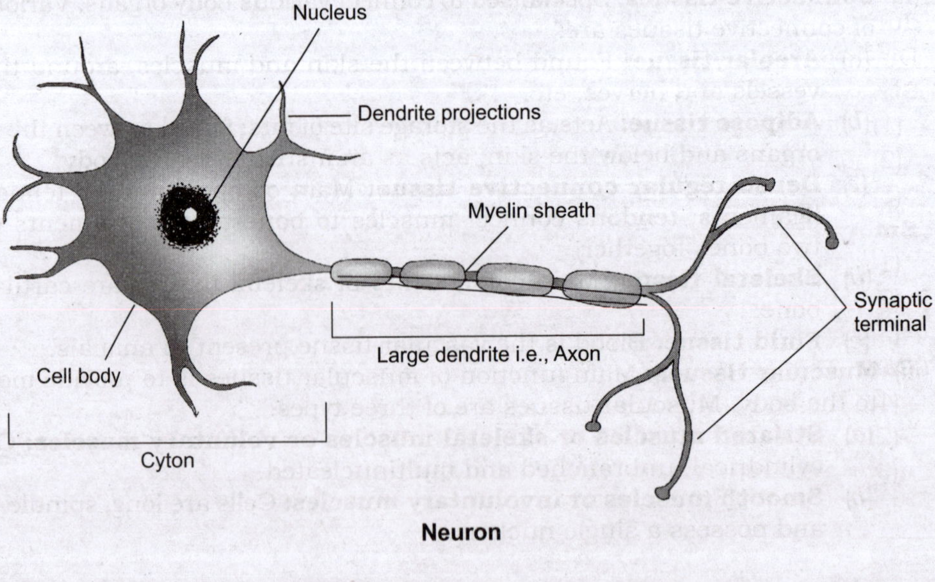

Neuron

Q9. Give three features of cardiac muscles.

Ans. Feature of cardiac muscles

(1) Heart muscles (cardiac muscles) are cylindrical, branched and uninucleated

(2) They are striated muscle fibres.

(3) They are involuntary muscles, cannot be controlled by us.

Q10. What are the functions of areolar tissue?

Ans. Areolar tissue are connective tissues found in animal. It is found between skin and muscles, around blood vessels and nerves and in the bone marrow.

It fills the space inside the organs, supports internal organs and helps in the repair of tissues.

NCERT TEXTUAL QUESTIONS SOLVED

Q1. Define the term "tissue".

Ans. Group of cells that are similar in structure and perform same function is called a tissue.

Q2. How many types of elements together make up the xylem tissue? Name them.

Ans. The xylem is made up of vessels, tracheids, xylem fibres and xylem parenchyma.

Q3. How are simple tissues different from complex tissues in plants?

Ans. Simple tissues are made up of **one type of cells** which coordinate to perform a common function.

Complex tissues are made up of **more than one type of cells.** All these coordinate to perform a common function.

Q4. Differentiate between parenchyma, collenchyma and sclerenchyma on the basis of their cell wall.

Ans. Parenchyma: The cells have thin cell walls made up of cellulose.

Collenchyma: The cells have cell walls thickened at the corners due to pectin deposition.

Sclerenchyma: Their walls are thickened due to lignin deposition.

Q5. What are the functions of stomata?

Ans. The outermost layer of the cell is called epidermis and is very porous. These pores are called stomata. These stomata help in **transpiration** and **exchange of gases** during photosynthesis and respiration.

Q6. Diagrammatically show the difference between the three types of muscle fibres.

Ans. Striated muscles

(1) They are connected to bones (Skeletal muscles).

(2) They are voluntary muscles.

(3) The cells are long, cylindrical, multinucleated and unbranched.

Smooth muscles

(1) They are found in alimentary canal and lungs.

(2) They are involuntary muscles.

(3) They are spindle in shape and have single nucleus.

Cardiac muscles

(1) They are found in heart.

(2) They are involuntary in action.

(3) They are branched and uninucleated.

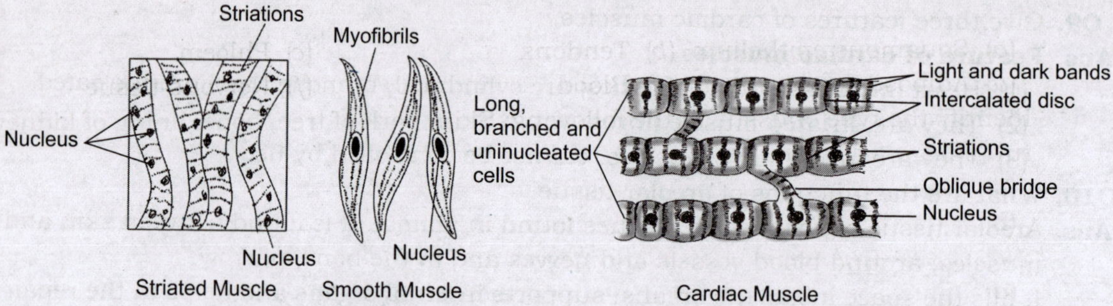

Q7. What is the specific function of the cardiac muscle?

Ans. Cardiac muscle show rhythmically contraction and relaxation throughout life and helps in pumping action of heart.

Q8. *Differentiate between striated, unstriated and cardiac muscles on the basis of their structure and location in the body.*

Ans.

Character	Striated Muscles	Unstriated Muscles	Cardiac Muscles
1. Shape	Cells are long, cylindrical and unbranched.	Cells are long with tapering ends and unbranched.	Cells are cylindrical in shape and branched.
2. Location in body	In hands, legs and skeletal muscles.	The wall of stomach, intestine, ureter and bronchi, etc.	In the heart.
3. Light and dark bands	Present.	Absent.	Present but less prominent.

Q9. Draw a labelled diagram of neuron.

Ans.

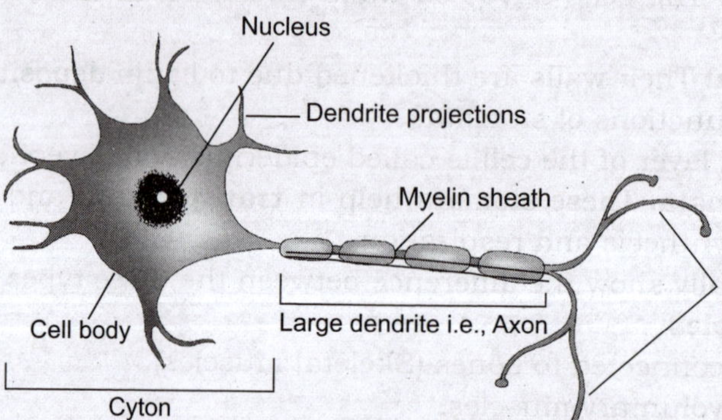

Neuron

Q10. Name the following:

(*a*) Tissue that forms the inner lining of our mouth.

(*b*) Tissue that connect muscle to bone in humans.

(*c*) Tissue that transports food in plants.

(*d*) Tissue that stores fat in our body.

(*e*) Connective tissue with a fluid matrix.

(*f*) Tissue present in the brain.

Ans. (*a*) Squamous epithelium (*b*) Tendons (*c*) Phloem
(*d*) Adipose tissue (*e*) Blood (*f*) Nervous tissue

Q11. Identify the type of tissue in the following: Skin, bark of tree, bone, lining of kidney tubule, vascular bundle.

Ans. (*a*) Skin—Striated squamous epithelium
(*b*) Bark of tree—Cork, protective tissue
(*c*) Bone—Connective tissue
(*d*) Lining of kidney tubule—Cuboidal epithelium tissue
(*e*) Vascular bundle—Conducting tissue or complex permanent tissue.

Q12. Name the regions in which parenchyma tissue is present.

Ans. In the pith of the roots and stems. When it contains chlorophyll, it is called chlorenchyma, found in green leaves. In aquatic plants, parenchyma contains large air cavities which help them to float. Such type of parenchyma is called aerenchyma.

Q13. What is the role of epidermis in plants?

Ans. Cells of epidermis forms a continuous layer without intercellular spaces. It protects all the parts of plants. Epidermis helps in absorption, secretion, transpiration, photosynthesis etc.

Q14. How does the cork act as a protective tissue?

Ans. Cork acts as a protective tissue because its cells are dead and compactly arranged without intercellular spaces. They have deposition of suberin on the walls that make them impervious to gases and water.

Q15. Complete the following chart:

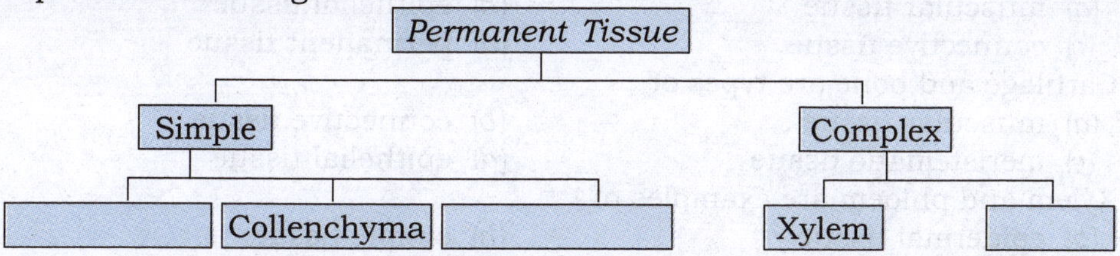

Ans.

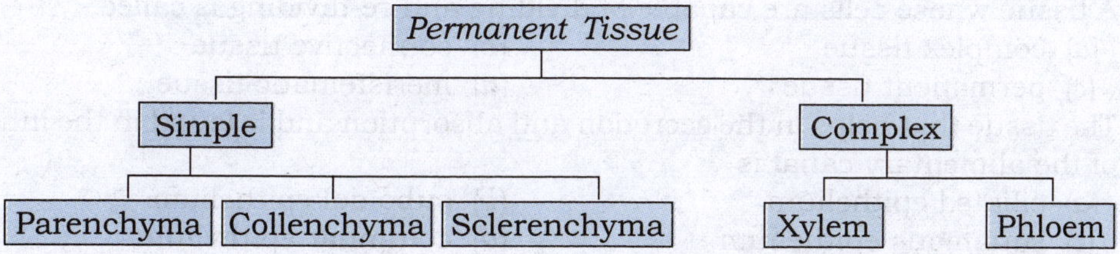

ADDITIONAL QUESTIONS SOLVED

I. Multiple Choice Questions

Choose the correct option:

1. The cells of cork are dead and have a chemical in their walls that makes them impervious to gases and water. The chemical is
(*a*) lignin (*b*) suberin (*c*) cutin (*d*) wax

2. The flexibility in plants is due to a tissue called
(*a*) chlorenchyma (*b*) parenchyma (*c*) sclerenchyma (*d*) collenchyma

3. The tissue present in the lining of kidney tubules and ducts of salivary glands is
   (*a*) squamous epithelium tissue (*b*) glandular epithelium tissue
   (*c*) cuboidal epithelium tissue (*d*) columnar epithelium tissue
4. The connective tissue that connects muscle to bone is called
   (*a*) ligament (*b*) tendon
   (*c*) cartilage (*d*) areolar
5. The tissue that helps in the movement of our body are
   (*a*) muscular tissue (*b*) skeletal tissue
   (*c*) nervous tissue (*d*) all of the above
6. Monocyte, basophil, eosinophil and neutrophil are the examples of different types of
   (*a*) red blood cells (*b*) white blood cells
   (*c*) areolar tissue (*d*) compact bone
7. The spindle shaped cells, uninucleated and unbranched are present in muscular tissue of
   (*a*) striated muscles (*b*) smooth muscles
   (*c*) cardiac muscle (*d*) both (*a*) and (*b*)
8. Sieve tubes and companion cells are present in
   (*a*) xylem (*b*) phloem
   (*c*) cork (*d*) cambium
9. The size of the stem increases in the width due to
   (*a*) apical meristem (*b*) intercalary meristem
   (*c*) primary meristem (*d*) lateral meristem
10. Blood and lymph are types of
   (*a*) muscular tissue (*b*) epithelial tissue
   (*c*) connective tissue (*d*) permanent tissue
11. Cartilage and bone are types of
   (*a*) muscular tissue (*b*) connective tissue
   (*c*) meristematic tissue (*d*) epithelial tissue
12. Xylem and phloem are examples of
   (*a*) epidermal tissue (*b*) simple tissue
   (*c*) protective tissue (*d*) complex tissue
13. A tissue whose cells are capable of dividing and re-dividing is called
   (*a*) complex tissue (*b*) connective tissue
   (*c*) permanent tissue (*d*) meristematic tissue
14. The tissue that helps in the secretion and absorption and is found in the inner lining of the alimentary canal is
   (*a*) ciliated epithelium (*b*) cuboidal epithelium
   (*c*) squamous epithelium (*d*) columnar epithelium

Ans. 1—(*b*), 2—(*d*), 3—(*c*), 4—(*b*), 5—(*d*), 6—(*b*), 7—(*b*), 8—(*b*), 9—(*d*), 10—(*c*), 11—(*b*), 12—(*d*), 13—(*d*), 14—(*d*).

II. Very Short Answer Type Questions

Q1. Name the tissues responsible for the movement of the body.

Ans. Muscle tissue and nervous tissue

Q2. How does neuron look like?

Ans. A neuron is the unit cell of nervous tissue. It is a thread-like structure with cell body and axon.

Q3. Name the types of simple tissues.

Ans. (*a*) Parenchyma (*b*) Collenchyma (*c*) Sclerenchyma

Q4. Name the types of complex tissues.
Ans. Xylem and phloem.
Q5. Where is apical meristem found?
Ans. It is present at the growing tips of stem and root, it increases the length of the stem and roots.
Q6. Which tissue make up the husk of coconut?
Ans. Sclerenchyma.
Q7. What are the constituents of phloem?
Ans. Phloem constitutes the sieve tubes, companion cell, phloem parenchyma and phloem fibres.
Q8. Define aerenchyma.
Ans. The cells of aerenchyma have air-filled large cavities present in parenchyma, and helps aquatic plants in floating.
Q9. What is the utility of tissues in multicellular organisms?
Ans. Tissves help in growth, organisation of different organs and performing different functions.
Q10. Name the two types of tissues.
Ans. Plant tissues and animal tissues.
Q11. Name the two types of plant tissue.
Ans. Meristematic tissue and permanent tissue.
Q12. What is differentiation?
Ans. The process of taking up a permanent shape, size and function by cells is called differentiation.
Q13. Name the three types of meristematic tissues.
Ans. The three types are:
(*a*) Apical tissue—tips of root and shoot
(*b*) Lateral tissue—sides of stem
(*c*) Intercalary tissue—at nodes
Q14. Where is apical tissue found?
Ans. Apical tissue is present at the tips of roots and stems.
Q15. Tissues present at the lateral surface of the stem are called apical tissues. Put (T) if true and put (F) if false.
Rewrite the answer if (F).
Ans. (F). Tissues present at the lateral surface of the stem are called lateral tissue.
Q16. Which tissues are present at the nodes of the plants?
Ans. Intercalary tissue.
Q17. What are the various types of blood cells?
Ans. There are three types:
(*a*) RBC's (*b*) WBC's and (*c*) Platelets.
Q18. What are tracheids?
Ans. Tracheids are elongated cells with tapering ends.
Q19. What are guard cells?
Ans. Each stomata is bounded by a pair of specialised kidney-shaped epidermal cells called guard cells.
Q20. Epithelial tissue is the simplest tissue. Write (F) for false or (T) for true.
Ans. (T).
Q21. What are the functions of cuboidal epithelium?
Ans. It helps in absorption, excretion, secretion and also provides mechanical support.
Q22. What does plasma contain?
Ans. The plasma contains proteins, salts and hormones.

Q23. What do you mean by differentiation?

Ans. The cells of permanent tissue loose the capacity to divide and attain a permanent shape, size and function.

Q24. How are simple tissues different from complex tissues in plant?

Ans. The simple tissues are made of one type of cells and complex tissues are made of one or more types of cells.

III. Short Answer Type Questions

Q1. Give four differences between bone and cartilage.

Ans.

Bone	*Cartilage*
1. Hard and non-flexible	1. Flexible not very hard
2. Porous	2. Non-porous
3. Blood vessels present	3. Blood vessels absent
4. Matrix made up of protein and mineral salts.	4. Matrix made up of proteins.

Q2. Give the functions of bone.

Ans. The functions of bone are:

(*i*) It provides shape to the body.
(*ii*) It provides skeletal support to the body.
(*iii*) It anchors the muscles.
(*iv*) It protects the vital body organs like brain, lungs, etc.

Q3. Give the functions of cartilage.

Ans. (*i*) It provides support and flexibility to the body parts.
(*ii*) It smoothens surface at joints.

Q4. Fill in the blanks:

(*i*) Water and minerals are conducted by ....
(*ii*) In higher plants food is conducted by ....
(*iii*) Blood is a .... tissue.
(*iv*) Bone consists of .... cells.
(*v*) Cartilage consists of .... cells.
(*vi*) Fibres are absent in .... type of connective tissue.

Ans. (*i*) Xylem (*ii*) Phloem (*iii*) Connective (*iv*) Osteocyte
(*v*) Chondrocyte (*vi*) Blood

Q5. What are the functions of areolar tissue?

Ans. **Functions are:**

(*i*) It helps in repair of tissues after an injury.
(*ii*) It also helps in combating foreign toxins.
(*iii*) It fixes skin to underlying muscles.

Q6. Give difference between xylem and phloem.

Ans.

Xylem	*Phloem*
1. It consists of mainly dead elements.	1. It consists of mainly living elements.
2. It conducts water and minerals.	2. It conducts food.
3. It provides mechanical strength to the plant.	3. It does not provide mechanical strength to the plant.

Q7. What are fibres?

Ans. Fibres consist of very long, narrow, flexible and thick cells. Example, jute and cotton fibre.

Q8. Name the tissues for the following:

(*a*) Stores fat in animal body.
(*b*) Divides and re-divides to grow in plants.
(*c*) Tissue that joins bone to bone.
(*d*) Covers the external surface of animal body.

Ans. (*a*) Adipose tissue (*b*) Meristematic tissue
(*c*) Ligament (*d*) Epithelial tissue.

Q9. What are stomata?

Ans. Stomata are small pores present on the surface of a leaf which helps in the exchange of gases during photosynthesis, respiration and transpiration.

Q10. Why does epidermal tissue have no intercellular space?

Ans. The epidermal (layer) tissue forms a protective outer covering and protects the internal parts of the plant. It aids in the protection against loss of water, mechanical injury and invasion by parasitic fungi.

For this protective role to play the continuation of cells is necessary, hence it does not have intercellular space.

Q11. Name and give the function of each cell of xylem.

Ans. Xylem consists of tracheids, vessels, xylem parenchyma and xylem fibres.

Tracheids and vessels—Allows the transport of water and minerals.

Xylem parenchyma—Stores food and helps in the sideways conduction of water.

Xylem fibres—Are supportive in function.

Q12. What is the function and location of stratified squamous epithelium?

Ans. Stratified squamous epithelium is present in the *skin*. The layers of cells are arranged to prevent *wear* and *tear*.

Q13. Give difference between ligament and tendon.

Ans.

Ligament	***Tendon***
1. Ligament helps in connecting bone to bone.	1. Tendon helps in connecting bone to muscles.
2. It is elastic and flexible.	2. It is strong and non-flexible.

Q14. Give difference between striated muscles and unstriated muscles.

Ans.

Striated Muscles	***Unstriated Muscles***
1. They are skeletal muscles.	1. They are smooth muscles.
2. They show alternate light and dark bands.	2. These muscles do not show such bands.
3. Voluntary muscles.	3. Involuntary muscle.
4. Cells are cylindrical and multinucleated.	4. Cells are tapering and uninucleated.

Q15. State the difference between bone and blood.

Ans.

Bone	***Blood***
1. It is a hard tissue.	1. It is a liquid tissue.
2. It consists of osteocytes.	2. It consists of plasma, RBC, WBC and blood platelets.
3. It helps in movement and support of the body.	3. It helps in the transport of substances.

Q16. Name all different types of tissues present in animal.

Ans. There are four main types of tissues present in animal.

(*a*) Epithelial tissue present on the outer and inner lining of the body.

(*b*) Muscular tissue are made up of muscles, help in movement.

(*c*) Connective tissue connects the different organs in the body.

(*d*) Nervous tissue consists of nerve cells and are present in the nervous system.

Q17. Why is blood called connective tissue?

Ans. The blood is composed of cells and plasma. Plasma is a fluid and cells like red blood cells, white blood cells and platelets are present in it. All these cells are connected due to plasma. It also transports absorbed nutrients, water gases like (O_2 and CO_2) to the different parts of the body and connects them.

Q18. Name three types of muscle tissues and give function of each.

Ans. Three types of muscle tissues are:

(*a*) Striated muscle (*b*) Smooth muscle (*c*) Cardiac muscle

(*a*) **Striated muscle:** These muscles show alternate light and dark bands or striations. They are voluntary muscles and present in skeletal tissues, help in movement of body and bones.

(*b*) **Smooth muscle:** These are involuntary muscles, control the movement of food in alimentary canal, contraction and relaxation of blood vessels. Present in iris, uterus etc.

(*c*) **Cardiac muscle:** These muscles are present in heart which help in the rhythmic contraction and relaxation of heart throughout the life.

Q19. State the difference between simple tissues of plants.

Ans. The simple tissues of plants are:

(*i*) Parenchyma (*ii*) Collenchyma (*iii*) Sclerenchyma

Parenchyma	*Collenchyma*	*Sclerenchyma*
1. The cells are living and thin walled.	The cells are living and thick at corners.	The cells are dead and thick walled due to lignin deposition.
2. The cells are oval, spherical or polygonal in shape.	The cells are elongated and thickened at corners.	The cells are long and narrow.
3. There is large, intercellular space between the cells.	There is very little intercellular space.	There is no intercellular space.

Q20. With the help of diagram show the difference between striated muscle fibre, smooth muscle fibre and cardiac muscle fibre.

Ans.

Striated Muscle	*Smooth Muscle*	*Cardiac Muscle*
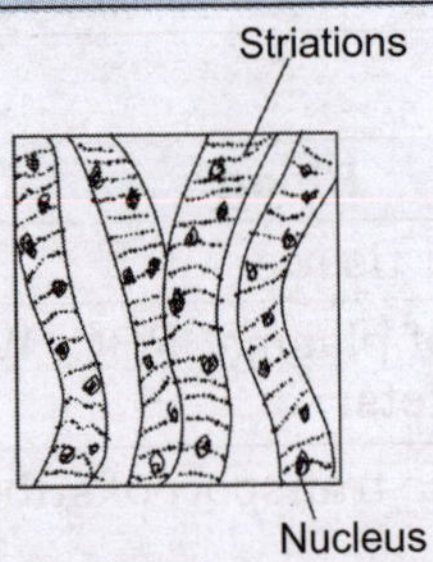	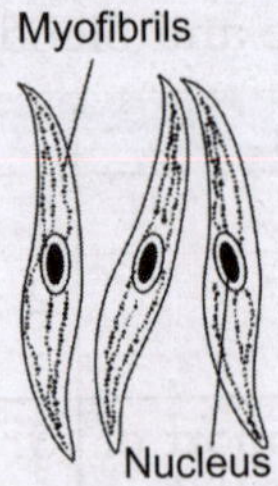	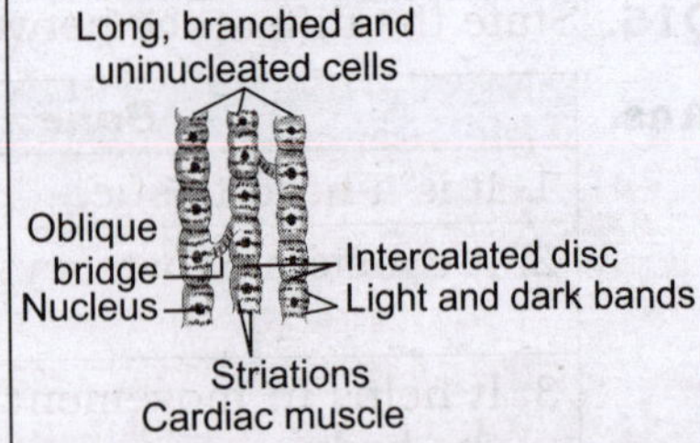

1. The cells are long, cylindrical, unbranched and multinucleated.	The cells are long with pointed ends and uni-nucleated.	The cells are cylindrical, branched and uninucleated.
2. The cells show alternate light and dark bands.	The cells do not have such light and dark bands.	The cells show alternate dark and light bands.
3. The muscles are voluntary	The muscles are involuntary.	The muscles are involuntary.

Q21. Name different types of meristematic tissue and draw diagram to show their location.

Ans. The 3 different types of meristematic tissue are:

(*a*) Apical meristem—Function: growth in length.

(*b*) Lateral meristem—Function: growth in thickness.

(*c*) Intercalary meristem—Function: growth in internodes.

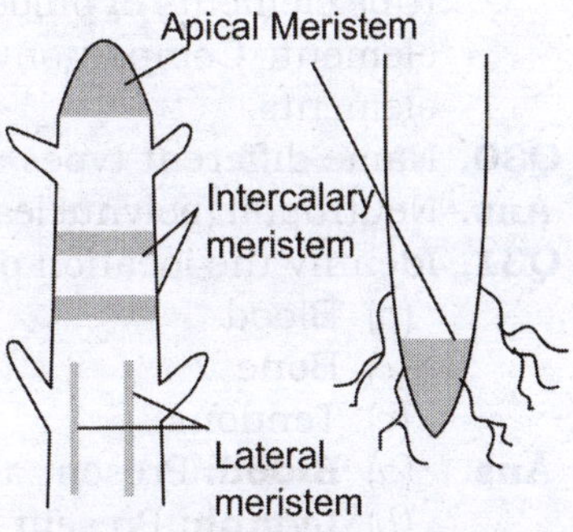

Location of meristematic tissue

Q22. Explain the structure, function and location of nervous tissue.

Ans. **Structure:** Nervous tissue consists of cells called nerve cells joined end to end (neurons). A neuron (nerve cell) consists of a cell body with nucleus and cytoplasm. From these cell body a long thin hair-like parts arise called axon and many short branched parts called dendrites.

Location: Nervous tissue are present in brain, spinal cord and nerves.

Function: Nervous tissue receives the stimuli and transmit the stimulus rapidly from one place to another within the body.

The nerve impulse allows us to move our muscles and respond to any stimuli.

Q23. Give the flow chart of plant tissues.

Ans.

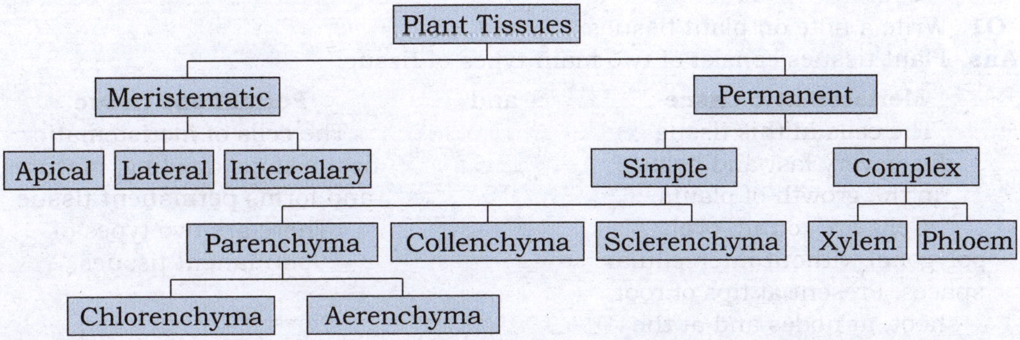

Q24. Name the tissue which allows easy bending in various parts of a plant.

Ans. Collenchyma is a kind of Simple permanent tissues Provides flexibility to parts of plant which bends thereby allowing easy bending in various parts of a plant.

Q25. Which structure protects the plant body against the invasion of parasites?

Ans. The upper layer of plant body, the dermal tissue and a hard cuticle covering protect the plant body from invasion of parasites and other harmful agents.

Q26. Which type of permanent tissue help the aquatic plants to float?

Ans. Aerenchyma is the type of parenchyma tissue that contains air cavities, makes the plant body light, which help the aquatic plants to float.

Q27. Epidermis in desert plants has a thin waxy coating of a chemical substance. Name the chemical.

Ans. Cutin which is a waxy polymer. Its waterproof, controls and limits the water loss in desert plants.

Q28. Name the part of phloem with perforated walls.

Ans. Sieve tubes of Phloem tissues are responsible for conduction of nutrients. Sieve tubes have perforated walls but lack a nucleus. Companion cells, phloem parenchyma and phloem fibers are other parts of phloem.

Q29. What are companion cells and are what are they associated with?

Ans. Companion cells are the specialized parenchyma cells associated with the sieve tube elements of phloem. They help in the development and function of a sieve-tube element. Companion cells move sugars and amino acids in and out of the sieve elements.

Q30. Name different types of white blood corpuscles.

Ans. Neutrophil (polynuclear leucocyte), Eosinophil, Basophil, Lymphocyte and Monocyte.

Q31. Identify the location of the following connective tissues.

(*a*) Blood (*b*) Lymph
(*c*) Bone (*d*) Cartilage
(*e*) Tendons.

Ans. (*a*) **Blood:** Present all over the body in blood vessels.
(*b*) **Lymph:** Present in lymph vessels.
(*c*) **Bone:** Present in all over body forming in endo-skeleton.
(*d*) **Cartilage:** Trachea, larynx, ear, tip of nose.
(*e*) **Tendons:** Connect muscles to bones.

Q32. How are muscles tissues related to nerve cells?

Ans. Muscles do not move on their own. They move only when they receive a nerve impulse. Motor neuron a type of nerve cell are connected to muscles which carry stimulus for muscle movement.

IV. Long Answer Type Questions

Q1. Write a note on plant tissues.

Ans. Plant tissues consist of two main types of tissue:

Meristematic tissue and **Permanent tissue**

Meristematic tissue
The cells in this tissue divide very fast and helps in the growth of plants. Cells are round, oval, polygonal without intercellular spaces. Present at tips of root, shoot, at nodes and at the sides of the stem.

Permanent tissue
The cells of meristematic tissue stops dividing, matures and forms permanent tissue. There are two types of permanent tissues.

Simple tissue
All cells are same in structure and perform same function. Types of simple tissue are parenchyma, collenchyma and sclerenchyma.

Complex tissue
It consists of group of different types of cells to perform same function. Types of complex tissue are xylem and phloem.

Parenchyma: Present in soft parts of the plant.
Collenchyma: Provides mechanical support to plant present in stalks.

Sclerenchyma: They provide strength and flexibility to the plants.
Xylem: Conduct water and minerals in plants from root to shoot. Consists of tracheids, vessels, xylem parenchyma and xylem fibres.
Phloem: Conduct food to all parts of plant. Consists of sieve tubes, companion cells, phloem parenchyma and phloem fibres.

Q2. Show the types of animal tissues using flow chart.

Ans.

Animal tissues

- Epithelial
  - → Squamous
  - → Cuboidal
  - → Columnar
  - → Ciliated
  - → Glandular
- Muscular
  - **Striated** — voluntary muscles
  - **Smooth** — involuntary muscles
  - **Cardiac** — heart muscles
- Connective
  - Fluid
    - → Blood
    - → Lymph
  - Skeletal
    - → Bone
    - → Cartilage
  - Proper
    - → Areolar
    - → Adipose
    - → Ligament
    - → Tendon
- Nervous (nerve cells)

Q3. What is connective tissue? Explain its types.

Ans. The connective tissue consists of different types of cells which perform same function.

The different types of connective tissue are:

- Proper connective tissue → Areolar, Adipose, Tendon and Ligament
- Fluid tissue → Blood and Lymph
- Skeletal tissue → Bone, Cartilage

Areolar connective tissue: It is found between the skin and muscles, around blood vessels and nerves and in the bone marrow.
Areolar tissue fills the space inside the organs. It supports internal organs and helps in repair of tissues.
Adipose tissue: Adipose tissue stores fat, found below the skin and between internal organs. The cells of this tissue are filled with fat globules. It acts as insulator due to fat storage.
Blood: It has a fluid called plasma, in plasma are present red blood cells, white blood cells and platelets. Blood flows all over the body and helps in the transport of gases, digested food, hormones and waste material to and from different parts of the body.
Lymph: Lymph carries digested fat and lot of white blood cells in the plasma.
Bone: It forms the framework that supports the body. It supports the different parts of our body. It is strong and non-flexible tissue.

Cartilage: It is present in nose, ear, trachea and larynx. It smoothens bone surfaces at joints.

Tendon: It connects bone and muscles. These tissues are fibrous, flexible and has lot of strength.

Ligament: It connects bone to bone. It is elastic and has lot of strength.

Q4. Describe 'epidermis' in plants.

Ans. Epidermis forms the entire outermost layer of the plant. It is made up of single cell layer. It protects all the internal parts of the plant.

On aerial parts, epidermis secretes waxy, water-resistant layer on their outer surface. This helps in protection against loss of water, mechanical injury and invasion of parasitic fungi.

In leaves, epidermis consists of small pores called stomata. These pores helps in the transpiration and exchange of gases, like oxygen and carbon dioxide for plants during photosynthesis and respiration.

In roots, epidermis have long hair-like parts that provide greater surface for water absorption.

In desert plants, epidermis has a thick waxy coating of cutin which acts as a water proofing agent.

Q5. Explain the "complex tissue" of plants.

Ans. Complex tissues are made up of more than one type of cells. All these cells co-ordinate to perform common function. These are—xylem and phloem.

Both are conducting tissues and form a vascular bundle.

Xylem consists of—tracheids, vessels, xylem parenchyma and xylem fibres. Most of these cells are dead. Tracheids and vessels helps in water transportation, parenchyma stores food and helps in the sideways conduction of water and fibres are mainly supportive in function.

Phloem is made up of four types of elements—sieve tubes, companion cells, phloem fibres and phloem parenchyma. It helps in the transportation of food in both the directions, i.e. from leaves to roots and to other parts of the plant.

V. Activity-based Questions

1.
- Take two glass jars and fill them with water.
- Now, take two onion bulbs and place one on each jar, as shown in the figure given below.
- Observe the growth of roots in both the bulbs for a few days.
- Measure the length of roots on day 1, 2 and 3.
- On day 4, cut the root tips of the onion bulb in jar 2 by about 1cm. After this, observe the growth of roots in both the jars and measure their lengths each day for five more days and record the observations in tables, like the table below:

Length	*Day 1*	*Day 2*	*Day 3*	*Day 4*	*Day 5*	*Day 6*	*Day 7*
Jar 1	3 cm	3.5 cm	4 cm	4.5 cm	5 cm	5.2 cm	5.4 cm
Jar 2	3 cm	3.5 cm	4 cm	4.5 cm	3.5 cm	3.5 cm	3.5 cm

From the above observations, answer the following questions:

(*a*) Which of the two onions has longer roots? Why?

(*b*) Do the roots continue growing even after we have removed their tips?

(*c*) Why would tips stop growing in jar 2 after we cut them?

Ans. (*a*) The onion in jar 1 has longer roots, as the growth of roots continues in it due to intact root tips.

(*b*) The roots did not continue to grow in jar 2 after cutting down their tips.

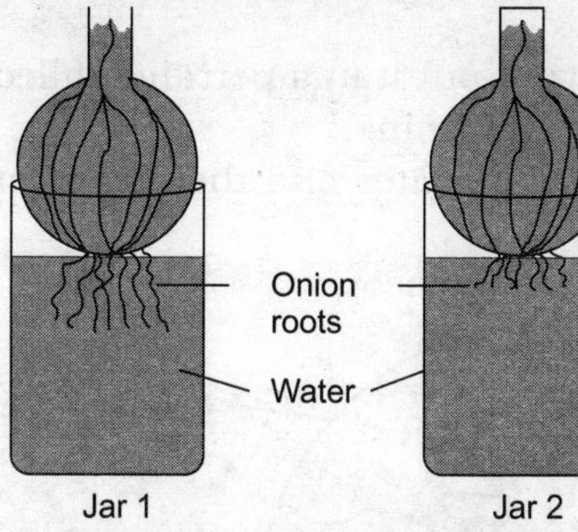

Growth of roots in onion bulb

(*c*) The tips of root stopped growing in jar 2 because the tips of these roots were cut down and the tissues which helps in the growth of roots *i.e.*, meristematic tissues were removed from it.

2. • Take a plant stem and with the help of a teacher cut it into very thin slices or sections.

• Now, stain the slices with safranin. Place one neatly cut section on a slide, and put a drop of glycerine.

• Cover with a cover-slip and observe under a microscope. Observe the various types of cells and their arrangement.

• Answer the following on the basis of your observations:

(*a*) Are all cells similar in structure?

(*b*) How many types of cells can be seen?

(*c*) Can we think of reasons why there would be so many types of cells?

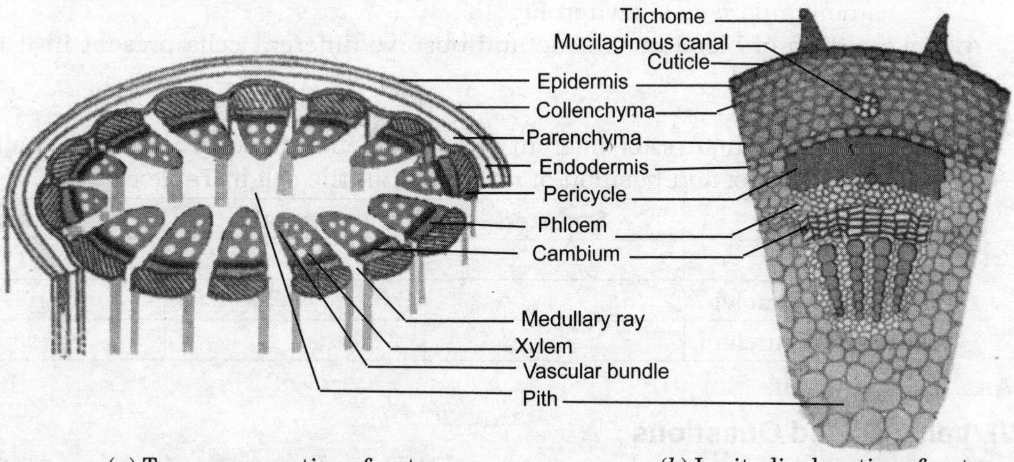

(*a*) Transverse section of a stem (*b*) Logitudinal section of a stem

Ans. (*a*) No, all cells are not similar in structure, variety of cells with different shape and size are noticed.

(*b*) Ten different types of cells in the slide are seen.

(*c*) Yes, there are variety of cells so that each group of cell does a specific role in the overall growth of plant.

3. • Take a freshly plucked leaf of Rheo.

• Stretch and break it by applying pressure.

- While breaking it, keep it stretched gently so that some peel or skin projects out from the cut.
- Remove this peel and put it in a petridish filled with water.
- Add a few drops of safranin.
- Wait for a couple of minutes and then transfer it onto a slide. Gently place a cover slip over it.
- Observe it under a microscope.

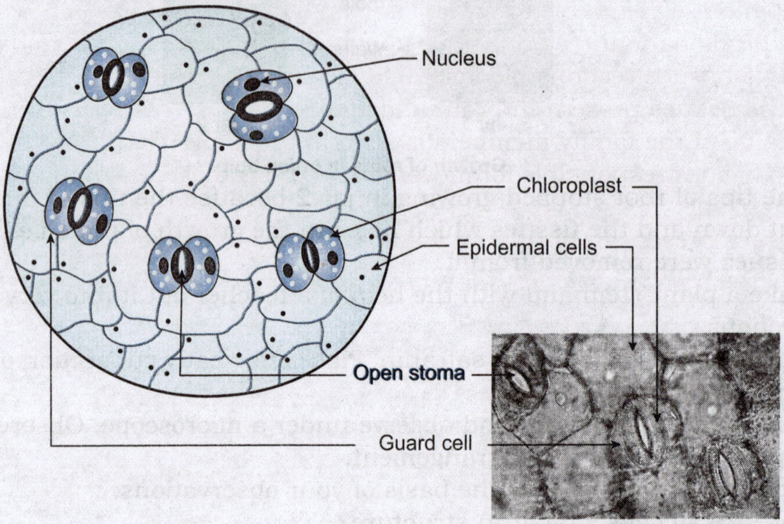

Ans. (*a*) The slide shows epidermal cells with stomatal pores as shown in Fig. (*a*).
(*b*) On focusing stomata pores under microscope. We can see guard cells and stomata pore as shown in Fig. (*b*).

4. Take a drop of blood on a slide and observe different cells present in it under a microscope.

Ans. Do it yourself.

5. Compare the structures of different types of mucular tissues. Note down their shape, number of nuclei and position of nuclei within the cell in Table 6.1.

Features	***Striated***	***Smooth***	***Cardiac***
Shape			
Number of nuclei			
Position of nuclei			

Ans. Do it yourself.

VI. Value-Based Questions

Q1. A group of students completed the project of finding the botanical names of all the trees present in the school campus. They prepared metal plates with names carved on it, to fix it on the plant trunks. Shreya was concerned that if the metal plate is fixed into tree many cells of the tree may get damaged. But the group members explained her that the outer layer of trunk does not have living cells and there won't be any damage to the tree.

(*a*) What type of cells are present on the outer layer of the bark/tree trunk?
(*b*) How does the cork act as a protective tissue?

(c) What value of the group is seen in the above cast?

Ans. (a) On the outer layer of the tree trunk/bark all thick layer of dead cells is present which acts as a protective tissue.

(b) In cork, all cells are dead without intercellular spaces, the walls of the cells have deposition of suberin.

(c) The students in a group show team effort, peer learning and co-operative behaviour.

Q2. A paralytic patient was unable to walk. The family member of the patient took the utmost care of the patient.

(a) Name two tissues responsible for the movement of a body.

(b) Name the tissues present in brain and spine.

(c) What value of the family members is seen in the above case?

Ans. (a) The two tissues responsible for movement of the body are muscular tissue and nervous tissue.

(b) The tissues present in brain and spine are nervous tissues.

(c) The family members showed the value of being caring, responsible, dutiful and kind.

VII. Practical Based Questions (Solved)

Q1. How will you identify cardiac muscles cells under a microscope?

Ans. Cardiac muscle cells are short, branched and striated. These are usually uninucleated.

Q2. Which substance is responsible for thickening of sclerenchyma walls?

Ans. Lignin. It gives mechanical strength to the cell wall of sclerenchymatous cells. Suberin is present in the bark of a tree and makes the cells impervious to water and gases. Pectin is a polysaccharide. Cutin is a waxy polymer.

Q3. If you are given a slide of parenchymatous tissue. What are the main distinguishing features that you will observe?

Ans. (i) All cells are same in size and length.

(ii) Corners of the cells show intercellular spaces.

(iii) Each cell shows prominent nucleus and a large central vacuole.

(iv) Each cell has thin cell walls.

(v) Intercellular spaces are present in between the cells.

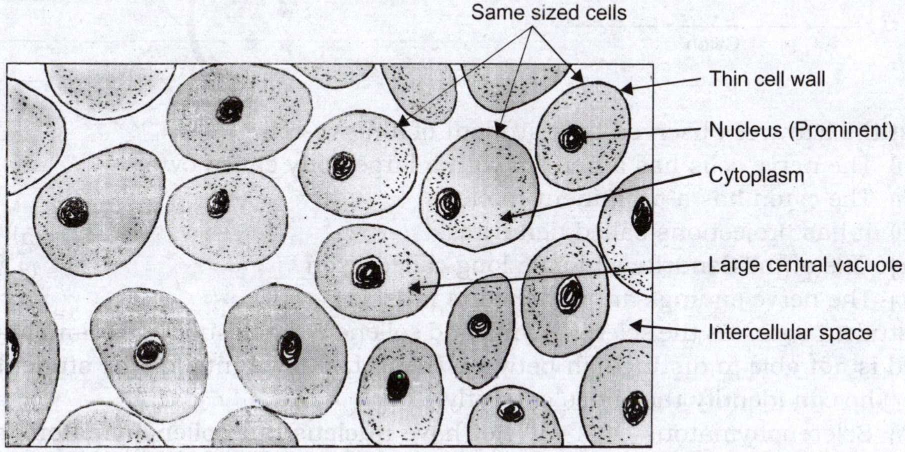

Parenchyma tissue (T.S.)

Q4. If you have to identify the animal tissue; striated muscles what distinguishing features will you observe under the microscope in the slide.

Ans. (*i*) These muscles show long cylindrical fibres.

(*ii*) The cells are multinucleated.

(*iii*) The muscles show alternate dark and light bands.

(*iv*) The cells are surrounded and held by connective tissue.

(*v*) The cells are surrounded by a membrane called as sarcolemma.

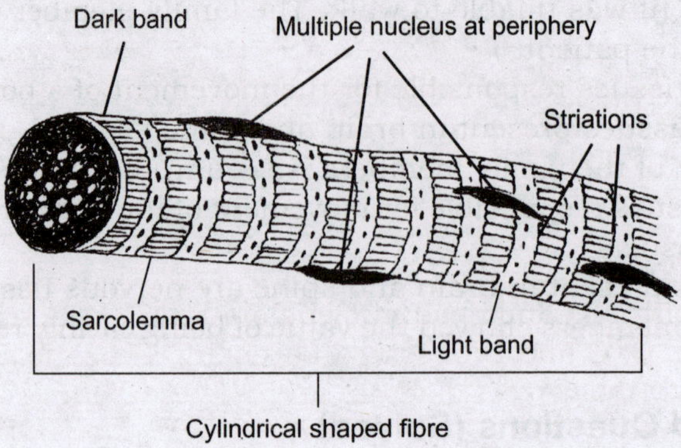

Q5. Draw the nerve cell as you observe under the microscope and label its four parts.

Ans.

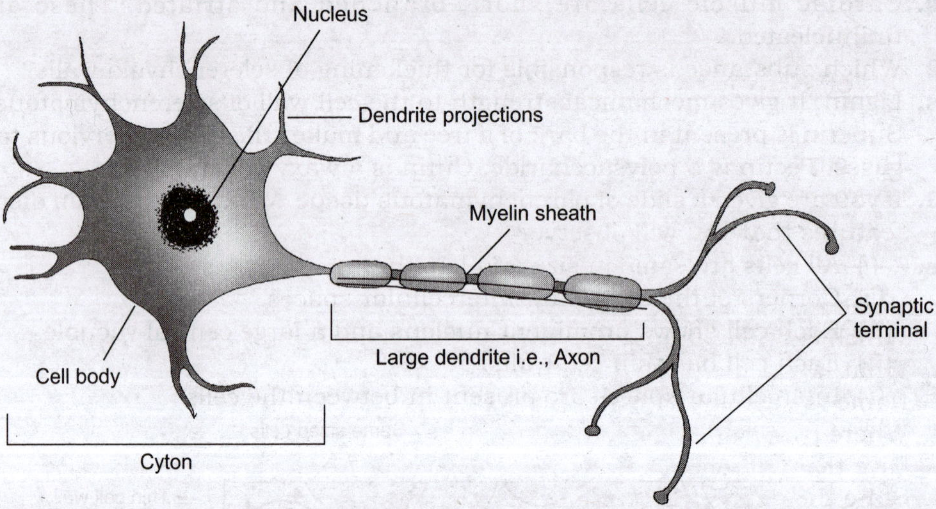

Q6. List the features observed by a student of a nerve cell.

Ans. (*i*) The nerve cells has a neuron with a large body called cyton.

(*ii*) The cyton has a prominent nucleus.

(*iii*) It has projections called dendrites.

(*iv*) One of the dendrite which is long called axon.

(*v*) The nerve endings are attached to muscles.

Q7. A student observes the sclerenchyma and collenchyma tissue slides simulataneously and is not able to distinguish between them. List few hints for the student so that he/she can identify the slides correctly.

Ans. (*a*) Sclerenchymatous cells will not have nucleus but collenchymatous cells will show prominent nucleus in it.

(*b*) Both the cells have thick cell wall but collenchymatous cells are living and the other ones have dead cells.

Q8. State the characteristics of striated muscle fibre.

Ans. These muscle fibres are unbranched with striations. They show light and dark bands. The cells are multinucleated. The cells are surrounded by a membrane called as sarcolemma.

Q9. From the given diagrams, how can you identify the diagram of Sclerenchyma tissue?

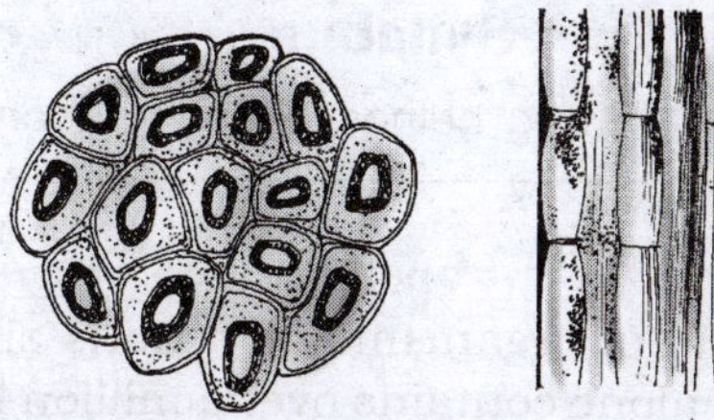

Ans. Thick cell wall with pits and dead nucleus are seen in sclerenchyma.

Q10. Four students A, B, C and D observed Parenchyma tissue and draw the following diagrams. Identify the correct diagram and state reason.

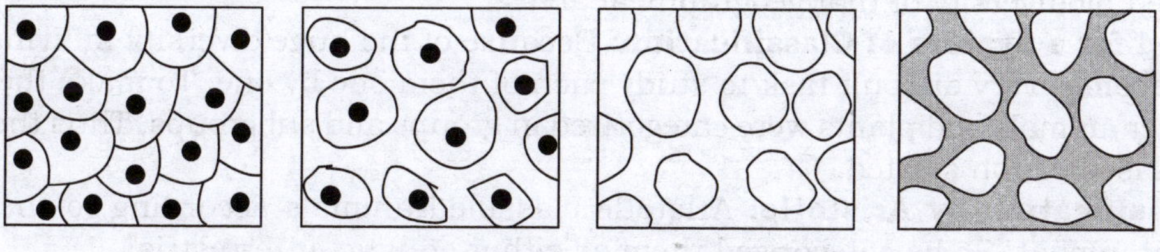

Ans. The correct diagram is drawn by B. The cells of parenchyma should show the intercellular space and nucleus in it.

TEST YOUR SKILLS

Q1. Name the tissue responsible for the movement of the body.
Q2. Which tissue makes up the husk of coconut?
Q3. What is aerenchyma?
Q4. Name the constituents of phloem.
Q5. Where is apical tissue found?
Q6. Give the difference between bone and cartilage.
Q7. State the difference between xylem and phloem.
Q8. What is the function of ligament and tendon?
Q9. Name three types of muscle tissues and give function of each.
Q10. Explain the structure, function and location of nervous tissue. Draw diagram.
Q11. Draw a flow chart of animal tissue.

❑❑❑

7 Diversity in Living Organisms

Syllabus

Diversity, Classification of living beings, Plant kingdom, Animal kingdom.

Facts that Matter

- **Diversity:** This earth is full of organisms of various shapes and sizes. The largest Phylum of animal kingdom alone contains over a million species. There are varieties of plants, right from small grasses to tall Eucalyptus trees. This variety in living beings is called diversity.
- **Biodiversity:** The variety of animals and plants living in a given geographical area is called biodiversity of that geographical area.
- **Need for a System of Classification:** Because of the huge diversity in living beings it becomes very difficult task to study each of them one by one. To make their study easier animals and plants were categorized in groups and subgroups. Thus the system of classification started.
- **Classification by Aristotle:** Aristotle classified animals according to their living environment. So he categorized them as either aquatic or terrestrial.
  – **Drawbacks of Aristotle's Classification:** Both in sea as well as on land we can find animals and plants. Moreover, there are very small animals, like sea-horse, along with large animals, like whale. So, this was not a good basis of classification.
- **Basis of Classification**

(a) Presence or Absence of Nucleus in Cells

Prokaryotes: Those organisms which have cells without well defined nucleus are called prokaryotes.

Eukaryotes: Those organisms which have cells with well defined nucleus are called eukaryotes. Presence of nucleus and membrane-bound organelles give better efficiency to cells.

(b) Number of Cells in an Organism

Unicellular: Those organisms having single cell are termed as unicellular organisms. In them the single cell is responsible for carrying out all necessary functions to maintain life.

Multicellular: Those organisms having more than one cell are called multicellular organisms. Because of more number of cells there can be some division of labour to gain more efficiency.

(c) Mode of Nutrition

Autotrophs: Organisms producing their own food are called autotrophs. All green plants are autotrophs. They have a pigment (chlorophyll) in green parts which facilitates photosynthesis.

Heterotrophs: Organisms dependent on either plants or animals are called heterotrophs. They don't have chlorophyll. All animals, fungi and certain bacteria and protozoa belong to this group.

(d) Level of Organisation in Body

In multicellular organisms which are small, like hydra particular group of cells are assigned a particular function. But in larger organisms, tissues group to form an organ, which in turn make organ system. For example, in human beings there are separate systems for performing specific tasks.

Even in larger plants there is separate root system for conduction of water and minerals, leaf for photosynthesis and flowers for reproduction.

Based on these characters organisms can be further classified into various sub-groups.

- **Evolutionary Relationship or Phylogenetic Relationship**
  Charles Darwin wrote a book 'The Origin of Species' in 1859 and gave his theories of evolution. As per his theories all organisms have evolved from unicellular organisms. Primitive body designs came early in evolutionary history leading to more complex designs. This gave rise to such a huge diversity in life forms. Because of common ancestors all organisms are related. The closer evolutionary relation between two organisms is also one of the basis of classification of organisms.
- **The Hierarchy of Classification—Groups**
  Biologists, such as Ernst Haeckel (1894), Robert Whittaker (1959) and Carl Woese (1977) have tried to classify all living organisms into broad categories, called kingdoms.
- **Whittaker's Five Kingdom Classification**
  Monera, Protista, Fungi, Plantae, Animalia.
- **Further Levels of Classification Beyond Kingdom**
  – Phylum (for animals)/Division (for plants)
  – Class, Order, Family, Genus, Species
- Thus, by separating organisms on the basis of a hierarchy of characteristics into smaller and smaller groups, we arrive at the basic unit of classification, which is a 'species'. Broadly, a species includes all organisms that are similar enough to breed and perpetuate.
- **Monera**
  – These organisms do not have a defined nucleus or organelles, and are unicellular.
  – Cell wall is present in some organisms of this group.
  – Nutrition: Autotrophic or heterotrophic
  – Examples: Bacteria and blue green algae.
- **Protista**
  – Unicellular eukaryotic organisms.
  – Locomotion: By hair-like cilia or whip-like flagella for moving around in some members.
  – Nutrition: Autotrophic or heterotrophic.
  – Examples: Algae, protozoans (*Plasmodium*, *Entamoeba*)
- **Fungi**
  – Heterotrophic eukaryotic organisms.
  – Nutrition: Saprophytic they use decaying organic materials as food.
- Lichens: Some fungi live in a symbiotic relationship with cynobacteria. They are called lichens. The algal part provides food and the fungal part provides minerals and substratum.
- **Plantae**
  – Multicellular eukaryotes with cell walls.
  – Nutrition: Autotrophs use chlorophyll for photosynthesis.
- **Animalia**
  – Multicellular eukaryotes without cell walls.
  – Nutrition Heterotrophs.

- **Classification of Kingdom Plantae**

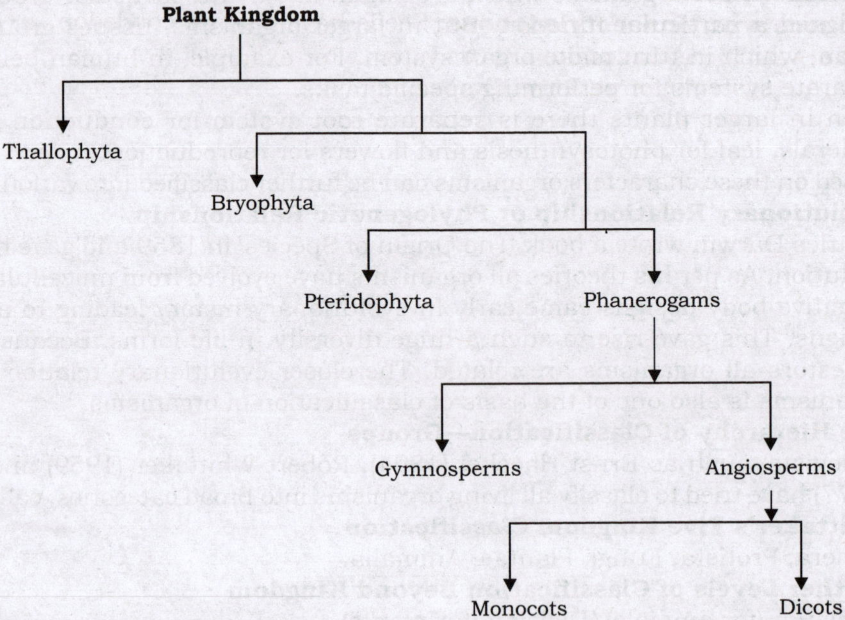

- **Thallophyta or Algae:** Plants that do not have well-differentiated body design fall in this group. The plants in this group are commonly called algae. These plants are predominantly aquatic. Examples are *Spirogyra, Ulothrix, Cladophora* and *Chara*.
- **Bryophyta:** These are called the amphibians of the plant kingdom. The plant body is commonly differentiated to form stem and leaf-like structures. However, there is no specialized tissue for the conduction of water and other substances from one part of the plant body to another. Examples are moss (*Funaria*) and *Marchantia*.
- **Pteridophyta**: The plant body is differentiated into roots, stem and leaves and has specialized tissue for the conduction of water and other substances from one part of the plant body to another. Some examples are *Marsilea*, ferns and horse-tails.

> **Important:** The thallophytes, the bryophytes and the pteridophytes have naked embryos that are called spores. The reproductive organs of plants in all these three groups are very inconspicuous, and they are therefore called 'cryptogamae', or 'those with hidden reproductive organs'.
> On the other hand, plants with well differentiated reproductive tissues that ultimately make seeds are called phanerogams. Seeds are the result of the reproductive process. They consist of the embryo along with stored food, which serves for the initial growth of the embryo during germination.

- **Gymnosperms:** The plants of this group bear naked seeds and are usually perennial, evergreen and woody. Examples are pines and deodar.
- **Angiosperms:** This word is made from two Greek words: *angio* means covered and *sperma*—means seed. The seeds develop inside an organ which is modified to become a fruit. These are also called flowering plants. Plant embryos in seeds have structures called cotyledons.
- **Cotyledons:** Cotyledons are called 'seed leaves' because in many instances they emerge and become green when the seed germinates.

The angiosperms are divided into two groups on the basis of the number of cotyledons present in the seed.

(*a*) **Monocots or Monocotyledonous:** Seeds have a single cotyledon.

(*b*) **Dicots or Dicotyledonous:** Seeds have two cotyledons.

- **Classification of Kingdom Animalia:** Kingdom Animalia is further classified into several following phylum. Each phylum has it own classess, sub-classess orders, families, etc.

(*a*) **Porifera**

– These are non-motile animals attached to some solid support which comprises calcium carbonate, silica.

– There are holes or 'pores', all over the body. These lead to a canal system that helps in circulating water throughout the body to bring in food and oxygen.

– Animals are covered with a hard outside layer or skeleton which comprises of spicules or collagen of both.

– They have very minimal differentiation and division into tissues.

– Examples: Sponges

(*b*) **Coelenterata**

– Aquatic animals.

– There is a cavity in the body hence the name Coelenterate (coelom means cavity).

– Body is made of two layers of cells.

– Examples: *Hydra*, Jellyfish

(*c*) **Platyhelminthes**

– The body is bilaterally symmetrical, meaning that the left and the right halves of the body have the same design.

– There are three layers of cells from which differentiated tissues can be made, that is why such animals are called triploblastic.

– There is no true internal body cavity or coelom, in which well developed organs can be accommodated.

– The body is flattened dorsiventrally, meaning from top to bottom, that is why these animals are called flatworms.

– They are either free-living or parasitic.

– Examples: *Planaria*, Liverfluke

(*d*) **Nematoda**

– Body is bilaterally symmetrical and triploblastic.

– Body is cylindrical rather than flattened.

– False body cavity or a pseudocoelom, is present.

– These are very familiar as parasitic worms causing diseases, such as the worms causing elephantiasis (filarial worms) or the worms in the intestines (roundworm or pinworms).

– Examples: *Ascaris, Wuchereria*

(*e*) **Annelida**

– These are bilaterally symmetrical and triploblastic.

– True body cavity present.

– Body is divided into many ring like segments, hence the name annelida.

– Examples: Earthworms, Leech

(*f*) **Arthropoda**

– The largest group of animals.

– These are bilaterally symmetrical and segmented.

– There is an open circulatory system, and so the blood does not flow in well defined blood vessels.

– They have jointed legs (the word 'arthropod' means 'jointed legs').
– Examples: Ants, Cockroach, Grasshopper, Scorpion

(*g*) **Mollusca**
– These are bilaterally symmetrical.
– Reduced coelomic cavity.
– The soft body is covered with a hard shell made of calcium carbonate.
– Examples: Snails, Mussels.

(*h*) **Echinodermata**
– In Greek, *echinos* means hedgehog, and *derma* means skin. Thus, these are spiny skinned organisms.
– Exclusively free-living marine animals.
– Triploblastic animals with coelomic cavity.
– They have a peculiar water-driven tube system that they use for moving around.
– Skeleton made of calcium carbonate.
– Examples: Starfish and Sea urchins

(*i*) **Protochordata**
– These animals are bilaterally symmetrical, triploblastic and have a coelom.
– In addition, they show a new feature of body design, namely a notochord, at least at some stages during their lives.

> The notochord is a long rod-like support structure (chord=string) that runs along the back of the animal separating the nervous tissue from the gut. It provides a place for muscles to attach for ease of movement.

Examples: *Balanoglossus*, *Herdmania* and *Amphioxus*.

(*j*) **Vertebrata**

These animals have a true vertebral column and internal skeleton, allowing a completely different distribution of muscle attachment points to be used for movement. Vertebrates are bilaterally symmetrical, triploblastic, coelomic and segmented, with complex differentiation of body tissues and organs. All chordates possess the following features:

(*i*) Notochord (*ii*) Dorsal nerve cord (*iii*) Triploblastic
(*iv*) Paired gill pouches (*v*) Coelomate

Vertebrates are grouped into five classes:

(*i*) **Pisces**
– Body is streamlined and has fins and tail for swimming.
– Skin is covered with scales.
– Skeleton can be made of bone or cartilage.
– Intake of oxygen is by gills.
– Cold-blooded animals.
– Two-chambered heart is present.
– Examples: Fishes like Rohu, Tuna, Shark

(*ii*) **Amphibia**
– They are adapted to live both on land and water.
– Respiration is through either gills or lungs.
– Three-chambered heart is present.
– Examples: Frogs, Toads, Salamander

(*iii*) **Reptilia**

- These are crawling animals.
- Skin is rough and modified to withstand extreme temperatures.
- Heart is three chambered in most, while four chambered in crocodiles.
- Cold-blooded animals.
- Examples: Lizards, Turtles, Snakes

(*iv*) **Aves**

- Body is covered with feathers and forelimbs are modified for flying.
- Breathing is through lungs.
- Warm blooded animals.
- Four-chambered heart is present.
- Examples: Sparrow, Eagle, Crow, Parrot

(*v*) **Mammalia**

- Mammary glands are present which produce milk to nurture young ones.
- Skin is covered with hairs and has sweat glands and sebaceous (oil) glands.
- Warm-blooded animals with four-chambered heart.
- Most animals are viviparous (giving birth to live young ones), some are oviparous (producing eggs).
- Examples: Man, Horse, Kangaroo, Lion

- **Conventions for writing the scientific names:**
  1. The name of the genus begins with a capital letter.
  2. The name of the species begins with a small letter.
  3. When printed, the scientific name is given in italics.
  4. When written by hand, the genus name and the species name have to be underlined separately.

NCERT IN-TEXT QUESTIONS SOLVED

Q1. Why do we classify organisms?

Ans. We classify organisms for easier and convenient study of variety of lifeforms.

Q2. Give three examples of the range of variations that you see in life-forms around you.

Ans. (*a*) Small cat and big cow

(*b*) Grass and banyan tree

(*c*) Black crow and green parrot

Q3. Which do you think is a more basic characteristic for classifying organisms?

(*a*) the place where they live.

(*b*) the kind of cells they are made of. Why?

Ans. Classification based on the kind of cells they are made of is more basic as there can be wide variations in organisms living in a given place, hence it can't be basic characteristic of classifying organisms.

Q4. What is the primary characteristic on which the main broad division of organisms is made?

Ans. Nature of cell is the primary characteristic on which the main broad division of organisms is decided. Based on this criterion life forms can be classified into prokaryotes or eukaryotes.

Q5. On what bases are plants and animals put into different categories?

Ans. Mode of nutrition and presence or absence of cell walls.

Q6. Which organisms are called primitive and how are they different from the so-called advanced organisms?

Ans. Organisms with simple cellular structure and no division of labour are called primitive. Advanced organisms, like mammals have millions of cells and there are different organs and organ system for different biological functions.

Q7. Will advanced organisms be the same as complex organisms? Why?

Ans. Yes, advanced organisms means greater degree of evolution which leads to more complexity.

Q8. What is the criterion for classification of organisms as belonging to kingdom Monera or Protista?

Ans. It is the presence or absence of a well defined nucleus. Monera has no nuclear membrane, while Protista shows well defined nucleus.

Q9. In which kingdom will you place an organism which is single-celled, eukaryotic and photosynthetic?

Ans. Protista.

Q10. In the hierarchy of classification, which grouping will have the smallest number of organisms with a maximum of characteristics in common and which will have the largest number of organisms?

Ans. In the hierarchy of classification, species will have the smallest number of organisms with a maximum of characteristics in common and kingdom will have the largest number of organisms.

Q11. Which division among plants has the simplest organisms?

Ans. Thallophyta or algae.

Q12. How are pteridophytes different from the phanerogams?

Ans. Pteridophytes have naked embryo and inconspicuous reproductive organ whereas phanerogams have well-differentiated reproductive organs and covered embryo.

Q13. How do gymnosperms and angiosperms differ from each other?

Ans. Seeds are naked in gymnosperms and are covered in angiosperms.

Q14. How do porifera animals differ from coelenterate animals?

Ans.
- Animals from Porifera show cellular level of organisation, while those from Coelenterata show tissue level of organisation.
- In Porifera there is no division of labour, while in Coelenterata some division of labour is seen.
- Porifera do not have coelom, while coelenterata have coelom.

Q15. How do annelid animals differ from arthropods?

Ans.

Arthropoda	***Annelida***
Exoskeleton present.	No skeleton.
Body is segmented into head, thorax and abdomen.	Body is segmented into rings.
Sexes are usually separate.	Sexes may be united (Hermaphrodite) or separate.

Q16. What are the differences between amphibians and reptiles?

Ans.

Amphibia	*Reptilia*
1. Adapted to live in water and land, can breathe by skin in water.	Can live in water but need to come to surface to breathe in oxygen.
2. Skin is moist and soft.	Skin is hardened.
3. Respiration is either through gills or lungs.	Respiration is through lungs.
4. Can jump.	Move by crawling.
5. Development is indirect through tadpole stage.	Development is direct with no intermediate stage in life cycle

Q17. What are the differences between animals belonging to the Aves group and those in the mammalia group?

Ans.

Amphibia	*Reptilia*
1. Body is covered with feathers.	Body is covered with hair.
2. Beak is present, teeth absent.	Teeth present, beak absent.
3. Forelimbs modified for flying.	Forelimbs modified for various activities.
4. Hollow bones for flying.	No hollow bones.
5. Streamlined body.	Body is not streamlined, except in whales, dolphins.

NCERT TEXTUAL QUESTIONS SOLVED

Q1. What are the advantages of classifying organisms?

Ans. **Advantages of classification:**

- Better categorization of living beings based on common characters.
- Easier study for scientific research.
- Better understanding of human's relation and dependency on other organisms.
- Helps in cross breeding and genetic engineering for commercial purposes.

Q2. How would you choose between two characteristics to be used for developing a hierarchy in classification?

Ans. Gross character will form the basis of start of the hierarchy and fine character will form the basis of further steps of single hierarchy.

Example:

- Presence of vertebral column in human beings can be taken under vertebrata.
- Presence of four limbs makes them members of Tetrapoda.
- Presence of mammary glands keeps them under mammalia.

Q3. Explain the basis for grouping organisms into five kingdoms.

Ans. **Basis of Classification:**

(*a*) Number of cells: unicellular or multicellular.
(*b*) Complexity of cell structure : Prokaryote & Eukaryote.
(*c*) Presence or absence of cell wall
(*d*) Mode of nutrition
(*e*) Level of organization

Q4. What are the major divisions in the Plantae? What is the basis for these divisions?

Ans. Major Divisions of Kingdom Plantae:

Division	*Basis for classification*
Thallophyta or Algae	Thallus like body, plant body is not differentiated into roots, stems etc.
Bryophyta	Body is divided into leaf and stem, lack vascular tissue.
Pteridophyta	Body is divided into root, stem and leaf, lack seeds.
Gymnosperm	Seed bearing, naked seeds, lack flowers.
Angiosperm	Seed bearing covered seeds, produce flowers.

Q5. How are the criteria for deciding divisions in plants different from the criteria for deciding the subgroups among animals?

Ans. In plants basic structure of their body is a major criteria based on which Thallophytes are different from Bryophytes. Apart from this absence or presence of seeds is another important criteria. Gymnosperms and angiosperms are further segregated based on if seeds are covered or not. It is clear that it is the morphological character which makes the basis for classification of plants.

In animals classification is based on more minute structural variations. So in place of morphology, cytology forms the basis. Animals are classified based on layers of cells, presence or absence of coelom. Further higher the hierarchy animals are classified based on presence or absence of smaller features, like presence or absence of four legs.

Q6. Explain how animals in Vertebrata are classified into further subgroups.

Ans. Vertebrata is divided into two superclasses, viz. Pisces and Tetrapoda. Animals of Pisces have streamlined body with fins and tails to assist in swimming. Animals of Tetrapoda have four limbs for locomotion.

Tetrapoda is further classified into following classes:

(*a*) Amphibia: Are adapted to live in water and on land. Can breathe oxygen through skin when under water.

(*b*) Reptilia: These are crawling animals. Skin is hard to withstand extreme temperatures.

(*c*) Aves: Forelimbs are modified into wings to assist in flying. Beak is present. Body is covered with feathers.

(*d*) Mammalia: Mammary glands present to nurture young ones. Skin is covered with hair. Most of the animals are viviparous.

ADDITIONAL QUESTIONS SOLVED

I. Very Short Answer Type Questions

Q1. Who wrote the book "The Origin of Species"?

Ans. Charles Darwin in 1859.

Q2. Who proposed the classification of organisms into five kingdoms?

Ans. Robert Whittaker (1959).

Q3. Define species.

Ans. All organisms that are similar to breed and perpetuate.

Q4. Give example of the organism belonging to Monera and Protista Kingdom.

Ans. Monera—*Anabaena*, blue-green algae

Protista—*Euglena*, *Paramecium*, *Amoeba*

Q5. Name the appendages used for movement by organism belonging to Protista kingdom.
Ans. *Paramecium*–Cilia
Euglena – Flagella
Amoeba – Pseudopodia
Q6. What is lichen?
Ans. The symbiotic association of fungi and blue-green algae, is called **lichen**.
Q7. What is symbiotic relationship?
Ans. It is a relationship between two organisms in which both of them are benefitted, *e.g.*, fungi gets food from blue-green algae and in return blue-green gets shelter *[lichens]*.
Q8. What is saprophytic nutrition?
Ans. The organisms using dead and decaying organic matter as food are said to show saprophytic nutrition.
Q9. Give simple classification of plant kingdom.
Ans.

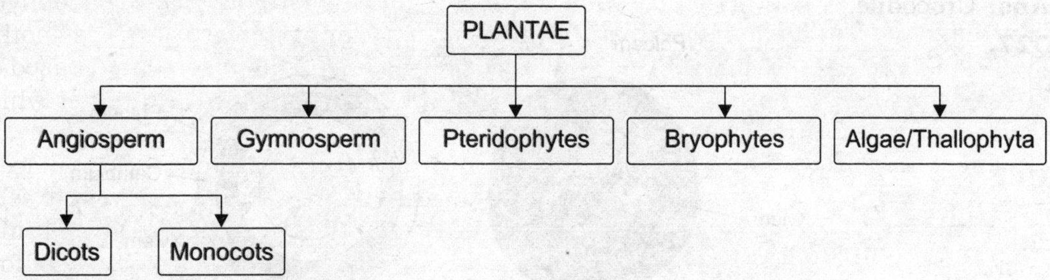

Q10. Name the plant amphibian.
Ans. Bryophyta *e.g. Funaria* (Moss).
Q11. What are cryptogamae?
Ans. The plants with inconspicuous reproductive organs are called cryptogamae, *e.g.*, fern.
Q12. Give examples of pteridophyte.
Ans. *Marsilea* and Fern.
Q13. Name the reproductive organ of plants.
Ans. Flower.
Q14. What are gymnosperms?
Ans. The group of plants that bear naked seeds *e.g.*, pines, deodar.
Q15. What are angiosperms?
Ans. The group of plants with covered seeds are called angiosperms. These are flowering plants.
Q16. What are cotyledons?
Ans. Plant embryos in seeds have structures called cotyledons. Cotyledens are also known as seed leaves.
Q17. Name the phylum of an animals with pores on it.
Ans. Porifera *e.g.*, sponge.
Q18. Name the phylum of Jellyfish.
Ans. Coelenterata or Cnidaria.
Q19. What is the meaning of triploblastic?
Ans. Animals which have three layers of cells from which differentiated tissues can be made.
Q20. What is bilateral symmetry?
Ans. When the left and right halves of the body have the same design it is called bilateral symmetry.

Q21. What is the meaning of "cold-blooded animal"?

Ans. Those animals who show the variation in their body temperature according to the surroundings are called cold-blooded animals. *E.g.*, fish, amphibians, reptiles.

Q22. Name two mammals that lay eggs.

Ans. Platypus and echidna.

Q23. Name three mammals that live in water.

Ans. Whale, Platypus and Dolphins.

Q24. Name a fish with skeleton made up of cartilage.

Ans. Shark.

Q25. Name two fish which have skeleton made up of both bone and cartilage.

Ans. Tuna and rohu.

Q26. Name the reptile with four-chambered heart.

Ans. Crocodile.

Q27.

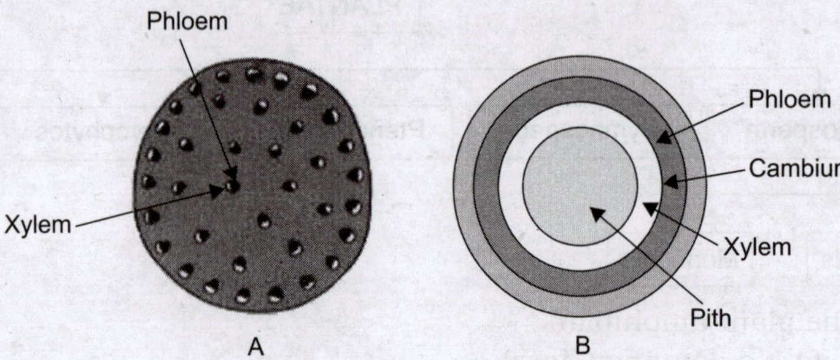

Identify the monocot and dicot vascular bundles given above.

Ans. A is monocot and B is dicot.

Q28. Name the phylum in which the animals have water vascular system.

Ans. Echinodermata eg star fish.

Q29. Name the largest group of animals. Write the salient features of this group.

Ans. The largest group of animals are arthropods. They have joint appendages.

Q30. To which group in the hierarchy of classification does the saprophytes belong. Why are they named so?

Ans. Saprophytes belong to kindom fungi. Example Mucor.

II. Short Answer Type Questions

Q1. Give the characteristics of Monera.

Ans. (*a*) Organisms are unicellular, do not have a defined nucleus.

(*b*) Organisms may have cell wall or may not have cell wall.

(*c*) Mode of nutrition is either autotrophic or heterotrophic.

Q2. Give the characteristics of Protista.

Ans. (*a*) Organsims are unicellular and eukaryotic.

(*b*) Use appendages for locomotion like cilia, flagella, etc.

(*c*) Nutrition is either autotrophic or heterotrophic.

(*d*) *E.g.*, algae, protozoa.

Q3. What are hermaphrodites? Give two examples.

Ans. When an organism has both the sexes, *i.e.,* it can produce both sperms and eggs are called hermaphrodites. Example: Sponges, earthworms.

Q4. Give the difference between thallophyta and bryophyta.

Ans.

Thallophyta	***Bryophyta***
Body is thallus like not differentiated into root, stem. *Example: Spirogyra.*	Plant body is differentiated into stem and leaf like structures. *Example:* Moss.

Q5. Give the difference between monocots and dicots.

Ans.

Monocots	***Dicots***
1. Seeds with one cotyledon.	Seeds with two cotyledons.
2. Leaves have parallel venation.	Leaves have reticulate venation.
3. Root system—fibrous.	Root system—tap root.

Q6. Give the difference between two types of symmetry that animals show.

Ans. **Symmetry—**Bilateral and Radial

Bilateral Symmetry	***Radial Symmetry***
Any organism that has same design on left and right halves of the body. *Example:* Earthworm, spider, cockroach.	Any organisms with a body design such that it can be divided into two equal halves from any radius. *Example:* Starfish, sea urchin.

Q7. Differentiate between vertebrates and invertebrates.

Ans.

Vertebrates	***Invertebrates***
1. Notochord is present.	Notochord is absent.
2. True internal skeleton present.	No true internal skeleton present.

Q8. Name the phylum of the following animals:

(*a*) Tapeworm (*b*) Starfish (*c*) Jellyfish (*d*) Octopus

Ans. (*a*) Tapeworm – Platyhelminthes (*b*) Starfish – Echinodermata

(*c*) Jellyfish – Coelenterata (*d*) Octopus – Mollusca

Q9. Identify the phylum for the following characteristics given below:

(*a*) Organisms with joint appendages.

(*b*) Organisms are generally flat worms.

(*c*) Body is segmented.

(*d*) Skin of organisms is full of spikes.

Ans. (*a*) Arthropoda (*b*) Platyhelminthes

(*c*) Annelida (*d*) Echinodermata

Q10. State the features of all chordates.

Ans. All chrodates possess the following features:

(*i*) Have a notochord (*ii*) Have a dorsal nerve chord

(*iii*) Are triploblastic (*iv*) Have paired gill pouches

Q11. Give general characteristics of Porifera.

Ans. (*a*) Animals with pores all over the body.

(*b*) Body is not well differentiated.

(*c*) Non-motile animals, remain attached to solid support.

(*d*) Body is covered with hard outer skeleton. Example, sponges.

Q12. How are pores or holes all over the body of Porifera important?

Ans. The pores or holes present all over the body of the organisms lead to a canal system that helps in circulating water throughout the body to bring in food and oxygen.

Q13. *Give general characteristics of 'Platyhelminthes'?*

Ans. (*a*) These are flat worms.

(*b*) Most of them are parasites.

(*c*) Animals are triploblastic

(*d*) No true internal body cavity.

E.g., Tapeworm, *Planaria,* Liver fluke.

Q14. Give specific characteristics of Coelenterata.

Ans. (*a*) Water living animals.

(*b*) Body is made of two layers of cells.

(*c*) Some of them live in colonies (corals), while others have solitary life-span (*Hydra*).

(*d*) Body cavity present.

Q15. Give the characteristics of Arthropoda with 2 examples.

Ans. (*a*) Arthropoda means 'jointed legs'.

(*b*) Animals are bilaterally symmetrical and segmented.

(*c*) It has an open circulatory system.

(*d*) This is the largest group of animals.

Example: Spider, scorpions, crabs, houseflies.

Q16. Give the characteristic features of Echinodermata.

Ans. (*a*) Spikes present on skin.

(*b*) Free living, marine animals.

(*c*) Triploblastic and have a coelomic cavity.

(*d*) Have a peculiar water-driven tube system used for moving around.

(*e*) Have hard calcium carbonate structure that is used as a skeleton.

Example, Starfish, sea urchin.

Q17. Give the characteristics of mammals.

Ans. (*a*) Mammals are warm-blooded animals.

(*b*) Four-chambered heart.

(*c*) Mammary glands for production of milk to nourish their young ones.

(*d*) Skin has hairs, sweat glands and oil glands.

(*e*) Most of them produce their young ones (viviparous).

Q18. What are the conventions followed for writing the scientific names?

Ans. The conventions followed while writing the scientific names are:

1. The name of the genus begins with a capital letter.
2. The name of the species begins with a small letter.
3. When printed, the scientific name is given in italics.
4. When written by hand, the genus name and the species name have to be underlined separately.

Q19. Differentiate between algae and fungi.

Ans.

Algae	*Fungi*
1. Contain chlorophyll (green in colour).	1. Do not contain chlorophyll (non-green)
2. Autotrophic nutrition.	2. Heterotrophic nutrition.
3. Food is stored in the form of starch.	3. Food is stored in the form of glycogen.

Q20. Name the phylum of the following organisms. whose exclusive characteristics is given below:

(*a*) Hollow bones (*b*) Jointed appendages

(*c*) Flat worm (*d*) Round worms, parasitic

(*e*) Soft body, muscular marine animal (*f*) Radially symmetrical, spiny skin.

Ans. (*a*) Phylum chordata, subphylum—vertebrata, class—Aves

(*b*) Phylum—Arthropoda
(*c*) Phylum—Platyhelminthes
(*d*) Phylum—Aschelminthes or Nematoda
(*e*) Phylum—Mollusca
(*f*) Phylum—Echinodermata

Q21. Give the characteristics of amphibians.

Ans. Amphibians are vertebrates that lives on land and in water.
(*a*) They are cold-blooded.
(*b*) Heart is three-chambered.
(*c*) Fertilization is external.
(*d*) Respiration through lungs on land and through moist skin when in water.
Example, Frog, Toads

Q22. Give the characteristics of Aves.

Ans. (*a*) Aves/birds can fly.
(*b*) Streamlined body.
(*c*) Hollow and light bones.
(*d*) Forelimbs are modified into wings.
(*e*) Warm-blooded animals, heart with four chambers.
(*f*) Egg laying animals.
(*g*) Beak is present and teeth are absent.

Q23. Why do most of the amphibians lay their eggs in water and reptiles lay their eggs on land?

Ans. Amphibians lay their eggs in water because the tadpoles or young ones that hatch out of egg has gills at initial stages, that allows them to breathe in water.
In case of reptiles the young ones that hatch out does not have gills and the hatching of eggs requires warmth that is given by the mother reptile.

Q24. Give the hierarchy of 5 kingdom classification of living world.

Ans.

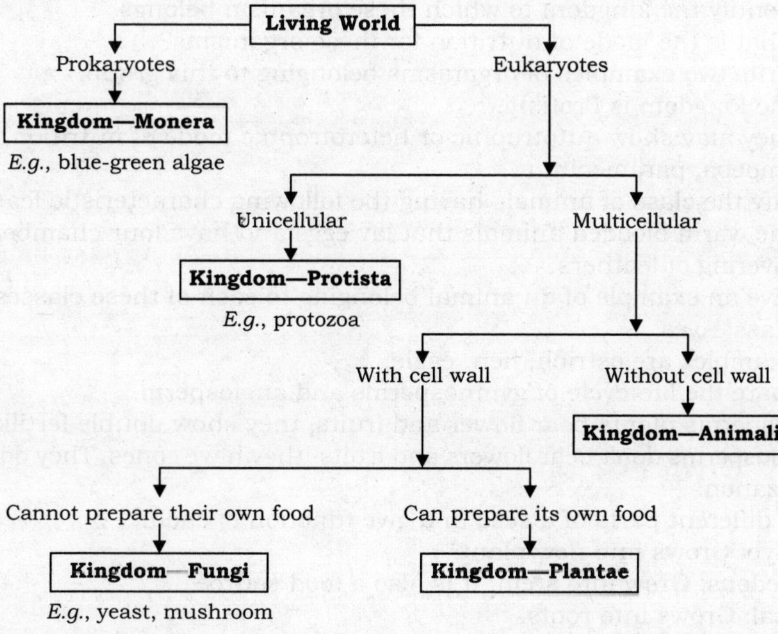

Q25. Give one example of each
(*a*) Asymmetry,bilateral and radial symmetry.

(b) Acoelomate,pseudocoelomate and haemocoelomate.

Ans. (a) In asymmetrical the body cannot be divided into two equal halves and in radial symmetry the body can be divided into two halves.

(b) Acoelomate: Body has no coelom eg. Sponges and flat worms,
Pseudocoelomate: The animals in this group have false cavity eg. nematodes.
Haemocoelomate: The body cavity is filled with blood eg. arthropods

Q26. What is the other name given to flowering plants? Classify them on the basis of number of cotyledons.

Ans. Angiosperms are flowering plants. They are classified as monocot and dicot. Monocot are the ones that bear seeds with single cotyledon and dicots are those which bear seeds with two cotyledons.

Q27. What is meant by symbiotic relationship? Give example.

Ans. Symbiotic relationship is a give and take relationship in which both the organisms associated are benefitted with each other. Eg. Lichen in which algae and fungi are associated.

Q28. Distinguish between

(a) Monera and Protista on the basis of nucleus.
(b) Fungi and plantae on the basis of mode of nutrition.
(c) Gymnosperm and angiosperm on the basis of seeds.

Ans. (a) Monera is prokaryotic, does not have well defined nucleus and Protista is eukaryotic with well-defined nucleus.

(b) Fungi are saprophytes, Plantae are autotrophs.

(c) Gymnosperms have naked seeds and the angiosperms have seeds enclosed in the fruit.

Q29. A group in classification includes many kind of unicellular eukaryotic organisms. Some of them use appendages, such as hair like cilia, flagella for moving around. Answer the following questions based on the information given above:

(a) Identify the kingdom to which these organism belongs.
(b) What is the mode of nutrition for these organisms?
(c) Write two examples of organisms belonging to this group.

Ans. (a) The kingdom is Protista.

(b) They may show autotrophic or heterotrophic mode of nutrition.

(c) Amoeba, paramecium.

Q30. Identify the class of animals having the following characteristic features.

(a) The warm blooded animals that lay eggs and have four chambered heart and a covering of feathers.
(b) Give an example of an animal belonging to each of these classes.

Ans. (a) Class: Aves.

(b) Examples are ostrich, hen, eagle.

Q31. Compare the life-cycle of gymnosperms and angiosperm.

Ans. Angiosperms plants bear flower and fruits, they show double fertilization.
Gymnosperms don't bear flowers and fruits- they have cones. They don't show double fertilization.

Q32. State different parts of a seed and give function of each?

Ans. Embryo: Grows into new plant.
Cotyledons: Grow into stem. It is also a food source.
Radical: Grows into roots.
Endosperm: Food storage.

Q33. Explain the fertilization process in angiosperms.

Ans. Double fertilization takes place in which a male egg fuses with a female egg to form zygote(2n) which then develops into embryo. The other male egg fuses with two cells (nuclei) present at the center of embryo sac (ovule) to form endospore (3n) that acts as food reserve.

Q34. Name the different Groups of Mammals which includes some variation in their lifestyle. With one example.

Ans. (*i*) Egg-laying mammals : Platypus
(*ii*) Pouched mammals : Kangaroo
(*iii*) Grass eating mammal: elephant
(*iv*) Flesh-eating mammals : Tiger
(*v*) Aquatic mammals : Dolphin
(*vi*) Flying mammals: Bat

III. Long Answer Type Questions

Q1. What is the importance of classification?

Ans. Classification is important because:

(*a*) Classification makes the study of wide variety of organisms, systematic and easier.
(*b*) It projects a picture of all organisms and their interrelation with each other.
(*c*) It provides a base for the study of other branches of biology.
(*d*) It is useful in the study of ecology, which deals with the inter-relation of an organism with their environment.
(*e*) It helps to establish a hierarchy of groups of organisms.

Q2. What are the characteristic features of mammals?

Ans. Characteristics features of mammals:

(*a*) Body is covered with hair.
(*b*) Skin is provided with sweat and sebaceous glands.
(*c*) Heart is four-chambered.
(*d*) Fertilization is internal.
(*e*) Females have mammary glands to produce milk to nourish their young ones.
(*f*) External ear—pinna present.
(*g*) Eyes have eye lids.
(*h*) Warm-blooded.
(*i*) Respiration through lungs.
(*j*) Body cavity divided into thorax and abdomen by muscular diaphragm.

Q3. *What are the characteristic features of reptiles?*

Ans. The characteristics of reptiles:

(*a*) Dry, scaly and impermeable skin.
(*b*) Respiration through lungs.
(*c*) Cold-blooded
(*d*) Internal fertilization.
(*e*) Heart is three chambered.
(*f*) Two pairs of pentadactyl limbs are present.

Q4. What are the basis for classification of organisms?

Ans. The basis for classification are:

(*a*) Presence or absence of nucleus.
(*b*) Organisms are unicellular or multicellular.
(*c*) Level of organisation.
(*d*) Autotrophic or heterotrophic mode of nutrition.
(*e*) Of the organisms that perform photosynthesis (Plants), their level or organisation of the body.
(*f*) Of the animals, how does the individuals body develop and organise its different parts.

Q5. Give the classification of plant kingdom.

Ans.

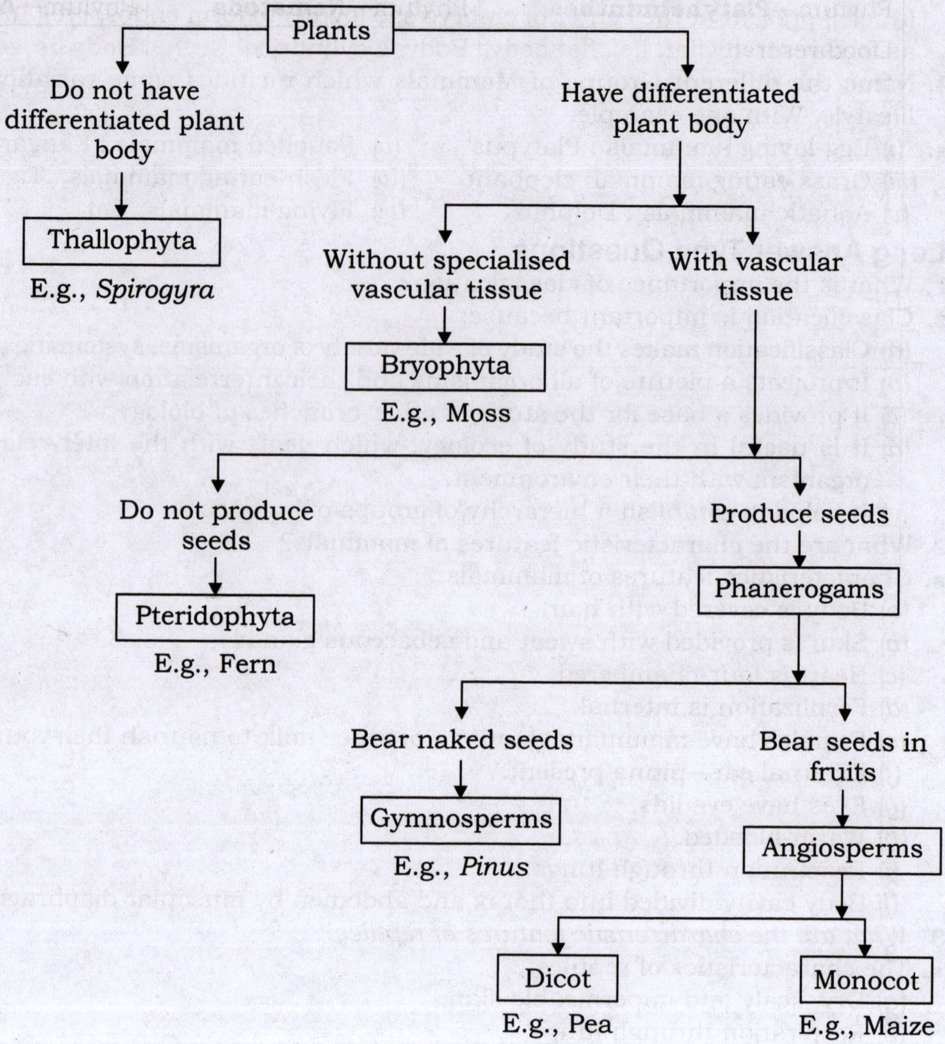

Q6. Give the characteristics of flat worms, round worms and segmented worm. Give their phylum.

Ans.

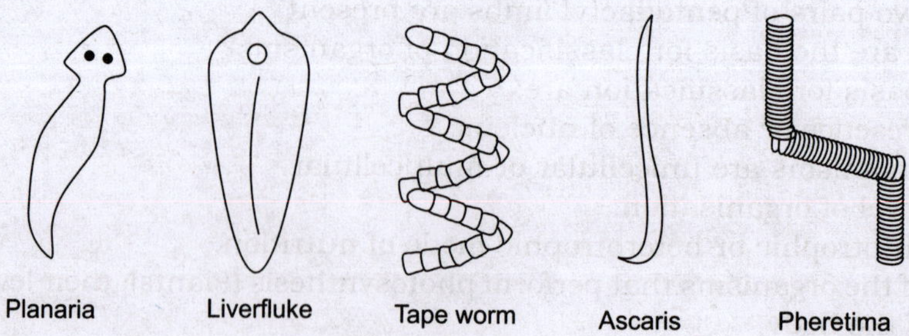

Types of Worms

Flat worms	***Round worms***	***Segmented worm***
Phylum—**Platyhelminthes**	Phylum—**Nematoda**	Phylum—**Annelida**
Dorsoventrally flat, i.e., flat body from top to bottom.	Body is cylindrical.	Body is segmented from head to tail.
No true body cavity.	Pseudocoelom (Sort of body cavity).	True body cavity.
Mostly hermaphrodite, i.e., male and female sex organs present in the same individual.	Sexes are separate.	May be unisexual or bisexual.

Q7. Differentiate (5 points) between monocot and dicot plants.

Ans.

Monocot Plants	***Dicot Plants***
1. Fibrous root system	Tap root system
2. Parallel venation	Reticulate venation.
3. Seeds with one cotyledon	Seeds with two cotyledons
4. Vascular bundles are scattered.	Vascular bundles are arranged in rings.
5. Flowers are trimerous	Flowers are pentamerous or tetramerous

Q8. Give the outline classification of animal kingdom.

Ans. **Animal kingdom**

Chordata (Vertebrate)

Class

1. Pisces
2. Amphibia
3. Reptilia
4. Aves
5. Mammalia

Non-chordata Invertebrate Phylum

1. **Porifera:** Body with pores, aquatic, sessile, asexual reproduction. Example, Sponge.
2. **Cnidaria:** Diploblastic, stinging cells. Example, Jellyfish, *Hydra*.
3. **Platyhelminthes:** Flat worms, free living or parasitic. Example, Tape worm.
4. **Aschelminthes:** Round worms. Example, *Ascaris*.
5. **Annelida:** Segmented worm. Example, Earthworm, Leech
6. **Arthropoda:** Joint appendages. Example, Spider, Cockroach
7. **Mollusca:** Soft muscular animals. Example, Pila, Octopus.
8. **Echinodermata:** Hedgehog skin. Example, Starfish, sea urchin.
9. **Protochordata:** Between invertebrates and chordata. Example, *Balanoglossus*.

Q9. List four distinguishing features between porifera and coelenterate animals.

Ans.

Porifera Animals	***Coelenterate Animals***
1. These organisms have holes (pores) all over their body.	These organisms have body cavity called coelenteron with a single opening.
2. Their body is made up of single layer of cells.	Their body is made up of two layer of cells.

3. The body design of these animals have very minimum differentiation and division into tissues.	They show more body design differentiation.
4. These have a characteristic canal system to helps in circulating water through the body to bring in food and oxygen.	These have a characteristic feature of cavity in the body.

Q10. Fill in the following table to compare bryophytes, ferns, gymnosperms and angiosperms.

	Bryophytes	**Pteridophytes**	**Gymnosperms**	**Angiosperms**
Flowers and Fruits				
Vascular tissue				
Seeds				
Branched sporophytes				
Mode of transfer of male gamete				
Type of fertilization				
Examples				

Ans.

	Bryophytes	**Pteridophytes**	**Gymnosperms**	**Angiosperms**
Flowers and Fruits	No	No	No	Yes
Vascular tissue	No	Yes	Yes	yes
Seeds	No	No	Yes - naked	Yes - covered
Branched sporophytes	No	Yes	Yes	Yes
Mode of transfer of male gamete	Moisture	Moisture	Wind	Wind, animals, birds, insects
Type of fertilization	Normal	Normal	Normal	Double
Examples	Moss	Ferns	Cones	Sunflower

Q11. Give reason to justify the following statements:

(*i*) Platypus and echidna lay eggs but are considered as mammals.

(*ii*) Crocodiles have four chambered heart but are still reptiles.

Ans. (*i*) Mammals show the following characteristics:

Warm-blooded vertebrate animal of a class that is distinguished by the possession of hair or fur, females secrete milk for the nourishment of the young, and (typically) give birth to live young ones. Platypus and echidna shows all the other characteristics except they lay eggs

(*ii*) Reptiles show the following characteristics:

They are distinguished by having a dry scaly skin and typically laying soft-shelled eggs on land. Crocodile shows all the other characteristics except it has four chambered heart like mammals.

Q12. Explain different forms of pollination and seed dispersal and also talk about the importance of co-evolution in animals and plants.

Ans. Pollination can occur by insects, birds, mammals etc.

For this the flowers need to be colorful and attractive, have good fragrance or may be bad odour in few. The flowers should also have more nectar.

The animals need to be able to see colors, get attracted to the nectar and smell the flower.

Seed dispersal: The fruit and seeds serve as a food to many animals. The seeds that are hard does not get digested in the animals body and is removed as waste. Some of the seeds have special structures so they stick to the body of the animals and are transferred.

The co-existence of plants and animals is seen in the above explanation where plants get pollinated and the seeds get dispersed only because of animals in most of the cases. At the same time the animals also get food from the plants.

V. Activity- Based Questions

1.
- Soak seeds of green gram, wheat, maize, peas and tamarind. Once they become tender, try to split the seed. Do all the seeds break into two nearly equal halves?
- The seeds that do are the dicot seeds and the seeds that don't are then monocot seeds.
- Now take a look at the roots, leaves and flowers of these plants.
- Are the roots, tap roots or fibrous?
- Do the leaves have parallel or reticulate venation?
- How many petals are found in the flowers of these plants?
- Can you write down further characteristics of monocots and dicots on the basis of these observations?

Ans.

Characteristics	*Green gram*	*Wheat*	*Maize*	*Peas*	*Tamarind*
1. Roots	Tap root	Fibrous root	Fibrous root	Tap root	Tap root
2. Cotyledon	Dicotyledon	Monocotyledon	Monocotyledon	Dicotyledon	Dicotyledon
3. Venation in leaves	Reticulate	Parallel	Parallel	Reticulate	Reticulate
4. Vascular bundle	In a ring	Scattered	Scattered	In a ring	In a ring
5. Flowers	Pentamerous	Trimerous	Trimerous	Pentamerous	Pentamerous

2.
- We have heard of '*desi*' cows and Jersey cows.
- Does a *desi* cow look like a Jersey cow?
- Do all *desi* cows look alike.

- Will we be able to identify a Jersey cow in a crowd of *desi* cows that don't look like each other?
- What is the basis of our identification?

Ans. 1. *Desi* cow is different in size and colour.
2. Most of the *desi* cows look alike, not all.
3. Yes, Jersey cow can be spotted from the group.
4. Basis of identification:
Size, horn shape, skin colour, height, etc.

3. Find out the names of the following animals and plants in as many languages as you can.

Ans. It is difficult to remember names of a species in different languages. This problem means there was a need for some system to create uniform naming convention: Hence system of nomenclature and classification was devised.

Animals	*Plants*
1. Frog—*Rana tigrina*	1. Touch me not—*Mimosa pudica.*
2. Human—*Homo sapiens*	2. Neem—*Azadirachta indica.*
3. Peacock—*Paro cristatus*	3. Maize—*Zea mays.*
4. Honeybee—*Apis cerena, Apis indica.*	

VI. Value-Based Questions

Q1. Many medicinal plants every year are getting extinct. A group of students who had gone for educational trip clicked photographs of endangered plants. These photograph were used by the school laboratory to study these plants.
(*a*) Name two endangered plants.
(*b*) Name any one medicinal plant and give its medicinal use.
(*c*) What value of students is reflected in the above act?

Ans. (*a*) Two endangered plants are:
(*i*) *Euphrasia* (*ii*) *Ulmus rubra*
(*b*) Aloe-vera. Juice of Aloe-vera is used in case of indigestion, treating skin infection etc.
(*c*) Students are caring citizens, shows responsible behaviour.

Q2. Due to global warming coral is getting diminished in all the oceans/water bodies. People in Lakshadweep island protects their corals by not allowing people/tourist to scape few pieces away.
(*a*) Name the phylum of coral.
(*b*) What is coral made up of?
(*c*) What values of people in Lakshadweep island is reflected?

Ans. (*a*) Phylum of coral is coelenterata.
(*b*) Coral is made up of calcium carbonate.
(*c*) People in Lakshadweep island reflect the value of being responsible citizen, respecting environment and nature.

VII. Practical Based Questions (Solved)

Q1. Name an aquatic reptile. How many chambers are there in the heart of: (*i*) lizard; (*ii*) crocodile?

Ans. Sea snake, sea turtle.
(*i*) three chambers (*ii*) four chambers

Q2. Monocot and dicots differ in the way their vascular systems are arranged. In monocots, the vascular bundles are scattered throughout the stem. In dicots, the vascular bundles are arranged in a ring. Draw the vascular bundles of both types.

Ans.

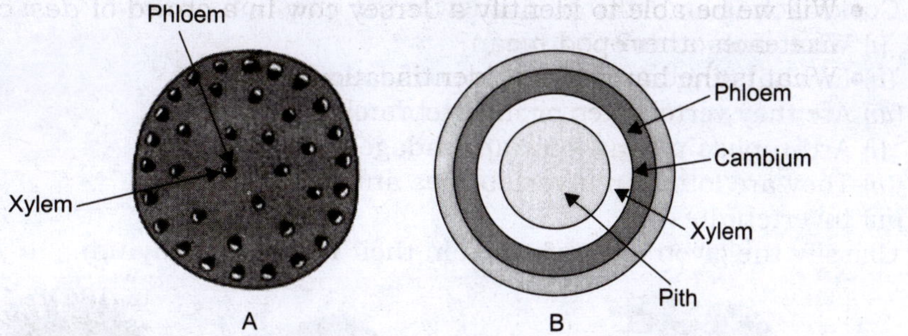

Q3. List three characteristics of all arthropods.

Ans. (*i*) Bilateral symmetry (*ii*) Joint legs

(*iii*) Body is segmented

Q4. Insects like butterfly, mosquitoes have similar body structure but have different wings. Answer the question below:

(*i*) Name the three body segments of insects.

(*ii*) How many legs do insects have and which body segment are they attached to?

(*iii*) How many antennae do insects have?

(*iv*) Name the insect's jaws.

(*v*) Do all insects have wings?

(*vi*) Where are wings attached to on an insect?

Ans. (*i*) The head, thorax and abdomen (*ii*) Three pairs of legs, thorax

(*iii*) one pair (*iv*) mandible

(*v*) No, eg. Lice and silverfish (*vi*) thorax

Q5. Name and Label the following parts of a grasshopper:

(*i*) Openings for respiration: spiracle

(*ii*) Organs for flight: wings

(*iii*) Used for touch and smell: antennae

(*iv*) Last section of the insect's body: abdomen

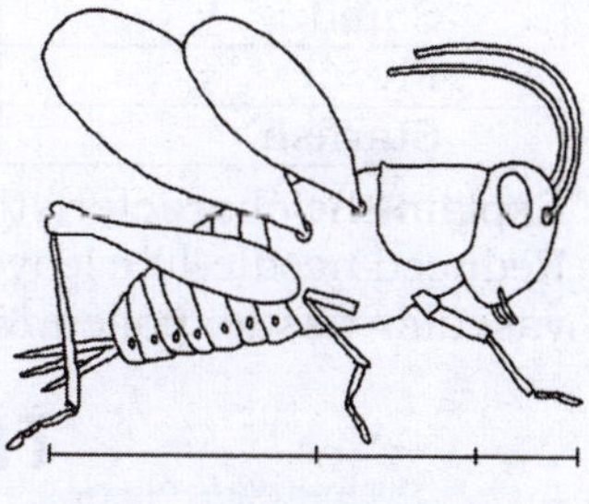

Ans.

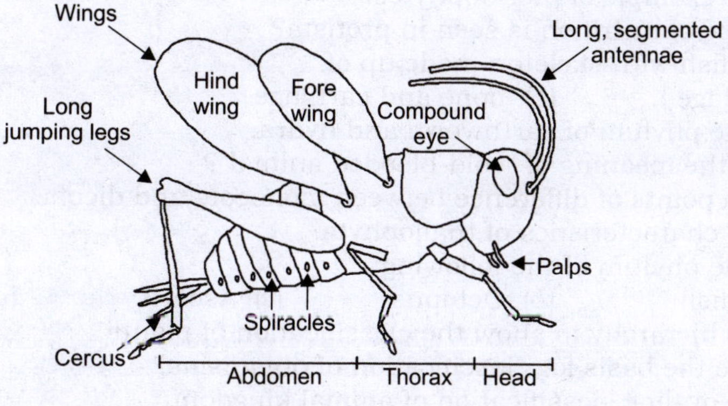

Q6. Cockroach is an arthropod, answer the questions below:

(*i*) What does arthropod mean?

(*ii*) In what kingdom are arthropods found?

(*iii*) Are they vertebrates or invertebrates?

Ans. (*i*) Arthropods means joint appendages

(*ii*) They are found in invertebrates animal kingdom

(*iii*) Invertebrates

Q7. Classify the given invertebrates in their respective phylum.

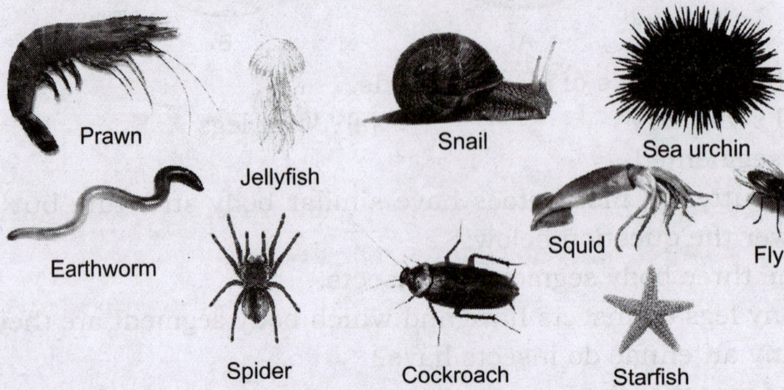

Ans.

Invertebrate Animals	***Invertebrate Phylum***
Jellyfish	Cnidarin
Sea urchin	Echinoderm
Prawn	Arthropod
Snail	Mollusc
Cockroach	Arthropod
Earthworm	Annelia
Spider	Arthropod
Squid	Mollusca
Fly	Arthropod
Starfish	Echinderm

Q8. Explain the characteristics of conifers.

Ans. Reduced needle-like leaves, pollination is wind-dependent, almost all are evergreen, vascular tissue, pollen & seeds usually naked borne in cones.

TEST YOUR SKILLS

Q1. Give one example of pteridophytes.

Q2. What type of nutrition is seen in protista?

Q3. Name a fish with skeleton made up of:

(*a*) cartilage (*b*) bone and cartilage

Q4. Name the phylum of earthworm and hydra.

Q5. What is the meaning of "cold-blooded animal"?

Q6. Give two points of difference between monocots and dicots.

Q7. Give the characteristics of thallophyta.

Q8. Name the phylum of the following:

(*a*) Jellyfish (*b*) Octopus (*c*) Ascaris (*d*) Spider

Q9. Give the hierarchy to show the classification of plants.

Q10. What are the basis for classification of organisms?

Q11. Give the outline classification of animal kingdom.

❑❑❑

8 Motion

Syllabus

Motion, Uniform motion, Non-uniform motion, Speed, Acceleration

Facts that Matter

- An object is said to be in motion when its position changes with time.
- We describe the location of an object by specifying a reference point. Motion is relative. The total path covered by an object is said to be the distance travelled by it.
- The shortest path/distance measured from the initial to the final position of an object is known as the **displacement**.
- **Uniform motion:** When an object covers equal distances in equal intervals of time, it is said to be in uniform motion.
- **Non-uniform motion:** Motions where objects cover unequal distances in equal intervals of time.
- **Speed:** The distance travelled by an object in unit time is referred to as speed. Its unit is m/s.
- **Average speed:** For non-uniform motion, the average speed of an object is obtained by dividing the total distance travelled by an object by the total time taken.

$$\text{Average speed } (v) = \frac{\text{Total distance travelled (s)}}{\text{Total time taken (t)}}$$

- **Velocity:** Velocity is the speed of an object moving in definite direction. S.I. unit is m/s.

$$\text{Average velocity} = \frac{\text{initial velocity} + \text{final velocity}}{2}$$

$$\therefore \quad v_{av} = \frac{u+v}{2} \qquad u = \text{initial velocity}$$

$$v = \text{final velocity}$$

- **Acceleration:** Change in the velocity of an object per unit time.

$$\text{Acceleration } a = \frac{v-u}{t} \quad \text{S.I. unit is m/s}^2$$

- **Graphical representation of motions**

(i) Distance-time graph

For a distance-time graph time is taken on x-axis and distance is taken on y-axis.

[**Note:** All independent quantities are taken along the x-axis and dependent quantities are taken along y-axis.]

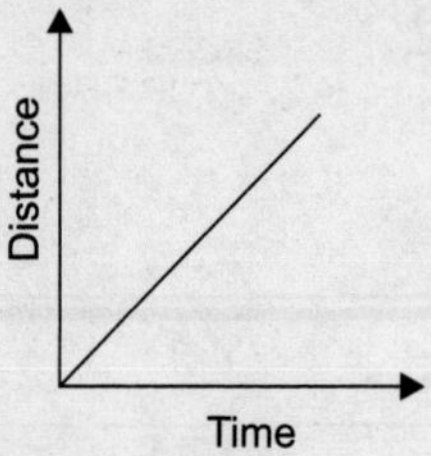

Uniform speed

$\left(\text{speed} = \frac{\text{distance}}{\text{time}}\right)$

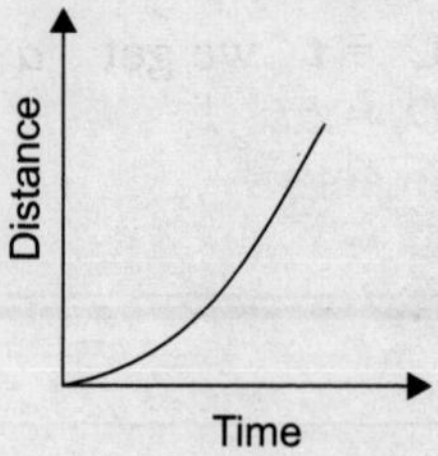

Non-uniform speed

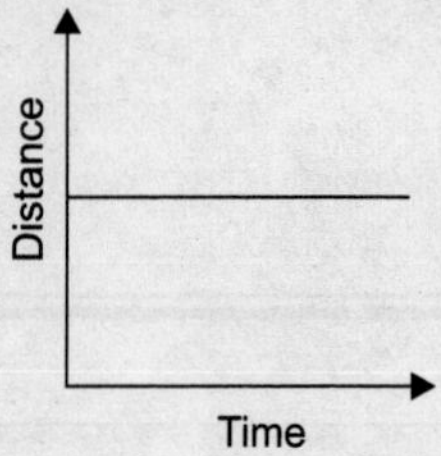

Stationary

(*ii*) Velocity-time graph

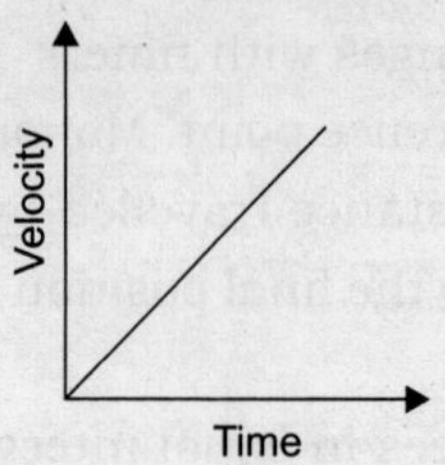

Uniform acceleration

$\left(a = \frac{v}{t}\right)$

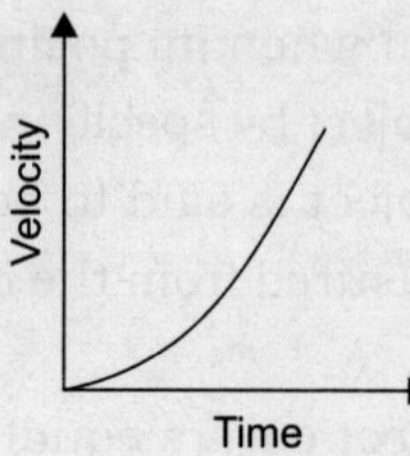

Non-uniform acceleration

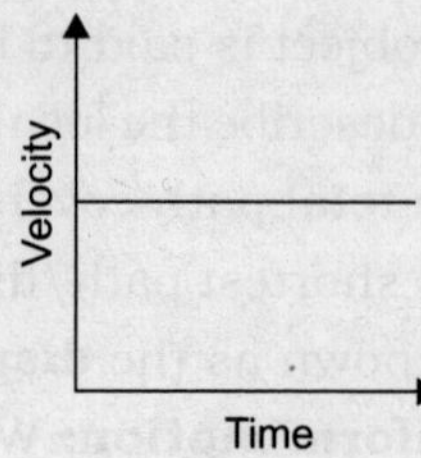

Uniform motion or no acceleration

- **Equations of motion by graphical method**

(*i*) Velocity-time relation:

$$v = u + at$$

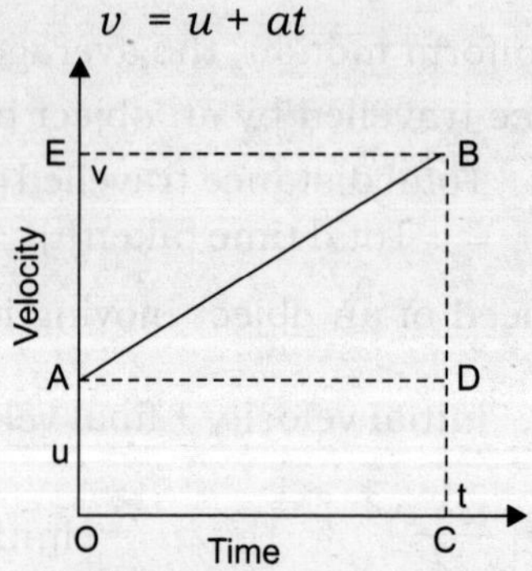

$$OA = CD = u$$
$$OE = CB = v$$
$$OC = AD = t$$
$$BD = BC - DC \quad \text{(Change in velocity)}$$

AD is parallel to *OC*.

$\therefore \quad BC = BD + DC = BD + OA$

$\therefore \quad BC = v \text{ and } OA = u$

We get $\quad v = BD + u$

$\therefore \quad BD = v - u \qquad \ldots(1)$

In velocity-time graph, slope gives acceleration.

$$\therefore \quad a = \frac{\text{Change in Velocity}}{\text{time taken}} = \frac{BD}{AD} = \frac{BD}{OC}$$

$\because \quad OC = t$ we get $\left| \; a = \dfrac{BD}{t} \right.$

$\therefore \quad BD = at$ ...(2)

Substituting (2) in (1) we get

$$BD = v - u$$
$$at = v - u$$
$$\therefore \quad \boxed{v = u + at}$$

(*ii*) Equation for position-time relation:

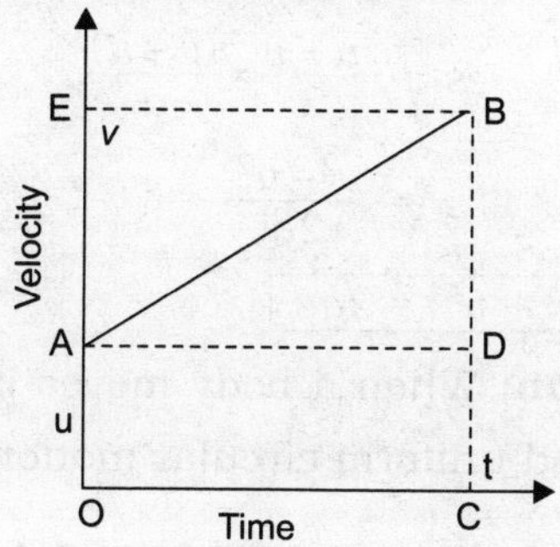

Let us assume,

s = distance travelled by the object

t = time t

a = uniform acceleration.

$\therefore$ Distance travelled by the object is given by area enclosed with *OABC* in the graph.

$\therefore \quad s$ = area OABC (which is a trapezium)

= (area of rectangle *OADC*) + (area of ΔABD)

$= (OA \times OC) + \dfrac{1}{2}\ (AD \times BD)$

Substituting $OA = u, \quad OC = AD = t$ and $BD = at$ (from equation 2)

We get $s = ut + \dfrac{1}{2}\ (t \times at)$

$$\therefore \quad \boxed{s = ut + \frac{1}{2}\ at^2}$$

(*iii*) Equation for position–velocity relation:

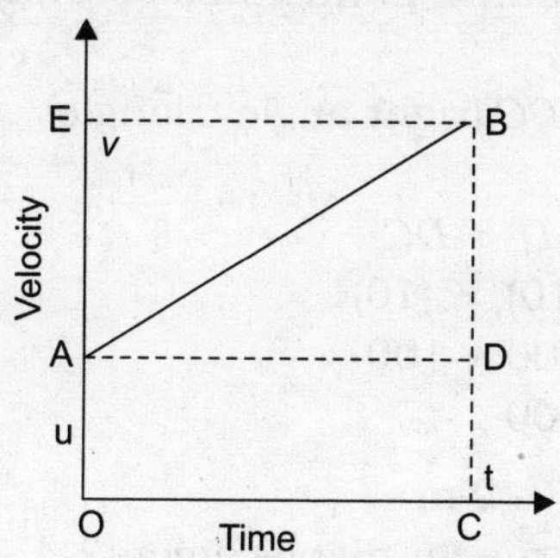

s = distance travelled by the object

t = in time t

a = uniform acceleration

$\therefore \quad s$ = area enclosed by trapezium *OABC*

$$\therefore \quad s = \frac{(OA + BC) \times OC}{2}$$

$$\because \quad OA = u, \quad BC = v \quad \text{and} \quad OC = t.$$

$$\therefore \quad s = \frac{(u + v)t}{2} \qquad \text{...(1)}$$

Slope $t = \frac{v - u}{a}$ from the graph ...(2)

Substitute value of 't' in (1)

$$\therefore \quad s = \frac{u + v}{2} \times \frac{(v - u)}{a}$$

$$s = \frac{v^2 - u^2}{2a}$$

$$\therefore \quad \boxed{v^2 - u^2 = 2as}$$

- **Uniform circular motion:** When a body moves in a circular path with uniform speed, its motion is called uniform circular motion.

NCERT IN-TEXT QUESTIONS SOLVED

Q1. An object has moved through a distance. Can it have zero displacement? If yes, support your answer with an example.

Ans. Yes, the object inspite of moving through a distance can have zero displacement. *Example,* if an object travels from point 'A' and reaches to the same point 'A', then its displacement is '0'.

Q2. A farmer moves along the boundary of a square field of side 10 m in 40 s. What will be the magnitude of displacement of the farmer at the end of 2 minutes 20 seconds from his initial position?

Ans. Total distance = perimeter of square = 4 × 10 m = 40 m

Time taken = 40 s

∴ Total time taken by the farmer = 2 min 20 seconds = 140 seconds

∴ 140 ÷ 40 = 3.5

∴ The farmer completes 3 and a half round of the square. *i.e.,* if he starts from A he reaches point 'C' after 2 minutes 20 seconds.

∴ Displacement is AC.

To find AC, assume ΔADC (right angle triangle)

∴ In ΔADC

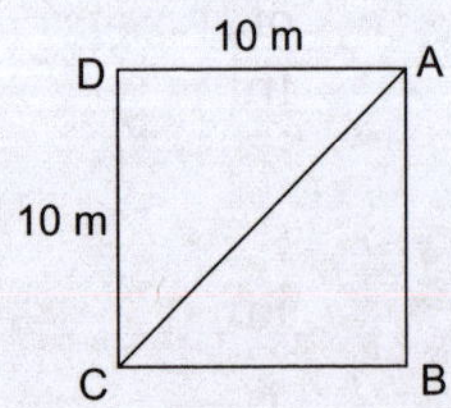

$$AC^2 = AD^2 + DC^2$$

$$\therefore \quad AC^2 = (10)^2 + (10)^2$$

$$AC^2 = 100 + 100$$

$$AC^2 = 200$$

$$\therefore \quad AC = 10\sqrt{2} \text{ m}$$

Q3. Which of the following is true for displacement?

(*a*) It cannot be zero.

(*b*) Its magnitude is greater than the distance travelled by the object.

Ans. (*a*) False (*b*) False

Q4. Distinguish between speed and velocity.

Ans.

Speed	*Velocity*
1. The distance travelled by a moving body per unit time is called its speed.	1. The distance travelled by moving body in a particular direction per unit time is velocity.
2. It is scalar quantity.	2. It is a vector quantity.

Q5. Under what condition(s) is the magnitude of average velocity of an object equal to its average speed?

Ans. The magnitude of average velocity of an object is equal to its average speed if the object moves in a straight line in a particular direction.

Q6. What does the odometer of an automobile measure?

Ans. The odometer of an automobile measure the distance travelled by a vehicle.

Q7. What does the path of an object look like when it is in uniform motion?

Ans. It is a straight line.

Q8. During an experiment, a signal from a spaceship reached the ground station in five minutes. What was the distance of the spaceship from the ground station? The signal travels at the speed of light, that is 3×10^8 ms^{-1}.

Ans. Time taken = 5 minutes = 5×60 sec = 300 sec

Speed of signal u = 3×10^8 m/s

Distance = ?

$$\text{Speed} = \frac{\text{distance}}{\text{time}} \quad \therefore \text{distance} = \text{speed} \times \text{time}$$

$\therefore$ Distance = $3 \times 10^8 \times 300$

= 9×10^{10} m.

Q9. When will you say a body is in

(*i*) uniform acceleration? (*ii*) non-uniform acceleration?

Ans. (*i*) **Uniform acceleration:** If the velocity of a body changes by equal amounts in equal interval of time, howsoever small or large these intervals may be, the acceleration is said to be uniform. Acceleration due to gravity is an example of uniform acceleration.

(*ii*) **Non-uniform acceleration:** If velocity changes by unequal amount in equal interval of time or if the direction of motion changes then the acceleration is said to be non-uniform. Acceleration of a train running from one station to another is a non-uniform acceleration.

Q10. A bus decreases its speed from 80 km h^{-1} to 60 km h^{-1} in 5 s. Find the acceleration of the bus.

Ans. Initial velocity u = 80 km/h

$$= \frac{80 \times 1000}{60 \times 60} \text{ m/s} = 22.22 \text{ m/s}$$

Final velocity $$v = 60 \text{ km/h} = \frac{60 \times 1000}{60 \times 60} = 16.66 \text{ m/s}$$

Time t = 5s

$\therefore$ a = ?

$$a = \frac{v-u}{t} = \frac{16.06 - 22.22}{5} = -1.11 \text{ m/s}^2$$

$\therefore$ The acceleration of bus is -1.11 m/s^2.

Q11. A train starting from a railway station and moving with uniform acceleration attains a speed 40 km h^{-1} in 10 minutes. Find its acceleration.

Ans.

$$u = 0$$

$$v = 40 \text{ km/h} = \frac{40 \times 1000}{60 \times 60} = 11.11 \text{ m/s.}$$

$$t = 10 \text{ minutes} = 10 \times 60 = 600 \text{ s}$$

$$a = ?$$

$$\therefore \quad a = \frac{v - u}{t} = \frac{(11.11 - 0)}{600} = 0.018 \text{ m/s}^2$$

Q12. What is the nature of the distance-time graphs for uniform and non-uniform motion of an object?

Ans. For uniform motion, distance-time graph is a straight line.

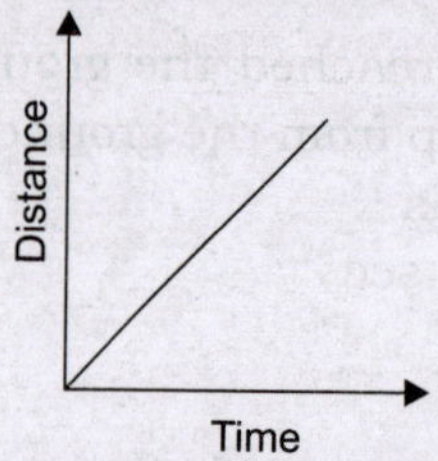

For non-uniform motion, distance-time graph is a curved line.

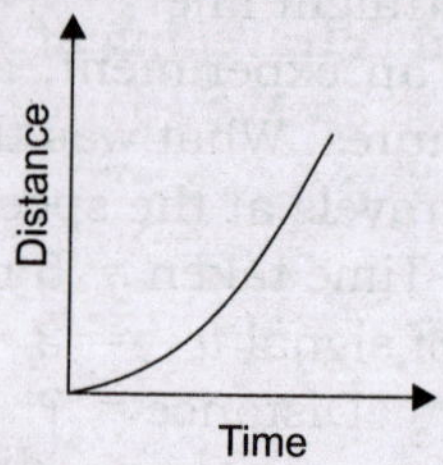

Q13. What can you say about the motion of an object whose distance-time graph is a straight line parallel to the time axis?

Ans. The body is at rest.

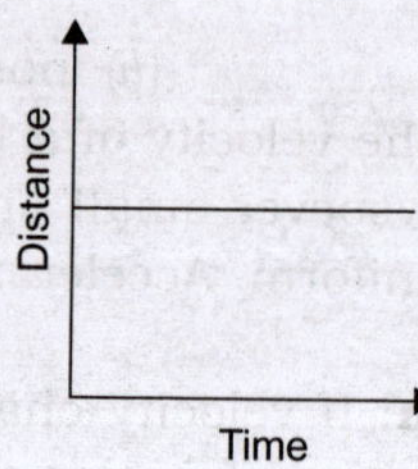

Q14. What can you say about the motion of an object if its speed-time graph is a straight line parallel to the time axis?

Ans.

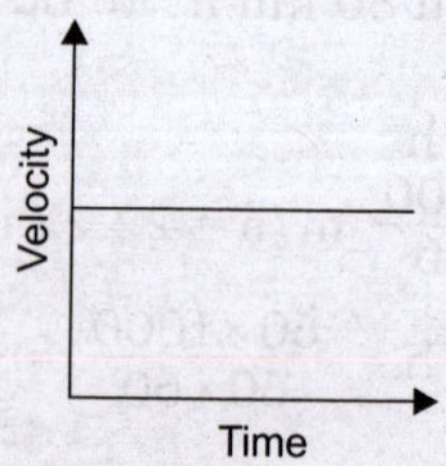

The body is moving with a uniform speed and zero acceleration.

Q15. What is the quantity which is measured by the area occupied below the velocity-time graph?

Ans. Distance travelled.

Q16. A bus starting from rest moves with a uniform acceleration of 0.1 ms^{-2} for 2 minutes. Find (a) the speed acquired, (b) the distance travelled.

Ans.
$u = 0$
$a = 0.1\ m/s^2$
$t = 2$ minute $= 2 \times 60 = 120$ s.

(i) $v = ?$
(ii) $s = ?$

(i)
$$v = u + at$$
$$v = 0 + 0.1 \times 120$$
$$v = 12\ m/s.$$

(ii)
$$v^2 - u^2 = 2as$$
$$(12)^2 - (0)^2 = 2 \times 0.1 \times s$$
$$\therefore \quad 144 = 0.2\ s$$
$$\therefore \quad s = \frac{144}{0.2} = 720\ m$$

The speed acquired is 12 m/s and the distance travelled is 720 m.
The speed acquired is 12 m/s and the distance travelled is 720 m.

Q17. A train is travelling at a speed of 90 km h^{-1}. Brakes are applied so as to produce a uniform acceleration of -0.5 ms^{-2}. Find how far the train will go before it is brought to rest.

Ans.
$$u = 90\ km/h = \frac{90 \times 1000}{60 \times 60} = 25\ m/s$$
$a = -0.5\ m/s^2$
$v = 0$
$s = ?$
$$v^2 - u^2 = 2as$$
$$0 - (25)^2 = 2 \times (-0.5)\ s$$
$$\therefore \quad s = \frac{-(25)^2}{2(-0.5)} = \frac{-625}{-1.0} = 625\ m.$$

Q18. A trolley, while going down an inclined plane, has an acceleration of 2 cm s^{-2}. What will be its velocity 3 s after the start?

Ans.
$a = 2\ cm/s^2$
$t = 3$ s
$v = ?$
$u = 0$
$$v = u + at$$
$$= 0 + 2 \times 3$$
$$v = 6\ cm/s.$$

The velocity of a trolley 3 s after the start will be 6 cm/s.

Q19. A racing car has a uniform acceleration of 4 ms^{-2}. What distance will it cover in 10 s after start?

Ans.
$a = 4\ m/s^2$
$t = 10$ s
$s = ?$
$u = 0$
$$\therefore \quad s = ut + \frac{1}{2}at^2 = (0 \times 10) + \frac{1}{2} \times 4 \times (10)^2 = 0 + \frac{1}{2} \times 4 \times 100$$
$$s = 200\ m.$$

The distance covered in 10 s by the car is 200 m.

Q20. A stone is thrown in a vertically upward direction with a velocity of 5 ms^{-1}. If the acceleration of the stone during its motion is 10 ms^{-2} in the downward direction, what will be the height attained by the stone and how much time will it take to reach there?

Ans.
$$u = 5\text{ m/s}$$
$$v = 0$$
$$a = -10\text{ m/s}^2$$
$$s = ?$$
$$t = ?$$
$$v = u + at$$
$$0 = 5 + (-10)\,t$$
$$-5 = -10t$$
$$\therefore \quad t = \frac{5}{10} = 0.5\text{ sec.}$$
$$t = 0.5\text{ s}$$
$$v^2 - u^2 = 2as$$
$$(0)^2 - (5)^2 = 2\,(-10) \times s$$
$$-25 = -20 \times s$$
$$\therefore \quad s = \frac{25}{20} = 1.25\text{ m}$$
$$s = 1.25\text{ m}$$

The height attained by the stone is 1.25 m and time required to reach there is 0.5 s.

NCERT TEXTUAL QUESTIONS SOLVED

Q1. An athlete completes one round of a circular track of diameter 200 m in 40 s. What will be the distance covered and the displacement at the end of 2 minutes 20 s?

Ans. Diameter = 200 m, $r = \frac{d}{2} = 100$ m

Time for one round = 40 s

Distance travelled in 2 minutes and 20 s

$$= (2 \times 60) + 20 = 140\text{ s}$$

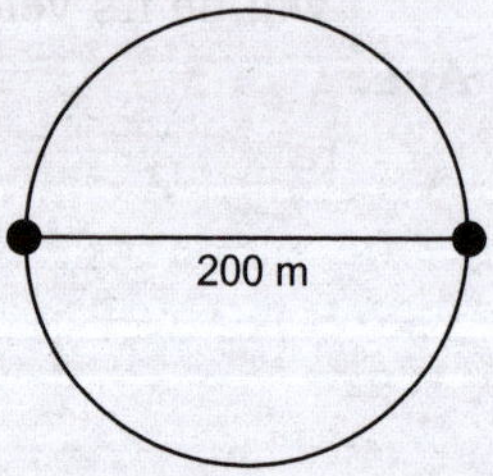

$$\therefore \quad \frac{140}{40} = 3.5\text{ rounds}$$

Distance travelled = Circumference of the circle × 3.5

$$= 2\,\pi r \times 3.5$$
$$= 2 \times \frac{22}{7} \times 100 \times 3.5 = 2200\text{ m}$$

Displacement after 3.5 revolution

= diameter of the track

= 200 m.

Q2. Joseph jogs from one end A to the other end B of a straight 300 m road in 2 minutes 30 seconds and then turns around and jogs 100 m back to point C in another 1 minute. What are Joseph's average speeds and velocities in jogging (a) from A to B and (b) from A to C?

Ans. (*a*) From A to B

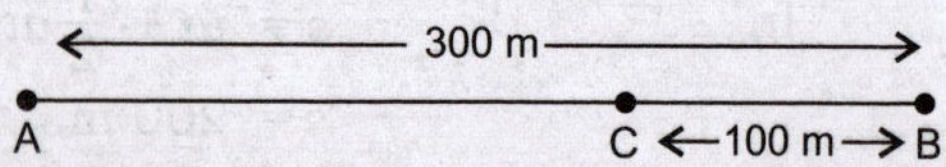

Time for $A \rightarrow B$ = 2 min 30 sec

= 2 × 60 + 30

= 150 sec

$$\text{Average speed} = \frac{\text{total distance}}{\text{time interval}} = \frac{300}{150} = 2 \text{ m/s}$$

$$\text{Average velocity} = \frac{\text{displacement}}{\text{time interval}} = \frac{300}{150} = 2 \text{ m/s}$$

(*b*) From *A* to *C*

Total distance = *A* to *B* + *B* to *C* = (300 + 100) = 400 m

Time taken = 150 + 60 = 210 sec

$$\therefore \quad \text{Average speed} = \frac{\text{total distance}}{\text{time interval}} = \frac{400}{210} = 1.9 \text{ m/s}$$

$$\therefore \quad \text{Average velocity} = \frac{\text{displacement}}{\text{time interval}} = \frac{400}{210} = 0.95 \text{ m/s}$$

Q3. Abdul, while driving to school, computes the average speed for his trip to be 20 km h^{-1}. On his return trip along the same route, there is less traffic and the average speed is 30 km h^{-1}. What is the average speed for Abdul's trip?

Ans. $$\text{Average speed} = \frac{\text{total distance}}{\text{time}}$$

∴ Let the distance from Abdul's home to school = *x* km

∴ While driving to school

$$\text{Average speed} = \frac{\text{distance}}{\text{time}}$$

$$20 \text{ km/h} = \frac{x}{t_1}$$

While on his return trip

$$\text{Average speed} = \frac{\text{distance}}{\text{time}}$$

$$30 \text{ km/h} = \frac{x}{t_2}$$

$$\therefore \quad \text{Total distance} = x + x = 2x$$

$$\therefore \quad \text{Total time } (t_1 + t_2) = \frac{x}{20} + \frac{x}{30} = \frac{3x + 2x}{60} = \frac{5x}{60}$$

$$\therefore \quad \text{Average speed} = \frac{2x}{\frac{5x}{60}} = \frac{2x \times 60}{5x} = 24 \text{ km/h.}$$

Q4. A motorboat starting from rest on a lake accelerates in a straight line at a constant rate of 3.0 ms^{-2} for 8.0 s. How far does the boat travel during this time?

Ans.

$$u = 0$$

$$a = 3.0 \text{ m/s}^2$$

$$t = 8 \text{ s}$$

$$s = ut + \frac{1}{2}at^2 = 0 \times t + \frac{1}{2}(3)(8)^2$$

$$s = \frac{1}{2} \times 3 \times 64 = 96 \text{ m.}$$

∴ Boat travelled a distance of 96 m.

Q5. A driver of a car travelling at 52 km h^{-1} applies the brakes and accelerates uniformly in the opposite direction. The car stops in 5 s. Another driver going at 3 km h^{-1} in another car applies his brakes slowly and stops in 10 s. On the same graph paper plot the speed versus time graphs for the two cars. Which of the two cars travelled farther after the brakes were applied?

Ans. $$\text{Initial speed of first driver} = \frac{52 \times 1000}{60 \times 60} = 14.44 \text{ m/s}$$

$$\text{Initial speed of second driver} = \frac{3 \times 1000}{60 \times 60} = 0.833 \text{ m/s}$$

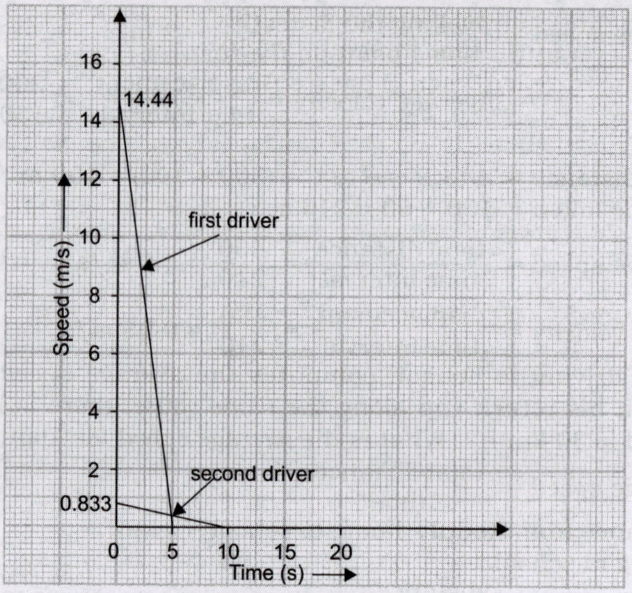

Distance covered by first driver = $\frac{1}{2} \times 14.44 \times 5 = 36.1$ m

Distance covered by second driver = $\frac{1}{2} \times 0.833 \times 10 = 4.165$ m

Hence, distance travelled by first car is more.

Q6. Figure given below shows the distance-time graph of three objects A, B and C, study the graph and answer the following questions.

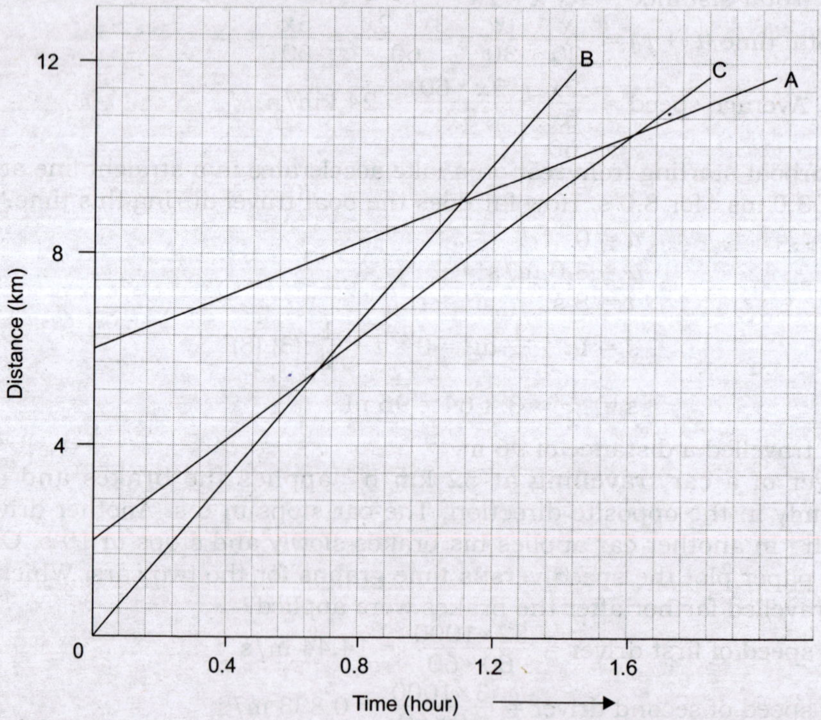

(*a*) Which of the three is travelling the fastest?
(*b*) Are all three ever at the same point on the road?
(*c*) How far has C travelled when B passes A?
(*d*) How far has B travelled by the time it passes C?

Ans. (*a*) *B* is travelling fastest.
(*b*) No, three lines do not meet at any point.
(*c*) When *B* passes *A*, *C* is at a distance approximately 8 km from origin.
(*d*) By the time *B* passes *C*, it has travelled 5.5 km.

Q7. A ball is gently dropped from a height of 20 m. If its velocity increases uniformly at the rate of 10 ms^{-2}, with what velocity will it strike the ground? After what time will it strike the ground?

Ans.

$s = 20$ m.
$u = 0$
$a = 10$ m/s^2
$t = ?$
$\therefore \quad v = u + at$
$= 0 + 10 \times 2$
$v = 20$ m/s.

$s = ut + \frac{1}{2}at^2$
$(20) = 0 \times t + \frac{1}{2}(10)t^2$
$20 = \frac{1}{2} \times 10t^2$
$t^2 = \frac{20 \times 2}{10}$
$t^2 = 4$
$\therefore \quad t = 2$ s.

The ball will strike the ground after 2 s with the velocity of 20 m/s.

Q8. The speed-time graph for a car is shown in the figure given below.

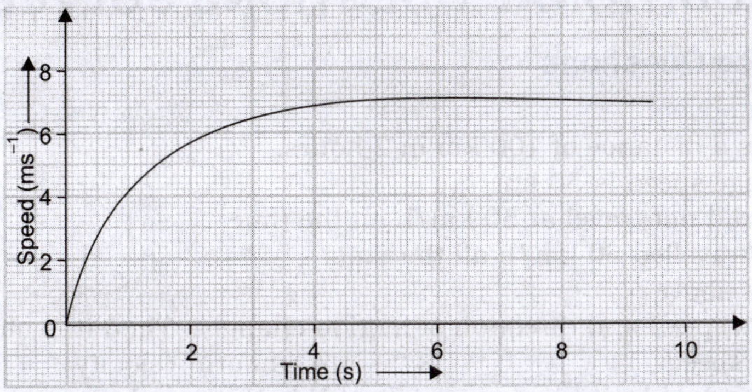

(*a*) Find how far does the car travel in the first 4 seconds. Shade the area on the graph that represents the distance travelled by the car during the period.
(*b*) Which part of the graph represents uniform motion of the car?

Ans. (*a*) The distance travelled by car in the first 4 seconds is approximately 12 m.

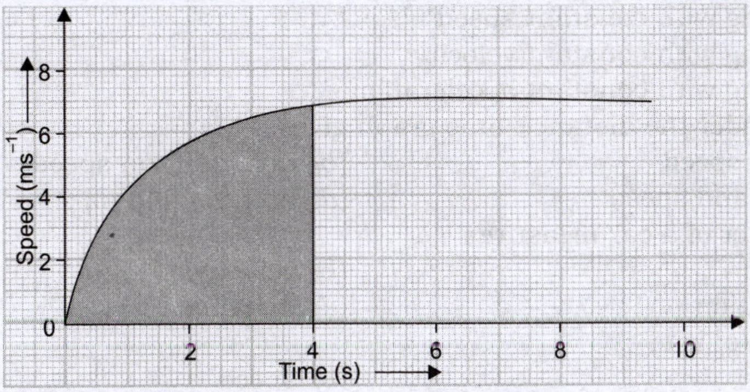

(*b*) The uniform motion of the car is shown after 5.5 s.

Q9. State which of the following situations are possible and give an example for each of these:

(*a*) an object with a constant acceleration but with zero velocity

(*b*) an object moving with an acceleration but with uniform speed

(*c*) an object moving in a certain direction with an acceleration in the perpendicular direction.

Ans. (*a*) Free fall due to gravity

(*b*) Not possible

(*c*) Object moving in a circular path

Q10. An artificial satellite is moving in a circular orbit of radius 42250 km. Calculate its speed if it takes 24 hours to revolve around the earth.

Ans.

$$\text{Radius of the orbit} = 42250 \text{ km} = 42250 \times 1000 \text{ m}$$

$$\text{Time taken for one revolution} = 24 \text{ hours} = 24 \times 60 \times 60 \text{ sec}$$

$$\text{Speed} = ?$$

$$\therefore \quad \text{Speed} = \frac{\text{distance}}{\text{time}} = \frac{2\pi r}{\text{time}}$$

$$= 2 \times \frac{22}{7} \times \frac{42250 \times 1000}{24 \times 60 \times 60}$$

$$\text{Speed} = 3073.74 \text{ m/s.}$$

ADDITIONAL QUESTIONS SOLVED

I. Multiple Choice Questions

Choose the correct option:

1. A car travels a distance of 100 km in 2 hours.

(*a*) Its average speed is 50 km/h.

(*b*) The car did not travel at 50 km/h all the time.

(*c*) The car travelled 50 km/h all the time.

(*d*) all of the above

2. If an object's speed and direction of motion changes. Then it is moving with

(*a*) uniform speed (*b*) uniform velocity

(*c*) non-uniform velocity (*d*) both (*b*) and (*c*)

3. The distance-time graph of an object is shown in the figure given below. The object is

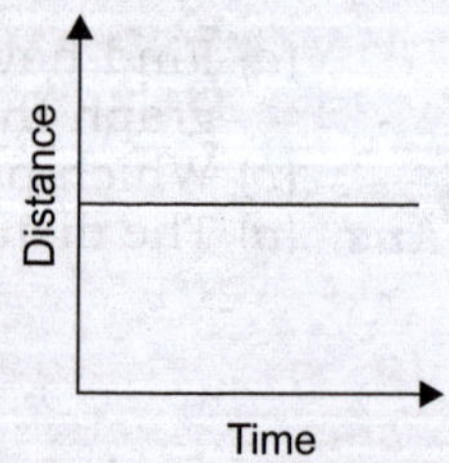

(*a*) at rest

(*b*) is making with constant speed

(*c*) is making with constant velocity

(*d*) is making with constant acceleration

4. The area under the distance-time graph gives

(*a*) uniform speed (*b*) non-uniform speed

(*c*) velocity and speed (*d*) both (*a*) and (*b*)

5. The odometer of a car measures

(*a*) speed (*b*) velocity

(*c*) acceleration (*d*) distance

6. The unit m/s^2 is of

(*a*) velocity (*b*) speed

(*c*) acceleration (*d*) deceleration

7. The velocity-time graph represents
   (*a*) body is in uniform motion
   (*b*) body is stationary
   (*c*) distance travelled by the body
   (*d*) none of these

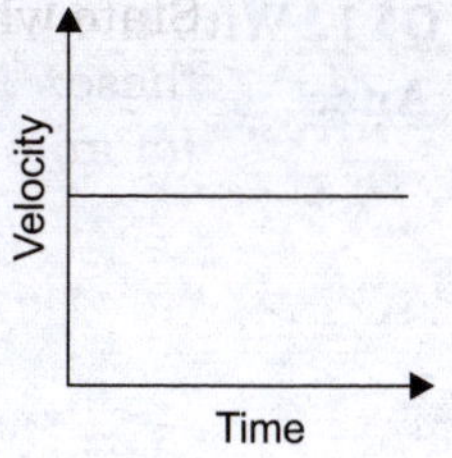

8. The area under velocity-time graph gives a physical quantity whose unit is
   (*a*) m/s   (*b*) m/s^2
   (*c*) m   (*d*) m^2
9. If a particle moves with a constant speed, the distance-time graph is
   (*a*) straight line   (*b*) curved line
   (*c*) horizontal line to time   (*d*) parallel line to velocity
10. An object moving with uniform circular motion shows
   (*a*) constant acceleration   (*b*) constant velocity
   (*c*) constant change in direction   (*d*) constant change in motion

Ans. 1—(*a*), 2—(*c*), 3—(*a*), 4—(*d*), 5—(*d*), 6—(*c*), 7—(*a*), 8—(*c*), 9—(*a*), 10—(*c*).

II. Very Short Answer Type Questions

Q1. Define uniform motion.

Ans. When an object covers equal distances in equal intervals of time, it is said to be in uniform motion.

Q2. Define speed.

Ans. It is defined as the distance travelled by an object in unit time. Its unit is m/s.

Q3. Define average speed.

Ans. The total distance travelled by an object divided by the total time taken.

Q4. Define velocity.

Ans. Velocity is the speed of an object moving in definite direction.

Q5. Define acceleration.

Ans. Change in the velocity of an object per unit time.

$$a = \frac{v-u}{t}, \quad \text{S.I. unit is } m/s^2.$$

Q6. While plotting a distance-time graph, why do we plot time on x-axis.

Ans. While plotting a distance time graph, we should plot time on x-axis as, all independent quantities are plotted on x-axis.

Q7. What is odometer?

Ans. Odometer is a device fitted in the automobiles to show the distance travelled.

Q8. Draw a distance-time graph that represents uniform speed.

Ans.

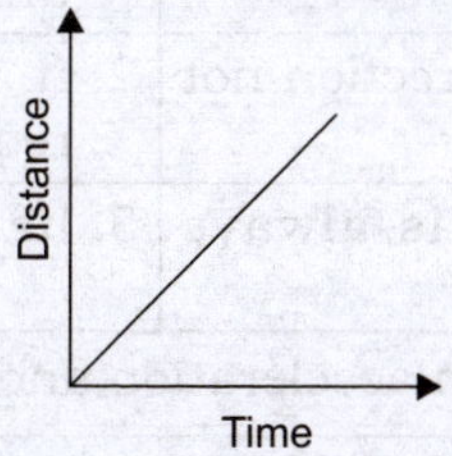

Q9. What does the area under velocity-time graph represent?

Ans. The area under the velocity-time graph represents the displacement.

Q10. A body travels a distance from A to B its physical quantity is measured to be 15 m/s. Is it speed or velocity? Give reason for the answer.

Ans. The physical quantity is – 15 m/s. It represents velocity because sign of speed cannot be a negative. Negative sign indicates the opposite direction.

Q11. With the help of distance-time graph show that the object is stationary.

Ans.

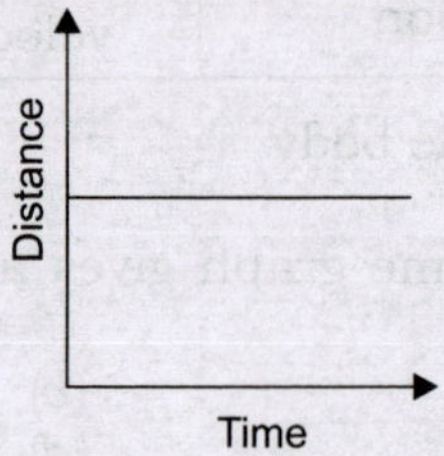

Q12. What type of velocity-time graph will you get for a particle moving with a constant acceleration?

Ans. For a particle moving with a constant acceleration velocity-time graph will be a straight line inclined to x-axis.

Q13. Define uniform circular motion.

Ans. When a body moves in a circular path with uniform speed, its motion is called uniform circular motion.

Q14. What is deceleration?

Ans. When the speed of an object decreases, the object is said to be decelerating. In this case the direction of acceleration is opposite to the velocity of the object.

Q15. A car travels with a speed of 30 km/h and then returns back with a speed of 50 km/h. Find average speed of the car.

Ans. Average speed = $\frac{30+50}{2}$ = 40 km/h.

III. Short Answer Type Questions

Q1. Give the difference between distance and displacement.

Ans.

Distance	*Displacement*
1. It is the total path covered by an object.	1. It is the shortest path measured from initial position to final position.
2. It does not need direction.	2. It needs direction.
3. It cannot be '0'.	3. It can be '0'.

Q2. Give the difference between speed and velocity.

Ans.

Speed	*Velocity*
1. It is the distance travelled by an object per unit time.	1. It is the displacement of the body per unit time.
2. It is scalar quantity, direction not required.	2. It is a vector quantity, direction is required.
3. Its unit is m/s and is always positive.	3. Its unit is m/s and can be negative.

Q3. Give the difference between acceleration and deceleration.

Ans.

Acceleration	*Deceleration*
1. It is change in velocity per unit time. It is always positive.	1. It is change in velocity per unit time. It is always negative.
2. In this case, the velocity keeps increasing.	2. In this case the increased velocity starts decreasing.

3. $u < v$, initial velocity is less than final velocity $u = 0$.	3. $u > v$, final velocity is less than the initial velocity $v = 0$.

Q4. Differentiate between velocity and acceleration.

Ans.

Velocity	***Acceleration***
1. The rate of change of position of body is called velocity.	1. It is the rate of change of velocity.
2. S.I. unit is m/s.	2. S.I. unit is m/s^2.

Q5. With the help of graph, show the uniform acceleration and uniform retardation of a body.

Ans.

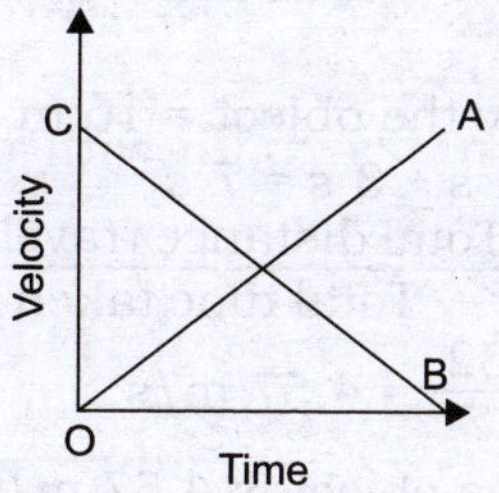

OA – shows uniform acceleration.
CB – shows uniform retardation.

Q6. What conclusion do you draw about acceleration of the particle in motion from given velocity-time graph?

(*a*)

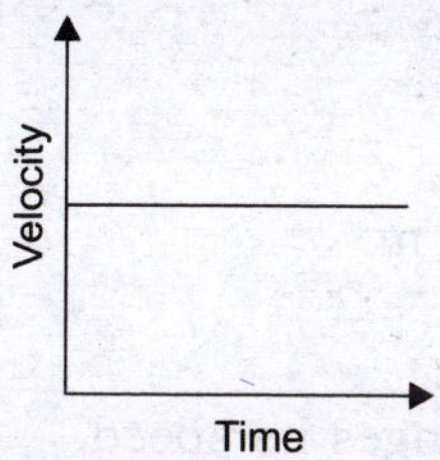

(*b*)

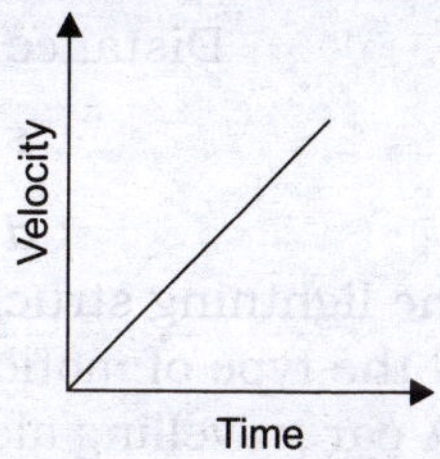

Ans. (*a*) No acceleration
(*b*) Uniform acceleration

Q7. A car accelerates uniformly from 20 km/h to 35 km/h in 5 s. Calculate (i) the acceleration and (ii) the distance covered by the car in that time.

Ans.

$$u = 20 \text{ km/h} = 5.5 \text{ m/s}$$
$$v = 35 \text{ km/h} = 9.72 \text{ m/s}$$
$$t = 5 \text{ s.}$$
$$a = \frac{v-u}{t} = \frac{9.7-5.5}{5}$$
$$a = \frac{4.2}{5} = 0.84 \text{ m/s}^2.$$

(*ii*) The distance covered by the car

$$s = ut + \frac{1}{2}at^2 = 5.5 \times 5 + \frac{1}{2}(0.84)(5)^2$$
$$= 27.5 + \frac{1}{2} \times 0.84 \times 25$$
$$= 27.5 + 10.5$$
$$s = 38 \text{ m.}$$

Q8. The odometer of a car reads 1800 km at the start of a trip and 2400 km at the end of the trip. If the trip took 10 h. Calculate the average speed of the car in km/h and m/s.

Sol. Distance covered by the car

$$s = 2400 - 1800 = 600 \text{ km.}$$

Trip time = 10 hr

Average speed = ?

(*i*) $V_{av} = \frac{s}{t} = \frac{600 \text{ km}}{10} = 60 \text{ km/h.}$

(*ii*) In m/s (60 km/h) = $\frac{60 \times 1000}{60 \times 60} = 16.7 \text{ m/s.}$

The average speed of the car in km/h = 60 km/h and in m/s is 16.7 m/s.

Q9. An object travels 16 m in 4 s and then another 16 m in 3 s. What is the average speed of the object?

Ans. Total distance travelled by the object = 16 m + 16 m = 32 m

Total time taken = $4\ s + 3\ s = 7\ s$

$\therefore$ Average speed = $\frac{\text{Total distance travelled}}{\text{Total time taken}}$

$= \frac{32}{7} = 4.57 \text{ m/s.}$

$\therefore$ The average speed of the object is 4.57 m/s.

Q10. It took 2 s after lightning for the sound of thunder to reach you. How far did the lightning struck?

Ans. Speed of sound is 346 m/s in air.

Time = 2 *s*

$\therefore$ Distance = ?

$$s = \frac{d}{t}$$

$\therefore$ $d = s \times t = 346 \times 2 = 692$ m.

$\therefore$ The lightning struck 692 m away.

Q11. Find the type of motion in the following case :

(*a*) A car travelling along a straight road, changes its speed.
(*b*) An athlete running a 100 m race.
(*c*) Moon revolving around the earth.
(*d*) An ant moving on the floor.

Ans. (*a*) Non-uniform motion (*b*) Uniform motion
(*c*) Uniform circular motion (*d*) Non-uniform motion

Q12. What conclusion do you draw about acceleration of the particle in motion from given velocity-time graphs.

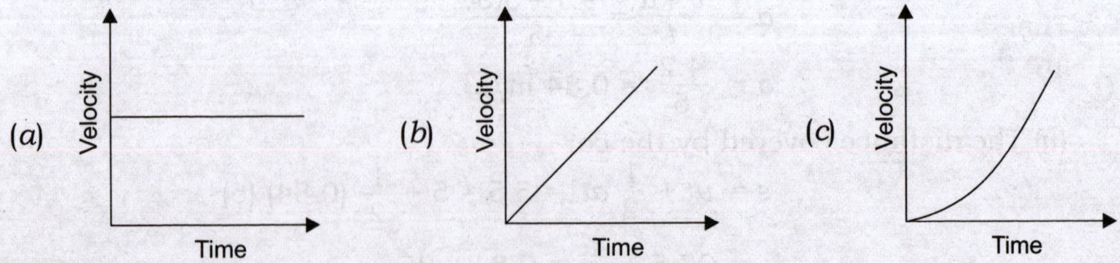

Ans. (*a*) No acceleration
(*b*) Uniform acceleration
(*c*) Non-uniform acceleration

Q13. Derive the equation for velocity-time relation ($v = u + at$) by graphical method.

Ans. Let the initial velocity of a body be $u = OA = CD$.

The final velocity of a body be $v = OE = CB$

Time $t = OC = AD$

AD is parallel to OC

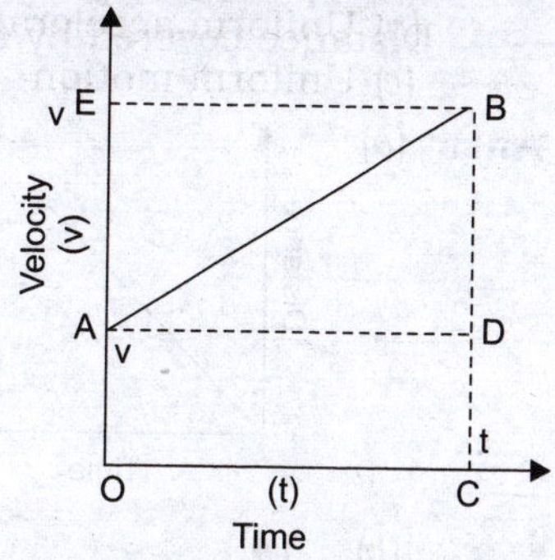

$$BC = BD + DC$$
$$= BD + OA$$
$$\therefore \quad v = BD + u$$
$$\therefore \quad BD = v - u \quad \text{...(1)}$$

In velocity-time graph, slope gives acceleration.

$$\therefore \quad a = \frac{BD}{AD} = \frac{BD}{OC}$$
$$OC = t,$$

we get
$$a = \frac{BD}{t}$$
$$\therefore \quad BD = at \quad \text{...(2)}$$

Substitute (2) in (1) we get.

$$BD = v - u$$
$$at = v - u$$
$$\therefore \quad v = u + at$$

Q14. How can we get speed from distance-time graph?

Ans. Let us assume that an object moves with a uniform speed. The distance-time graph will be a straight line.

Let d_1 be the distance covered in time t_1

Let d_2 be the distance covered in time t_2

$\therefore$ $d_2 - d_1$ will be the distance covered in $t_2 - t_1$

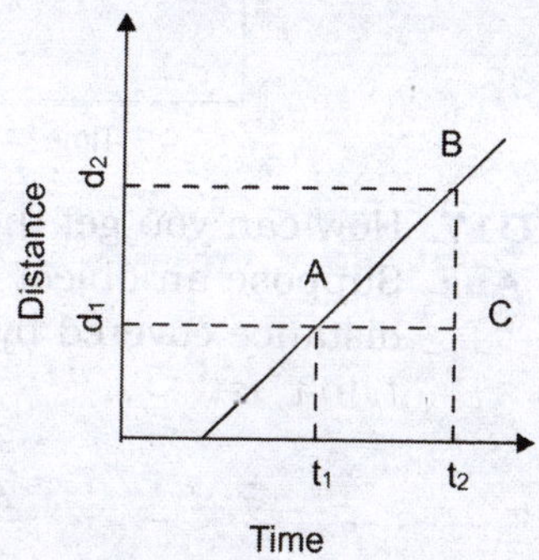

$$\therefore \text{ Speed of the object} = \frac{\text{distance covered}}{\text{time taken}}$$

$$v = \frac{d_2 - d_1}{t_2 - t_1} = \frac{BC}{AC}$$

But here $\dfrac{BC}{AC}$ = slope of the graph

Conclusion:

To find the speed from distance-time graph we can get its slope which is equal to the speed of the object.

Q15. Represent a graph that shows the following:

(*a*) Uniform speed (*b*) Non-uniform speed

(*c*) Stationary object

Ans. Time is taken on x-axis as it is independent quantity and all dependent quantities are taken along y-axis.

(*a*)

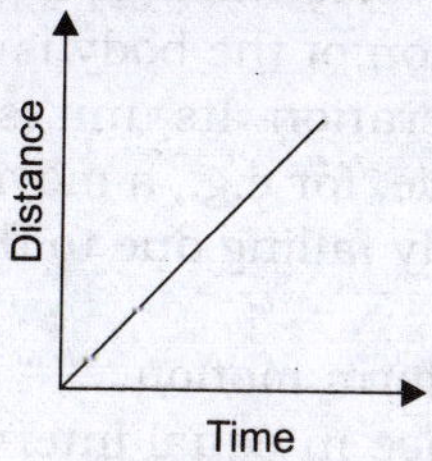

Uniform speed

(*b*)

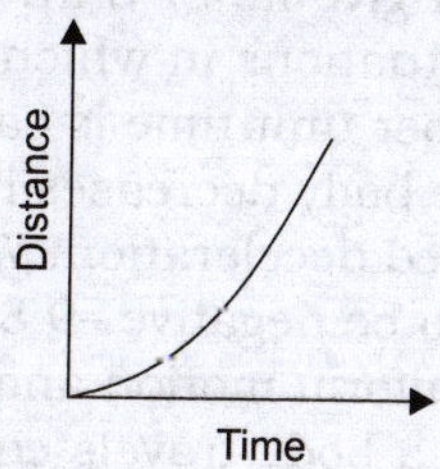

Non-uniform speed

(*c*)

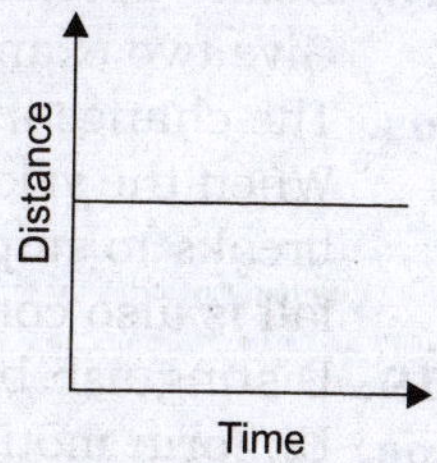

Stationary object

Q16. Draw graph to show the following:

(*a*) Uniform acceleration (*b*) Non-uniform acceleration

(*c*) Uniform motion

Ans. (*a*)

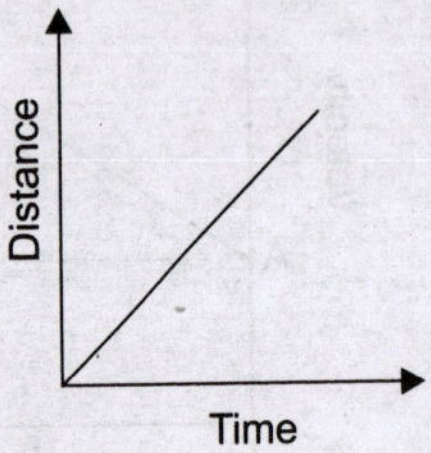

Uniform acceleration—A body travels equal distances in equal intervals of time.

(*b*)

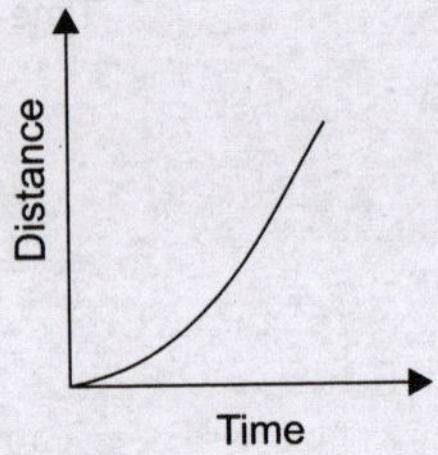

Non-uniform acceleration—A body travels unequal distances in equal intervals of time.

(*c*)

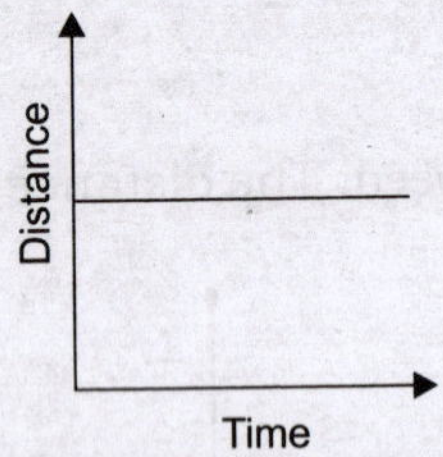

Uniform motion or zero acceleration—A body moves with constant speed in same line.

Q17. How can you get the distance travelled by on object from its speed-time graph?

Ans. Suppose an object is moving with a same speed v, the distance covered by this object when it was at (point A) t_1 to t_2 is:

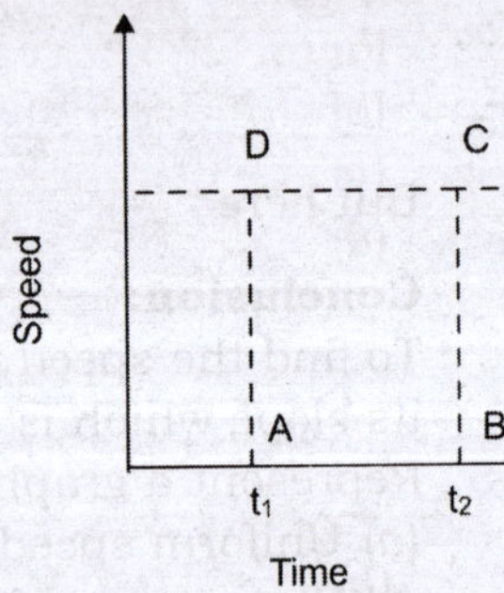

$$AB = t_2 - t_1$$

$$AD = BC = v$$

$$\because \quad v = \frac{\text{distance}}{\text{time}}$$

$$\therefore \quad \text{distance} = v\,(t_2 - t_1)$$

$$= AD \,.\, AB$$

$$\therefore \quad s = \text{area of rectangle } ABCD.$$

∴ To find the distance travelled by a body from its speed-time graph, we need to find the area enclosed by the graph.

Q18. Define acceleration and give its SI unit. When is acceleration of a body negative? Give two examples of situations in which acceleration of the body is negative.

Ans. The change in velocity per unit time is called acceleration. Its unit is m/s^2. When the velocity of the body decreases it is negative, for e.g., a moving car applies breaks to stop, it is called deceleration. When a body falling due to the gravity, free fall is also considered to be negative $-9.8 m/s^2$.

Q19. Distinguish between uniform motion and non- uniform motion.

Ans. Uniform motion: When a body travels equal distance in equal intervals of time, is called uniform motion.

Non-uniform motion: When a body travels unequal distance in equal intervals of time it is called non-uniform motion.

Q20. The below data shows the speedometer readings of a car. Calculate the acceleration of the car.

Time	Speedometer
8:10 am	40 km/h
8:30 am	75 km/h

Ans. Acceleration = $\frac{v-u}{t}$

$$a = \frac{75-40}{0.34} = \frac{35}{0.34}$$

$$= 102.94 \text{ m/s}^2$$

Q21. Velocity-time graph for the motion of an object in a straight path is a straight line parallel to the time axis. Comment on any two analysis from such a graph.

Ans. The nature of the motion is uniform.

The object is not accelerating.

Q22. Draw the shape of the distance-time graph for uniform and non-uniform motion of object.

Ans.

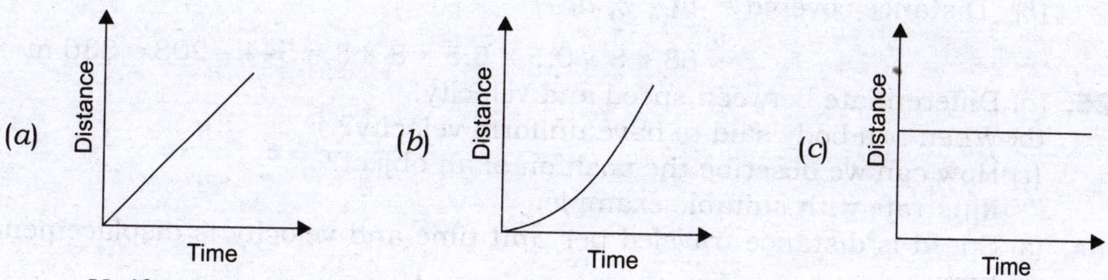

Uniform speed — Non-uniform speed — Stationary object

Q23. A bus of starting from rest moves with uniform acceleration of 0.5 ms^{-2} for 2 minutes. Find

(*a*) the speed acquired.

(*b*) the distance travelled.

Ans. (*a*)

$$a = \frac{v-u}{t}$$

$$0.5 = \frac{v-0}{120s}$$

$$120 \times 0.5 = v$$

$$v = 60 \text{ m/s}$$

(*b*)

$$s = ut + \frac{1}{2}at^2$$

$$s = 0 \times 120 + \frac{1}{2} \times 0.5 \times (120)^2$$

$$= \frac{1}{2} \times 0.5 \times 120 \times 120 = 3600 \text{ m}$$

$$= 3.6 \text{ km}$$

Q24. A car accelerates uniformly from 50 km/h to 85 km/h in 10 seconds. Calculate

(*a*) acceleration in m/s^2.

(*b*) distance covered by the car in metres during the given time of interval.

Ans. (*a*) $a = 85 - 50 = 35 \text{ km/h} = 35 \times \frac{1000}{3600} = 9.73\text{m/s}$

$a = 9.73\text{m/s}$

$50\text{km/h} = 13.89 \text{ m/s}$

$85\text{km/h} = 23.62 \text{ m/s}$

(*b*) There are two ways to find the distance covered by the car in $t = 10$ seconds.

(*i*) $x = \frac{1}{2}(v + u)\text{t} = 0.5\ (23.62 + 13.89)10$

$= 187.6 \text{ m}$

(*ii*) $x = \frac{1}{2}at^2 + ut = 0.5 \times 0.973 \times 100 + 13.89 \times 10$

$= 48.5 + 138.9 = 187.4 \text{ m}$

Q25. A vehicle decelerates from 68 ms^{-1} to 16 ms^{-1} in 8 sec. Calculate

(*a*) the deceleration and

(*b*) the distance covered by the car in that time.

Ans. (*a*) $a = \frac{v-u}{t};$

$= \frac{16-68}{8} = -6.5 \text{ m/s}^2$

(*b*) Distance covered $= ut + \frac{1}{2}at^2$

$= 68 \times 8 - 0.5 \times 6.5 \times 8 \times 8 = 544 - 208 = 336 \text{ m}$

Q26. (*a*) Differentiate between speed and velocity.

(*b*) When is a body said to have uniform velocity?

(*c*) How can we describe the position of an object?

Illustrate with suitable example.

Ans. (a) Speed is distance traveled per unit time and velocity is displacement per unit time.

(*b*) Uniform velocity: when a body travels equal distance in equal intervals of time.

(*c*) The position of an object is described by the displacement shown by an object from its original position. For e.g., a boy travels in a circular track from a start point and reaches the finish point which is the same point. Hence the displacement is zero.

Q27. Define the term displacement. Is it a vector quantity or a scalar quantity?

Ans. The distance moved by a body from its mean position is called displacement. It is a vector quantity.

Q28. What is circular motion? Is circular motion an acceleration motion?

Ans. Uniform circular motion can be described as the motion of an object in a circle at a constant speed. Yes, as an object moves in a circle, it constantly changes its direction.

Q29. A car is travelling with a speed of 90km/h. The driver applied the brakes and retards the car uniformly. The car is stopped in 10sec. Find:

(*a*) The acceleration of car.

(*b*) Distance before it stops after applying breaks.

Ans. Here $u = 90\frac{km}{h} = \frac{90 \times 1000}{60 \times 60}\frac{m}{s} = 25\frac{m}{s}, t = 10 \text{ sec and } v = 0$

(*a*) Acceleration of the car $= \frac{(0-25)\,m/s}{10 \text{ s}} = -2.5 \text{ m/s}^2$

(*b*) $s = ut + \frac{1}{2}at^2 = 25 \times 10 + 0.5 \times 2.5 \times 10 \times 10$

$= 250 - 125 = 125 \text{ m}$

Q30. Give two examples of a situation when the displacement can be zero.

Ans. (a) The displacement can be zero if the start point of the object is same as the end point.

(b) The body reaching the same point after travelling a particular distance. A body in circular motion.

IV. Long Answer Type Questions

Q1. (a) What is motion?

(b) State types of motion.

(c) Derive the unit for acceleration.

Ans. (a) **Motion:** An object is said to be in motion when its position changes with time. We describe the location of an object by specifying a reference point. Motion is relative.

The total path covered by an object is said to be the distance travelled by it.

(b) **There are two types of motion:** Uniform motion and non-uniform motion.

Uniform motion: When an object covers equal distances in equal intervals of time, it is said to be in uniform motion.

Non-uniform motion: Motion where object cover unequal distances in equal intervals of time.

(c) **Acceleration**, 'a' is change in velocity per unit time.

$$a = \frac{v-u}{t} = \frac{\text{m/s}}{\text{s}}$$

$$\therefore \quad a = \text{m/s}^2$$

Q2. (a) What is uniform circular motion?

(b) An athlete runs on a circular track, whose radius is 50 m with a constant speed. It takes 50 seconds to reach point B from starting point A. Find

(i) the distance covered (ii) the displacement

(iii) the speed.

Ans. (a) When a body moves in a circular path with uniform speed, its motion is called uniform circular motion.

(b)
$$\text{Radius} = 50 \text{ m}$$
$$\text{Time} = 50 \text{ s}$$

(i) The distance covered by an athlete A to B *i.e.*, semicircle of the track

$$\therefore \quad \text{circumference} = 2\pi r$$
$$\text{circumference-half} = \pi r$$
$$= \frac{22}{7} \times 50$$
$$\text{distance} = 157.14 \text{ m}$$

(ii) Displacement from $A - B$ is diameter AB

$$d = 2r$$
$$d = 2 \times 50 = 100 \text{ m}$$

(iii)
$$\text{Speed} = ?$$
$$\text{Speed} = \frac{\text{distance}}{\text{time}} = \frac{157.14}{50} = 3.143$$
$$\therefore \quad \text{Speed} = 3.143 \text{ m/s.}$$

V. Activity-Based Questions

1. Discuss whether the walls of your classroom are at rest or in motion.

Ans. The walls of the classroom are at rest.

2. • Have you ever experienced that the train in which you are sitting appears to move while it is at rest?
• Discuss and share your experience.

Ans. The train in which we are sitting appears to move while it is at rest, this we can feel if the vehicles move besides the train.
If one sees any object to be in motion near the train it appears that train is in motion although it is at rest.

3. • Take a metre scale and a long rope.
• Walk from one corner of a basket ball court to its opposite corner along its sides.
• Measure the distance covered by you and magnitude of the displacement.
• What difference would you notice between the two in this case?

Ans. The distance covered by me while walking from one corner of a basketball court to its opposite corner along its sides is more *i.e.,* A to B and B to $C \rightarrow 2x$.
The magnitude of the displacement is from A to C. Which is much less than the distance travelled.

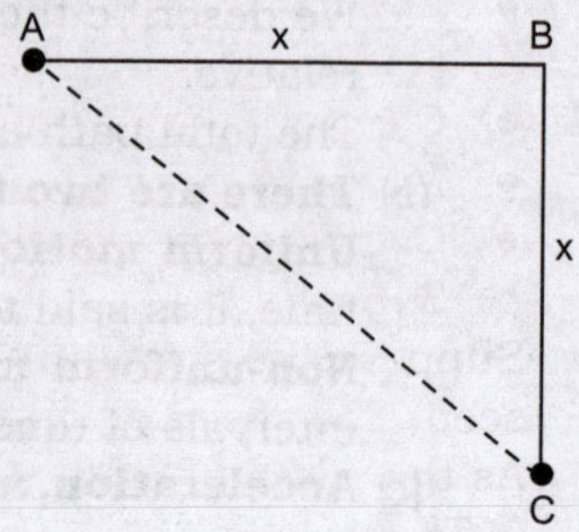

4. • Automobiles are fitted with a device that shows the distance travelled. Such a device is known as an odometer. A car is driven from Bhubaneswar to New Delhi. The difference between the final reading and the initial reading of the odometer is 1850 km.
• Find the magnitude of the displacement between Bhubaneswar and New Delhi by using the road map of India.

Ans. To find the magnitude of displacement there are two ways:
• Find the aerial distance from atlas.
• Measure straight distance between two places and convert the measurement as per scale given in the map.

5. • The data regarding the motion of two different objects A and B are given in table below.
• Examine them carefully and state whether the motion of the objects is uniform or non-uniform.

Time	***Distance travelled by object A in m***	***Distance travelled by object B in m***
9:30 am	10	12
9:45 am	20	19
10:00 am	30	23
10:15 am	40	35
10:30 am	50	37
10:45 am	60	41
11:00 am	70	44

Ans. Object A travels equal distances in equal intervals of time. Hence A is showing uniform motion.
Object B travel unequal distances in equal intervals of time. Hence B is showing non-uniform motion.

6. • Measure the time it takes you to walk from your house to your bus stop or the school. If you consider that your average walking speed is 4 km/h, estimate the distance of the bus stop or school from your house.

Ans. The time it takes to walk from my house to the school is 30 minutes—30 × 60 s

Average walking speed is 4 km/h = $\frac{4 \times 1000}{60 \times 60}$ m/s

$$\text{Distance} = ?$$

$$\therefore \quad \text{Speed} = \frac{\text{Distance}}{\text{Time}}$$

$$\therefore \quad \text{Distance} = \text{Speed} \times \text{Time}$$

$$= \frac{4 \times 1000}{60 \times 60} \times 30 \times 60 = 2 \times 1000 \text{ m} = 2000 \text{ m} = 2 \text{ km}$$

$$\text{Distance} = 2 \text{ km}$$

7. • At a time when it is cloudy, there may be frequent thunder and lightning. The sound of thunder takes some time to reach you after you see the lightning.

- Can you answer why this happens?
- Measure this time interval using a digital wrist watch or a stop watch.
- Calculate the distance of the nearest point of lightning. (Speed of sound in air = 346 m/s.)

Ans. Suppose the sound of thunder took 0.28 second to reach after the lightning was seen. The speed of light is 3×10^8 m/s and the speed of sound in air is 346 m/s. As the speed of light is much more than the speed of sound, it reaches fast.

∴ The distance of the nearest point of lightning is

$$\text{Speed} = \frac{\text{Distance}}{\text{Time}}$$

$$346 \text{ m/s} = \frac{\text{Distance}}{0.28 \text{ s}}$$

$$\therefore \quad \text{Distance} = 346 \times 0.28$$

$$\text{Distance} = 96.88 \text{ m}$$

8. • In your everyday life you come across a range of motions in which

(*a*) acceleration is in the direction of motion,

(*b*) acceleration is against the direction of motion,

(*c*) acceleration is uniform,

(*d*) acceleration is non-uniform.

- Can you identify one example each for the above type of motion?

Ans. (*a*) A car moving on a road.

(*b*) A ball thrown up.

(*c*) Fan blades rotating

(*d*) Wind mill at times moves fast when the wind speed is more and becomes slow when the wind speed decreases.

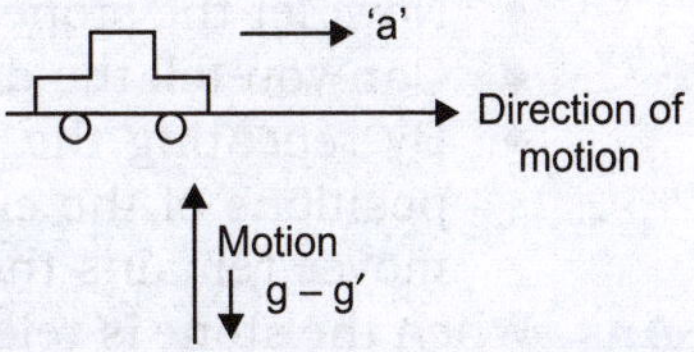

9. • The time of arrival and departure of a train at three stations *A*, *B* and *C* and the distance of stations *B* and *C* from station *A* are given in the table.

Distances of stations B and C from A and times of arrival and departure of the train			
Station	***Distance from A (km)***	***Time of arrival (hours)***	***Time of departure (hours)***
A	0	08:00	08:15
B	120	11:15	11:30
C	180	13:00	13:15

- Plot and interpret the distance-time graph for the train assuming that its motion between any two stations is uniform.

Ans.

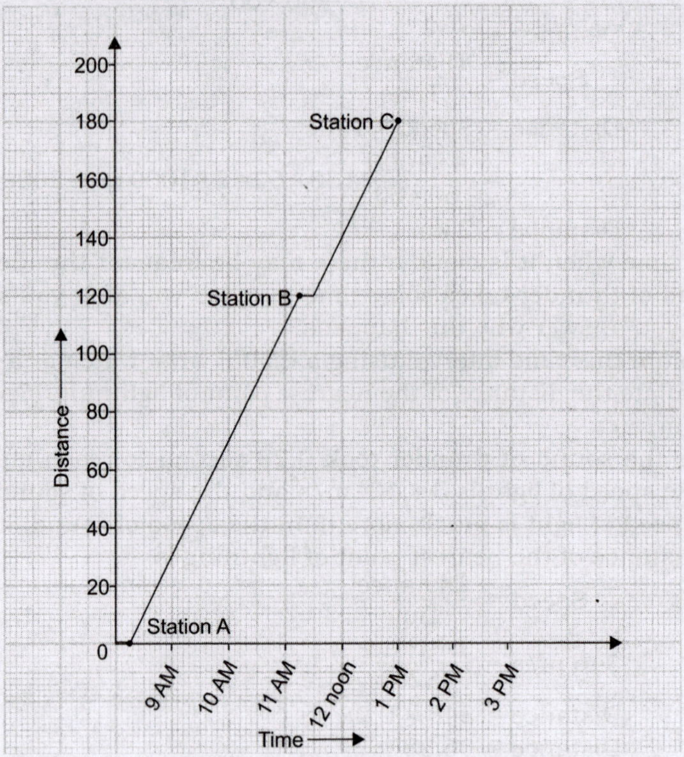

- As the distance time graph of a train between station A and B; and B and C is a straight line, so the train is moving with a uniform speed between the two stations.

10. • Take a piece of thread and tie a small piece of stone at one of its end. Move the stone to describe a circular path with constant speed by holding the thread at the other end as shown in figure.

- Now, let the stone go by releasing the thread.
- Can you tell the direction in which the stone moves after it is released?
- By repeating the activity for a few times and releasing the stone at different positions of the circular path, check whether the direction in which the stone moves remains the same or not.

Ans. When the stone is released. It moves along a straight line, tangential, to the circular path.

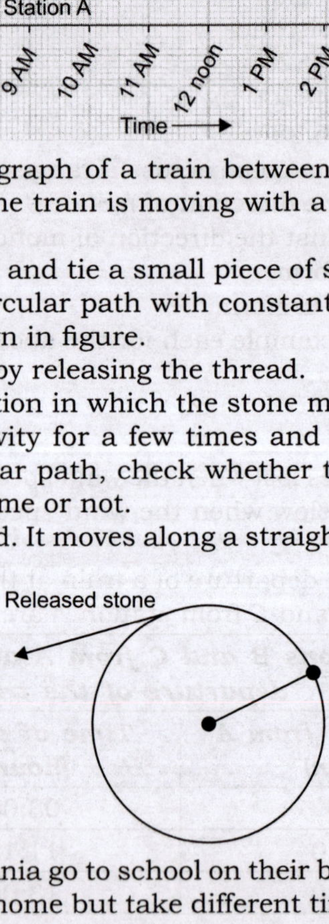

11. • Feroz and his sister Sania go to school on their bicycles. Both of them start at the same time from their home but take different time to reach the school although they follow the same route. The table below shows the distance travelled by them in different time.

Distance covered by Feroz and Sania at different time on their bicycles		
Time	***Distance travelled by Feroz (km)***	***Distance travelled by Sania (km)***
8:00 am	0	0
8:05 am	1.0	0.8
8:10 am	1.9	1.6
8:15 am	2.8	2.3
8:20 am	3.6	3.0
8:25 am	–	3.6

- Plot the distance-time graph for their motions on the same scale and interpret.

Ans.

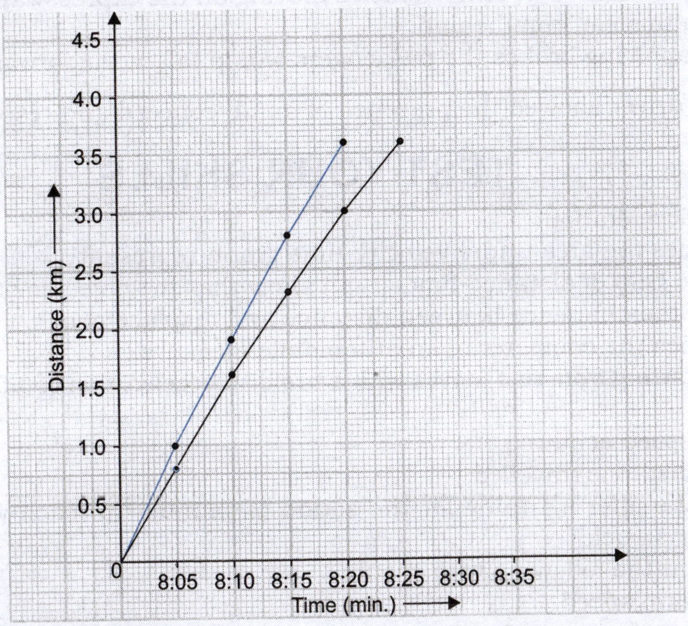

Both Feroz and Sania started at 8 am to travel and reach their school, the distance covered by them is 3.6 km.

Feroz reaches the school at 8:20 am and Sania reaches at 8:25 am.

The graph plotted to their motion on distance-time graph shows that the speed of Feroz is more than that of Sania.

VI. Value-Based Questions

Q1. A water tanker was completely filled with water. Abhishek saw the driver covering the mouth of the tanker with the lid. He immediately stopped the driver from doing so and told him that the tanker while moving can lose balance and overturn/ topple.

(*a*) Why will the tanker overturn if its lid is closed?

(*b*) If the moving tanker with more than half-filled with water, applies sudden brake in which direction will the water fall.

(*c*) What value of Abhishek is seen in the above case?

Ans. (*a*) The moving tanker completely filled with water is in inertia of motion, both water and tanker experiences momentum. On applying sudden brakes the tanker will come to rest but the water will continue to remain in motion and hence the tanker will lose the balance and topple.

(*b*) The water will fall forward.

(*c*) Abhishek showed the value of being intelligent, helpful and caring.

Q2. A car was moving at a speed of 120 km/h on an expressway, suddenly the tyre of the car got punctured and burst. The driver of the car did not apply sudden brakes but he slowed down his vehicle and finally stopped at a road side choosing the appropriate place. All the passengers in the car were shocked but glad with the driver's decision.

(*a*) What would have happened if the driver applied sudden brakes?

(*b*) On applying brakes in which direction would the passengers fall?

(*c*) What value of driver is seen in this act?

Ans. (*a*) If the driver would have applied sudden brakes then all the passengers would get hurt and even other vehicles moving on the expressway would have collided with this car from behind.

(*b*) On applying brakes the passengers would fall in the forward direction.

(*c*) The driver showed the presence of mind, concern and responsible behaviour.

TEST YOUR SKILLS

Q1. Define acceleration.

Q2. What does the area under velocity-time graph represent?

Q3. With the help of distance-time graph show that the object is stationary.

Q4. What is the difference between distance and displacement?

Q5. What does the odometer of an automobile measure?

Q6. A bus starting from rest moves with a uniform acceleration of 0.5 m/s^2 for 4 minutes. Find:

(*a*) the speed acquired.

(*b*) the distance travelled.

Q7. It took 2 s after lightning for the sound of thunder to reach you, how far did the lightning struck?

Q8. Represent the following with graph:

(*a*) Uniform speed

(*b*) Non-uniform speed

Q9. Derive the equation for velocity-time relation by graphical method.

Q10. (*a*) What is motion?

(*b*) State types of motion.

(*c*) Derive the unit of acceleration.

Q11. A car accelerates uniformly from 20 km/h to 35 km/h in 5 s. Calculate

(*a*) the acceleration.

(*b*) the distance covered by the car in that time.

❑❑❑

9 Force and Laws of Motion

Syllabus

Force, Newton's three laws of motion, Inertia, Conservation of momentum.

Facts that Matter

- **Force:** It is a push or pull on an object that produces acceleration in the body on which it acts. S.I. unit of force is Newton.
- A force can do three things on a body.
  (*a*)It can change the speed of a body.
  (*b*)It can change the direction of motion of a body.
  (*c*)It can change the shape and size of a body.
- **Balanced forces:** Forces are said to be balanced forces if they nullify one another and their resultant force is zero.

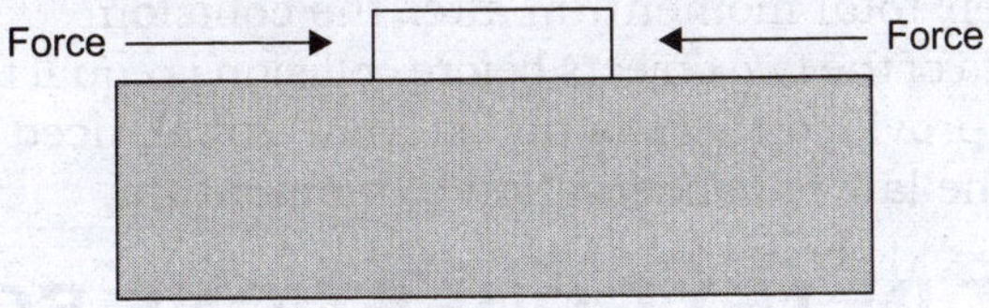

Balanced Force

- **Unbalanced forces:** When two opposite forces acting on a body, move a body in the direction of the greater force or forces which brings motion in a body are called as unbalanced forces.
- **First law of motion:** An object remains in a state of rest or of uniform motion in a straight line unless acted upon by an external unbalanced force.
- **Inertia:** The natural tendency of an object to resist a change in its state of rest or of uniform motion is called inertia.
  The mass of an object is a measure of its inertia.
  Its S.I. unit is kg.
  A body with greater mass has greater inertia.
- **Frictional force:** The force that always opposes the motion of objects is called force of friction.
- **Second law of motion:** The rate of change of momentum of an object is proportional to the applied unbalanced force in the direction of the force.
  Mathematically,

$$F \propto \frac{p_2 - p_1}{t} \text{ or } \frac{m(v-u)}{t} \text{ or } ma$$

$$F = k\,ma \text{ (where } k \text{ is a proportionality constant)}$$

$$F = ma \qquad (\because\ k = 1)$$

- **Momentum:** The momentum of an object is the product of its mass and velocity and has the same direction as that of the velocity. Its S.I. unit is kg m/s.

$$(p = mv)$$

1 Newton: A force of one Newton produces an acceleration of 1 m/s² on an object of mass 1 kg.

$$1\text{N} = 1\,\text{kg m/s}^2$$
$$(F = ma)$$

- **Third law of motion:** To every action, there is an equal and opposite reaction and they act on two different bodies.
- **Conservation of momentum:** If the external force on a system is zero, the momentum of the system remains constant *i.e.,* in an isolated system, the total momentum remains conserved.

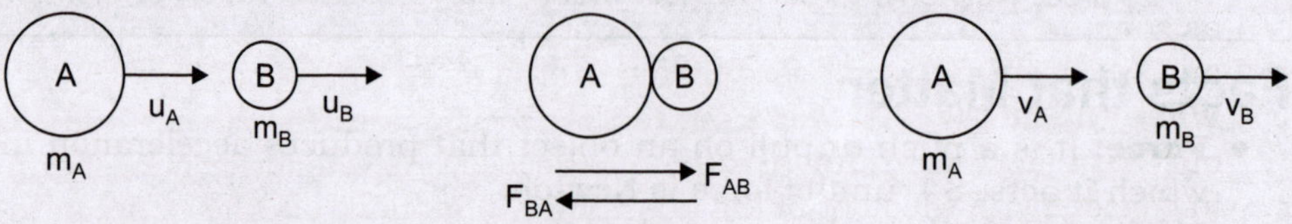

Before collision During collision After collision

Suppose A and B are two balls, they have mass m_A and m_B and initial velocities u_A and u_B as shown in above figure before collision. The two bodies collide and force is exerted by each body. There is change in their velocities due to collision.
$(m_Au_A + m_Bu_B)$ is the total momentum of the two balls A and B before collision and $(m_Av_A + m_Bv_B)$ is their total momentum after the collision.
The sum of momenta of the two objects before collision is equal to the sum of momentum after the collision, provided there is no external unbalanced force acting on them. This is known as the law of conservation of momentum.

NCERT IN-TEXT QUESTIONS SOLVED

Q1. Which of the following has more inertia:
(*a*) a rubber ball and a stone of the same size?
(*b*) a bicycle and a train?
(*c*) a five-rupees coin and a one-rupee coin?

Ans. (*a*) A stone of the same size (*b*) a train (*c*) a five-rupees coin
As the mass of an object is a measure of its inertia, objects with more mass have more inertia.

Q2. In the following example, try to identify the number of times the velocity of the ball changes.
"A football player kicks a football to another player of his team who kicks the football towards the goal. The goalkeeper of the opposite team collects the football and kicks it towards a player of his own team".
Also identify the agent supplying the force in each case.

Ans.

Agent supplying the force	*Change in velocity of ball*
1. First player kicks a football.	→ Velocity from '0' changes to '*u*'
2. Second player kicks the football towards the goal.	→ Velocity changes again
3. The goalkeeper collects the football.	→ Velocity becomes 0
4. Goalkeeper kicks it towards a player of his team.	→ Change in velocity takes place

The velocity of football changed four times.

Q3. Explain why some of the leaves may get detached from a tree if we vigorously shake its branch.

Ans. When the tree's branch is shaken vigorously the branch attain motion but the leaves stay at rest. Due to the inertia of rest, the leaves tend to remain in its position and hence detaches from the tree to fall down.

Q4. Why do you fall in the forward direction when a moving bus apply brakes to stop and fall backwards when it accelerates from rest?

Ans. **When a moving bus applies brakes to stop:** When the bus is moving, our body is also in motion, but due to sudden brakes, the lower part of our body comes to rest as soon as the bus stops. But the upper part of our body continues to be in motion and hence we fall in forward direction due to inertia of motion.

When the bus accelerates from rest we fall backwards: When the bus is stationary our body is at rest but when the bus accelerates, the lower part of our body being in contact with the floor of the bus comes in motion, but the upper part of our body remains at rest due to inertia of rest. Hence we fall in backward direction.

Q5. If action is always equal to the reaction, explain how a horse can pull a cart?

Ans. The third law of motion states that action is always equal to the reaction but they act on two different bodies.

In this case the horse exerts a force on the ground with its feet while walking, the ground exerts an equal and opposite force on the feet of the horse, which enables the horse to move forward and the cart is pulled by the horse.

Q6. Explain, why is it difficult for a fireman to hold a hose, which ejects a large amount of water at a high velocity.

Ans. The water that is ejected out from the hose in the forward direction comes out with a large momentum and equal amount of momentum is developed in the hose in the opposite direction and hence the hose is pushed backward. It becomes difficult for a fireman to hold a hose which experiences this large momentum.

Q7. From a rifle of mass 4 kg, a bullet of mass 50 g is fired with an initial velocity of 35 m/s. Calculate the initial recoil velocity of the rifle.

Ans. (m_1) Mass of rifle = 4 kg

(m_2) Mass of bullet = 50 g = 0.05 kg

(v_2) Velocity of bullet = 35 m/s

(v_1) Recoil velocity of rifle = ?

According to the law of conservation of momentum

Momentum of rifle = momentum of bullet

$$m_1 v_1 = m_2 v_2$$

$$4\,\text{kg} \times v_1 = 0.05 \times 35\ \text{m/s}$$

$$\therefore \quad v_1 = \frac{0.05 \times 35}{4} = \frac{1.75}{4}$$

$$v_1 = 0.4375\ \text{m/s}$$

$\therefore$ Recoil velocity of rifle = 0.4375 m/s

Q8. Two objects of masses 100 g and 200 g are moving along the same line and direction with velocities of 2 m/s and 1 m/s respectively.

They collide and after the collision the first object moves at a velocity of 1.67 m/s. Determine the velocity of the second object.

Ans.

$$m_1 = 100\ \text{g} = 0.1\,\text{kg}$$

$$m_2 = 200\ \text{g} = 0.2\,\text{kg}$$

$$u_1 = 2\,\text{m/s}$$

$$u_2 = 1 \text{ m/s}$$

After collision $v_1 = 1.67 \text{ m/s}$

$$v_2 = ?$$

$$m_1u_1 + m_2u_2 = m_1v_1 + m_2v_2$$

$$(0.1 \times 2) + (0.2 \times 1) = (0.1 \times 1.67) + (0.2 \times v_2)$$

$$\therefore \quad 0.2 + 0.2 = 0.167 + 0.2v_2$$

$$0.4 - 0.167 = 0.2v_2$$

$$\frac{0.4 - 0.167}{0.2} = v_2$$

$$\therefore \quad v_2 = \frac{0.233}{0.2} = 1.165 \text{ m/s}$$

$\therefore$ The velocity of the second object is 1.165 m/s.

NCERT TEXTUAL QUESTIONS SOLVED

Q1. An object experiences a net zero external unbalanced force. Is it possible for the object to be travelling with a non-zero velocity? If yes, state the conditions that must be placed on the magnitude and direction of the velocity. If no, provide a reason.

Ans. When an object experiences a net zero external unbalanced force, in accordance with second law of motion its acceleration is zero. If the object was initially in a state of motion, then in accordance with the first law of motion, the object will continue to move in same direction with same speed. It means that the object may be travelling with a non-zero velocity but the magnitude as well as direction of velocity must remain unchanged or constant throughout.

Q2. When a carpet is beaten with a stick, dust comes out of it. Explain.

Ans. The carpet with dust is in state of rest. When it is beaten with a stick the carpet is set in motion, but the dust particles remain at rest. Due to inertia of rest the dust particles retain their position of rest and falls down due to gravity.

Q3. Why is it advised to tie any luggage kept on the roof of a bus with a rope?

Ans. In moving vehicle like bus, the motion is not uniform, the speed of vehicle varies and it may apply brake suddenly or takes sudden turn. The luggage will resist any change in its state of rest or motion, due to inertia and this luggage has the tendency to fall sideways, forward or backward.

To avoid the fall of the luggage, it is tied with the rope.

Q4. A batsman hits a cricket ball which then rolls on a level ground. After covering a short distance, the ball comes to rest. The ball slows to a stop because

(*a*) the batsman did not hit the ball hard enough.

(*b*) velocity is proportional to the force exerted on the ball.

(*c*) there is a force on the ball opposing the motion.

(*d*) there is no unbalanced force on the ball, so the ball would want to come to rest.

Ans. (*c*) there is a force on the ball opposing the motion.

Q5. A truck starts from rest and rolls down a hill with a constant acceleration. It travels a distance of 400 m in 20 s. Find its acceleration. Find the force acting on it if its mass is 7 tonnes (Hint : 1 tonne = 1000 kg).

Ans. $u = 0 \text{ m/s}$ $\quad m = 7$ tonnes

$s = 400$ m $\quad = 7 \times 1000 \text{ kg} = 7000$ kg

$t = 20$ s

$a = ?$

$$F = ?$$

$$s = ut + \frac{1}{2}at^2$$

$$400 = (0 \times 20) + \frac{1}{2}a\,(20)^2$$

$$\frac{400 \times 2}{(20)^2} = a \qquad \therefore a = 2\,m/s^2$$

Force → $F = ma$

$= 7000 \times 2 = 14000$ N

Q6. A stone of 1kg is thrown with a velocity of 20 ms^{-1} across the frozen surface of a lake and comes to rest after travelling a distance of 50 m. What is the force of friction between the stone and the ice?

Ans.

$m = 1$ kg

$u = 20\,m/s$

$s = 50$ m

$v = 0$

$F = ?$

$a = ?$

$$v^2 - u^2 = 2as$$

$$(0)^2 - (20)^2 = 2a(50)$$

$$\therefore -400 = 100\,a$$

$$\therefore a = \frac{-400}{100} = -4\ m/s^2$$

Force of friction, $F = m \times a$

$= 1\text{ kg} \times -4\ m/s^2$

$= -4$ N

Q7. A 8000 kg engine pulls a train of 5 wagons, each of 2000 kg, along a horizontal track. If the engine exerts a force of 40000 N and the track offers a friction force of 5000 N, then calculate:

(*a*) the net accelerating force; and

(*b*) the acceleration of the train.

Ans. (*a*) The net accelerating force = Force exerted by the engine – friction force

= 40000 N – 5000 N

= 35000 N

(*b*) The acceleration of the train (a) = ?

$F = 35000$ N

Mass of train = Mass of 5 wagons + Engine

$= 5 \times 2000 + 8000$

= 10000 kg + 8000 kg = 18000 kg

$\therefore$ $F = ma$

$35000 = 18000 \times a$

$$\therefore a = \frac{35000}{18000} = 1.94\ m/s^2$$

Q8. An automobile vehicle has a mass of 1500 kg. What must be the force between the vehicle and road if the vehicle is to be stopped with a negative acceleration of 1.7 ms^{-2}?

Ans.

mass = 1500 kg

$a = -1.7\ m/s^2$

$F = ?$

$F = m \times a$

$= 1500 \times (-1.7)$

$= -2550$ N

The force between the vehicle and road is – 2550 N.

Q9. What is the momentum of an object of mass m, moving with a velocity v?

(*a*) $(mv)^2$ (*b*) mv^2 (*c*) $1/2\ mv^2$ (*d*) mv

Ans. (*d*) mv

Q10. Using a horizontal force of 200 N, we intend to move a wooden cabinet across a floor at a constant velocity. What is the friction force that will be exerted on the cabinet?

Ans.

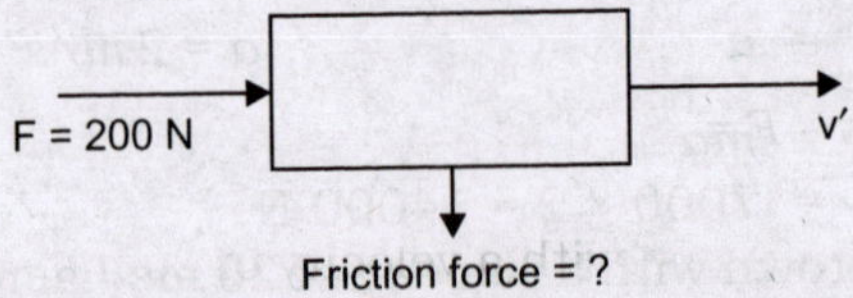

As the wooden cabinet moves across the floor at a constant velocity and the force applied is 200 N. Hence the frictional force that will be exerted on the cabinet will be less than 200 N.

Q11. Two objects each of mass 1.5 kg, are moving in the same straight line but in opposite directions. The velocity of each object is 2.5 ms^{-1} before the collision during which they stick together. What will be the velocity of the combined object after collision?

Ans.

Mass of the objects $m_1 = m_2 = 1.5\,\text{kg}$

Velocity of first object $u_1 = 2.5\ \text{m/s}$

Velocity of second object $u_2 = -2.5\ \text{m/s}$

Momentum before collision $= m_1u_1 + m_2u_2 = (1.5 \times 2.5) + (1.5 \times -2.5) = 0$

Mass after collision $= m_1 + m_2 = 1.5 + 1.5 = 3.0$ kg

After collision $v = ?$

According to law of conservation of momentum

Momentum before collision = Momentum after collision

$0 = 3 \times v$

$\therefore \quad v = 0$ m/s

Q12. According to the third law of motion when we push on an object, the object pushes back on us with an equal and opposite force. If the object is a massive truck parked along the roadside, it will probably not move. A student justifies this by answering that the two opposite and equal forces cancel each other. Comment on this logic and explain why the truck does not move.

Ans. The mass of truck is too large and hence its inertia is too high. The small force exerted on the truck cannot move it and the truck remains at rest. For the truck to attain motion, an external large amount of unbalanced force need to be exerted on it.

Q13. A hockey ball of mass 200 g travelling at 10 ms^{-1} is struck by a hockey stick so as to return it along its original path with a velocity at 5 ms^{-1}. Calculate the magnitude of change of momentum occurred in the motion of the hockey ball by the force applied by the hockey stick.

Ans.

Mass of ball m = 200 g = 0.2 kg

Initial speed of ball u = 10 m/s

Final speed of ball v = – 5 m/s

Initial momentum of the ball = mu = 0.2 kg × 10 m/s = 2 kg m/s

Final momentum of the ball = mv

= 0.2 kg × (– 5 m/s)

= – 1 kg m/s

Hence, change in momentum = Difference in the momentum = – 1 – 2 = – 3 kg m/s

Q14. A bullet of mass 10 g travelling horizontally with a velocity of 150 ms^{-1} strikes a stationary wooden block and comes to rest in 0.03 s. Calculate the distance of penetration of the bullet into the block. Also calculate the magnitude of the force exerted by the wooden block on the bullet.

Ans. $m = 10 \text{ g} = \frac{10}{1000} = 0.01 \text{ kg}$

$u = 150 \text{ m/s}$

$v = 0 \text{ m/s}$

$t = 0.03 \text{ s}$

$v = u + at$

$0 = 150 + a(0.03)$

$a = \frac{-150}{0.03} = -5000 \text{ m/s}^2$

$s = ?$

$F = ?$

$v^2 - u^2 = 2as$

$\therefore \quad (0)^2 - (150)^2 = 2 \times 5000 \times s$

$\therefore \quad s = \frac{150 \times 150}{2 \times 5000} = \frac{22500}{10000}$

$s = 2.25 \text{ m}.$

$\therefore$ The penetration distance of the bullet in the wooden block = 2.25 m.

Magnitude of force $F = ma = 0.01 \times (-5000)$

$F = -50 \text{ N}.$

Q15. An object of mass 1 kg travelling in a straight line with a velocity of 10 ms^{-1} collides with, and sticks to, a stationary wooden block of mass 5 kg. Then they both move off together in the same straight line. Calculate the total momentum just before the impact and just after the impact. Also, calculate the velocity of the combined object.

Ans. $m_1 = 1 \text{ kg}$

$v_1 = 10 \text{ m/s}$

Mass of wooden block = 5 kg

$m_2 = 5 \text{ kg} + 1 \text{ kg (combined object)} = 6 \text{ kg}$

Velocity of combined object = $v_2 = ?$

p_1 and p_2 = ?

Momentum before impact $p_1 = m_1 v_1$

$= 1 \times 10 = 10 \text{ kg m/s}$

$\therefore$ Momentum before impact = Momentum after impact

$m_1 v_1 = m_2 v_2$

$10 \text{ kg m/s} = 6\, v_2$

$\therefore \quad \frac{10}{6} = v_2$

$\therefore \quad v_2 = 1.67 \text{ m/s}$

Q16. An object of mass 100 kg is accelerated uniformly from a velocity of 5 ms^{-1} to 8 ms^{-1} in 6 s. Calculate the initial and final momentum of the object. Also, find the magnitude of the force exerted on the object.

Ans. $m = 100 \text{ kg}$

$u = 5 \text{ m/s}$

$v = 8 \text{ m/s}$

$t = 6 \text{ s}$

$p_1 = ?$

$p_2 = ?$

$$F = ?$$

$\therefore$ Initial momentum $p_1 = mu$

$= 100 \times 5 = 500 \text{ kg m/s}$

Final momentum $p_2 = mv$

$= 100 \times 8 = 800 \text{ kg m/s}$

Force exerted on the object $F = ma = 100\left(\frac{v-u}{t}\right) = 100\left(\frac{8-5}{6}\right) = 100 \times \frac{3}{6}$

$F = 50 \text{ N}$

Q17. Akhtar, Kiran and Rahul were riding in a motorcar that was moving with a high velocity on an expressway when an insect hit the windshield and got stuck on the windscreen. Akhtar and Kiran started pondering over the situation. Kiran suggested that the insect suffered a greater change in momentum as compared to the change in momentum of the motorcar (because the change in the velocity of insect was much more than that of the motorcar). Akhtar said that since the motorcar was moving with a larger velocity, it exerted a larger force on the insect. And as a result the insect died. Rahul while putting an entirely new explanation said that both the motorcar and the insect experienced the same force and a change in their momentum. Comment on these suggestions.

Ans. Rahul gave the correct reasoning and explanation that both the motorcar and the insect experienced the same force and a change in their momentum. As per the law of conservation of momentum

When two bodies collide:

Initial momentum before collision = Final momentum after collision

$$m_1u_1 + m_2u_2 = m_1v_1 + m_2v_2$$

The equal force is exerted on both the bodies but, because the mass of insect is very small it will suffer greater change in velocity.

Q18. How much momentum will a dumb-bell of mass 10 kg transfer to the floor if it falls from a height of 80 cm? Take its downward acceleration to be 10 ms^{-2}.

Ans. Mass of dumb-bell = 10 kg

Height, $h = 80 \text{ cm} = 0.8 \text{ m}$

$g = 10 \text{ m/s}^2$

$u = 0$

$v^2 - u^2 = 2gh$

$v^2 - (0)^2 = 2 \times 10 \times 0.8$

$v^2 = 16$

$\therefore$ $v = 4 \text{ m/s}$

Momentum $p = mv = 10 \times 4 = 40 \text{ kg m/s}$

ADDITIONAL EXERCISE

Q1. The following is the distance-time table on an object in motion:

Time in seconds	*Distance in metres*
0	0
1	1
2	8
3	27
4	64
5	125
6	216
7	343

(a) What conclusion can you draw about the acceleration? Is it constant, increasing, decreasing, or zero?

(b) What do you infer about the forces acting on the object?

Ans. (a) As per given table initial speed of the object is zero. Applying the relation

$$s = ut + \frac{1}{2}at^2 \quad or \quad s = \frac{1}{2}at^2 \text{ (because } u = 0)$$

We have $a = \frac{2s}{t^2}$

$\therefore$ For 1st second $a_1 = \frac{2s_1}{t_1^2} = \frac{2 \times 1}{1^2} = 2 \text{ ms}^{-2}$

For first 2 second $a_2 = \frac{2s_2}{t_2^2} = \frac{2 \times 8}{2^2} = 4 \text{ ms}^{-2}$

For first 3 seconds $a_3 = \frac{2s_3}{t_3^2} = \frac{2 \times 27}{3^2} = 6 \text{ ms}^{-2}$

and so on.

Thus it is clear that the acceleration is increasing with time.

(b) According to the Newton's 2nd law of motion, force F is directly proportional to acceleration. Therefore, the forces acting on the object are increasing with time, since acceleration is increasing with time.

Q2. Two persons manage to push a motorcar of mass 1200 kg at a uniform velocity along a level road. The same motorcar can be pushed by three persons to produce an acceleration of 0.2 ms^{-2}. With what force does each person push the motorcar? (Assume that all persons push the motorcar with the same muscular effort.)

Ans. Let each person applies a force F on a motorcar of mass, $m = 1200$ kg.

When two persons push the car, they just manage to move it at a uniform velocity. It means that their combined force $2F$ is just balanced by force of friction due to road and car moves with a uniform velocity.

When three persons push the car, they apply a total force $3F$ on the car.

Now net unbalanced force on the car = force applied by three persons – frictional force

$$= 3F - 2F = F$$

As now acceleration $a = 0.2 \text{ ms}^{-2}$, hence

$$F = ma = 1200 \times 0.2 = 240 \text{ N}$$

Hence each person pushes the car with a force of 240 N.

Q3. A hammer of mass 500 g, moving at 50 ms^{-1}, strikes a nail. The nail stops the hammer in a very short time of 0.01 s. What is the force of the nail on the hammer?

Ans. Mass of hammer m = 500 g = 0.5 kg

Initial velocity of hammer u = 50 ms^{-1}

Final velocity of hammer v = 0 and time t = 0.01 s

$\therefore$ Acceleration of the hammer, $a = \frac{v-u}{t} = \frac{0-50}{0.01} = -5000 \text{ ms}^{-2}$

$\therefore$ Force applied by the hammer on nail

$$F = ma = (0.5) \times (-5000) = -2500 \text{ N}$$

$-ve$ sign of force suggests that the force is opposing the motion of hammer.

$\therefore$ Force applied by the nail on hammer = 2500 N

Q4. A motorcar of mass 1200 kg is moving along a straight line with a uniform velocity of 90 km/h. Its velocity is slowed down to 18 km/h in 4 s by an unbalanced external force. Calculate the acceleration and change in momentum. Also calculate the magnitude of the force required.

Ans. Here mass of motor car $m = 1200\,\text{kg}$

Initial velocity of car, $u = 90\,\text{km/h} = 90 \times \frac{5}{18}\,\text{ms}^{-1} = 25\,\text{ms}^{-1}$

Final velocity of car, $v = 18\,\text{kmh}^{-1} = 18 \times \frac{5}{18} = 5\,\text{ms}^{-1}$

and time $t = 4\text{s}$

Acceleration $a = \frac{v-u}{t} = \frac{5-25}{4} = -5\,\text{ms}^{-2}$

Change in momentum of car

$$mv - mu = m(v-u)$$
$$= 1200(5-25) = -24000\ \text{kg ms}^{-1}$$

Magnitude of force $F = ma = 1200 \times (-5) = -6000\,\text{N}$

$-ve$ sign of acceleration, charge in momentum and force suggests that the force is opposing the motion of motor car.

Q5. A large truck and a car, both moving with a velocity of magnitude v, have a head-on collision and both of them come to a halt after that. If the collision lasts for 1 s:

(*a*) Which vehicle experiences the greater force of impact?

(*b*) Which vehicle experiences the greater change in momentum?

(*c*) Which vehicle experiences the greater acceleration?

(*d*) Why is the car likely to suffer more damage than the truck?

Ans. (*a*) During head on collision forces applied by truck and car are action-reaction forces. Hence both vehicles experience same (equal) force of impact.

(*b*) Here initial velocity of both car and truck is same equal to v and final velocity of both is zero. But mass of truck is much more than that of car, hence change in momentum of truck is more than change in momentum of car.

(*c*) For same force of impact, the acceleration of car will have greater magnitude because its mass is less.

(*d*) Car suffers more damage than the truck, as acceleration of car is more, its velocity falls to zero in a shorter time and consequently, its momentum changes in a shorter time.

ADDITIONAL QUESTIONS SOLVED

I. Multiple Choice Questions

Choose the correct option:

1. The S.I. unit of force is

(*a*) kg m/s (*b*) g m/s^2 (*c*) Newton (*d*) Newton-meter

2. The product of mass and velocity gives a physical quantity

(*a*) force (*b*) inertia (*c*) momentum (*d*) Newton

3. The rate of change of momentum of an object is proportional to

(*a*) mass of the body (*b*) velocity of the body

(*c*) net force applied on the body (*d*) none of these

4. If two balls of different masses are dropped on sand, the depths of penetration is same if:

(*a*) heavier ball is dropped faster than lighter ball

(*b*) lighter ball is dropped faster than heavier ball

(*c*) the product 'mv' is same for both bodies

(*d*) none of these

5. The coin remains at rest in the figure shown. This is due to

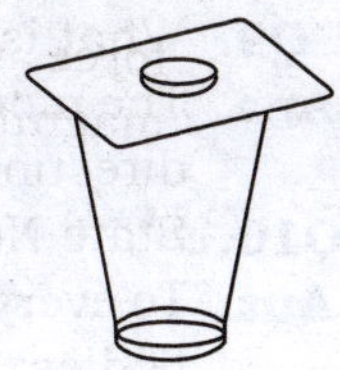

(*a*) inertia of rest
(*b*) two forces act on the coin which balance each other
(*c*) no unbalanced force acts on it
(*d*) all of these

6. A force of 50 N moves a body.
(*a*) Frictional force exerted on the body is less than 50 N
(*b*) Frictional force exerted on the body is more than 50 N
(*c*) None of these
(*d*) Both (*a*) and (*b*)

7. Fielder giving a swing while catching a ball is an example of
(*a*) inertia (*b*) momentum
(*c*) Newton's II law of motion (*d*) Newton's I law of motion

8. Action and reaction forces
(*a*) acts on same body (*b*) act on different bodies
(*c*) act in same direction (*d*) both (*a*) and (*c*)

9. When we stop pedaling the bicycle it stops because
(*a*) the earths gravitational force acts on it
(*b*) it is not accelerated
(*c*) no unbalanced force acts on it
(*d*) frictional force acts on it

10. A football and a stone has same mass
(*a*) both have same inertia (*b*) both have same momentum
(*c*) both have different inertia (*d*) both have different momentum

Ans. 1—(*c*), 2—(*c*), 3—(*c*), 4—(*c*), 5—(*d*), 6—(*a*), 7—(*c*), 8—(*b*), 9—(*d*), 10—(*a*).

II. Very Short Answer Type Questions

Q1. Define force.
Ans. It is a push or pull on an object that produces acceleration in the body on which it acts.

Q2. What is S.I. unit of force?
Ans. S.I. unit of force is Newton.

Q3. Define one Newton.
Ans. A force of one Newton produces an acceleration of 1 m/s^2 on an object of mass 1 kg.

$$1 \text{ N} = 1 \text{ kg m/s}^2$$

Q4. What is balanced force?
Ans. When forces acting on a body from the opposite direction do not change the state of rest or of motion of an object, such forces are called balanced forces.

Q5. What is frictional force?
Ans. The force that always opposes the motion of an object is called force of friction.

Q6. What is inertia?
Ans. The natural tendency of an object to resist a change in their state of rest or of uniform motion is called inertia.

Q7. State Newton's first law of motion.
Ans. An object remains in a state of rest or of uniform motion in a straight line unless acted upon by an external unbalanced force.

Q8. State Newton's second law of motion.
Ans. The rate of change of momentum of an object is proportional to the applied unbalanced force in the direction of the force.

Q9. What is momentum?

Ans. The momentum of an object is the product of its mass and velocity and has the same direction as that of the velocity. The S.I. unit is kg m/s. ($p = mv$)

Q10. State Newton's III law of motion.

Ans. To every action, there is an equal and opposite reaction and they act on two different bodies.

Q11. Which will have more inertia a body of mass 10 kg or a body of mass 20 kg?

Ans. A body of mass 20 kg will have more inertia.

Q12. Name the factor on which the inertia of the body depends.

Ans. Inertia of a body depends upon the mass of the body.

Q13. Name two factors which determine the momentum of a body.

Ans. Two factors on which momentum of a body depend is mass and velocity. Momentum is directly proportional to the mass and velocity of the body.

Q14. What decides the rate of change of momentum of an object?

Ans. The rate of change of momentum of an object is proportional to the applied unbalanced force in the direction of force.

Q15. The diagram shows a moving truck. Forces A, B, C and D are acting on the truck. Name the type of forces acting on a truck.

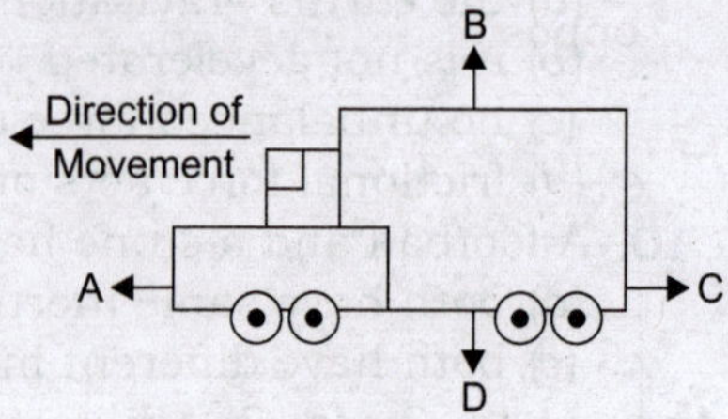

Ans. The forces A, B, C and D acting on the truck are:

A ⟶ driving force

B ⟶ reacting force

C ⟶ frictional force

D ⟶ weight/gravitational force

Q16. A 68 kg runner exerts a force of 59 N. What is the acceleration of the runner?

Ans. $m = 68$ kg, F = 59N, a = ?

$$F = ma,$$
$$59 = 68a$$
$$\Rightarrow \quad a = \frac{59}{68} = 0.87 \text{ m/s}^2$$

Q17. A trolley is dragged across an ice covered lake. The box accelerates at 0.08 m/s^2 and is pulled by a 47 N force. What is the mass of the box?

Ans. $a = 0.08$ m/s^2, F = 47N, m = ?

$$F = ma,$$
$$47 = m(0.08)$$
$$\Rightarrow \quad m = \frac{47}{0.08} = 587.5 \text{ kg}$$

Q18. A tennis ball, 0.314 kg, is accelerated at a rate of 164 m/s^2 when hit by a professional tennis player. What force does the player's tennis racket exert on the ball?

Ans. $m = 0.314$ kg, $a = 164$ m/s^2, F = ?

$$F = ma = (0.314)(164) = 51.50 \text{ N}$$

Q19. A coolie exerts a force of 628 N on a luggage trolley. Later, the mass of the trolley is increased by a factor of 3.8. If the coolie exerts the same force, how does the new acceleration compare to the old one?

Ans.

$$a = \frac{F}{m}$$
$$\Rightarrow \quad a = 628\text{N}/3.8$$
$$= 165.26 \text{ N}$$

Q20. What is the mass of a runner whose weight is 648 N?

Ans. $g = 9.80 \text{ m/s}^2$, W = 648N,

$$W = mg \quad \Rightarrow m = \frac{W}{g} \quad \Rightarrow \quad m = \frac{648}{9.8}$$

$$m = 66.12 \text{ kg}$$

Q21. When you jump, the Earth is pushed away from you. Use a formula to explain why this movement of the Earth isn't noticed.

Ans. $a = \frac{F}{m}$ the Earth has lot of mass that its acceleration is tiny.

Q22. Compare the force on a cricket ball by a bat with the force exerted by the ball on the bat.

Ans. The force has the same magnitude but opposite direction.

Q23. A cart is being moved by a certain net force. If more force is applied on the cart, doubling its mass, state by how much the acceleration changes.

Ans. It will be half.

Q24. A hammer is hitting a nail. Compare the force on the nail; with the force on the hammer.

Ans. The forces acting on nail and on hammer are equal in magnitude (strength) but opposite in direction.

III. Short Answer Type Questions

Q1. State the difference in balanced and unbalanced force.

Ans.

Balanced force	***Unbalanced force***
1. Forces acting on a body from the opposite directions are same.	1. Forces acting on a body from two opposite directions are not same.
2. It does not change the state of rest or of motion of an object.	2. It do change the state of rest or of motion of an object.

Q2. What change will force bring in a body?

Ans. Force can bring following changes in the body:

(*i*) It can change the speed of a body.

(*ii*) It can change the direction of motion of a body.

(*iii*) It can change the shape of the body.

Q3. When a motorcar makes a sharp turn at a high speed, we tend to get thrown to one side. Explain why?

Ans. It is due to law of inertia. When we are sitting in car moving in straight line, we tend to continue in our straight-line motion. But when an unbalanced force is applied by the engine to change the direction of motion of the motorcar. We slip to one side of the seat due to the inertia of our body.

Q4. Explain why it is dangerous to jump out of a moving bus.

Ans. While moving in a bus our body is in motion. On jumping out of a moving bus our feet touches the ground and come to rest. While the upper part of our body stays in motion and moves forward due to inertia of motion and hence we can fall in forward direction.

Hence, to avoid this we need to run forward in the direction of bus.

Q5. Why do fielders pull their hand gradually with the moving ball while holding a catch?

Ans. While catching a fast moving cricket ball, a fielder on the ground gradually pulls his hands backwards with the moving ball. This is done so that the fielder increases the time during which the high velocity of the moving ball decreases to zero. Thus, the acceleration of the ball is decreased and therefore the impact of catching the fast moving ball is reduced.

Q6. In a high jump athletic event, why are athletes made to fall either on a cushioned bed or on a sand bed?

Ans. In a high jump athletic event, athletes are made to fall either on a cushioned bed or on a sand bed so as to increase the time of the athlete's fall to stop after making the jump. This decreases the rate of change of momentum and hence the force.

Q7. How does a karate player breaks a slab of ice with a single blow?

Ans. A karate player applies the blow with large velocity in a very short interval of time on the ice slab which therefore exerts large amount of force on it and suddenly breaks the ice slab.

Q8. What is law of conservation of momentum?

Ans. Momentum of two bodies before collision is equal to the momentum after collision. In an isolated system, the total momentum remain conserved.

Q9. Why are roads on mountains inclined inwards at turns?

Ans. A vehicle moving on mountains is in the inertia of motion. At a sudden turn there is a tendency of vehicle to fall off the road due to sudden change in the line of motion hence the roads are inclined inwards so that the vehicle does not fall down the mountain.

Q10. For an athletic races why do athletes have a special posture with their right foot resting on a solid supporter?

Ans. Athletes have to run the heats and they rest their foot on a solid supports before start so that during the start of the race the athlete pushes the support with lot of force and this support gives him equal and opposite push to start the race and get a good start to compete for the race.

Q11. Why do you think it is necessary to fasten your seat belts while travelling in your vehicle?

Or

How are safety belts helpful in preventing any accidents?

Ans. While we are travelling in a moving car, our body remains in the state of rest with respect to the seat. But when driver applies sudden breaks or stops the car our body tends to continue in the same state of motion because of its inertia. Therefore, this sudden break may cause injury to us by impact or collision. Hence, safety belt exerts a force on our body to make the forward motion slower.

Q12. Explain how momentum gets conserved in collision of two bodies.

Ans. Consider two bodies *i.e.*, balls *A* and *B*, the mass and initial velocities are $m_A u_A$ and $m_B u_B$ respectively before collision. The two bodies collide and force is exerted by each body. There is change in their velocities due to collision.

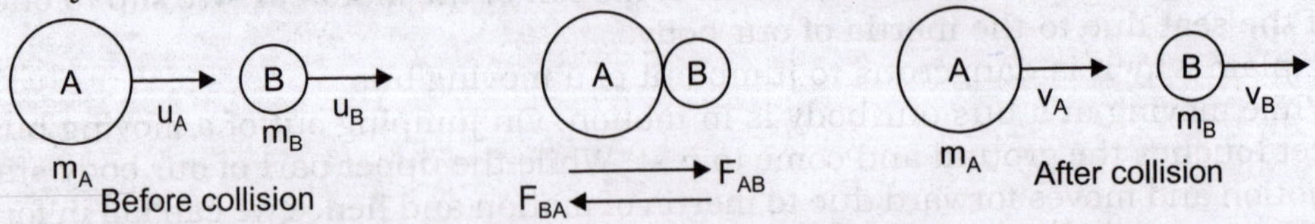

The momentum of ball *A* before collision is $m_A u_A$ and final momentum is $m_A v_A$.

The rate of change of momentum, during the collision for 'A' will be $m_A \frac{(v_A - u_A)}{t}$.

Initial momentum of B is $m_B u_B$ and final momentum is $m_B v_B$.

Rate of change of momentum of B will be $m_B \frac{(v_B - u_B)}{t}$.

According to the third law of motion, the force F_{AB} exerted by ball *A* on ball *B* and the force F_{BA} exerted by the ball *B* on ball *A* must be equal and opposite to each other.

Therefore

$$F_{AB} = F_{BA}$$

or $$m_A \frac{(v_A - u_A)}{t} = m_B \frac{(v_B - u_B)}{t}$$

$\therefore$ $$m_A u_A + m_B u_B = m_A v_A + m_B v_B$$

$\therefore$ $(m_A u_A + m_B u_B)$ is the total momentum of the two balls A and B before collision and $(m_A v_A + m_B v_B)$ is their total momentum after collision.

$\therefore$ The total momentum of the two balls remains unchanged or conserved provided no other external force acts.

Q13. When you kick a football it flies away but when you kick a stone you get hurt why?

Ans. This is because stone is heavier than football and heavier objects offer larger inertia. When we kick a football its mass is less and inertia is also less so force applied by our kick acts on it and hence it shows larger displacement but in case of stone, it has larger mass and offers larger inertia. When we kick (action) the stone it exerts an equal and opposite force (reaction) and hence it hurts the foot.

Q14. If a person jumps from a height on a concrete surface he gets hurt. Explain.

Ans. When a person jumps from a height he is in state of inertia of motion. When he suddenly touches the ground he comes to rest in a very short time and hence the force exerted by the hard concrete surface on his body is very high, and the person gets hurt.

Q15. What is the relation between Newton's three laws of motion?

Ans. Newton's first law explains about the unbalanced force required to bring change in the position of the body.

Second law states/explains about the amount of force required to produce a given acceleration.

And Newton's third law explains how these forces acting on a body are interrelated.

Q16. Give any three examples in daily life which are based on Newton's third law of motion.

Ans. Three examples based on Newton's third law are :

1. **Swimming:** We push the water backward to move forward.
   action – water is pushed behind
   reaction – water pushes the swimmer ahead
2. **Firing gun:** A bullet fired from a gun and the gun recoils.
   action – gun exerts force on the bullet
   reaction – bullet exerts an equal and opposite force on the gun
3. **Launching of rocket**
   action – hot gases from the rocket are released
   reaction – the gases exert upward push to the rocket

Q17. *A bullet of mass 20 g is horizontally fired with a velocity 150 m/s from a pistol of mass 2 kg. What is the recoil velocity of the pistol?*

Ans.

Bullet	**Pistol**
m_1 mass = 20 g = 0.02 kg	$m_2 = 2\,kg$
$u_1 = 0$	$u_2 = 0$
$v_1 = +150\,m/s$	$v_2 = ?$

Total momentum of the pistol and bullet before firing, when the gun is at rest

$$= m_1 u_1 + m_2 u_2$$
$$= (0.02 \times 0) + (2 \times 0)$$
$$= 0\,kg\,m/s$$

Total momentum of the pistol and bullet after it is fired

$$= m_1 v_1 + m_2 v_2$$
$$= (0.02\,kg \times 150) + (2\,kg \times v) = 3 + 2v$$

$\therefore$ Total momentum after firing = Total momentum before firing

$$3 + 2v = 0$$

$$\therefore \quad v = \frac{-3}{2} = -1.5 \text{ m/s}$$

Negative sign indicates that the direction in which the pistol would recoil is opposite to that of bullet.

Q18.

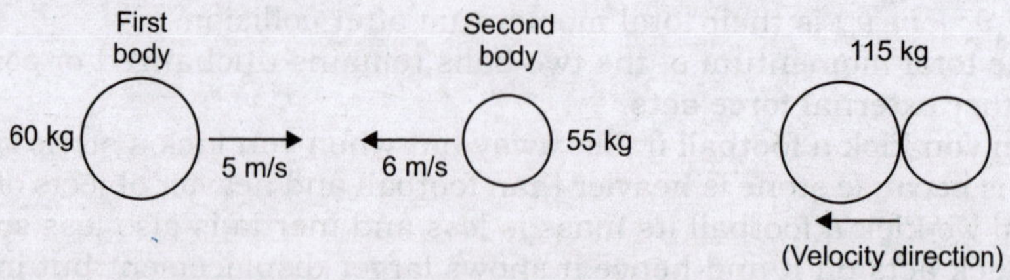

Two bodies as shown in the figure collide with each other and join thereafter. With what velocity will they move after combining together?

Ans. $m_1 = 60$ kg $\quad m_2 = 55$ kg

$u_1 = +5$ m/s positive direction $\quad u_2 = -6$ m/s negative direction

$v = ?$

Total momentum of two bodies before collision

$$= m_1u_1 + m_2u_2$$
$$= 60 \times 5 + 55 \times (-6)$$
$$= -30 \text{ kg m/s}$$

If v is the velocity of two joined bodies. After collision, the total momentum will be

$$= m_1v_1 + m_2v_2 \quad (\because v_1 = v_2)$$
$$= (m_1 + m_2)\, v$$
$$= (60 + 55) \text{ kg} \times v \text{ m/s} = 115\, v$$

$\therefore$ According to law of conservation of momentum

$$m_1u_1 + m_2u_2 = m_1v_1 + m_2v_2$$
$$-30 \text{ kg m/s} = 115\, v$$
$$\therefore \quad v = \frac{-30}{115} = -0.26 \text{ m/s}$$

$\therefore$ Two bodies will move with velocity 0.26 m/s in the direction of the second body.

Q19. The surface gravity of the Sun is 274 m/s². How many Earth's g is this?

Ans.

$$g = 9.80 \text{ m/s}^2,$$
$$g_{Sun} = 274 \text{ m/s}^2,$$
$$274/9.8 = 27.96 \text{ times of Earth gravity}$$

Q20. A parked car is pushed with a force of 342 N from rest. How far does the car travel in 12 seconds? Its mass is 989 kg. How far does the car travel now if the pushing force is doubled?

Ans. F = 342N, $v_o = 0$, $x = ?$, $t = 12$s, $m = 989$ kg,

$$F = ma$$
$$342 = 989a,$$
$$a = 0.3458 \text{ m/s}^2,$$
$$x = (v_o)t + \frac{1}{2}at^2 = 0 + \frac{1}{2}(0.3458)(12)^2 = 24.90 \text{ m}$$

If the pushing force is doubled then the acceleration is doubled. Because the relationship between x and a is linear, if the acceleration is doubled then the distance is also doubled. Therefore, the car will travel 49.80 m.

Q21. A 1027 kg truck is resting at a stop light. The truck moves with a force of 1528 N for 22 s. Then the truck travels at a constant velocity for 10 seconds. Finally, the truck stops with a force of 4056 N. Calculate the distance travelled by truck during this journey.

Ans. m = 1027 kg, F = 1528 N

$F = m \times a \Rightarrow 1528 = 1027 \times a \Rightarrow a = 1.487 \text{ m/s}^2$

$v = u + at = 0 + 1.487 \times 22$ $[\because u = 0, t = 22s]$

$= 32.73$ m/s

Now, $v^2 = u^2 + 2as \Rightarrow 1071.58 = 0 + 2 \times 1.49 \times s$

$\Rightarrow s = 360.318$ m

Distance travelled in 10 sec.

Distance = Speed × time = 32.73 × 10 = 378.30 m

Again $F = m \times a \Rightarrow 4056 = 1027 \times a \Rightarrow a = 3.95 \text{ m/s}^2$

Now $v^2 = u^2 - 2as \Rightarrow (0)^2 = 1071.39 - 7.9\ s$

$\Rightarrow s = 135.62$ m

Total distance = 360.32 m + 378.30 m + 135.62 = 874.22 m.

Q22. Skydivers experience terminal speed.

(*a*) State what terminal speed is and how it occurs.

(*b*) Explain the effect opening a parachute has on the skydiver's terminal speed

Ans. (*a*) The speed at which a falling object's weight is cancelled by air resistance is called terminal speed.

(*b*) Air friction increases with speed. Once the force of friction equals weight, the net force on the skydiver is zero.

Q23. Two students are standing on the roller skates and pulling on a rope:

(*a*) The student on the left is pulling with 432 N. State how much force the student on the right is pulling with.

(*b*) The student on the left and his boat have a total mass of 103 kg, and the friction of the land is 98.1 N. Calculate the acceleration of the student on the left.

Ans. (*a*) 432 N.

(*b*) Net force on the student is 432 – 98.1 = 333.9N

$$u = \frac{F}{m} = \frac{333.9}{103} = 3.24 \text{ ms}^{2} \text{ to the right}$$

Q24. A big luggage bag was thrown from an aircraft on the ground.

(*a*) State the magnitude of the acceleration of the bag as soon as it is dropped.

(*b*) After falling for some time, the bags acceleration is zero, but it is still falling. Explain, using net forces, how and why this happened.

Ans. (*a*) 9.8 ms^{-2}.

(*b*) Air resistance increases with speed. Eventually the air resistance equals weight, so the net force is zero (hence acceleration is zero).

Q25. If a bird feather and a feather made of metal are dropped on earth, the bird feather takes much longer to reach the ground. Explain why the bird feather falls slower than the feather made of metal.

Ans. The metal feather has more inertia, so the force of air resistance has less effect. The metal feather has more weight, so its net force is greater.

Q26. (*a*) Explain how much force is required to stop an object with the force then to start it moving.

(*b*) State the effect friction would have on these forces.

Ans. (*a*) It is the same. The inertia of an object is the same no matter what its speed is.

(*b*) Friction makes it easier to slow things down as it is a force which opposes motion.

Q27. If a trolley is initially at rest it takes a lot of force to get it moving and then a much smaller consistent force to keep it moving at constant speed.

(*a*) If the force of friction acting on a moving trolley is 15.42 N, state the force required to maintain a constant velocity.

(*b*) State the net force on the trolley at constant velocity.

(*c*) If the trolley is accelerated to a faster speed and then maintain its motion at that speed. Explain the effect this would have on the force required to maintain constant speed.

Ans. (*a*) 15.42 N (*b*) 0 N

(*c*) Greater, since the trolley is moving faster and friction is proportional to speed.

Q28. In a frictionless environment/vacuum, two objects with different masses will experience different forces due to gravity but the same acceleration. Explain.

Ans. The force due to gravity (weight) is proportional to mass (W = *mg*), so heavier objects have more force due to gravity. The acceleration is inversely proportional to mass $a = F/m$, so heavier objects need more force to experience the same acceleration (they have more inertia).

Q29. If you are in a plane travelling at 600 km/h and a hand bag falls from an overhead compartment:

(*a*) Explain why the hand bag doesn't go towards the back of the plane.

(*b*) State the hand bags horizontal speed relative to the ground.

(*c*) State the hand bags horizontal speed relative to you.

Ans. (*a*) No force is acting on it which would change its speed, so it continues at the speed of the plane.

(*b*) 600 km/h. (*c*) 0 km/h.

Q30. When you are weighing yourself standing next to the table. If you push yourself down on the table , the scales read less, and if you pull the table, the scales read more. Explain, using Newton's third law.

Ans. When you push down on the table, the table pushes you upward. This tends to lift you off the scales and decrease the reading on the scale. If you pull the table , it will push you downwards and increase the reading.

Q31. If somebody weighs 500N on Earth, calculate how much the same person weighs on Planet X, where the acceleration of gravity is $26 ms^{-2}$.

Ans. The person's mass is 500 ÷ 9.8 = 51 kg,

So his weight on Planet X is 51 × 26 = 1326 N.

IV. Long Answer Type Questions

Q1. Explain Newton's second law of motion and with the help of an example show how it is used in sports.

Ans. **Newton's second law of motion:** The rate of change of momentum of an object is proportional to the applied unbalanced force in the direction of the force.

Let us assume :

Object of mass *m*, is moving along a straight line with an initial velocity '*u*', It is uniformly accelerated to velocity *v* in time '*t*' by the application of force, *F* throughout the time '*t*'.

Initial momentum of the object = $P_1 = mu$

Final momentum of the object = $P_2 = mv$

The change in momentum $\propto P_2 - P_1$

$\propto mv - mu = m(v - u)$

The rate of change of momentum $\propto \dfrac{m(v-u)}{t}$

$$\therefore \quad \text{Applied force } F \propto \frac{m(v-u)}{t}$$

$$F = \frac{km(v-u)}{t}$$

$$\therefore \quad F = kma \qquad \because a = \frac{v-u}{t}$$

k = constant of proportionality

F = kg m/s^2 = Newton

Use of second law of motion in sports:

In **cricket field**, the fielder gradually pulls his hands backward while catching a ball. The fielder catches the ball and gives swing to his hand to increase the time during which the high velocity of the moving ball decreases to zero.

The acceleration of the ball is decreased and therefore the impact of catching the fast moving ball is reduced.

If not done so, then the fast moving ball will exert large force and may hurt the fielder.

Q2. State all 3 Newton's law of motion. Explain inertia and momentum.

Ans. Newton's I law of motion: An object remains in a state of rest or of uniform motion in a straight line unless acted upon by an external unbalanced force.

Newton's II law of motion: The rate of change of momentum of an object is proportional to the applied unbalanced force in the direction of the force.

Newton's III law of motion: To every action, there is an equal and opposite reaction and they act on two different bodies.

Inertia: The natural tendency of an object to resist a change in their state of rest or of uniform motion is called inertia.

Momentum: The momentum of an object is the product of its mass and velocity and has the same direction as that of the velocity. Its S.I. unit is kg m/s.

$$p = m \times v$$

Q3. Define force. Give its unit and define it. What are different types of forces?

Ans. Force: It is a push or pull on an object that produces acceleration in the body on which it acts.

A force can do 3 things on a body

(*a*) It can change the speed of a body.

(*b*) It can change the direction of motion of a body.

(*c*) It can change the shape of the body.

The S.I. unit of force is Newton.

Newton: A force of one Newton produces an acceleration of 1 m/s^2 on an object of mass 1 kg.

$$1\text{N} = 1\,\text{kg m/s}^2$$

$$\text{Force} = \text{mass} \times \text{acceleration}$$

Types of forces:

(*i*) *Balanced force:* When the forces acting on a body from the opposite direction do not change the state of rest or of motion of an object, such forces are called balanced forces.

(*ii*) *Unbalanced force:* When two opposite forces acting on a body move a body in the dirction of the greater force or change the state of rest, such forces are called as unbalanced force.

(*iii*) *Frictional force:* The force that always opposes the motion of object is called force of friction.

Q4. What is inertia? Explain different types of inertia. Give three examples in daily life which shows inertia.

Ans. Inertia: The natural tendency of an object to resist change in their state of rest or of motion is called inertia.

The mass of an object is a measure of its inertia. Its S.I. unit is kg.

Types of inertia:

Inertia of rest: The object at rest will continue to remain at rest unless acted upon by an external unbalanced force.

Inertia of motion: The object in the state of uniform motion will continue to remain in motion with same speed and direction unless it is acted upon by an external unbalanced force.

Three examples of inertia in daily life are:

(*i*) When we are travelling in a vehicle and sudden brakes are applied we tend to fall forward.

(*ii*) When we shake the branch of a tree vigorously, leaves fall down.

(*iii*) If we want to remove the dust from carpet we beat the carpet so that dust fall down.

Q5. Consider the two forces acting on a person standing on the ground; the downward pull of gravity and the upward push of the ground.

(*a*) Explain whether the forces are equal and opposite.

(*b*) Explain whether the forces are an action-reaction pair.

Ans. (*a*) They are equal and opposite but the forces are not acting on two different bodies, the forces in question are on the same body.

(*b*) There are two action-reaction pairs which combine to make the effect – gravity provides the Earth-person attraction and the normal perpendicular force provides the Earth-person repulsion it is equal and opposite to prevent the person sinking into the Earth.

V. Activity-Based Questions

1.
- Set a five-rupees coin on a stiff card covering an empty glass tumbler standing on a table as shown in the figure.
- Give the card a sharp horizontal flick with a finger. If we do it fast then the card shoots away, allowing the coin to fall vertically into the glass tumbler due to its inertia.
- The inertia of the coin tries to maintain its state of rest even when the card flows off.

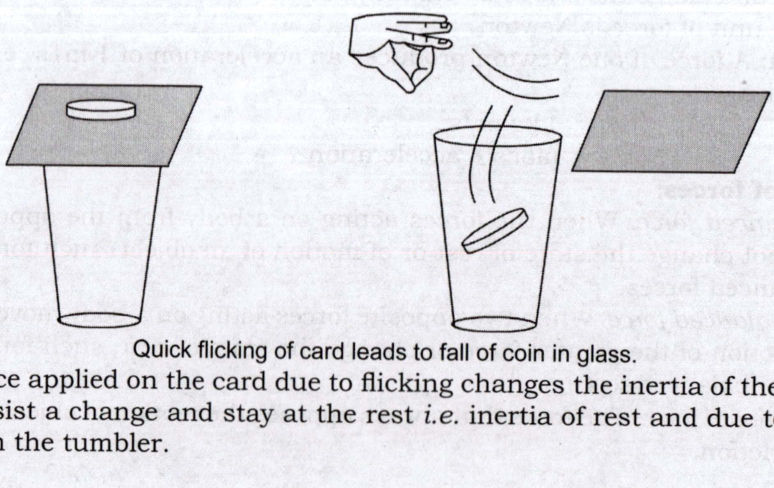

Quick flicking of card leads to fall of coin in glass.

Ans. The force applied on the card due to flicking changes the inertia of the card but the coin resist a change and stay at the rest *i.e.* inertia of rest and due to gravity falls down in the tumbler.

2. • Make a pile of similar carom coins on a table, as shown in the figure.
• Attempt a sharp horizontal hit at the bottom of the pile using another carom coin or striker. If the hit is strong enough the bottom coin moves out quickly. Once the lowest coin is removed, the inertia of the other coins makes them 'fall' vertically on the table.

Ans. **Inertia:** It is the tendency of a body to maintain its state of rest or of motion.

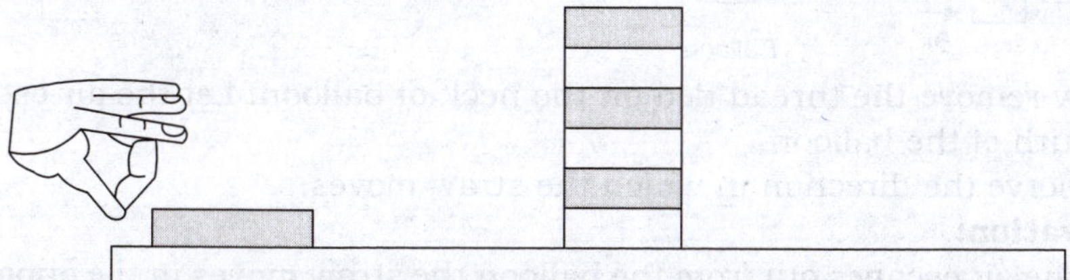

3. • Place a water-filled tumbler on a tray.
• Hold the tray and turn around as fast as you can.
• We observe that the water spills. Why?

Ans. The water-filled in tumbler and tray are at rest. On moving/turning around the tray at faster speed the water spills because the tray and the tumbler comes into motion while the water in the tumbler remain at inertia of rest.

4. • Request two children to stand on two separate carts as shown on the next page.
• Give them a bag full of sand or some other heavy object. Ask them to play a game of catch with the bag.
• Does each of them experience an instantaneous force as a result of throwing the sand bag?
• You can paint a white line on cartwheels to observe the motion of the two carts when the children throw the bag towards each other.

Ans. Yes, in this case each of them receives an instantaneous reaction as a result of throwing the sand bag.
This activity explain Newton's III law of motion *i.e.*, the force is exerted forward in throwing the bag full of sand and the person who is throwing it gets pushed backward.

Action and reaction taking place simultaneously on two different bodies

5. • Take a big rubber balloon and inflate it fully. Tie its neck using a thread. Also using adhesive tape, fix a straw on the surface of this balloon.
• Pass a thread through the straw and hold one end of the thread in your hand or fix it on the wall.
• Ask your friend to hold the other end of the thread or fix it on a wall at some distance. The arrangement is shown in the figure below.

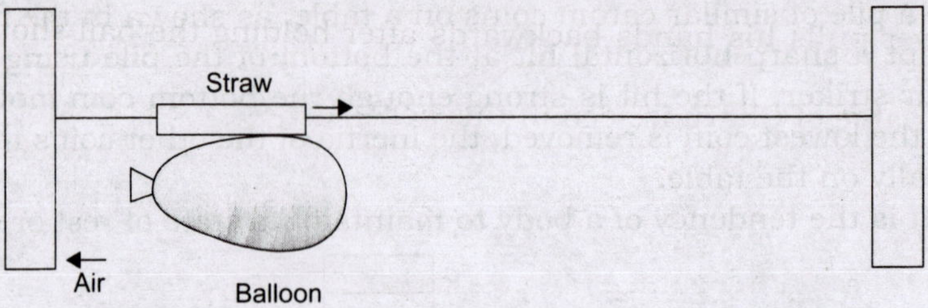

- Now remove the thread tied on the neck of balloon. Let the air escape from the mouth of the balloon.
- Observe the direction in which the straw moves.

Observation:

When the air escapes out from the balloon the straw moves in the opposite direction of the air moved out of the balloon.

This activity explains the law of conservation of momentum and Newton's III law of motion.

Initial momentum = Final momentum

6. - Take a test tube of good quality glass material and put a small amount of water in it. Place a stop cork at the mouth of it.
   - Now suspend the test tube horizontally by two strings or wires as shown in the figure on next page.
   - Heat the test tube with a burner until water vaporises and the cork blows out.
   - Observe that the test tube recoils in the direction opposite to the direction of the cork.

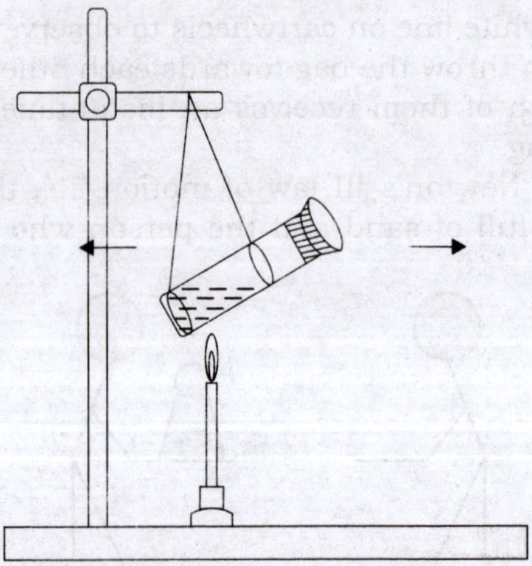

Observation:

The cork is pushed out in forward direction by the hot steam. The test tube is pushed in the backward direction.

It explain Newton's III law of motion and conservation of momentum.

VI. Value-Based Questions

Q1. Class V students were playing cricket with the cork ball in the school campus. Charu a senior student told them about the accidents that can occur due to cork ball in the campus and also advised them to bring soft cosco ball to play the game.

(*a*) Why it was safe to play with soft ball and not with hard cork ball?

(*b*) A player pulls his hands backwards after holding the ball shot at high speed. Why?

(*c*) What value of Charu is seen in this act?

Ans. (*a*) The soft ball will have less inertia as compared to the heavy ball and it would not hurt the players.

(*b*) By pulling the hand backwards it reduces the force exerted by the ball on hands.

(*c*) Charu showed the value of being responsible and helpful by nature.

Q2. Saksham saw his karate expert friend breaking a slate. He tried to break the slate but Saksham's friend stopped him from doing so and told him that it would hurt, one needs lot of practice in doing so.

(*a*) How can a karate expert break the slate without any injury to his hand?

(*b*) What is Newton's third law of motion?

(*c*) What value of Saksham's friend is seen in the above case?

Ans. (*a*) A karate player applies the blow with large velocity in a very short interval of time on the slate, therefore large force is exerted on the slate and it breaks.

(*b*) To every action there is an equal and opposite reaction, both act on different bodies.

(*c*) Saksham's friend showed the value of being responsible and caring friend.

TEST YOUR SKILLS

Q1. Define one Newton.

Q2. What is inertia?

Q3. What is momentum?

Q4. What is balanced force?

Q5. Give one application of Newton's III law of motion.

Q6. Why are roads on mountains inclined inwards at turns?

Q7. What change will a force bring in a body?

Q8. Why do you think it is necessary to fasten your seat belts while travelling in your vehicle?

Q9. From a rifle of mass 4 kg, a bullet of mass 50 g is fired with an initial velocity of 35 m/s. Calculate the initial rccoil velocity of the rifle.

Q10. A stone of 1 kg is thrown with a velocity of 20 m/s across the frozen surface of a lake and comes to rest after travelling a distance of 50 m. What is the force of friction between the stone and the ice?

Q11. Explain Newton's second law of motion and with the help of example show how it is used in sports.

❑❑❑

10 Gravitation

Syllabus

Gravitation, Universal law of gravitation, Force of gravitation of the earth (gravity), Acceleration due to gravity, Mass and weight, Free fall, Thrust and pressure. Archimedes' principle, buoyancy, elementary idea of relative density.

Facts that Matter

- **Universal law of gravitation:** Every object in the universe attracts every other object with a force which is proportional to the product of their masses and inversely proportional to the square of the distance between them.
  The force is along the line joining the centres of two objects.

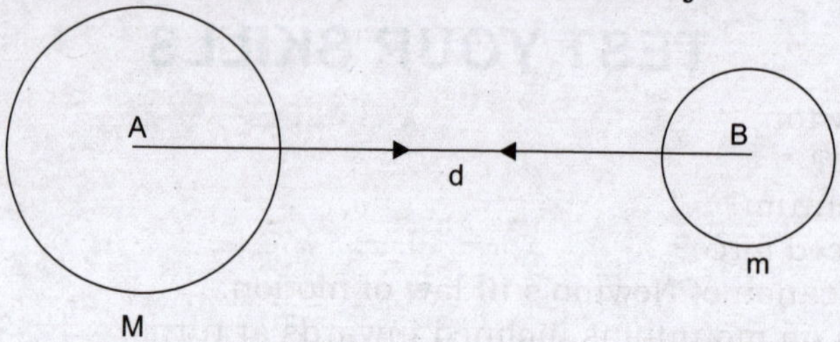

Gravitational force between two uniform objects is directed along the line joining their centres.

Let two objects A and B of masses M and m lie at a distance of d from each other as shown in the figure.
Let F be the force of attraction between two objects. According to the universal law of gravitation

$$F \propto \frac{Mm}{d^2}$$

$$F = G\frac{Mm}{d^2} \quad \because \quad G = \text{universal gravitational constant}$$

$$G = \frac{Fd^2}{Mm}$$

- G is called a universal constant because its value does not depend on the nature of intervening medium or temperature or any other physical variable.

  S.I. unit of $G = \text{Nm}^2/\text{kg}^2$

  Value of $G = 6.673 \times 10^{-11}\ \text{Nm}^2/\text{kg}^2$

  (Found by Henry Cavendish)

- **Importance of universal law of gravitation**
  Universal law of gravitation successfully explained several phenomena like :
  (*i*)the force that binds us to the earth.
  (*ii*)the motion of moon around the earth.
  (*iii*)the motion of planets around the Sun.
  (*iv*)the tides due to the moon and the Sun.

- **Free fall**

When an object falls down towards the earth under the gravitational force alone, we say the object is in free fall.

The velocity of a freely falling body changes and is said to be accelerated.

This acceleration is called acceleration due to gravity, denoted by 'g'. Unit is m/s^2.

As $F = ma \quad (\because a = g) \quad \ldots(i)$

$F = mg \quad \ldots(ii)$

and $F = G\dfrac{Mm}{d^2}$ (from Universal law of gravitation) $\ldots(iii)$

From (*ii*) and (*iii*)

$$\therefore \quad mg = G\frac{Mm}{d^2}$$

$$\therefore \quad g = \frac{GM}{d^2}$$

M = Mass of the earth

d = Distance between the object and the earth

G = Gravitational constant

If the object is placed on the earth then $d = R$

(R = radius of the earth)

$$\therefore \quad g = \frac{GM}{R^2} \quad \text{i.e. } g \propto \frac{1}{R^2} \quad \ldots(iv)$$

Earth is not a sphere, it is flattened at poles.

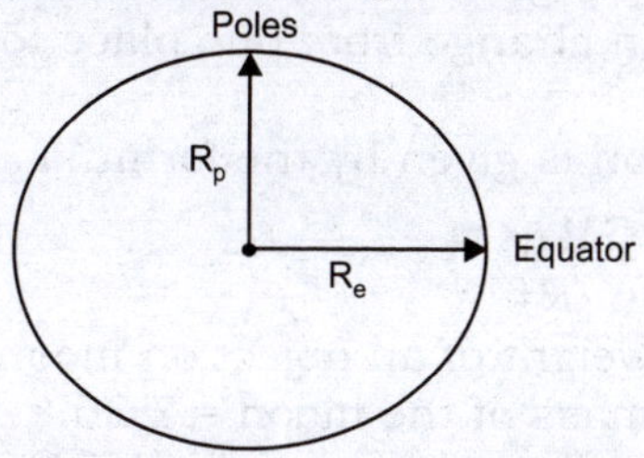

Hence R_p – Radius at pole and R_e – Radius at equator

$$R_e > R_p$$

$$g \propto \frac{1}{R^2} \quad \text{[Using (iv)]}$$

∴ The value of 'g' is more at poles = (9.9 m/s^2)

and less at equator = (9.8 m/s^2)

Calculation of value of *g*

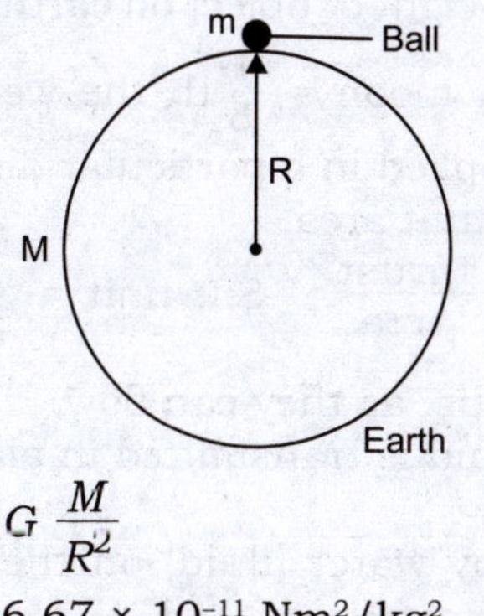

$$g = G\frac{M}{R^2}$$

$$G = 6.67 \times 10^{-11} \text{ Nm}^2/\text{kg}^2$$

$M = 6 \times 10^{24}$ kg (Mass of the earth)

$R = 6.4 \times 10^{6}$ m

On substituting the given values

$$g = \frac{6.67 \times 10^{-11} \text{Nm}^2 \text{kg}^{-2} \times 6 \times 10^{24} \text{kg}}{(6.4 \times 10^6 \text{m})^2}$$

$g = 9.8$ m/s^2.

Motion of objects under the influence of gravity 'g' does not depend on the mass of the body. All objects small, big, heavy, light, hollow or solid fall at same rate.

- The three equations of motion viz.

  (*i*) $v = u + at$ (*ii*) $s = ut + \frac{1}{2}at^2$ (*iii*) $v^2 - u^2 = 2as$ are true for motion of objects under gravity. For free fall, value of acceleration $a = g = 9.8$ ms^{-2}.
- If an object is just let fall from a height then in that case $u = 0$ and $a = g = 9.8$ m/s^2.
- If an object is projected vertically upward with an initial velocity u, then $a = -g = -9.8$ ms^{-2} and the object will go to a maximum height h where its final velocity becomes zero (*i.e.*, $v = 0$).
- **Mass:** Mass of an object is the measure of its **inertia.** It is the matter present in it. It remains the same everywhere in the universe.
- **Weight:** The force of attraction of the earth on the object is known as the weight of the object. Its S.I. unit is Newton.

  $W = m \times g$

  The weight of an object can change from one place to the other, from one planet to the other.

  Weight of an object on moon is given by the formula

  $$W_m = \frac{GM_m \times m}{R_m^2}$$

  W_m = weight of an object on moon

  M_m = mass of the moon = 7.36×10^{22}

  R_m = radius of the moon = 1.74×10^{6}

  $G = 6.67 \times 10^{-11}$ Nm^2/kg^2

  $$\therefore \quad W_m = G\frac{7.36 \times 10^{22} \text{kg} \times \text{m}}{(1.74 \times 10^6 \text{m})^2}$$

  $W_m = 2.431 \times 10^{10}$ G × m

  and $W_e = 1.474 \times 10^{11}$ G × m

  $$\therefore \quad \frac{W_m}{W_e} = \frac{\text{Weight of object on moon}}{\text{Weight of object on earth}} = \frac{2.431 \times 10^{10} Gm}{1.474 \times 10^{11} Gm} = \frac{1}{6}.$$

  $\therefore$ Weight of an object on moon = $\frac{1}{6}$th the weight of an object on the earth.
- **Thrust:** It is the net force applied in a particular direction. Its S.I. unit is N.
- **Pressure:** It is the force per unit area.

  $$\text{Pressure} = \frac{\text{thrust}}{\text{area}}, \quad \text{S.I. unit} = \frac{N}{m^2} = \text{Pascal (Pa)}$$
- **Pressure in fluids**

  All liquids and gases are fluids, as they can flow.

  The pressure exerted by a fluid is transmitted in all direction.
- **Buoyancy**

  The upward force exerted by water (fluid) on the body is known as upthrust or buoyancy.

The magnitude of the buoyant force depends on the density of the fluid.

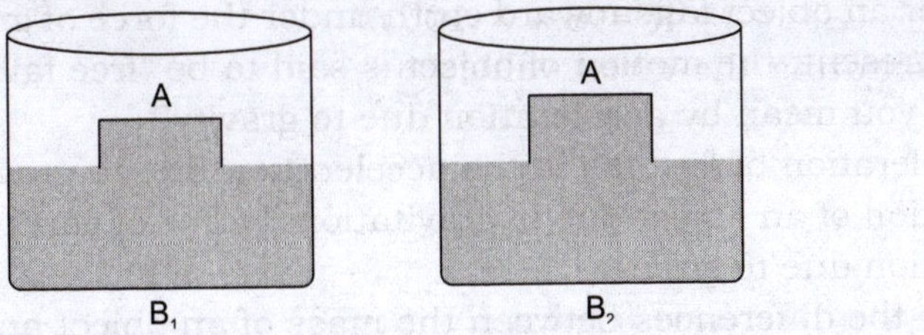

A – Wooden block
B_1 – Beaker with tap water
B_2 – Beaker with salty water

The buoyant force exerted in B_2 is more as compared to B_1. It is because the density of B_2 water is more.

The object may float, sink or remain half submerged and half above water, the density of the fluid and object decides this.

- If the density of object is **less** than the fluid, then it will **float** on the liquid.
- If the density of object is **more** than the fluid, then it will **sink** in the liquid.
- If the density of object is **same** as the density of fluid, then it will **half float** and **half sink**.

- **Archimedes' principle:** When a body is immersed fully or partially in a fluid, it experiences an upward force that is equal to the weight of the fluid displaced by it.
- **Its applications are:**

  (*i*) Used in designing ships and submarines,
  (*ii*) In lactometers to find purity of milk.
  (*iii*) In hydrometer to determine density of liquid.

$$\textbf{Relative density} = \frac{\text{density of a substance}}{\text{density of water}}$$

It has no unit.

NCERT IN-TEXT QUESTIONS SOLVED

Q1. State the universal law of gravitation.

Ans. Every object in the universe attracts every other object with a force which is proportional to the product of their masses and inversely proportional to the square of the distance between them. The force is along the line joining the centres of two objects

$$F \propto \frac{Mm}{d^2} \text{ or } F = \frac{GMm}{d^2}$$

Q2. Write the formula to find the magnitude of the gravitational force between the earth and an object on the surface of the earth.

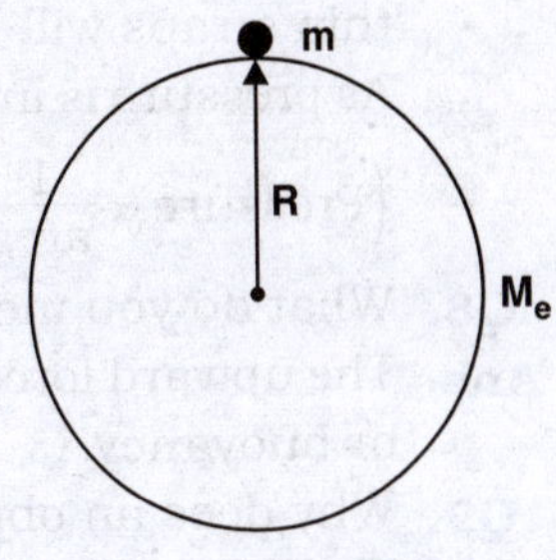

Ans. The gravitational force between the earth and an object on its surface

M_e = Mass of the earth
R = Radius of the earth
m = Mass of an object

$$\therefore \quad F \propto \frac{M_e m}{R^2}$$

$$\therefore \quad \boxed{F = G\frac{M_e m}{R^2}} \qquad \because G = \text{Gravitational constant}$$

Q3. What do you mean by free fall?

Ans. Whenever an object falls toward earth under the force of gravity alone and no other force is present, the motion of object is said to be "free fall".

Q4. What do you mean by acceleration due to gravity?

Ans. The acceleration of free fall is the acceleration due to gravity. We can also say the acceleration of an object due to gravitational force of earth acting on it is known as acceleration due to gravity.

Q5. What are the differences between the mass of an object and its weight?

Ans.

Mass	*Weight*
1. Mass of a body is the measure of its inertia.	1. Weight of the body is the force with which it is attracted towards the earth ($W = m \times g$).
2. Its S.I. unit is kg.	2. Its S.I unit is Newton.
3. It remains constant everywhere and it cannot be zero.	3. Its value changes from place to place and it can be zero.
4. It can be measured by beam-balance.	4. It can be measured by spring balance.
5. It has only magnitude i.e. it is a scalar quantity.	5. It has both magnitude and direction i.e. it is a vector quantity.

Q6. Why is the weight of an object on the moon 1/6 th its weight on the earth?

Ans. The weight of an object depends on '*g*' acceleration due to gravity, and the value of '*g*' on earth and moon is not same.

$$g = \frac{GM}{R^2}$$

The mass and radius of the earth is more than the mass and radius of the moon.

As $W = G\frac{Mm}{R^2}$, the weight of a body on the earth is 6 times more than theweight of a same body on moon.

Q7. Why is it difficult to hold a school bag having a strap made of a thin and strong string?

Ans. The force exerted by a thin and strong string is distributed to very less area and hence the force applied due to the bag is more, the pressure exerted on the body by thin straps will be more and hence will be more painful.

As pressure is inversely proportional to area, if the area is reduced pressure increases

$\left(\text{Pressure} \propto \frac{1}{\text{area}}\right)$

Q8. What do you mean by buoyancy?

Ans. The upward force exerted by any fluid (liquid, gas) on an object is known as upthrust or buoyancy.

Q9. Why does an object float or sink when placed on the surface of water?

Ans. The density of the object and water decides the floating or sinking of the object in water.

The density of water is 1 gm/cm^3.

- If the density of an object is less than the density of water then the object will float.
- If the density of an object is more than the density of water then the object will sink.

Q10. You find your mass to be 42 kg on a weighing machine. Is your mass more or less than 42 kg?

Ans. The weighing machine actually measures the mass of the body. Hence the mass reading of 42 kg given by a weighing machine is same as the actual mass of the body. As mass is the quantity of inertia, it remains the same.

Q11. You have a bag of cotton and an iron bar, each indicating a mass of 100 kg when measured on a weighing machine. In reality, one is heavier than other. Can you say which one is heavier and why?

Ans. The heaviness of the bag can be given by density

$$\text{Density} = \frac{\text{mass}}{\text{volume}}$$

Mass of both cotton bag and iron bag is same. But the volume of cotton bag is more than the iron bag.

Hence density is inversely proportional to volume. The bag of iron will be heavier.

NCERT TEXTUAL QUESTIONS SOLVED

Q1. How does the force of gravitation between two objects change when the distance between them is reduced to half?

Ans.
$$F \propto \frac{1}{d^2}$$

if d is reduced to $\frac{1}{2}$

$$\therefore \quad F \propto \frac{1}{\left(\frac{1}{2}\right)^2} \quad \therefore \quad F \propto \frac{4}{1}$$

The force of gravitation becomes 4 times more.

Q2. Gravitational force acts on all objects in proportion to their masses. Why then, a heavy object does not fall faster than a light object?

Ans. The heavy object when falls, the acceleration due to gravity 'g' is acting on it, which is independent of the mass of the body.

$$g = \frac{Gm}{R^2}$$

Therefore, a heavy object doesn't fall faster than a light object.

Q3. What is the magnitude of the gravitational force between the earth and a 1 kg object on its surface? [Mass of the earth is 6×10^{24} kg and radius of the earth is 6.4×10^6 m].

Ans. The magnitude of the gravitational force between earth and an object is given by the formula.

$$F = \frac{GMm}{R^2}$$

$$m = 1 \text{ kg}, \quad M = 6 \times 10^{24} \text{ kg.}$$

$$R = 6.4 \times 10^6 \text{ m}, \quad G = 6.67 \times 10^{-11} \text{ Nm}^2/\text{kg}^2$$

$$\therefore \quad F = \frac{6.67 \times 10^{-11} \text{ Nm}^2/\text{kg}^2 \times 6 \times 10^{24} \text{kg} \times 1 \text{ kg}}{(6.4 \times 10^6 \text{m})^2}$$

$$\therefore \quad F = 9.8 \text{ N}$$

Q4. The earth and the moon are attracted to each other by gravitational force. Does the earth attract the moon with a force that is greater or smaller or the same as the force with which the moon attracts the earth? Why?

Ans.

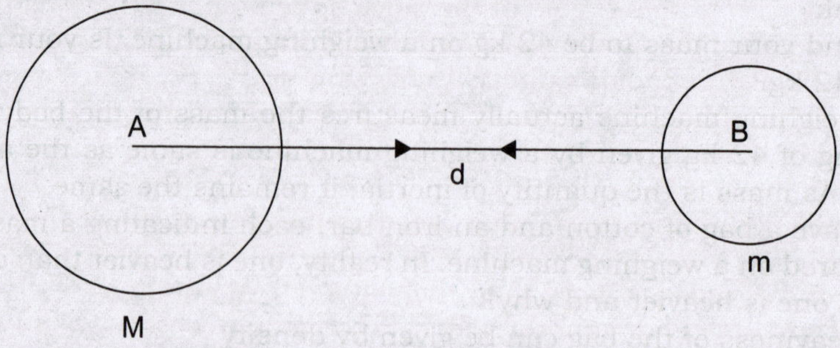

Gravitational force $F = G\frac{M_e M_m}{d^2}$

The value of F is same for earth and the moon. Both the bodies will exert the same amount of force on each other.

As per universal law of gravitation, every body attracts the other body with some force and this force is same for both the bodies called gravitational force.

Q5. If the moon attracts the earth, why does the earth not move towards the moon?

Ans. According to the universal law of gravitation both moon and earth attract each other with a force that is directly proportional to the product of their masses and inversely proportional to the square of distance between them.

The force of attraction of moon on the earth is present, but the earth does not appear to move towards the moon as the mass of the earth is large and the distance between the moon and earth is so large, even if the earth is attracted/moves towards the moon it is negligible, cannot be seen.

Q6. What happens to the force between two objects, if

(*i*) the mass of one object is doubled?

(*ii*) the distance between the objects is doubled and tripled?

(*iii*) the masses of both objects are doubled?

Ans. (*i*) If the mass of one object is doubled, the force between two objects will be doubled (increases)

(*ii*) If the distance between the objects is doubled the force between two objects will be one-fourth and if the distance will be tripled, the force will be one-ninth (1/9).

(*iii*) If the masses of both objects are doubled the force will be 4 times.

As $F \propto \frac{Mm}{d^2}$

Q7. What is the importance of universal law of gravitation?

Ans. The universal law of gravitation explains several phenomena:

(*i*) it explains about the force that binds the earth,

(*ii*) the motion of the moon around the earth,

(*iii*) the motion of planets around the Sun, and

(*iv*) the tides due to the moon and the Sun.

Q8. What is the acceleration of free fall?

Ans. The acceleration of free fall is, when the body falls due to earth's gravitational pull, its velocity changes and is said to be accelerated due to the earth's gravity and it falls freely called as free fall. This acceleration is calculated to be 9.8 m/s^2.

Q9. What do we call the gravitational force between the earth and an object?

Ans. The gravitational force between the earth and an object is called force due to gravity. It is measured as the weight of an object.

Q10. Amit buys few grams of gold at the poles as per the instruction of one of his friends. He hands over the same when he meets him at the equator. Will the friend agree with the weight of gold bought? If not, why?
[Hints: The value of g is greater at the poles than at the equator.]

Ans. Weight of the body is given by the formula

$$W = mg$$

It depends on the value of 'g' *i.e.*, acceleration due to gravity.
The weight of gold at poles = $W_p = m \times g$ (poles)
Value of g at poles is more than the value of g at equator.
The weight of gold at equator = $W_e = m \times g$ (equator)

$$\therefore \quad W_p > W_e.$$

The weight at pole of the same gold is found to be more as compared to the weight at the equator.
Hence, the friend will not agree with the weight of the gold bought.

Q11. *Why will a sheet of paper fall slower than one that is crumpled into a ball?*

Ans. A sheet of paper has larger surface area and while falling down it has to overcome the force exerted by air/wind current called as air resistance.
The crumpled paper has smaller surface area and it has to overcome very less amount of air current.
The air resistance offered to plain sheet is more than the resistance to crumpled sheet. Hence, the sheet of paper fall slower than the crumpled one.

Q12. *Gravitational force on the surface of the moon is only 1/6 as strong as gravitational force on the earth. What is the weight in Newtons of a 10 kg object on the moon and on the earth?*

Ans. Mass of the object = 10 kg
Weight of the object on earth = $W = m \times g$

$$\therefore \quad W = 10 \times 9.8$$
$$W = 98 \text{ N}$$

Weight of the object on moon = $\frac{1}{6}$ th the weight on the earth.
As the gravitational force on the surface of the moon is only $\frac{1}{6}$ th as strong as gravitational force on the surface of the earth.

$\therefore$ Weight of the object on moon = $\frac{98}{6}$ = 16.3 N
Weight on earth = 98 N
Weight on moon = 16.3 N

Q13. A ball is thrown vertically upwards with a velocity of 49 m/s. Calculate
(*i*) the maximum height to which it rises,
(*ii*) the total time it takes to return to the surface of the earth.

Ans. (*i*) Initial velocity, $u = 49$ m/s
Final velocity, $v = 0$ m/s
$a = g = -9.8$ m/s^2
(going against the gravity)
Height (h) = Distance = s = ?

$$\therefore \quad v^2 - u^2 = 2gs$$
$$0^2 - (49)^2 = 2(-9.8) \times s$$
$$\therefore \quad s = \frac{(49)\times-(49)}{2(-9.8)} = 122.5 \text{ m}$$

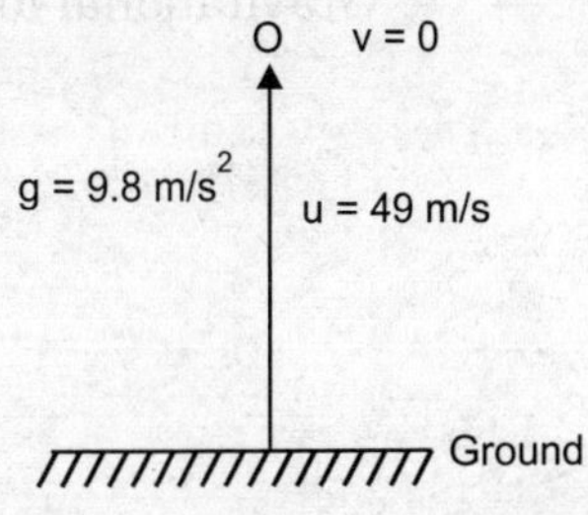

(*ii*) Time taken, $t = ?$

$$v = u + gt$$

$$\therefore \quad 0 = 49 + (-9.8) \times t$$

$$\therefore \quad t = \frac{-49}{-9.8} = 5 \text{ s}$$

Total time taken to return the surface of the earth by the ball is 5 s + 5 s = 10 s.

Q14. A stone is released from the top of a tower of height 19.6 m. Calculate its final velocity just before touching the ground?

Ans. Data

$$u = 0 \text{ m/s}$$

$$v = ?$$

$$h = s = 19.6 \text{ m}$$

$$g = 9.8 \text{ m/s}^2 \quad \text{(falling down)}$$

$$v^2 - u^2 = 2gs$$

$$v^2 - (0)^2 = 2 \times 9.8 \times 19.6$$

$$\therefore \quad v^2 = 19.6 \times 19.6$$

$$\therefore \quad v = 19.6 \text{ m/s}$$

The final velocity just before touching the ground is 19.6 m/s.

Q15. A stone is thrown vertically upward with an initial velocity of 40 m/s. Taking g = 10 m/s², find the maximum height reached by the stone. What is the net displacement and the total distance covered by the stone?

Ans.

$$u = 40 \text{ m/s}$$

$$g = -10 \text{ m/s}^2 \quad \text{(going against gravity)}$$

$$h = s = ?$$

$$v = 0$$

$$v^2 - u^2 = 2gs$$

$$(0)^2 - (40)^2 = 2(-10) \times s$$

$$\therefore \quad s = \frac{-(40 \times 40)}{2(-10)}$$

$$\therefore \quad s = 80 \text{ m}$$

Net displacement of the stone = 0 (As the stone falls, back to the same point.)

Total distance covered by stone = 80m (up) + 80m (down)

= 160 m

Q16. Calculate the force of gravitation between the earth and the Sun, given that the mass of the earth = 6×10^{24} kg and of the Sun = 2×10^{30} kg. The average distance between the two is 1.5×10^{11} m.

Ans.

$$M_e = 6 \times 10^{24} \text{ kg}, \quad G = 6.67 \times 10^{-11} \text{ Nm}^2/\text{kg}^2$$

$$M_s = 2 \times 10^{30} \text{ kg}$$

$$d = 1.5 \times 10^{11} \text{ m}$$

$$\therefore \text{ Gravitational force } F = G\frac{M_e M_s}{d^2}$$

$$\therefore \quad F = \frac{6.67 \times 10^{-11} Nm^2/kg^2 \times 6 \times 10^{24} kg \times 2 \times 10^{30} kg}{(1.5 \times 10^{11} m)^2}$$

$$= \frac{80.04 \times 10^{-11+24+30}}{2.25 \times 10^{22}} = \frac{80.04}{2.25} \times 10^{21}$$

$$= 3.56 \times 10^{22} \text{ N.}$$

Q17. A stone is allowed to fall from the top of a tower 100 m high and at the same time another stone is projected vertically upwards from the ground with a velocity of 25 m/s. Calculate when and where the two stones will meet.

Ans. $h = 100$ m

time, $t = ?$ $\quad g = 10 \text{ m/s}^2$

Height covered by the falling stone = s_1

$$\therefore \quad s_1 = ut + \frac{1}{2}gt^2$$

$$\therefore \quad s_1 = 0 \times t + \frac{1}{2}(10)\,t^2$$

$$\therefore \quad s_1 = 5t^2 \qquad ...(1)$$

The distance covered by the stone thrown upward = s_2

$g = -10$ m/s

$u = 25$ m/s

$$s_2 = ut + \frac{1}{2}gt^2$$

$$\therefore \quad s_2 = 25t + \frac{1}{2}(-10)t^2$$

$$\therefore \quad s_2 = 25t - 5t^2 \qquad ...(2)$$

Total height given = 100 m

$$\therefore \quad s_1 + s_2 = 100 \text{ m}$$

$$5t^2 + (25t - 5t^2) = 100 \text{ m}$$

$$\therefore \quad 25t = 100 \text{ m}$$

$$t = \frac{100}{25} = 4 \text{ seconds} \qquad ...(3)$$

Putting the value of equation (3) in equation (1), we get

$$\therefore \quad s_1 = 5t^2$$

$$= 5 \times (4)^2 = 80 \text{ m}$$

∴ The two stones will meet after 4 seconds when the falling stone has covered a height of 80 m.

Q18. A ball thrown up vertically returns to the thrower after 6 s. Find

(*a*) the velocity with which it was thrown up,

(*b*) the maximum height it reaches, and

(*c*) its position after 4 s.

Ans. $u = ?$

$v = 0$

$g = -9.8 \text{ m/s}^2$ (thrown upward)

Total time = 6 s (to go up and down)

∴ Time for upward journey = $\frac{6}{2} = 3$ s.

(*a*)

$$v = u + gt$$

$$0 = u + (-9.8) \times 3$$

$$u = 29.4 \text{ m/s}$$

(*b*) Maximum height, $h = s = ?$

$$\therefore \quad s = ut + \frac{1}{2}gt^2 = (29.4 \times 3) + \frac{1}{2}(-9.8)(3)^2$$

$$= 88.2 + \frac{1}{2}(-88.2) = 88.2 - 44.1$$

$$h = 44.1 \text{ m}$$

(c) Position after 4 s

$$t = 4 \text{ s}$$

$$\therefore \quad s = ut + \frac{1}{2}gt^2$$

$$s = (29.4 \times 4) + \frac{1}{2}(-9.8) \times (4)^2 = 117.6 + \frac{1}{2}(-156.8)$$

$$= 117.6 - 78.4 = 39.2 \text{ m.}$$

∴ Position after 4 s = 39.2 m from the top.

Q19. In what direction does the buoyant force on an object immersed in a liquid act?

Ans. The buoyant force on an object immersed in a liquid acts upwards, i.e. opposite to the direction of the force exerted by the object.

Q20. Why does a block of plastic released under water come up to the surface of water?

Ans. The floating or sinking of a body in the water is decided by the density of both the body and water's buoyant force acting on the body.

The density of plastic is less than the water and the buoyant force exerted by water on the plastic block is greater than the force exerted by plastic on the water.

Q21. The volume of 50 g of a substance is 20 cm^3. If the density of water is 1 gcm^{-3}, will the substance float or sink?

Ans.

Mass = 50 g

Volume = 20 cm^3

$$\text{Density} = \frac{\text{mass}}{\text{volume}}$$

$$\therefore \text{Density of a given substance} = \frac{50 \text{ g}}{20 \text{ cm}^3} = 2.5 \text{ g/cm}^3$$

Density of water = 1 g/cm^3

As the density of a given substance is more than the density of water. The substance will sink in water.

Q22. The volume of a 500 g sealed packet is 350 cm^3. Will the packet float or sink in water if the density of water is 1g cm^{-3}? What will be the mass of the water displaced by this packet?

Ans. Mass of the packet = 500 g

Volume of the packet = 350 cm^3

Density of the packet = ?

$$\text{Density} = \frac{\text{mass}}{\text{volume}} = \frac{500 \text{ g}}{350 \text{ cm}^3} = 1.428 \text{ g/cm}^3.$$

Density of water = 1 g/cm^3

The packet will sink in water as the density of packet is greater than the density of water.

Mass of the water displaced by this packet

= Volume of the packet × Density of water = 350 cm^3 × 1 g/cm^3

= 350 g

ADDITIONAL QUESTIONS SOLVED

I. Multiple Choice Questions

Choose the correct option:

1. A body of mass 1 kg is attracted by the earth with a force equal to
   (a) 9.8 N (b) 1 N (c) 6.67×10^{11} (d) 9.8 m/s
2. The value of '*g*'
   (a) increases as we go above the earth's surface
   (b) decreases as we go to the centre of the earth
   (c) remains constant everywhere
   (d) is more at equator and less at poles

3. A ball is thrown up, the value of 'g' will be

(*a*) zero (*b*) positive
(*c*) negative (*d*) negligible

4. The mass of body on moon is 40 kg, what is the weight on the earth?

(*a*) 240 kg (*b*) 392 N
(*c*) 240 N (*d*) 400 kg

5. The gravitational force between two objects is

(*a*) attractive at large distances only
(*b*) attractive at small distances only
(*c*) attractive at all distances
(*d*) attractive at large distances but repulsive at small distances.

6. The gravitation force causes

(*a*) tides (*b*) motion of moon
(*c*) none of the above (*d*) both (*a*) and (*b*)

7. The gravitational force between two objects is F. If masses of both the objects are halved without altering the distance between them, then the gravitational force would become

(*a*) $\frac{F}{4}$ (*b*) $\frac{F}{2}$
(*c*) F (*d*) $2F$

8. The Earth attracts the moon with a gravitational force of 10^{20} N. The moon attracts the earth with a gravitational force of

(*a*) less than 10^{20} N (*b*) 10^{20} N
(*c*) greater than 10^{20} N (*d*) 10^{-20} N

9. The distance between two bodies becomes 6 times more than the usual distance. Then the F becomes

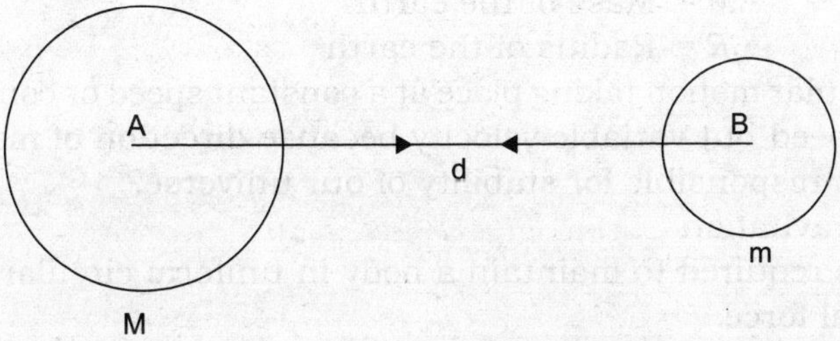

(*a*) 36 times (*b*) 6 times
(*c*) 12 times (*d*) $\frac{1}{36}$ times

10. Newton's law of gravitation applies to

(*a*) small bodies only (*b*) plants only
(*c*) all bodies irrespective of their size (*d*) for solar system

11. The device used to measure the purity of milk is

(*a*)hydrometer (*b*) lactometer
(*c*)hygrometer (*d*) maltometer

12. The cork floats while the nail sinks in the water, this is due to

(*a*) density of cork is more than nail
(*b*) density of nail is more than cork.
(*c*) density of cork is less than the density of water.
(*d*) density of iron is less than the density of water.

13. The relative density of silver is 10.8 and the density of water is 10^3 kg/m^2. The density of silver is

(a) 1.8×10^4 N/m^3 (b) 10.8×10^3 N/m^3

(c) 1.8×10^4 kg/m^3 (d) 10.8×10^4 kg/m^3

14. Buoyant force exerted by different fluids on a given body is

(a) same (b) different

(c) zero (d) negligible

15. Liquid *A* is denser than liquid *B*, a body of wood is dipped in both the liquids. The buoyant force experienced by the body in

(a) liquid *A* is more (b) liquid *B* is more

(c) liquid *A* is less (d) none of the above

Ans. 1—(a), 2—(b), 3—(c), 4—(b), 5—(c), 6—(d), 7—(a), 8—(b), 9—(d), 10—(c), 11—(b), 12—(c), 13—(b), 14—(b), 15—(a).

II. Very Short Answer Type Questions

Q1. Give the S.I. unit of G and its value.

Ans. S.I. unit of *G* and its value = 6.67×10^{-11} Nm^2/kg^2

Q2. Earth attracts apple from the tree and it falls but the earth does not appear to move towards the apple?

Ans. For a force of attraction, acceleration is inversely proportional to the mass of the object.

Hence the mass of an apple is negligible as compared to that of the earth.

So, we do not see the earth moving towards the apple.

Q3. $g = GM/R^2$, what does these symbols denote?

Ans.
g = acceleration due to gravity
G = Gravitational constant
M = Mass of the earth
R = Radius of the earth

Q4. Is uniform circular motion taking place at a constant speed or constant velocity? Why?

Ans. At constant speed but variable velocity because direction of motion is changing.

Q5. Which force is responsible for stability of our universe?

Ans. The force of gravitation

Q6. Which force is required to maintain a body in uniform circular motion?

Ans. The centripetal force.

Q7. What is the direction of centripetal force?

Ans. Towards the centre of circle.

Q8. Moon is revolving round the earth in a circular orbit and needs a centripetal force. From where does the force come?

Ans. Centripetal force for circular motion of moon is provided by the force of gravitational attraction due to Earth.

Q9. What is gravity?

Ans. Force of gravitational attraction on an object due to Earth.

Q10. An object is let free to fall from the top of a tower. What is its acceleration and what is its sign?

Ans. Acceleration is positive having a value $g = 9.8$ m/s^2.

Q11. How is 'g' on the surface of Earth related to 'G'?

Ans. $g = \frac{GM}{R^2}$, where M = mass of earth, R = radius of earth

Q12. A ball is projected vertically upwards with an initial velocity 'u' goes to a maximum height 'h' before coming to ground. What is the value of 'h'?

Ans. $h = \frac{u^2}{2g}$

Q13. How is weight of an object related to its mass?

Ans. Weight (W) = mass (m) × acceleration due to gravity (g).

Q14. State the S.I. unit of weight.

Ans. S.I. unit of weight is Newton (1N).

Q15. Is the value of 'g' same at all places on earth?

Ans. No, it varies from place to place.

Q16. What is the S.I. unit of thrust?

Ans. Newton.

Q17. What is the S.I. unit of pressure?

Ans. The S.I. unit of pressure = N/m^2 = Pascal.

Q18. Define thrust.

Ans. The net force exerted by a body in a particular direction is called thrust.

Q19. Define pressure.

Ans. The force exerted per unit area is called pressure.

Q20. Why is it easier to swim in sea water than in river water?

Ans. The density of sea water is more due to dissolved salts in it as compared to the density of river water. Hence the buoyant force exerted on the swimmer by the sea water is more which helps in floating and makes swimming easier.

Q21. Why a truck or a motorbike has much wider tyres?

Ans. The pressure exerted by it can be distributed to more area, and avoid the wear and tear of tyres.

Q22. Why are knives sharp?

Ans. To increase the pressure, area is reduced,

As pressure $\propto \frac{1}{\text{Area}}$ hence the pressure or force exerted on a body increases.

Q23. Why is the wall of dam reservoir thicker at the bottom?

Ans. The pressure of water in dams at the bottom is more, to withstand this pressure the dams have wider walls at the bottom, to increase the area.

Q24. Why do nails have pointed tips?

Ans. The force exerted when acts on a smaller area, it exerts larger pressure. So the nails have pointed tips.

Q25. While swimming why do we feel light?

Ans. The swimmer is exerted by an upward force by water, this phenomenon is called buoyancy and it makes the swimmer feel light.

Q26. Define density and give its unit.

Ans. The density of a substance is defined as mass per unit volume. Its unit is kg/m^3.

Q27. What is relative density?

Ans. The relative density of a substance is the ratio of its density to that of water.

$$\text{Relative density} = \frac{\text{density of a substance}}{\text{density of water}}$$

Q28. If a planet and a moon both experience the same force, explain why the moon's acceleration is noticeable while the planet's is not.

Ans. The moon has a much smaller mass, and acceleration is inversely proportional to mass, as shown by $a = \frac{F}{m}$.

III. Short Answer Type Questions

Q1. During free-fall what is the weight of a body. Give reason for the answer.

Ans. During free-fall the body gets accelerated. This acceleration is caused due to the earth's gravitational force. Hence the weight of the body is '0'.

Q2. Mass of a dog on earth is 40 kg, what is its mass on the moon?

Ans. Mass on earth = 40 kg.

Mass of the body is its inertia, which remains constant.

∴ Mass of the dog on moon = 40 kg.

Q3. Obtain a relation between 'g' and 'G'.

Ans. Consider an object of mass 'm' placed at the surface of earth. Their force of gravitation acting on the object due to earth is given by

$F = \frac{GMm}{R^2}$, where M = mass of earth and R = radius of earth

By Newton's second law $F = mg$, where g = acceleration of given object due to gravitational pull of earth.

$$mg = \frac{GMm}{R^2}$$

$$g = \frac{GM}{R^2}$$

Q4. Distinguish between force of gravity and gravitational force.

Ans. By gravitational force we mean force of gravitational attraction between any two objects in the universe whether the objects are light or heavy and irrespective of the distance between them.

Force of gravity is simply a special case of gravitational force and it means force of attraction between the object and the earth.

Q5. The mass of the body on earth is 60 kg what is its weight on earth and on moon?

Ans. Mass of the body on earth = 60 kg

Weight on earth = ?

$$W = m \times g \quad (g = 9.8 \text{ m/s}^2)$$
$$= 60 \times 9.8$$
$$= 588 \text{ N.}$$

Weight on moon = $\frac{1}{6}$th the weight on earth

$$= \frac{1}{6} \times 588$$
$$= 98 \text{ N.}$$

Q6. The mass of earth is 6×10^{24} kg and that of moon is 7.4×10^{22} kg. If the distance between the earth and the moon is 3.84×10^5 km. Calculate the force exerted by the earth on the moon. G = 6.67×10^{-11} Nm^2 kg^{-2}.

Ans. It is given that the mass of earth $M_e = 6 \times 10^{24}$ kg

Mass of moon $M_m = 7.4 \times 10^{22}$ kg

Distance between the earth and the moon $d = 3.84 \times 10^5$ km $= 3.84 \times 10^8$ m

$$G = 6.7 \times 10^{-11} \text{ Nm}^2 \text{ kg}^{-2}$$

∴ Gravitational force exerted by the earth on the moon

$$F = \frac{GM_e \cdot M_m}{d^2} = \frac{6.7 \times 10^{-11} \times 6 \times 10^{24} \times 7.4 \times 10^{22}}{(3.84 \times 10^8)^2}$$
$$= 2.01 \times 10^{20} \text{ N}$$

Q7. What is effect of shape of earth on value of 'g'?

Ans. The Earth is not a perfect sphere. The radius of earth increases from the poles to the equator. Hence, as per relation $g = \frac{GM}{R^2}$, where value of 'g' is greater at the poles and lesser at the equator.

Q8. An object is just dropped from a certain point to fall freely under gravity. Write the equation of motion.

Ans. In this case, initial velocity $u = 0$ and acceleration $a = + g$. Hence, the equation of motion are:

(i) $v = gt$ (ii) $s = \frac{1}{2}gt^2$ (iii) $v^2 = 2gs$

where 's' is the vertical distance covered below the point from where the object was just dropped.

Q9. What is the distance covered by a freely falling body during the first three seconds of its motion?

Ans. Here initial velocity $u = 0$, acceleration $a = g = 9.8$ ms^{-2} and $t = 3$ s

∴ Vertically downwards distance covered $h = \frac{1}{2}gt^2$

$$= \frac{1}{2} \times (9.8) \times 3^2 = 44.1 \text{ m}$$

Q10. A stone and feather are thrown from a tower. Both the objects should reach the ground at same time but it does not, give reason.

Ans. As per the motion of object due to 'g' gravitational pull of earth, both the bodies are acted upon by the same force of earth but the stone will fall first and then the feather. As feather being lighter, experiences the greater air resistance, so it will reach later.

Q11. Find the weight of Uma, who weighs 36 kg.

Ans. Mass of Uma $m = 36$ kg,

∴ Weight of Uma $W = mg = 36 \times 9.8$ N

$= 352.8$ N

Q12. Why do we feel uneasy when the ferry wheel moves downwards?

Ans. When we are in the ferry wheel and the swing moves down, our body gets accelerated due to the gravitational forces. This causes weightlessness due to the free fall.

Q13. Derive the formula for the universal law of gravitation.

Ans. Let two objects A and B of masses M and m, lie at a distance d from each other as shown in the figure.

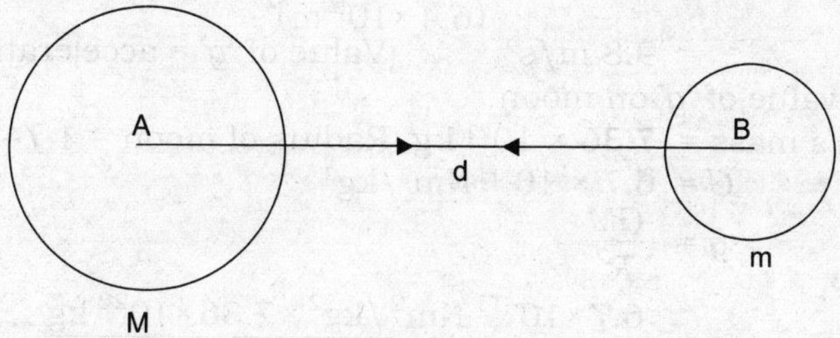

Let the force of attraction between two objects be F.

According to the universal law of gravitation, the force between two objects is directly proportional to the product of their masses.

$$F \propto Mm \quad \ldots(i)$$

And the force between two objects is inversely proportional to the square of distance between them,

$$F \propto \frac{1}{d^2} \qquad ...(ii)$$

$$\therefore \quad F \propto \frac{Mm}{d^2} \quad \text{from } (i) \text{ and } (ii)$$

$$\therefore \quad F = G\frac{Mm}{d^2} \qquad \because G = \text{Universal gravitational constant}$$

Q14. Give the difference between 'g' and 'G'.

Ans.

'g'	'G'
1. It is defined as acceleration due to gravity.	1. It is defined as universal gravitational constant.
2. Value of g = 9.8	2. Value of G = 6.67×10^{-11}
3. Unit = m/s^2	3. Unit = Nm^2/kg^2
4. It changes from place to place. At poles value of 'g' is more than at equator.	4. It remains constant.

Q15. Find the value of 'G', universal gravitational constant.

Ans.

$$F = G\frac{Mm}{d^2}$$

$$G = \frac{Fd^2}{Mm}$$

For any given value of M and m, mass of two objects, the distance between them is 'd' and the force 'F' exerted on the two bodies by each other is known as universal gravitational constant. The value of G will always be same.

i.e., $G = 6.67 \times 10^{-11}\ Nm^2/kg^2$.

Q16. Find the value of 'g', acceleration due to gravity.

Ans.

$$g = \frac{GM}{R^2}$$

$G = 6.7 \times 10^{-11}\ Nm^2/kg^2$ (constant)

$M = 6 \times 10^{24}$ kg (Mass of the earth)

$R = 6.4 \times 10^6$ m (Radius of the earth)

On substituting these values in the given equation

$$g = \frac{GM}{R^2}$$

$$= \frac{6.7 \times 10^{-11}\ Nm^2/kg^2 \times 6 \times 10^{24}\ kg}{(6.4 \times 10^6\ m)^2}$$

$= 9.8\ m/s^2$ (Value of 'g' = acceleration due to gravity)

Q17. Calculate the value of 'g' on moon.

Ans. Moon's mass = 7.36×10^{22} kg, Radius of moon = 1.74×10^6 m

$G = 6.7 \times 10^{-11}\ Nm^2/kg^2$

$$g = \frac{GM}{R^2}$$

$$= \frac{6.7 \times 10^{-11}\ Nm^2/kg^2 \times 7.36 \times 10^{22}\ kg}{(1.74 \times 10^6 m)^2}$$

$$= \frac{49.312 \times 10^{11}}{3.027 \times 10^{12}} = 16.29 \times 10^{-1} = 1.63\ m/s^2.$$

$\therefore$ The value of 'g' on moon = $1.63\ m/s^2$

Q18. A car falls of a ledge and drops to the ground in 0.5 s. Let $g = 10\ ms^{-2}$.

(i) What is its speed on striking the ground?

(ii) What is its average speed during 0.5 s?

(iii) How high is the edge from the ground?

Ans. Here $u = 0$, $t = 0.5$ s and $a = g = +\ 10\ ms^{-2}$

(i) ∴ Final speed of car when striking the ground

$$v = u + at = 0 + gt = 10 \times 0.5 = 5\ ms^{-1}$$

(ii) Average speed $V_{av} = \dfrac{u+v}{2} = \dfrac{0+5}{2} = 2.5\ ms^{-1}$.

(iii) Height of the ledge = total distance covered by car

$$h = \frac{1}{2} gt^2 = \frac{1}{2} \times 10 \times (0.5)^2 = 1.25\ m$$

Q19. What is centripetal force? Explain it with an example.

Ans. When a body moves around the other body, the force that causes this acceleration and keeps the body moving along a circular path is acting towards the centre. This force is called the centripetal force. It means centre seeking force.

E.g., tie a stone to a thread and whirl it round as shown in the figure. The stone continues to move round as long as the string is held. On releasing the thread the centre binding force called as centripetal force is no more acting on it, the stone flies off along the straight line. This straight line will be a tangent to the circular path.

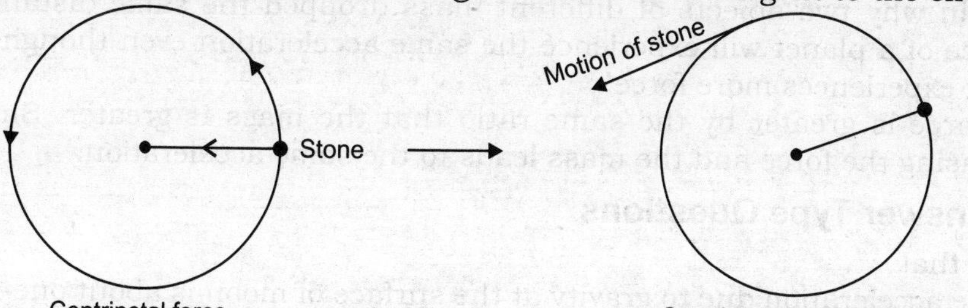

Centripetal force (A) Centripetal force is released (B)

Q20. A ship made of iron does not sink but the iron rod sinks in water, why?

Ans. The iron rod sinks due to high density and less buoyant force exerted by the water on it, but in case of ship the surface area is increased, the upthrust experienced by the body is more. So, it floats on water.

Q21. Camels can walk easily on desert sand but we are not comfortable walking on the sand. State reason.

Ans. Camel's feet are broad and the larger area of the feet reduces the force/ pressure exerted by the body on the sand. But when we have to walk on the same sand, we sink because the pressure exerted by our body is not distributed but is directional.

Q22. What is lactometer and hydrometer?

Ans. Lactometer is a device used to find the purity of a given sample of milk. Hydrometer is a device used to find the density of liquid.

Q23. The relative density of silver is 10.8. What does this mean?

Ans. It means that the density of silver is 10.8 times more than that of water.

Q24. The relative density of gold is 19.3. The density of water is $10^3\ kg/m^3$? What is the density of gold in S.I. unit?

Ans. Relative density of gold = 19.3

$$\text{Relative density of gold} = \frac{\text{Density of gold}}{\text{Density of water}}$$

∴ Density of gold = Relative density of gold × Density of water
$= 19.3 \times 10^3$ kg/m^3 = 19300 kg/m^3.

Q25. State Archimedes' principle.

Ans. **Archimedes' principle**—When a body is immersed fully or partially in a fluid, it experiences an upward force that is equal to the weight of the fluid displaced by it. It is used in designing of ships and submarines.

Q26. Two cork pieces of same size and mass are dipped in two beakers containing water and oil. One cork floats on water but another sink in oil. Why?

Ans. The cork floats on water because the density of cork is less than the density of water, and another cork sinks in the oil because the density of cork is more than the density of oil.

Q27. What are fluids? Why is Archimedes' principle applicable only for fluids? Give the application of Archimedes' principle.

Ans. Fluids are the substances which can flow *e.g.*, gases and liquids are fluids. Archimedes' principle is based on the upward force exerted by fluids on any object immersed in the fluid. Hence it is applicable only for fluids.

Applications of Archimedes' principle:

(*i*) It is used in designing of ship and submarine.

(*ii*) It is used in designing lactometer which is used to determine the purity of milk.

(*iii*) To make hydrometer that is used to determine the density of liquid.

Q28. Explain why two objects of different mass dropped the same distance from the surface of a planet will experience the same acceleration even though the heavier object experiences more force.

Ans. The force is greater by the same ratio that the mass is greater. Since F = *am*, increasing the force and the mass leads to the same acceleration.

IV. Long Answer Type Questions

Q1. Show that

(*a*) the acceleration due to gravity at the surface of moon is about one-sixth of that at the surface of the earth.

(*b*) the weight of the body on moon = 1/6 th the weight of the body on earth.

Ans. (*a*) The acceleration due to gravity '*g*' is given by the formula

$$g = \frac{Gm}{R^2} \qquad G = 6.67 \times 10^{-11}$$

Celestial Body	*Mass (kg)*	*Radius (m)*
Earth	5.98×10^{24}	6.37×10^6
Moon	7.36×10^{22}	1.74×10^6

g on earth

$$g_e = G\frac{M_e}{R_e^2}$$

$$g_e = G\frac{5.98 \times 10^{24}\,\text{kg}}{(6.37 \times 10^6\,\text{m})^2}$$

$$= 9.8 \text{ m/s}^2$$

g on moon

$$g_m = G\frac{M_m}{R_m^2}$$

$$g_m = G\frac{7.36 \times 10^{22}\,\text{kg}}{(1.74 \times 10^6\,\text{m})^2}$$

$$= 1.63 \text{ m/s}^2$$

The value of g on moon is 1.63 m/s^2

The value of g on earth is 9.8 m/s^2

∴ g on moon is $\frac{1}{6}$ th g on earth.

(*b*) Weight of the body is given by formula

$$W = m \times g$$

$\therefore$ Weight on earth $\qquad$ Weight on moon

$$W_e = m \times g_e \qquad W_m = m \times g_m$$

$$\frac{W_e}{W_m} = \frac{m\,g_e}{m\,g_m} \Rightarrow \frac{W_e}{W_m} = \frac{g_e}{g_m}$$

$$\therefore \frac{W_m}{W_e} = \frac{1.6\,m/s^2}{9.8\,m/s^2} = \frac{1}{6}$$

$\therefore$ Weight of the body on moon = $\frac{1}{6}$th the weight of the body on earth.

Q2. The acceleration of a freely falling body does not depend on the mass of the body. Show this by deriving an expression for the same.

Ans. Newton's law of gravitation states that every two bodies in the universe attract each other with a force which is directly proportional to the product of their masses and inversely proportional to the square of distance between them.

$$F = G\frac{Mm}{d^2} \qquad \ldots(i)$$

Newton's second law of motion shows that force is the product of mass and acceleration. Let *m* be the mass of the body, the gravitational force causes acceleration in it, is denoted by '*g*'

$$\therefore \quad F = mg \qquad \ldots(ii)$$

From (*i*) and (*ii*) we get

$$mg = G\frac{Mm}{d^2}$$

$\because$ M = mass of the earth

d = distance between the object and the earth

Let the object be on the surface of the earth. The distance $d = R$ (radius of the earth).

$$\therefore \quad mg = G\frac{M \times m}{R^2}$$

$$\therefore \quad g = \frac{GM}{R^2}$$

Q3. Establish a relationship between 'g' and 'G'.

Ans. 'g' is acceleration due to gravity.

The gravitational force 'F' is exerted on a body of mass '*m*', the body gets accelerated '*g*'

$$\therefore \quad F = mg \qquad \ldots(i)$$

'*G*' is the universal gravitational constant.

Newton's law of universal gravitational constant gives the formula

$$F = G\frac{Mm}{d^2} \qquad \ldots(ii)$$

when M = Mass of earth

m = mass of object

d = distance between the two bodies

From equation (*i*) and (*ii*) we get

$$mg = G\frac{Mm}{d^2}$$

For a body on the surface of earth

$$d = R \text{ (radius of the earth)}$$

$$\therefore \quad g = \frac{GM}{R^2} \qquad G = \frac{gR^2}{M}$$

Q4. With the help of an activity prove that the force acting on a smaller area exerts a larger pressure?

Ans. Consider a block of wood kept on a table top. The mass of the wooden block is 5 kg. Its dimension is 40 cm × 20 cm × 10 cm.

Now, we have to find the pressure exerted by the wooden block on the table top by keeping it vertically and horizontally.

The mass of the wooden block = 5 kg

Weight of the wooden block applies a thrust on the table top

$\therefore \quad \text{Thrust} = F = m \times g$

$= 5 \text{ kg} \times 9.8 \text{ m/s}^2 = 49 \text{ N}$

(case *a*)—When the wooden box is kept vertically with sides 20 cm × 10 cm.

Area of a side = length × breadth

= 20 cm × 10 cm

= 200 cm^2 = 0.02 m^2

$$\text{Pressure} = \frac{\text{Thrust}}{\text{Area}} = \frac{49 \text{ N}}{0.02 \text{ m}^2} = 2450 \text{ N/m}^2$$

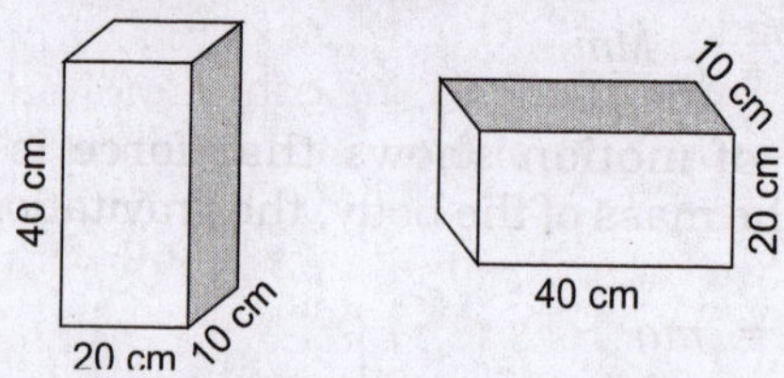

(case *b*)—When the block is kept horizontally with side 40 cm × 20 cm.

Area = length × breadth

= 40 cm × 20 cm

= 800 cm^2 = 0.08 m^2

$$\text{Pressure} = \frac{\text{Thrust}}{\text{Area}} = \frac{49 \text{ N}}{0.08 \text{ m}^2} = 612.5 \text{ N/m}^2$$

∴ The pressure exerted by the box in case (*a*) is more as compared to the pressure exerted in case (*b*).

The area is reduced and the pressure exerted is more.

This shows that pressure $\propto \frac{1}{\text{area}}$

Pressure will be larger if the area is reduced.

Application:

- Nails have pointed tips.
- Knives have sharp edges.
- Needles have pointed tips.

Q5. Calculate the gravitational force of a planet of mass 4.5 × 10^9 kg on a moon of mass 2.2 × 10^8 kg, if the distance between their centres is 6.8 × 10^7 m. Calculate the acceleration due to gravity on the surface of the given planet, given that it has a radius of 9.0 × 10^4 m.

Ans.
$$\text{F} = G\frac{m_1 m_2}{r^2} = 6.67 \times 10^{-11} \times \frac{4.5 \times 10^9 \times 2.2 \times 10^8}{(6.8 \times 10^7)^2} = 1.4 \times 10^{-8} \text{N}$$

The gravitational force is on the moon is 1.4 × 10^{-8} N (2 s.f.) towards the centre of the planet.

$$a = \frac{GM}{r^2} = \frac{6.67 \times 10^{-11} \times 4.5 \times 10^9}{(9.0 \times 10^4)^2} = 3.71 \times 10^{-11} \text{ ms}^{-2}$$

The acceleration at the surface of the planet is 3.7×10^{-11} ms^{-2} (2 s.f.) towards the planet's centre.

Q6. A buoyant force of 26 N acts on a piece of metal that is completely immersed in ethyl alcohol. What is the volume of the metal piece? The density of ethanol = 785.06 kg/m^3.

Ans. Buoyant force = density x volume x g

$$26N = 785.06 \times V \times 9.8$$

$$V = 3379.5\ cm^3$$

Q7. Find buoyant force on the lead block. Weight of lead block = 1.1 N, Volume of block = 10 cm^3. 1 cm^3 of water weighs 0.0098 N.

Ans. The lead displaces 10 cm^3 of water.

Buoyant force = weight of water displaced 10 cm^3 of water × 0.0098 N/cm^3

= 0.098 N.

V. Activity-Based Questions

1. • Take a piece of thread.
   • Tie a small stone at one end. Hold the other end of the thread and whirl it round, as shown in the figure.
   • Note the motion of the stone.
   • Release the thread.
   • Again, note the direction of motion of the stone.

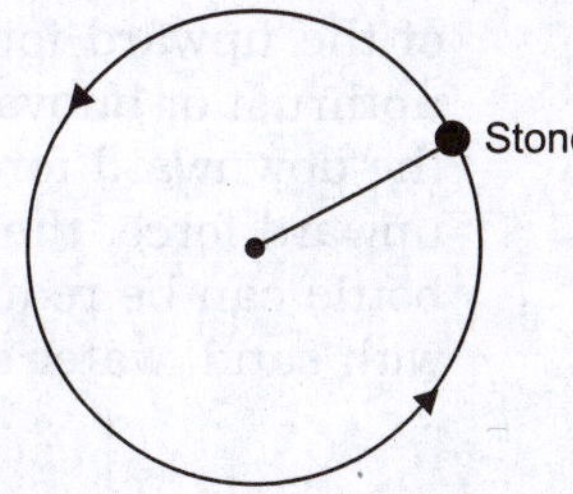

Observation: The motion gets accelerated and moves in a circular direction. When the thread is released the stone make a tangent to the circle and falls down.

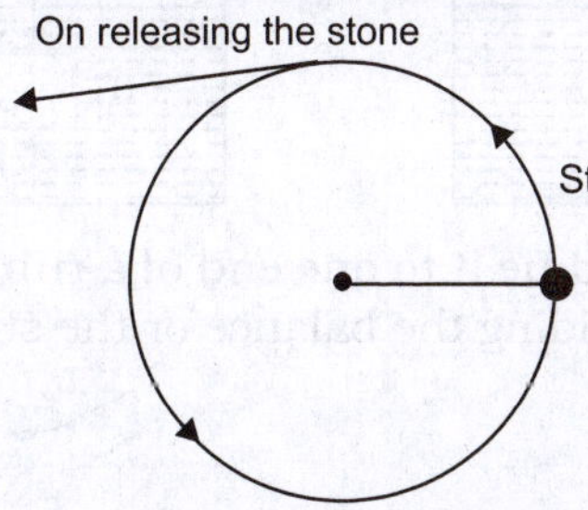

2. • Take a stone. • Throw it upwards.
   • It reaches a certain height and then it starts falling down.

   Observation: The stone is attracted by the earth hence it falls down due to earth's gravitational force '*g*'.

   The stone gets accelerated, when it goes upward its '*g*' is negative, when it falls towards the earth, '*g*' is positive.

3. • Take a sheet of paper and a stone. Drop them simultaneously from the first floor of building. Observe whether both of them reach the ground simultaneously.

Ans. Paper reaches the ground a little later than the stone. This is due to air-resistance. The air offers resistance due to friction to the motion of the falling objects. The resistance offered by air to the paper is more than the resistance offered to the stone.

• Repeat the above experiment in a glass jar from which air has been sucked out, the paper and stone would fall at the same rate.

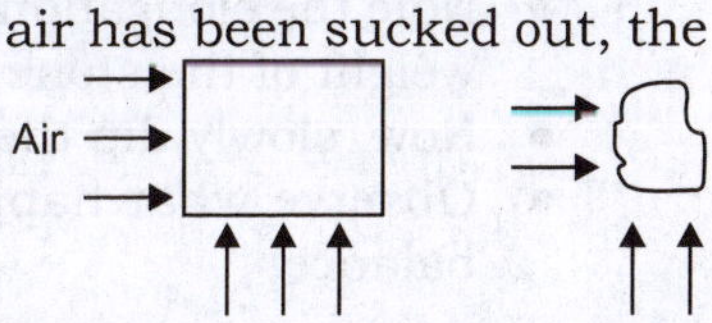

Result. When the earth attracts the paper's sheet and crumpled page, they experience acceleration during free fall. This acceleration experienced by an object is independent of its mass. Hence any object may be hollow or solid, big or small should fall at the same rate.

The air current offers resistance to the free-fall of the paper.

4. • Take an empty plastic bottle. Close the mouth of the bottle with an airtight stopper. Put it in a bucket filled with water. You see that the bottle floats.

- Push the bottle into the water. You feel an upward push. Try to push it further down. You will find it difficult to push deeper and deeper. This indicates that water exerts a force on the bottle in the upward direction. The upward force exerted by the water goes on increasing as the bottle is pushed deeper till it is completely immersed.
- Now, release the bottle. It bounces back to the surface.
- Does the force due to the gravitational attraction of the earth act on this bottle? If so, why doesn't the bottle stay immersed in water after it is released? How can you immerse the bottle in water?

Ans. Yes, the bottle is attracted downwards by the earth's gravitational force. On pushing the bottle with force in the water it does not remain there but comes up because of the upward force exerted by water on the bottle. This upward force is called upthrust or buoyant force. When the upward force or buoyant force is greater than the downward force '*g*' the bottle will float. But if downward force is greater than upward force, the bottle will sink. The upward force (buoyant force) acting on the bottle can be reduced by increasing the force on the bottle or by filling the bottle with sand, water etc.

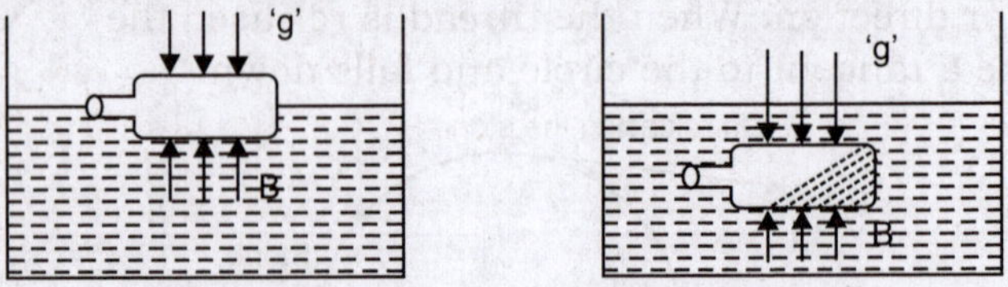

5. • Take a piece of stone and tie it to one end of a rubber string or a spring balance.

- Suspend the stone by holding the balance or the string as shown in the figure (*a*).

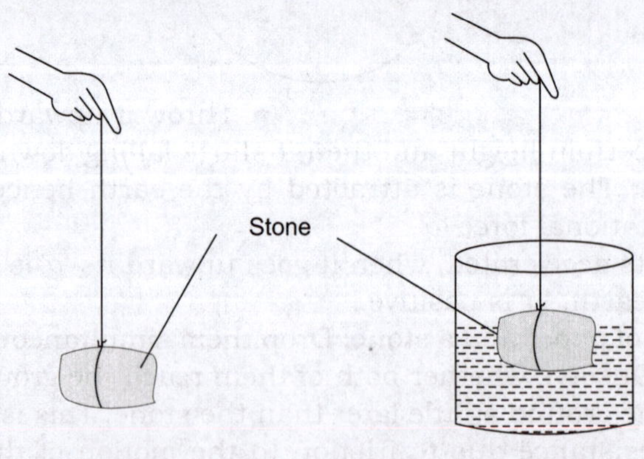

(*a*) (*b*)

- Note the elongation of the string or the reading on the spring balance due to the weight of the stone.
- Now, slowly dip the stone in the water in a container as shown in Fig. (*b*).
- Observe what happens to the elongation of the string or the reading on the balance.

Observations :

- In Fig. (*a*) the elongation of the string is 6 cm.
- In Fig. (*b*) when the stone is dipped in water the length of string reduced to 5 cm.
- The length of the string in case (*b*) decreases due to the upward force exerted by water on the stone called as buoyant force.

6. • Take a beaker filled with water.
- Take an iron nail and place it on the surface of the water.
- Observe what happens.

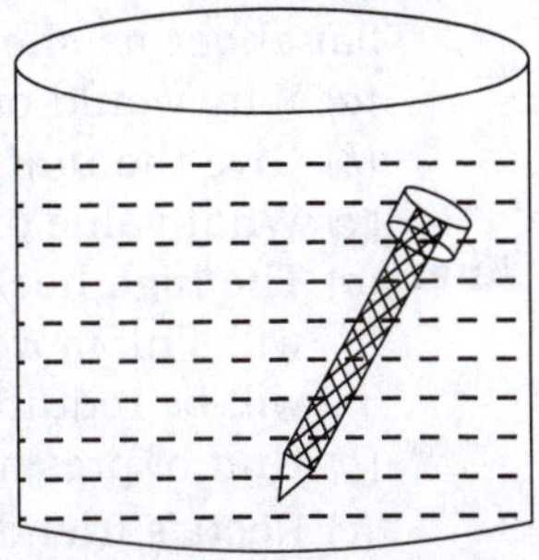

Ans. The iron nail sinks as the density of nail is more and the downward force exerted on nail is more than the buoyant force.

7. • Take a beaker filled with water.
- Take a piece of cork and an iron nail of equal mass.
- Place them on the surface of water.
- Observe what happens.

Ans. The iron nail sinks as the density of nail is more and the downward force exerted on nail is more than the buoyant force. The cork floats as the density of cork is less and the buoyant force exerted on it is more than the downward force.

VI. Value-Based Questions

Q1. Priya had a bad experience during the take off of the plane when she boarded it for the first time. Her friend assisted and helped her during the landing of plane. She told her to fasten the seat belt and involved her in gossip. Priya faced less problems while landing of the plane.

(*a*) Why do we tie our seat belts in moving cars or during landing/take off of the plane?

(*b*) What is free fall?

(*c*) What value of Priya's friend is seen in this act?

Ans. (*a*) We tie our seat belts to remain intact on the seat so that our body does not fall forward.

(*b*) When an object falls towards the earth under the gravitational force then we say that the object is in free fall.

(*c*) Priya's friend showed the value of concerned, sympathetic, responsible, and caring friend.

Q2. A goldsmith measured the purity of gold by using a special measuring device. He told the customer that there was impurity present in gold ornament that he wanted to buy and was not 22 carats but 18 carats jewellery.

(*a*) How can we find the purity of gold?

(*b*) What is the unit of relative density?

(*c*) What value of goldsmith is reflected in this act?

Ans. (*a*) The purity of gold can be obtained by knowing the density of the gold.

(*b*) Relative density does not have any unit.

(*c*) Goldsmith showed the value of honesty and trustworthy.

Q3. A milkman sold his milk in the city and always carried lactometer with him. The customers trusted him and his business flourished.

(*a*) What is lactometer?

(*b*) What is the principle of working of lactometer?

(*c*) What value of milkman is seen in this case?

Ans. (*a*) Lactometer is a device that measures the purity of milk.

(b) The principle of lactometer is 'Archimedes' principle'. It states that when a body is immersed fully or partially in a fluid, it experiences an upward force that is equal to the weight of the fluid displaced by it.

(c) Milkman is very honest and trustworthy.

Q4. Reeta was wearing a high heel shoes for a beach party, her friend told her to wear flat shoes as she will be tired soon with high heels and will not feel comfortable.

(a) Why would one feel tired with high heel shoes on beach?

(b) Give the unit of pressure.

(c) What value of Reeta's friend is seen in the above act?

Ans. (a) The high heel shoes would exert lot of pressure on the loose sand of beach and will sink more in the soil as compared to flat shoes. Hence large amount of force will be required to walk with heels.

(b) Unit of pressure is Pascal.

(c) Reeta's friend showed the value of being helpful, concerned and intelligent.

Q5. In the school fair, there was a game in which one need to find the heaviest ball without holding them in hand. Three balls were given and few disposable glasses were kept. Tarun saw his friend struggling to win the game but he was unable to find the heaviest ball. Tarun helped him by dipping the three balls one by one in the glasses full of water upto the brim and finally they won the game.

(a) Why did Tarun told his friend to dip the balls one by one in completely filled glass of water?

(b) Name the principle used here.

(c) What value of Tarun is reflected in this case?

Ans. (a) Tarun wanted to measure the amount of water displaced by each ball when dipped in water.

(b) The principle used is 'Archimedes' principle'.

(c) Tarun showed the value of being helpful, kind and intelligent.

VII. Practical Based Questions

Q1. Assume a 0.5 kg piece of wood that has volume ($1000cm^3$ or 1000mL), as shown in Figure when immersed in water what will be the observations? Answer the following questions.

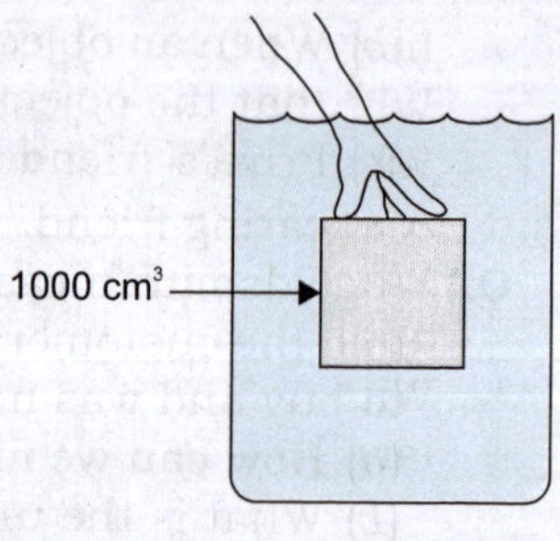

(a) What is the mass of 1L of water?

(b) What is the weight of 1L of water?

(c) What is the buoyant force acting on the block?

(d) What is the volume of water displaced by the piece of wood?

(e) What is the mass of water displaced by the piece of wood?

(f) What is the weight of water displaced by the piece of wood?

(g) What is weight of the piece of wood?

Ans. (a) Mass of 1L of water is 1000g = 1kg.

(b) Weight = $m \times g = 1 \times 9.8 = 9.8$ N.

(c) Buoyant Force = $1 \times 9.8 \times 1000 = 9800$ N.

(d) 1000 cm^3.

(e) 1000 g.

(f) W = $mg = 1 \times 9.8 = 9.8$ N.

(g) Weight of wood = $0.5 \text{ kg} \times 9.8 \text{ ms}^{-2} = 4.9$ N.

Q2. A 100 cm³ block of heavy metal that weighs 11 N is carefully submerged in water. One cm³ of water weighs 0.0098 N.

(*a*) What volume of water does the metal displace?

(*b*) How much does that volume of water weigh?

(*c*) What is the buoyant force on the metal?

(*d*) Will the lead metal sink or float in the water?

Ans. (*a*) 100 cm³.

(*b*) $0.0098 \times 100 = 0.98$ N.

(*c*) 0.98 N.

(*d*) Sink (∵ buoyant force < weight)

Q3. The 100 cm³ metal piece block is carefully submerged in a container of mercury that weighs 11N. One cm³ of mercury weighs 0.13 N.

(*a*) What volume of mercury is displaced?

(*b*) How much does that volume of mercury weigh?

(*c*) What is the buoyant force on the metal?

(*d*) Will the metal sinks or float in the mercury?

Ans. (*a*) 100 cm³.

(*b*) $0.13 \times 100 = 13$ N.

(*c*) 13 N.

(*d*) Float (∵ buoyant force > weight)

TEST YOUR SKILLS

Q1. With what force will the body of mass 1 kg get attracted to the earth?

Q2. If a ball is thrown up in the sky, what will happen to its value of 'g'?

Q3. Mass of a dog on earth is 40 kg, what will be its mass and weight on moon?

Q4. Give the difference between g and G.

Q5. Calculate the value of 'g', acceleration due to gravity.

Q6. Establish a relationship between '*g*' and 'G'.

Q7. What do you mean by buoyancy?

Q8. In what direction does the buoyant force on an object immersed in a liquid act?

Q9. Why is it easier to swim in sea water than in river water?

Q10. What is relative density?

Q11. A ship made of iron does not sink but the iron rod sinks in water, why?

Q12. What are fluids ? Why is Archimedes' principle applicable only for fluids ? Give the application of Archimedes' principle.

Q13. With the help of an activity prove that the force acting on a smaller area exerts a larger pressure?

❑❑❑

11 Work and Energy

Syllabus

Work done by a force, Energy, Power, Kinetic and potential energy, Law of conservation of energy.

Facts that Matter

- **Work:** When a force acts on an object and the object shows displacement, the force has done work on the object.
  Two conditions need to be satisfied for work to be done:
  (*i*) A force should act on the object
  (*ii*) The object must be displaced

  $$\text{Work} = \text{Force} \times \text{Displacement} = F \times S$$

  Unit of work done = Joule = Newton × metre

- 1 Joule work is said to be done when 1 Newton force is applied on an object and it shows the displacement by 1 meter.
  (Case I)
  If displacement is in the direction of the force

  $$W = F \times s$$

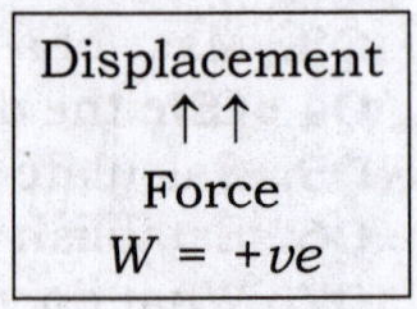

  If displacement is in the direction opposite to the force

  $$W = -F \times s$$

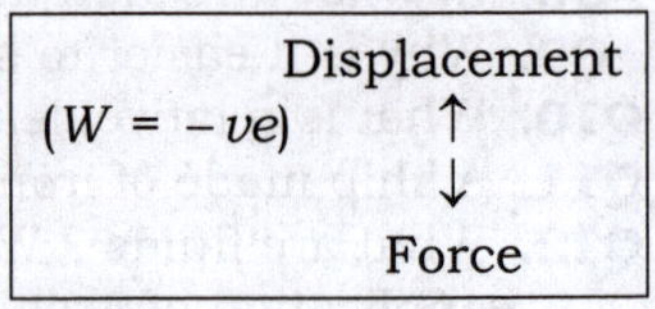

  (Case II)
  If displacement is perpendicular to the force, work done is zero.

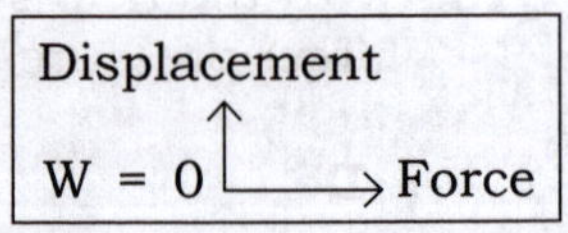

- **Energy**
  The capacity of a body to do work is called the energy of the body.

  Unit of energy = Joules
  1 kJ = 1000J

- **Forms of Energy:** The various forms of energy are potential energy, kinetic energy, heat energy, chemical energy, electrical energy and light energy.
- **Kinetic Energy:** Energy possessed by a body due to its motion. Kinetic energy of an object increases with its speed.
  Kinetic energy of body moving with a certain velocity = work done on it to make it acquire that velocity.

- **Derivation**

Let an object of mass m, moves with uniform velocity u, let us displace it by s, due to constant force F, acting on it

$\therefore$ Work done $\rightarrow$ $\quad W = F \times s \quad$ ... (*i*)

due to force the velocity changes to v, and the acceleration produced is a

$\therefore$ Relationship between v, u, a and s : $v^2 - u^2 = 2as$

$$\therefore \quad s = \frac{v^2 - u^2}{2a} \quad \text{... (ii)}$$

$$\text{and} \quad F = ma \quad \text{... (iii)}$$

Substitute (*ii*) and (*iii*) in (*i*), we get

$$W = F \times s$$

$$= ma \times \frac{v^2 - u^2}{2a}$$

$$W = \frac{1}{2} m(v^2 - u^2)$$

if $\quad u = 0$, (object starts at rest)

$$\therefore \quad W = \frac{1}{2} mv^2$$

Work done = Change in kinetic energy

$$\therefore \quad E_k = \frac{1}{2} mv^2$$

- **Potential Energy**

The energy possessed by a body due to its position or shape is called its potential energy.

- **Shape**

Position

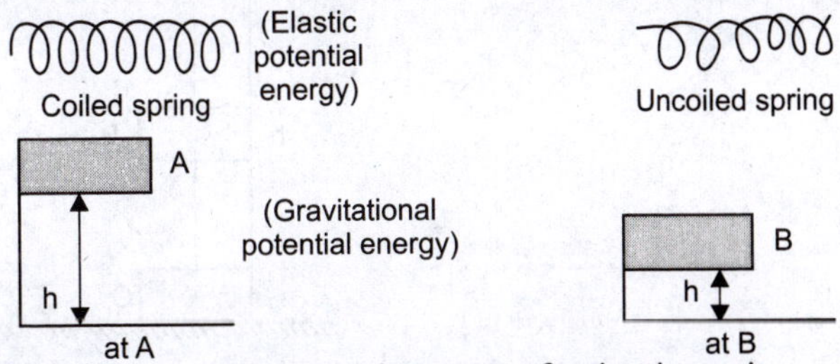

Greater energy due to compression in spring and due to greater height of the object.

Less energy due to rarefaction in spring and due to less height of the object.

- **Gravitational Potential Energy: (GP_E)**

When an object is raised through a height, work is said to be done on it against gravity. The energy possessed by such an object is called the gravitational potential energy.

$\therefore GP_E$ = work done in raising a body from the ground to a point against gravity.

- **Derivation**

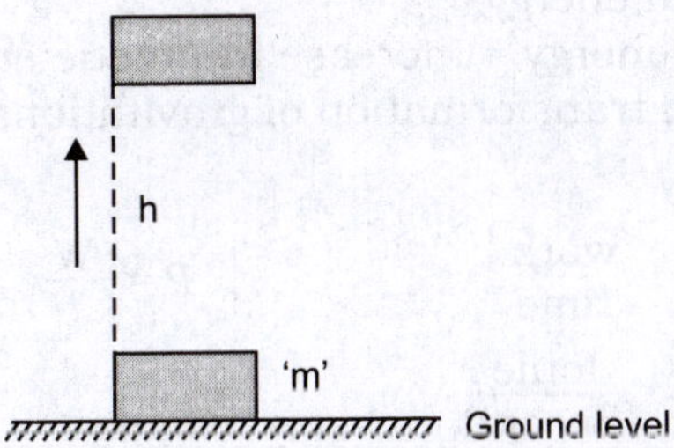

Consider a body with mass m, raised through a height h, from the ground,

Force required to raise the object = weight of object mg.

Object gains energy equal to the work done on it.

$\therefore$ Work done on the object against gravity is W.

$$\therefore \quad W = \text{force} \times \text{displacement} = mg \times h$$

$$W = mgh$$

$$\therefore \quad P_E = mgh$$

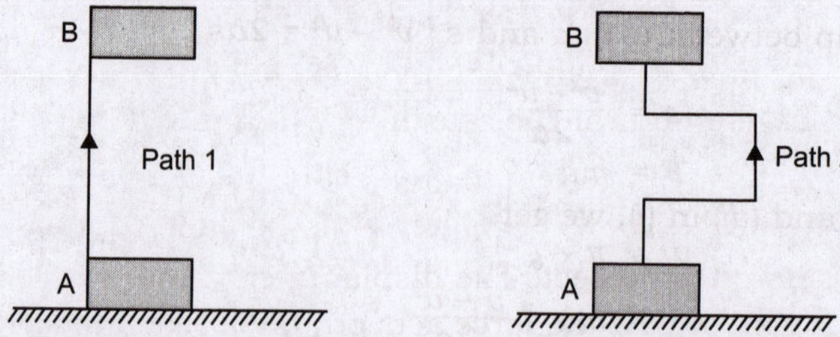

(i) (ii)

Work done in both the cases (*i*) and (*ii*) is same as a body is raised from position *A* to *B*, even if the path taken is different but the height attained is the same.

- **Mechanical Energy:** The sum of kinetic energy and potential energy is called mechanical energy.
- **Law of Conservation of Energy:**

Energy can neither be created nor destroyed, it can only be transformed from one form to another. The total energy before and after transformation remains the same.

Case (*i*)

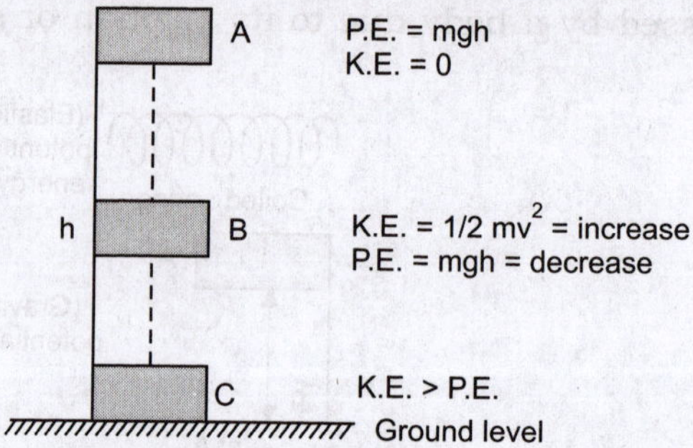

Potential energy + Kinetic energy = Constant (Mechanical energy)

A body of mass '*m*' is raised to height '*h*' at A its potential energy is maximum and kinetic energy is 0 as it is stationary.

When body falls at B, *h* is decreasing hence potential energy decreases and '*v*' is increasing hence kinetic energy is increasing.

When the body is about to reach the ground level, $h = 0$, v will be maximum hence kinetic energy > potential energy

$\therefore$ Decrease in potential energy = Increase in kinetic energy

This shows the continual transformation of gravitational potential energy into kinetic energy.

- **Power**

$$\text{Power} = \frac{\text{work}}{\text{time}} \qquad \therefore \; P = \frac{W}{t}$$

$$\text{Watt} = \frac{\text{Joules}}{\text{Second}}$$

1 kilowatt = 1000 watts

1 kilowatt = 1000 J/s

- **Commercial Unit of Energy**

Commercial unit of energy = 1 kilowatt hour (kWh)

$$\therefore \quad 1\ \text{kWh} = 1\ \text{kilowatt} \times 1\ \text{hour}$$
$$= 1000\ \text{watt} \times 3600\ \text{seconds}$$
$$= 3600000\ \text{Joule} \quad (\text{watt} \times \text{second})$$
$$1\ \text{kWh} = 3.6 \times 10^6\ \text{J.}$$
$$\therefore \quad \boxed{1\ \text{kWh} = 1\ \text{unit}}$$

The energy used in one hour at the rate of 1 kW is called 1 kWh.

NCERT IN-TEXT QUESTIONS SOLVED

Q1. A force of 7 N acts on an object. The displacement is, say 8 m, in the direction of the force. Let us take it that the force acts on the object through the displacement. What is the work done in this case?

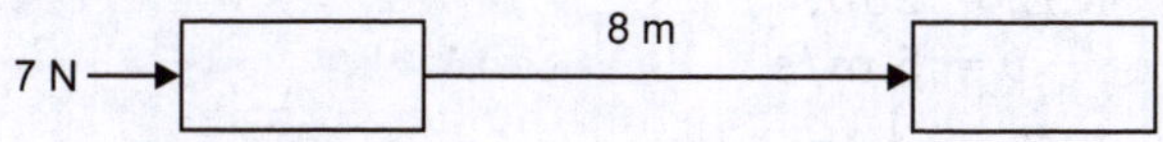

Ans.
$$F = 7\ \text{N}$$
$$s = 8\ \text{m}$$
$$W = F \times s$$
$$= 7\ \text{N} \times 8\ \text{m}$$
$$W = 56\ \text{J}$$

$\therefore$ Work done is 56 J.

Q2. When do we say that work is done?

Ans. Work is said to be done when force applied on an object shows the displacement in that object.

$$W = F \times s.$$

Q3. Write an expression for the work done when a force is acting on an object in the direction of its displacement.

Ans.
$$\text{Work done} = W$$
$$\text{Force} = F$$
$$\text{Displacement} = s$$

$\therefore$ Work done is equal to the product of the force and displacement.

$$\therefore \quad W = F \times s$$

Q4. Define 1 J of work.

Ans. 1 Joule of work is said to be done when force of 1 Newton acts on a body and shows displacement of 1 metre.

Q5. A pair of bullocks exerts a force of 140 N on a plough. The field being ploughed is 15 m long. How much work is done in ploughing the length of the field?

Ans.
$$\text{Force} = 140\ \text{N}$$
$$s = 15\ \text{m}$$
$$W = ?$$
$$\therefore \quad W = F \times s$$
$$= 140\ \text{N} \times 15\ \text{m} = 2100\ \text{Nm}$$
$$W = 2100\ \text{J}$$

$\therefore$ Work done in ploughing the length of the field is 2100 J.

Q6. What is the kinetic energy of an object?

Ans. The energy possessed by an object due to its motion is called kinetic energy of that object.

$$\text{K.E.} = \frac{1}{2}mv^2.$$

where m is mass of the object and v is velocity of the object.

Q7. Write an expression for the kinetic energy of an object.

Ans.
$$\text{K.E.} = \frac{1}{2}mv^2$$

where m = Mass of the object

v = Velocity of the object

Q8. The kinetic energy of an object of mass, m moving with a velocity of 5 ms^{-1} is 25J. What will be its kinetic energy when its velocity is doubled? What will be its kinetic energy when its velocity is increased three times?

Ans.
$$\text{K.E.} = 25\text{J},$$
$$v = 5 \text{ m/s}$$
$$\text{K.E.} = \frac{1}{2}mv^2$$
$$25 = \frac{1}{2}m(5)^2$$
$$\therefore \quad m = 2\text{kg}$$

(*i*) If velocity is doubled i.e., $v = 10\text{m/s}$, $m = 2\text{kg}$

$$\text{K.E.} = \frac{1}{2}mv^2 = \frac{1}{2}(2) \times (10)^2$$
$$= 100\text{J, K.E will become four times.}$$

(*ii*) If velocity is 3 times, $v = 15 \text{ m/s}, m = 2\text{kg}$

$$\text{K.E.} = \frac{1}{2}mv^2$$
$$= \frac{1}{2} \times 2 \times (15)^2$$
$$= 225\text{J, K.E will become nine times.}$$

Q9. What is power?

Ans. Power is defined as the rate of doing work.

$$P = \frac{\text{work}}{\text{time}}$$
$$P = \frac{\text{Joules}}{\text{Second}}$$
$$\text{watt} = \frac{\text{Joules}}{\text{Second}}$$

Q10. Define 1 watt of power.

Ans. Power is said to be 1 watt when 1 Joule of work is done in 1 second.

Q11. A lamp consumes 1000J of electrical energy in 10s. What is its power?

Ans.
$$P = ?$$
$$W = 1000\text{J}$$
$$t = 10 \text{ s}$$
$$P = \frac{W}{t} = \frac{1000}{10} = 100 \text{ watt}$$

$\therefore$ Power is 100 watt.

Q12. Define average power.

Ans. Average power is defined as the total energy consumed divided by the total time taken.

NCERT TEXTUAL QUESTIONS SOLVED

Q1. Look at the activities listed below. Reason out whether or not work is done in the light of your understanding of the term 'work'.

(a)Suma is swimming in a pond. (b) A donkey is carrying a load on its back.
(c)A wind-mill is lifting water from a well.
(d)A green plant is carrying out photosynthesis.
(e)An engine is pulling a train. (f) Food grains are getting dried in the sun.
(g)A sailboat is moving due to wind energy.

Ans. (*a*) Suma pushes water in backward direction and the displacement is in forward direction, work is said to be done.

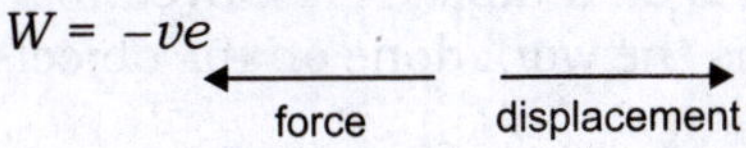

(*b*) Work done is 'zero'

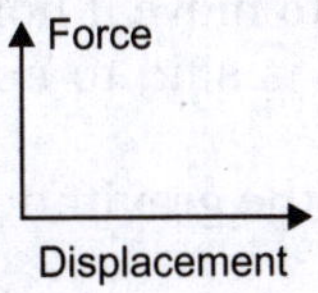

(*c*) Force ↑ ↑ Displacement of water W = +ve

(*d*) No displacement, hence no work is done

(*e*) Work is done

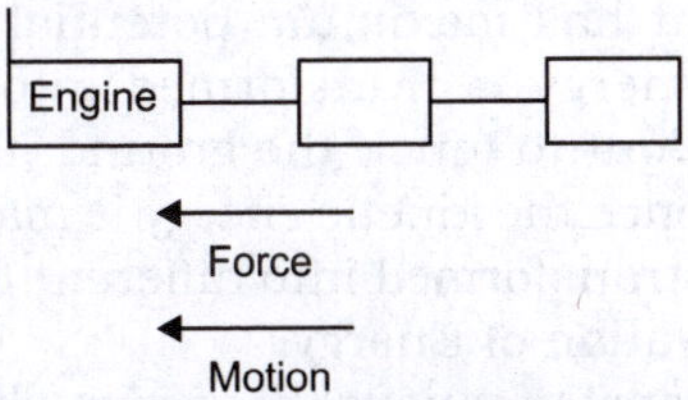

W = + ve

(*f*) No displacement, hence no work is done.

(*g*) Work is done

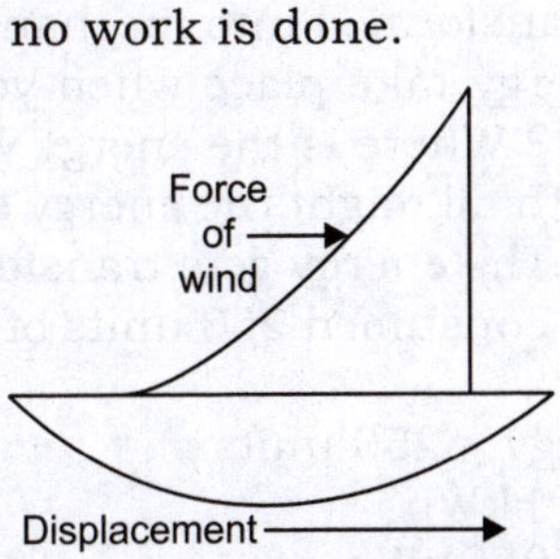

Q2. An object thrown at a certain angle to the ground moves in a curved path and falls back to the ground. The initial and the final points of the path of the object lie on the same horizontal line. What is the work done by the force of gravity on the object?

Ans. Work done by the force of gravity on the object is zero. Force of gravity acts in the vertical downward direction and the distance covered by the object is in the horizontal direction. As there is no displacement in the direction of force, hence the work done is zero.

Q3. A battery lights a bulb. Describe the energy changes involved in the process.

Ans. Chemical energy of battery → transformed into heat energy of bulb filament, which is further transformed into light energy.

Q4. Certain force acting on a 20 kg mass changes its velocity from 5 m/s to 2 m/s. Calculate the work done by the force.

Ans.

$$\text{mass} = 20\,\text{kg}$$
$$u = 5\,\text{m/s}$$
$$v = 2\,\text{m/s}$$
$$W = ?$$
$$W = F \times s = ma \times \left(\frac{v^2 - u^2}{2a}\right) = 20 \times \left(\frac{(2)^2 - (5)^2}{2}\right)$$
$$= 20 \times \left(\frac{4 - 25}{2}\right) = 10 \times (-21) = -210\,\text{J}$$

Q5. A mass of 10 kg is at a point A on a table. It is moved to a point B. If the line joining A and B is horizontal. What is the work done on the object by the gravitational force? Explain your answer.

Ans. Force acts on a body of mass 10 kg to move it horizontally from *A* to *B* as shown above. Work is said to be done on the object by the force.

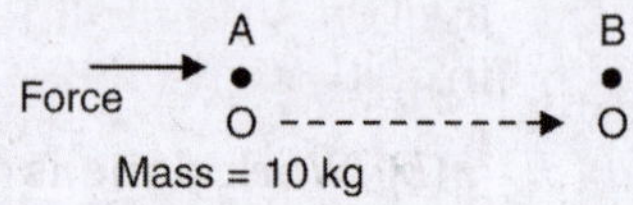

But the work done on the object by the gravitational force is zero.

Since work done by gravitational force depends upon change in vertical height.

Q6. The potential energy of a freely falling object decreases progressively. Does this violate the law of conservation of energy? Why?

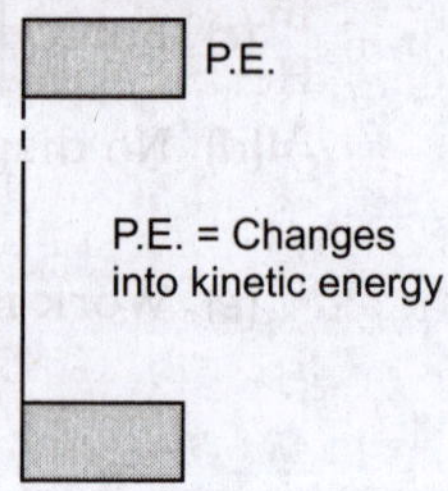

Ans. A body at a particular height has maximum potential energy, when it falls the potential energy is transformed into kinetic energy, when the object is about to touch the ground, the body has maximum velocity and hence the kinetic energy is maximum. Energy is not lost but it gets transformed into different forms. It abides by the Law of Conservation of Energy.

Q7. What are the various energy transformations that occur when you are riding a bicycle?

Ans. Muscular energy gets transformed into mechanical energy.

Q8. Does the transfer of energy take place when you push a huge rock with all your might and fail to move it? Where is the energy you spend going?

Ans. When rock is pushed with all might the energy does not allow the rock to move. No work is said to be done. The energy gets transformed in the form of heat energy.

Q9. A certain household has consumed 250 units of energy during a month. How much energy is this in joules?

Ans. Commercial unit of energy = 250 units

$$1\text{ unit} = 1\,\text{kWh}$$
$$\therefore \quad 250\text{ units} = 250\,\text{kWh}$$
$$1\,\text{kWh} = 3.6 \times 10^6\,\text{J}$$
$$\therefore \quad 250\text{ units} = 250 \times 3.6 \times 10^6\,\text{J}$$
$$\text{Energy in Joules} = 9 \times 10^8\,\text{J}$$

Q10. An object of mass 40 kg is raised to a height of 5 m above the ground. What is its potential energy? If the object is allowed to fall, find its kinetic energy when it is half-way down.

Ans.

$$\text{Mass} = 40\,\text{kg}$$

$h = 5\,\text{m}$

P.E. = ?

P.E. = $mgh = 40 \times 10 \times 5$ $\quad \because g = 10\,\text{m/s}^2$

P.E. = 2000 J

When the object falls the potential energy gets transformed into kinetic energy. When the object is half way down

P.E. will become half *i.e.,* $\frac{2000}{2} = 1000\,\text{J}$ and P.E. = K.E.

$\therefore$ Kinetic Energy = 1000 J

Q11. What is the work done by the force of gravity on a satellite moving around the earth? Justify your answer.

Ans. As the force acting on the body is perpendicular to the direction of displacement,

$\therefore$ Work done is zero.

Q12. Can there be displacement of an object in the absence of any force acting on it? Think. Discuss this question with your friends and teacher.

Ans. If an object is in a state of motion, then as per Newton's first law of motion in the absence of any external force acting on it, the object will maintain its motion along a given straight line. So the object will have displacement. However, if the object is initially at rest then there can be no displacement, the work done by person is zero.

Q13. A person holds a bundle of hay over his head for 30 minutes and gets tired. Has he done some work or not? Justify your answer.

Ans. Work is said to be done when force is applied on a body and the body shows the displacement.

In this case force is applied on hay bundle but there is no displacement of it. Hence no work is said to be done on the hay.

Q14. An electric heater is rated 1500 W. How much energy does it use in 10 hours.

Ans. Power = 1500 W $\rightarrow$ 1.5 kW

time = 10 hour

Energy = ?

Energy = Power $\times$ Time taken = $1.5 \times 10 = 15$ kWh

$\therefore$ Energy required = 15 kWh

Q15. Illustrate the law of conservation of energy by discussing the energy changes which occur when we draw a pendulum bob to one side and allow it to oscillate. Why does the bob eventually come to rest? What happens to its energy eventually? Is it a violation of the law of conservation of energy?

Ans.

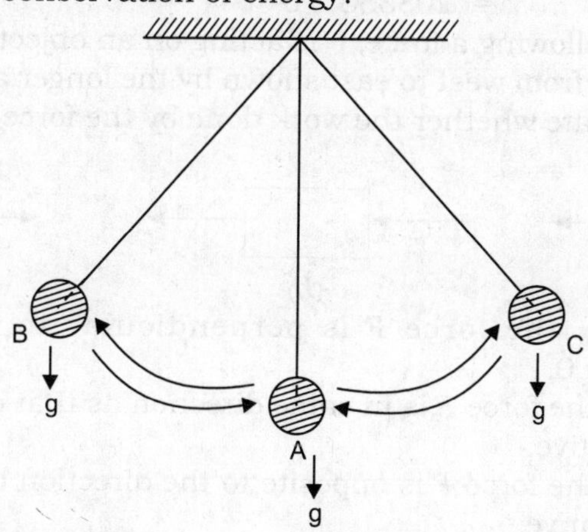

Let '*A*' be the mean position of pendulum. When it is raised to point '*B*' and released, it starts oscillating from B to A, A to C and back to A. It repeats this motion again and again.

At point B and C, height of pendulum is maximum, hence the potential energy at these points is maximum.

During oscillation, when pendulum moves from $B - A - C$, its maximum speed is at A, hence the maximum kinetic energy is at A, and potential energy at this point is minimum.

This shows the potential energy at B is transformed to kinetic energy at A and again this energy is transformed into potential energy at C.

This transformation of energy goes on and the pendulum oscillates, it does not violate the law of conservation of energy.

Bob comes to rest because there are three forces acting on it,

(*i*) Gravitational force exerted by earth 'g' which tries to bring the bob at rest.

(*ii*) Air resistance force that acts opposite the motion of pendulum.

(*iii*) Restoring force, the pendulum is tied at a point, the upward tension pull also tries to get the pendulum to its original position.

Q16. An object of mass, m is moving with a constant velocity, v. How much work should be done on the object in order to bring the object to rest?

Ans. The mass of the object = m

Velocity = v

$$\text{K.E.} = \frac{1}{2}mv^2$$ – This is the energy of the object with which the body is moving, hence same amount of energy is required to stop the body.

∴ Work done on the object in order to bring the object to rest

$$= \text{K.E.} = \frac{1}{2}mv^2$$

Q17. Calculate the work done required to be done to stop a car of 1500 kg moving at a velocity of 60 km/h.

Ans.

mass = 1500 kg

$$v = 60 \text{ km/h} = \frac{60 \times 1000}{60 \times 60} \text{ m/s} = \frac{50}{3} \text{ m/s}$$

Work done to stop a car = Energy required = K.E.

$$\therefore \quad \text{K.E.} = \frac{1}{2}mv^2 = \frac{1}{2} \times 1500 \times \left(\frac{50}{3}\right)^2$$

$$= 208333.3 \text{ J}$$

Q18. In each of the following a force, F is acting on an object of mass m. The direction of displacement is from west to east shown by the longer arrow. Observe the diagrams carefully and state whether the work done by the force is negative, positive or zero.

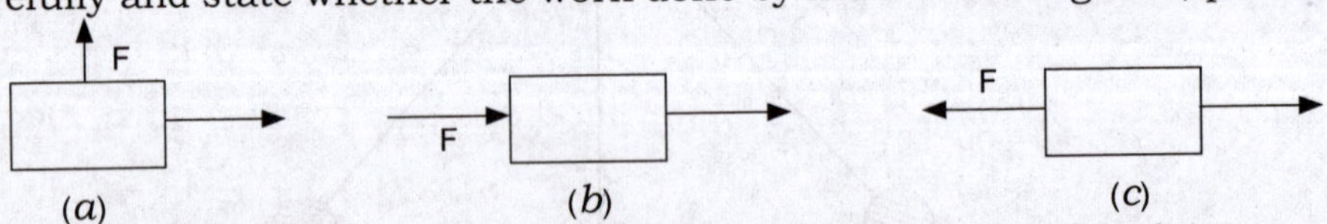

Ans. (*a*) In case (*a*), the force F is perpendicular to the displacement, hence work done = 0.

(*b*) In case (*b*), the force F is in same direction as that of displacement, hence work done is positive.

(*c*) In case (*c*), the force F is opposite to the direction of displacement, hence work done is negative.

Q19. Soni says that the acceleration in an object could be zero even when several forces are acting on it. Do you agree with her? Why?

Ans. Yes, when several forces are acting on a body, if the forces are opposite to each other, the acceleration produced can be zero.

Q20. Find the energy in kwh consumed in 10 hours by four devices of power 500 W each.

Ans.

$$\text{Power} = 500\,\text{W} = 0.5\,\text{kW}$$
$$\text{time} = 10\ \text{hours}$$
$$\text{Devices} = 4$$

$\therefore$ Energy consumed in kWh = 0.5 kW × 10 hours × 4 = 20 kWh

Q21. A freely falling object eventually stops on reaching the ground. What happens to its kinetic energy?

Ans. When a body is freely falling the energy remains conserved. Potential energy is transformed into kinetic energy. But when the body reaches the ground, its velocity, ($v = 0$) becomes zero. Hence the kinetic energy is also zero.

ADDITIONAL QUESTIONS SOLVED

I. Multiple Choice Questions

Choose the correct option:

1. The unit of work is joule. The other physical quantity that has same unit is
   (*a*) power (*b*) velocity
   (*c*) energy (*d*) force
2. The spring will have maximum potential energy when
   (*a*) it is pulled out (*b*) it is compressed
   (*c*) both (*a*) and (*b*) (*d*) neither (*a*) nor (*b*)
3. The energy possessed by an oscillating pendulum of a clock is
   (*a*) kinetic energy (*b*) potential energy
   (*c*) restoring energy (*d*) mechanical energy
4. The gravitational potential energy of an object is due to
   (*a*) its mass (*b*) its acceleration due to gravity
   (*c*) its height above the earth's surface (*d*) all of the above.
5. A ball is dropped from a height of 10 m.
   (*a*) Its potential energy increases and kinetic energy decreases during the falls.
   (*b*) Its potential energy is equal to the kinetic energy during the fall.
   (*c*) The potential energy decreases and the kinetic energy increases during the fall.
   (*d*) The potential energy is '0' and kinetic energy is maximum while it is falling.
6. If the velocity of a body is doubled its kinetic energy
   (*a*) gets doubled (*b*) becomes half
   (*c*) does not change (*d*) becomes 4 times
7. How much time will be required to perform 520 J of work at the rate of 20 W?
   (*a*) 24 s (*b*) 16 s
   (*c*) 20 s (*d*) 26 s
8. A student carries a bag weighing 5 kg from the ground floor to his class on the first floor that is 2 m high. The work done by the boy is
   (*a*) 1 J (*b*) 10 J
   (*c*) 100 J (*d*) 1000 J
9. The work done is '0' if
   (*a*) The body shows displacement in the opposite direction of the force applied.
   (*b*) The body shows displacement in the same direction as that of the force applied.
   (*c*) The body shows a displacement in perpendicular direction to the force applied.

(d) The body masses obliquely to the direction of the force applied.

10. One unit of electrical energy is equal to

(a) 3.6×10^5 J (b) 3.6×10^6 J

(c) 36×10^5 J (d) both (b) and (c)

Ans. 1—(c), 2—(c), 3—(d), 4—(d), 5—(c), 6—(d), 7—(d), 8—(c), 9—(c), 10—(b).

II. Very Short Answer Type Questions

Q1. Define work.

Ans. When a force acts on an object and the object moves, we say that the force has done work on the object.

$$W = F \times s$$

Q2. What is the unit of work done?

Ans. Joule.

Q3. Define 1 Joule of work.

Ans. When a force of 1 Newton acts on an object and the object moves a distance of 1 metre in the direction of the force, the work done by the force is 1 Joule.

Q4. Name two conditions required to do work.

Ans. Two conditions required to do work are force applied and displacement produced.

Q5. What is potential energy?

Ans. The energy possessed by a body due to its height or position is called potential energy.

Q6. Name 2 types of potential energy.

Ans. Gravitational potential energy and elastic potential energy

Q7. What is the formula of work and give the units of each symbol.

Ans. Formula → $W = F \times s$ ∴ W = work done

Units → Joule = Newton × Metre F = force

s = displacement

Q8. If the work done is 20 J and displacement is 2 m then find the force applied.

Ans.

$$W = F \times s$$
$$20 = F \times 2$$
$$\therefore \quad F = 10\,\text{N}$$

Q9. When we push a pebble lying on surface is work done?

Ans. On pushing a pebble lying on a surface, it moves through a distance so work is done.

Q10. Give the formula of kinetic energy and potential energy.

Ans. $\text{K.E.} = \frac{1}{2} mv^2$ P.E. = mgh

m = mass m = mass

v = velocity g = acceleration due to gravity

h = height

Q11. Name the energy stored when a rubber band is stretched?

Ans. On stretching a rubber band, potential energy is stored in it.

Q12. How many joules are there in 1 kJ?

Ans. 1000 Joules = 1 kJ

Q13. Define power.

Ans. Power is defined as the rate of doing work or the rate of transfer of energy.

$$P = \frac{W}{t}$$

Q14. What is the unit of power? Define it.

Ans. The unit of power is watt.

1 watt is the power of an agent which does work at the rate of 1 joule per second.

Q15. What is the commercial unit of energy? Define it.

Ans. The commercial unit of energy is kWh [kilowatt-hour]. 1 kWh is the energy used in one hour at the rate of 1000 J/s.

$$1\,\text{kWh} = 1\,\text{kW} \times 1\,\text{h}.$$

Q16. Convert 1 kWh into joules.

Ans.

$$\begin{aligned} 1\,\text{kWh} &= 1\,\text{kW} \times 1\,\text{h} \\ &= 1000\,\text{W} \times 3600\,\text{s} \\ &= 3600000\,\text{J} \\ &= 3.6 \times 10^6\,\text{J} \end{aligned}$$

Q17. What is mechanical energy?

Ans. The sum of kinetic energy and potential energy of an object is called its mechanical energy.

Q18. Give one example where work done on an object is zero.

Ans. A person walking horizontally straight with load on its head is said to be doing no work on the load.

This is because the direction of force acting on the load and the displacement seen is perpendicular.

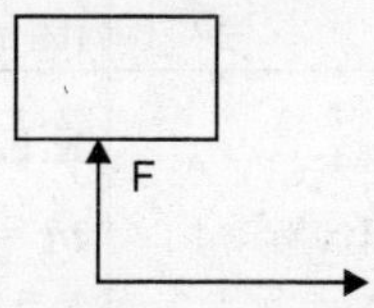

$W = 0$

Q19. Give one example where work done on an object is negative.

Ans. A person walking down the stairs with load on its head, the work done is negative as the force applied on the load is in opposite direction to its displacement.

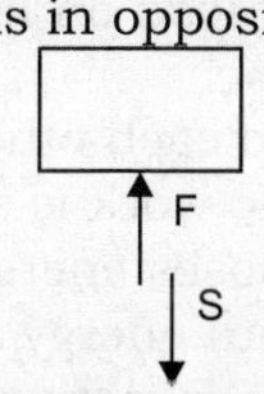

$W = -ve$

Q20.

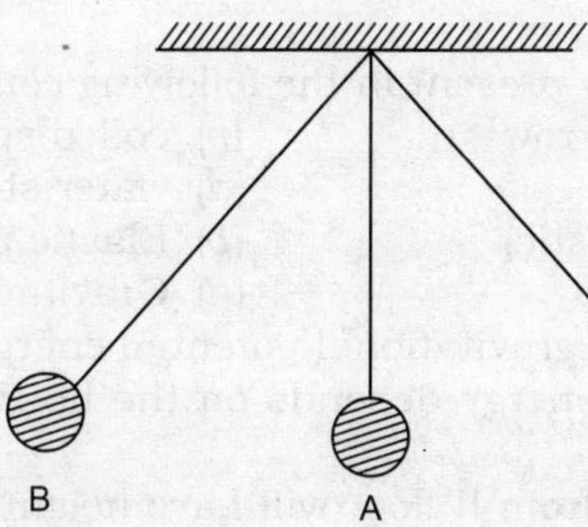

In the above figure a pendulum is shown oscillating from A to B, B to C and C to A. In its one oscillation state the position, where its kinetic energy is maximum.

Ans. A pendulum when raised to certain height and is at *B*, on releasing it from *B* it attains motion and hence its potential energy is transformed to kinetic energy. The maximum kinetic energy is at *A* when it is in motion.

Q21. A man does 60 J of work in 6 seconds. Calculate the power.

Ans. Power = $\frac{\text{work done}}{\text{time}} = \frac{60 \text{ J}}{6 \text{ s}}$

$\therefore$ Power = 10 watts.

Q22. What would happen to the kinetic energy of an object if its velocity is doubled?

Ans. Kinetic energy $\propto v^2$.

$\therefore$ If the velocity is doubled, kinetic energy will become 4 times more.

III. Short Answer Type Questions

Q1. What is gravitational potential energy?

Ans. The gravitational potential energy of an object at a point above the ground is defined as the work done in raising the object from the ground to that point against gravity.

G.P.E = mgh

Q2. Differentiate between potential energy and kinetic energy.

Ans.

Potential Energy	***Kinetic Energy***
1. Energy possessed by a body due to its height.	Energy is possessed by a body due to its motion.
2. P.E. = mgh m = mass g = acceleration due to gravity h = height	K.E = $\frac{1}{2}$ mv^2 m = mass v = velocity

Q3. Give two situations where energy is supplied but no work is done.

Ans. (*i*) A person pushing a heavy rock is using all the energy but if the rock does not move no work is done.

(*ii*) A person standing with heavy load on his head, energy is used/spent in doing this but no work is done.

Q4. How is work and energy related to each other?

Ans. An object having a capability to do work is said to possess energy.

The object which does the work loses energy and the object on which the work is done gains energy. The unit of both energy and work is Joule.

Q5. Give two examples in your daily life where you can see kinetic energy is doing work.

Ans. (*i*) Blowing wind

(*ii*) Rotating wheel

Q6. Name the form of energy present in the following conditions/situations:

(*a*) stretched bow and arrow (*b*) coiled spring

(*c*) a falling coconut (*d*) water stored in the dam

Ans. (*a*) Potential energy (Elastic) (*b*) Elastic potential energy

(*c*) Kinetic energy (*d*) Gravitational potential energy

Q7. On what factor does the gravitational potential energy depends?

Ans. Gravitational potential energy depends on the height from the ground level/zero level we choose.

Example, A ball tossed from II floor will have height h from its roof but from the I floor its height will be h'.

$\therefore h' > h$.

The potential energy of ball w.r.t. to I floor level is more as compared to the II floor.

Q8. Write the transformation of energy in the given cases.

(*a*) winds moving (*b*) an athlete running

(*c*) A coconut falling (*d*) playing of guitar

Ans. (*a*) Potential energy of wind to kinetic energy when it comes in motion.
(*b*) Muscular energy of athlete into kinetic energy.
(*c*) Potential energy into kinetic energy
(*d*) Potential energy (when guitar is plucked) to kinetic energy (when it shows the vibration)

Q9. Define work, give its unit. Give one example where work done is positive, zero and negative.

Ans. **Work:** Work is said to be done when force is applied on a body and it shows displacement. $W = F \times s$

Unit of work is Joule

Example:

(*a*) When we push a table in the direction of force. (Work done = positive)
(*b*) When the object is pushed/displaced in the direction opposite to the direction of force applied. (Work done = negative)
(*c*) When the displacement of the body is perpendicular to the direction of force applied. (Work done = '0')
Example, A person carrying load on its head and moving horizontally.

Q10. What is energy? Name different forms of energy. Give the unit of energy.

Ans. Energy is the capacity of a body to do work.

Different forms of energy are:

Potential energy, kinetic energy, heat energy, chemical energy, electrical energy, light energy, solar energy.

The unit of energy is Joules.

Q11. Two stones A and B of same mass fall from height h_1 and h_2 respectively on sand where $h_2 > h_1$. Which stone will exert more force on the sand and why? Name the energy present in it.

Ans. Stone *B* with height h_2 has more energy, potential energy is present in it, when the stone falls on the sand it exerts more force than stone A due to more energy transformation. When the stone falls all the potential energy present in it, is transformed into kinetic energy.

Q12. Derive the formula for kinetic energy.

Ans. Let an object of mass *m*, move with uniform velocity *u*.

Let us displace it by *s*, due to constant force *F*, acting on it.

Work done on the object of mass '*m*' is $W = F \times s$ ...(*i*)

Due to the force, velocity changes to *v* and the acceleration produced is '*a*'.

Relationship between *v*, *u*, *a* and *s* can be given by formula $v^2 - u^2 = 2as$

$$\therefore \quad s = \frac{v^2 - u^2}{2a} \quad ...(ii)$$

$$F = ma \quad ...(iii)$$

Substituting (*ii*) and (*iii*) in (*i*) we get

$$W = F \times s = ma \times \frac{v^2 - u^2}{2a}$$

$$W = \frac{1}{2} m (v^2 - u^2)$$

If $u = 0$, (object starts at rest)

$$W = \frac{1}{2} mv^2$$

Work done = Change in kinetic energy

$$\therefore \quad E_k = \frac{1}{2} mv^2.$$

Q13. Derive the formula for potential energy.

Ans. Consider a body with mass 'm' raised through a height 'h' from the ground level.

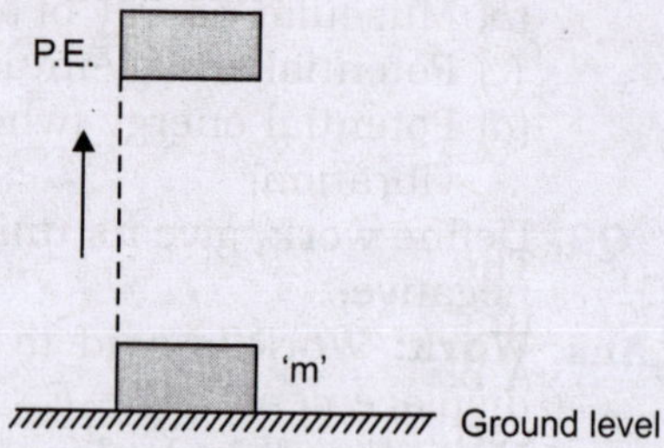

Force required to raise the object = weight of object, mg.

Object gains energy equal to the work done on it.

$\therefore$ Work done on the object against gravity be W.

$$\therefore \quad W = \text{force} \times \text{displacement}$$
$$= mg \times h$$
$$W = mgh$$
$$\therefore \quad \text{P.E.} = mgh$$

Q14. Define power, give its unit and define it.

Ans. Power is defined as the rate of doing work.

$$\text{Power} = \frac{\text{work done}}{\text{time taken}}, \quad \therefore \quad P = \frac{W}{t}$$

Unit → Watt

Definition of watt. When 1 Joule work is said to be done in 1 second, the power of the body doing work is said to be 1 watt.

Q15. Explain, law of conservation of energy.

Ans. Law of conservation of energy states that energy can neither be created nor destroyed but it can be transferred from one form to another. The total energy before and after transformation remains the same.

Let the body be at position A from the ground level. It has potential energy P_E. When the body falls down and reaches in the middle $P.E. = K.E.$ and when the body is just about to touch the ground its $K.E. > P.E.$ This shows that $P.E.$ is getting transferred into kinetic energy.

Q16. Two boys A and B were given a task to carry 20 kg load from ground level to height 10 m. A completed the work in 40 s and B in 60 s. Calculate the power in both the cases. Who has greater power?

Ans. $\text{Power} = \frac{\text{work}}{\text{time}}, \quad \text{Work} = m \times g \times h$

$$\therefore \quad \text{mass} = 20 \text{ kg}$$
$$\therefore \quad W = mgh$$
$$h = 10 \text{ m},$$
$$t_A = 40 \text{ s}$$
$$t_B = 60 \text{ s},$$
$$P_B = ?$$
$$g = 10 \text{ m/s}^2$$

$$P_A = \frac{W}{t_A} = \frac{20 \times 10 \times 10}{40}$$
$$P_A = 50 \text{ watt}$$

$$P_B = \frac{\text{work}}{\text{time}} = \frac{mgh}{t_B}$$
$$P_B = \frac{20 \times 10 \times 10}{60}$$
$$P_B = 33.34 \text{ watt}$$

$$P_A > P_B$$
$$50 \text{ W} > 33.34 \text{ W}$$

$\therefore$ Power of A is more than B.

Q17. An electrical appliance of 100 W is used for 3 h per day. Calculate the units of energy consumed per day and for a month.

Ans. Power of electrical appliance = 100 W = 0.1 kW

Time used = 3 h

Energy = power × time taken

= 0.1 kW × 3h

= 0.3 kWh

= 0.3 units (∵ 1 kWh = 1 unit)

The units of energy consumed per day = 0.3 units and for a month = 0.3 × 30 = 9 units.

Q18. A body possess potential energy of 460 J whose mass is 20 kg and is raised to a certain height. What is the height when g = 10 m/s²?

Ans. $P.E. = 460$ J

$m = 20$ kg

$g = 10 \text{ m/s}^2$

$h = ?$

$P.E. = mgh$

$460 = 20 \times 10 \times h$

$$h = \frac{460}{20 \times 10}$$

$h = 2.3$ m.

The height at which the object is raised from the ground is 2.3 m.

Q19. A mover pushes a 1700 N piano up a 4-metre ramp. How much work is done by the mover?

Ans. Work = Force × displacement

= 1700 × 4 = 6800 J

Q20. How much work is done when an engine generates 400 watts of power in 25 seconds?

Ans. $$\text{Power} = \frac{\text{work done}}{\text{time taken}}$$

Work = Power × time

= 400 × 25

= 10000 J

Q21. Why does an object float or sink when placed on the surface of the water?

Ans. When the density of the object is more than the density of water then the object sinks. If the density of an object is less, then the object will float on water. To change the density of an object we can change its volume by giving it different shapes and the same object that was sinking can be made to float on water.

Q22. What do you mean by thrust or buoyant force? What are the factors the buoyant force depends on?

Ans. Thrust: The upward force acting on an object is called thrust/buoyant force. Buoyant force depends on the mass on an object and is independent of the density of the object. It also depends on the volume displaced by an object.

Q23. A container of mass 300kg is raised by an electric motor through a height of 60m in 45 secs. Calculate:

(*a*) The weight of the container.

(*b*) The work done by the motor.

(*c*) The useful power of the motor. (Assume g = 10N/kg)

Ans. (*a*) The weight of the container = $m \times g$ = 300 × 10 = 3000 N.

(*b*) Work done by the container = F × s,

Hence W = 3000 N × 60 m – 180000J

(*c*) Power of the motor

$$P = \frac{\text{work done}}{\text{time}} = \frac{180000}{45} = 4000 \text{ Watt}$$

Q24. The diagram shows a pendulum which was released from position A. What forms of energy did the pendulum have at?

(*i*) A (*ii*) B (*iii*) C

Eventually the pendulum would stop moving. Explain what has happened to the initial energy of the pendulum?

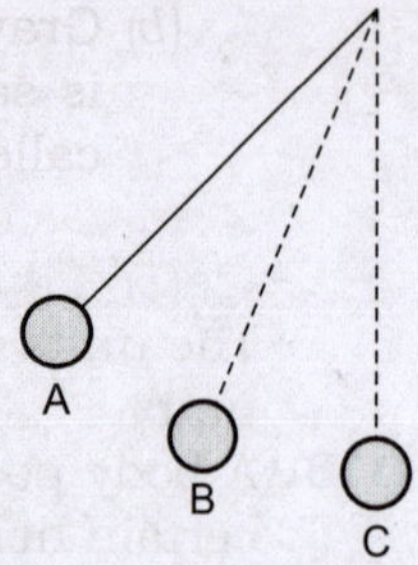

Ans. At A the pendulum is having gravitational potential energy, at C the pendulum has maximum kinetic energy as it is in the center of the oscillatory motion. At B the pendulum has equal potential and kinetic energy. The pendulum will eventually slow down and stop due to the air resistance.

Q25. An athlete of mass 54 kg is bouncing up and down on a trampoline.

(*a*) State the form of energy stored due to the stretching surface of the trampoline.

(*b*) The stretched surface of the trampoline begins to contract. The athlete is pushed vertically upwards and gets accelerates. At time *t*, when her upward velocity is 6.0 m/s, she loses contact with the surface. Calculate the kinetic energy at time *t*.

Ans. (*a*) The stretching surface of trampoline stores potential energy.

(*b*) Kinetic energy of the athlete will be K.E. = $\frac{1}{2}mv^2 = \frac{1}{2} \times 54 \times 6 \times 6 = 972$ J

Q26. In a power station, 2.05×10^8 kg of water is pumped up through a vertical height of 400 m.

(*a*) Calculate the weight of water.

(*b*) Calculate the gravitational potential energy gained by the water.

Ans. (*a*) Weight of water = mass × gravity = 2.05×10^8 kg × 10 m/s^2 = 2.05×10^9 N

(*b*) Gravitational potential energy = $m \times g \times h$

$= 2.05 \times 10^8 \times 10 \text{ N} \times 400 \text{ m} = 8.2 \times 10^{11}$ J.

Q27. A diver is at a depth of 40m beneath the surface of a sea. He carries a cylinder of high-pressure air on his back. Explain how the air molecules exert a pressure on the inside surface of the cylinder. The diver gradually uses up the air in the cylinder. Explain why the pressure falls.

Ans. The air molecules are in random motion in the cylinder and will exert pressure on the walls of the container. As the gas from the cylinder is used up by the diver the pressure inside the cylinder will decrease because the volume of the gas is decreased.

Q28. The cylinder is air tight and the temperature of the air in the cylinder is increased.

(*a*) State what happens to the volume of the air in the cylinder as a result of this temperature rise.

(*b*) Does the pressure inside the cylinder changes, give reason for your answer?

Ans. (*a*) The volume of air in the cylinder will increase as the molecules of the air gains heat energy and start moving away from each other.

(*b*) The pressure inside the cylinder will change as the molecules will hit more inside the cylinder and increase the pressure.

IV. Long Answer Type Questions

Q1. What is potential energy? Explain different types of potential energy.

Ans. Potential energy → The energy possessed by a body by virtue of its mass and height is called potential energy.

$$PE = mgh$$

Different types of potential energy are:

(*a*) Elastic Potential Energy: The energy possessed by a body when it is stretched is called elastic potential energy. Example: stretched bow, coiled spring, compressed slinky.

(*b*) Gravitational Potential Energy: When an object is raised to a certain height work is said to be done on it against gravity. The energy possessed by an object is called the gravitational potential energy. Example: Water raised in the dam.

Q2. (*a*) Define power. What is the S.I. unit of power and commercial unit of power?

(*b*) A tube light of 80 W is used for 8 hours per day. Calculate the unit of energy consumed in 1 day by the tube light.

Ans. (*a*) Power is the rate of doing work.

S.I. unit of power = watt

$$1 \text{ watt} = \frac{1\text{ J}}{1\text{ s}}$$

Commercial unit of power = kWh

$$1 \text{ kWh} = 3.6 \times 10^6 \text{ Joules.}$$

(*b*) Power of electric tube light = 80 W = 0.08 kW

Time used = 8 hour

$$\text{Energy} = \text{power} \times \text{time taken}$$
$$= 0.08 \times 8 = 0.64 \text{ kWh}$$
$$= 0.64 \text{ units.}$$

∴ The energy consumed per day = 0.64 units.

Q3. (*a*) List any 3 situations in your daily life where you can say work has been done.

(*b*) What work is said to be done to increase the velocity of a car from 15 km/h to 30 km/h, if the mass of the car is 1000 kg?

Ans. (*a*) 3 situations where work is done are:

(*i*) If a pebble lying on a surface is pushed, the pebble moves through a distance. In this situation work is said to be done.

(*ii*) If a girl pulls a trolley and the trolley moves through a distance. In this situation work is done.

(*iii*) If a book is lifted to a height, the force is applied and the book rises up, work is said to be done.

(*b*)

$$u = 15 \text{ km/h} = 15 \times \frac{5}{18}\frac{m}{s} = \frac{25}{6}\frac{m}{s}$$

$$v = 30 \text{ km/h} = 30 \times \frac{5}{18}\frac{m}{s} = \frac{25}{3}\frac{m}{s}$$

Mass = 1000 kg

W = ?

$$W = K.E. = \frac{1}{2}m(v^2 - u^2)$$

$$= \frac{1}{2} \times 1000 \times \left[\left(\frac{25}{3}\right)^2 - \left(\frac{25}{6}\right)^2\right] = \frac{1}{2} \times 1000 \times \left(\frac{625}{9} - \frac{625}{36}\right)$$

$$= \frac{1}{2} \times 1000 \times 625\left(\frac{4-1}{36}\right)$$

$$K.E. = \frac{1}{2} \times 1000 \times \frac{625}{12} = 26041.67 \text{ J}$$

∴ Work done = 26041.67 Joule

Q4. Explain the following:

(*a*) An object increases its energy when raised through a height.

(*b*) Energy is neither created nor destroyed then from where do we get energy.

(*c*) When we push the wall, the wall does not move and no work is done.

Ans. (*a*) An object has some mass '*M*', when it is raised through a certain height, energy is applied on it, this energy gets transformed and is gained by the stone hence its energy increases.

(*b*) Energy is present in every object in some or other form it exist in sun, planet, wind, water etc, the energy gets transformed and we get, because of its transformation into different form. For e.g., sun energy → plants convert it (due to chemical reaction) into food energy → we eat green vegetables products of plants, energy enters our body.

(*c*) Work is said to be done, when force is applied on the body and it moves to certain distance. When a wall is pushed there is no displacement and we say that work done is zero.

Q5. State and explain one example where (*i*) Kinetic energy is present in a body and is used; and (*ii*) Potential energy is present in a body and is used.

Ans. Kinetic energy is the energy present in a body by virtue of its motion.
When water is stored in a dam at particular height, we say it has maximum potential energy as the water is present at a height. When this water is allowed to fall down from a certain height, it is said to have kinetic energy. When the water falls on a turbine, the paddle wheels rotates to rotate the turbine. Hence the kinetic energy of water is used to push or rotate the turbine which is further used to produce the electricity.

Q6. A catapult toy has a spring attached to it as shown. The handle was pulled down to fully compress the spring and on release the metal ball of mass 0.1 kg (weight 1N) was projected 0.55 m vertically.

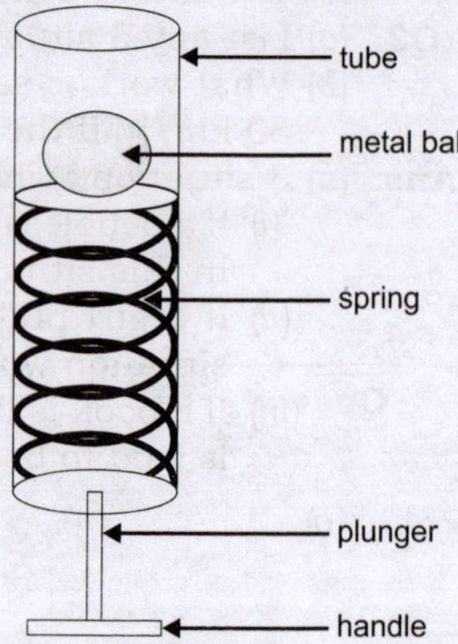

(*a*) (*i*) What type of energy is stored in a compressed spring?

(*ii*) What happens to this stored energy when the handle of the plunger is released?

(*b*) Calculate the maximum potential energy acquired by the metal ball from the catapult.
Write down the formula that you use and show your working. Take the acceleration due to gravity to be 10 m/s^2.

(*c*) Explain why the maximum potential energy gained by the metal ball is less than the original stored energy of the spring.

Ans. (*a*) (*i*) The energy stored in the compressed spring is potential energy.

(*ii*) The potential energy stored in the plunger is transformed into the mechanical energy.

(*b*) $P = mgh = 0.1 \times 10 \times 0.55 = 0.55$ J

(*c*) The spring is coiled and has the tendency to store more energy in the coils as more the coils more is the energy stored in it.

V. Activity-Based Questions

1.
- Push a huge rock. It does not move.
- Climb up a tall tree.
- Stand still with heavy load on the head.
- Push a table.

Questions:

1. What is the work being done on?
2. What is happening to the object?
3. Who (what) is doing the work?

Answers:

1. In case of tree climbing and pushing the table work is done.
2. The object shows displacement.
3. The energy used to apply force on a body is doing the work.

2. • Situations of doing work.

(*a*) Playing cricket, football.
(*b*) Cycling a cycle.
(*c*) Climbing a tall tree.
(*d*) Reading a book.

Question:

1. In which of the above cases work is being done?

Answer:

1. In situations (*a*), (*b*), (*c*) work is done as the displacement is seen in the bodies on which force is applied.

In case of (*d*) no work is said to be done, as the body is not having any displacement.

3. • Object is not displaced in spite of force applied on it.

Example: Pushing a wall, rock.

Question:

1. Is work done in the above examples?

Answer:

1. Here the energy is used on applying force on the wall and rock but the body does not show any displacement. The work is not done in this case.

4. • Lift an object up. Work is done by the force exerted by you on the object. The object moves upwards. The force you exerted is in the direction of displacement. However, there is the force of gravity acting on the objects.

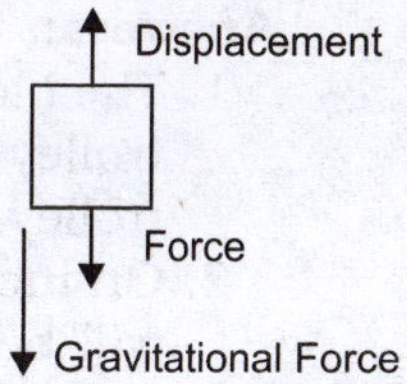

Questions:

1. Which work is called positive work?
2. Which work is called negative work?
3. Why a work is called a negative work?

Answers:

1. The force that is pushing the body upwards and the displacement is in the same direction (*i.e.*, upwards) so, it is **positive work.**
2. The gravitational force acting on the object is called negative work.
3. When the force acts opposite to the direction of displacement.

5. • Take a heavy ball. Drop it on a thick bed of sand. A wet bed of sand would be better. Drop the ball on the sand bed from the height of about 25 cm. The ball creates a depression.

- Repeat this activity from heights of 50 cm, 1 m and 1.5 m.
- Ensure that all the depressions are distinctly visible.
- Mark the depressions to indicate the height from which the ball was dropped.
- Compare their depths.

Questions:

1. Which one of them is deepest?
2. Which one is shallowest? Why?
3. What has caused the ball to make a deeper dent? Discuss and analyse.

Answers:

1. The ball that falls from the height of 1.5 m is deepest.
2. The ball that falls from the height of 50 cm is shallowest.

3. The ball placed at greater height possesses more potential energy than the ball at the lower height. Hence, the ball that falls from the height 1.5 m makes deeper dent.

6.
- Set up the apparatus as shown in the figure.

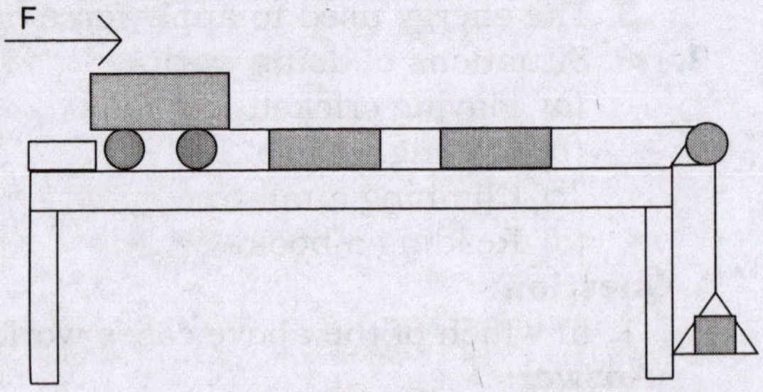

- Place a wooden block of known mass in front of the trolley at a convenient distance.
- Place a known mass on the pan so that the trolley starts moving.
- The trolley moves forward and hits the wooden block.
- Fix a stop on the table in such a manner that the trolley stops after hitting the block. The block gets displaced.
- Note down the displacement of the block. This means work is done on the block by the trolley as the block has gained energy.
- Repeat the activity by increasing the mass on the pan.
- In this activity, the moving trolley does work and hence it possesses energy.

Questions:

1. From where does the energy come in the block?
2. In which case is the displacement more?
3. In which case is the work done more?

Answers:

1. The block moves due to the energy possessed by the moving trolley. The moving trolley has gained energy called kinetic energy which is due to the motion of the trolley.
2. On increasing the mass on the pan the trolley is pulled further and the motion will be more and the kinetic energy possessed by the body is more hence the displacement is more in the second case.
3. In second case the work done is more as the displacement is more.

7.
- Take a rubber band.
- Hold it at one end and pull from the other. The band stretches.
- Release the band at one of the ends.
- What happens? The band will tend to regain its original length. Obviously the band had acquired energy in its stretched position.

Question:

1. How did it acquire energy when stretched?

Answer:

1. The energy is acquired by the rubber band due to work done on it by applying force/energy. The energy transferred to an object is stored as potential energy.

8.
- Take a slinky as shown below.
- Ask a friend to hold one of its ends.
- You hold the other end and move away from your friend. Now you release the slinky.

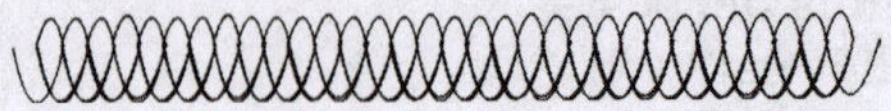

Questions:

1. What happened?
2. How did the slinky acquire energy when stretched?
3. Would the slinky acquire energy when it is compressed?

Answers:

1. When the slinky is released it gets compressed.
2. The energy is acquired by the slinky as work is done on stretching it.
3. When the slinky is compressed, work is done on it again as energy is required to compress it and this energy is transferred in the form of potential energy in the slinky.

9. • Take a toy car. Wind it using its key.
• Place the car on the ground.

Questions:

1. Did it move?
2. From where did it acquire energy?
3. Does the energy acquired depend on the number of windings?
4. How can you test this?

Answers:

1. The car moves as the spring gets uncoiled.
2. It acquired energy as work is done on it during the coiling of the spring, this energy gets transferred in the form of potential energy.
3. The energy acquired by the car depends on the number of windings, as more the winding more will be the work done on it and the energy stored in it is more.
4. We can test the energy acquired by the car by winding it and releasing the car. If the winding is less the car will travel smaller distance and if the winding is more the car will travel longer distance.

10. • Lift an object through a certain height.
The object can now do work. It begins to fall when released.
• This implies that it has acquired some energy. If raised to a greater height it can do more work and hence possesses more energy.

Question:

1. From where did it get the energy? Think and discuss.

Answer:

1. When the object is raised to certain height. The work is done on the object and the energy is acquired by the body. The transformation of energy takes place and the energy is stored in the form of potential energy.

11. • Take a bamboo stick and make a bow as shown in the figure.
• Place an arrow made of a light stick on it with one end supported by the stretched string.
• Now stretch the string and release the arrow.
• Notice the arrow flying off the bow. Notice the change in the shape of the bow.
• The potential energy stored in the bow due to the change of shape is thus used in the form of kinetic energy in throwing off the arrow.

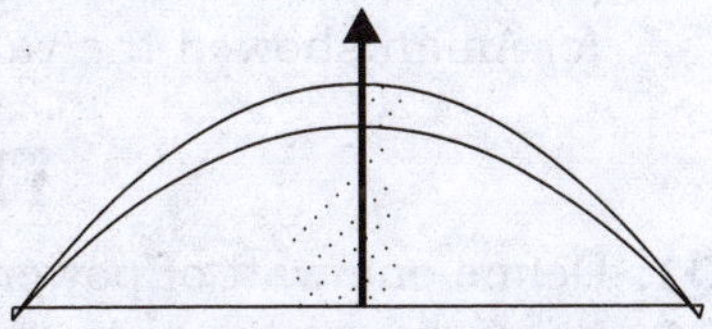
An arrow and the stretched string on the bow

Question:

1. What inference do you get from the above activity?

Answer:

1. An arrow and the stretched string on the bow possess potential energy when released this potential energy gets transferred into kinetic energy.

IV. Value-Based Questions

Q1. Apoorva saw few planter pot kept on the balcony sill of 4th floor in her building. She makes an effort and keeps all the planter pots down the sill.
(*a*) What type of energy is present in the pot kept on the 4th floor balcony sill?

(*b*) If the pot falls from the 4th floor, what type of energy will be seen in the falling pot?
(*c*) What value of Apoorva is reflected in the above act?

Ans. (*a*) The pot on the sill possesses potential energy.
(*b*) The falling pot possesses kinetic energy.
(c) Apoorva showed the value of moral responsibility and aware citizen.

Q2. Siddharth saw a lady labour who carried bricks on her head from one point of the construction site to the other end which was some 500 m far. He prepares a trolley for the labour to carry the bricks, to make her work easier.
(*a*) In carrying the bricks from point A to point B on head by lady labour in the construction site, is any work done by the labour?
(*b*) By pulling the trolley of bricks from point A to point B, is any work done?
(*c*) What value of Siddharth is seen in the above act?

Ans. (*a*) In carrying the bricks from point A to point B on head, by the lady no work is said to be done.
(*b*) By pulling the trolley of bricks, work is said to be done.
(*c*) Siddharth showed kindness, general awareness and sympathy.

Q3. Aman saw a sudden rise in the electricity bill for the month of January. He did the survey of electronic equipments used in his house and found that the electric room heater was used for longer hours to keep the room warm. The power of electric heater was 18000 watts. He suggested to use the heater intermittently and keep the warm air trapped in the room.
(*a*) Convert the power of room heater into kW and if it is used for one hour what is the work done by it.
(*b*) Convert 1 kWh into joules.
(*c*) What value of Aman is reflected in this act?

Ans. (*a*) The power of room heater is 18 kW.
Work done = ? $t = 1$ hour, $P = 18{,}000$ W

$$P = \frac{W}{t} \qquad \therefore \text{W} = P \times t = 18000 \times 3600 = 64800000 \text{ J}$$

$$\text{W} = 6.48 \times 10^7 \text{ J}$$

(*b*) 1 kWh = 3.6×10^6 J
(c) Aman showed the value of aware citizen.

TEST YOUR SKILLS

Q1. Define one watt of power.
Q2. Name two physical quantities whose unit is Joule.
Q3. What is gravitational potential energy?
Q4. What is the commercial unit of energy? Define it.
Q5. Give one example where work done on an object is negative.
Q6. What work is said to be done to increase the velocity of a car from 15 km/h to 30 km/h, if the mass of the car is 1000 kg?
Q7. A body possess potential energy of 460 J whose mass is 20 kg and is raised to a certain height. What is the height when g = 10 m/s^2.
Q8. An electric appliance of 100 W is used for 3 hours per day. Calculate the units of energy consumed per day and for a month.
Q9. Derive the formula for kinetic energy.
Q10. With pendulum as an example explain the law of conservation of energy.
Q11. Derive the formula for potential energy. ❑❑❑

12 Sound

Syllabus

Nature of sound and its propagation in various media, speed of sound, range of hearing in humans; ultrasound; reflection of sound; echo and SONAR.
Structure of the Human Ear (Auditory aspect only).

Facts that Matter

- Sound is a form of energy which produces a sensation of hearing in our ears.
- **Propagation of Sound**: Sound is produced by vibrating objects.
- **Medium:** The matter or substance through which sound is transmitted is called a medium. It can be solid, liquid or gas. Air is the most common medium for sound propagation.
- **Wave:** A wave is a disturbance that moves through a medium when the particles of the medium set neighbouring particles into motion. They in turn produce similar motion in others. The particles of the medium do not move forward themselves, but the disturbance is carried forward. This is what happens during propagation of sound in a medium, hence sound can be visualised as a wave. Sound waves are characterised by the motion of particles in the medium and are called mechanical waves.
- When a vibrating object moves forward, it pushes and compresses the air in front of it creating a region of high pressure. This region is called a compression (C), as shown in following figure. This compression starts to move away from the vibrating object. When the vibrating object moves backwards, it creates a region of low pressure called rarefaction (R).

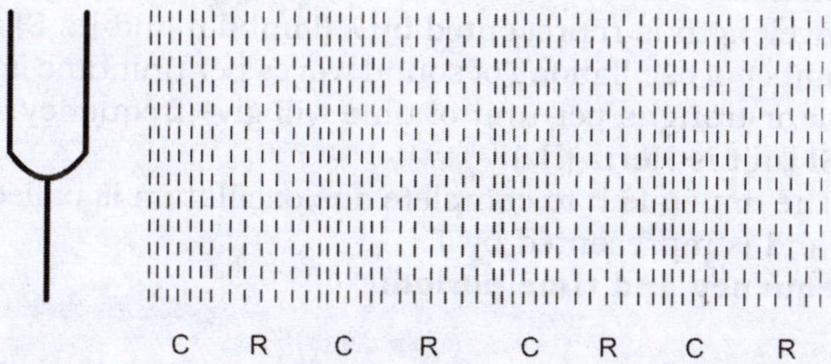

- As the object moves back and forth rapidly, a series of compressions and rarefactions is created in the air. These make the sound wave that propagates through the medium. Compression is the region of high pressure and rarefaction is the region of low pressure.
- **Experiment to show Sound needs a medium:**
  Activity:
  – Take an electric bell and airtight jar.
  – Fit the bell inside the jar and attach to battery.
  – With air still in jar ring the bell.
  – Now take out air by vaccumization.

– Ring the bell again.

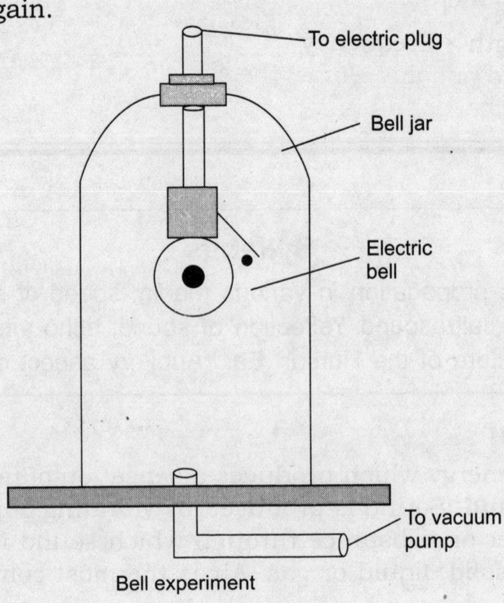

Bell experiment

Observation: Sound of bell can be heard when air is inside the jar. When air is taken out then sound cannot be heard.

Conclusion: This shows that presence of medium is necessary for propagation of sound waves.

- **Properties of Sound Waves:**

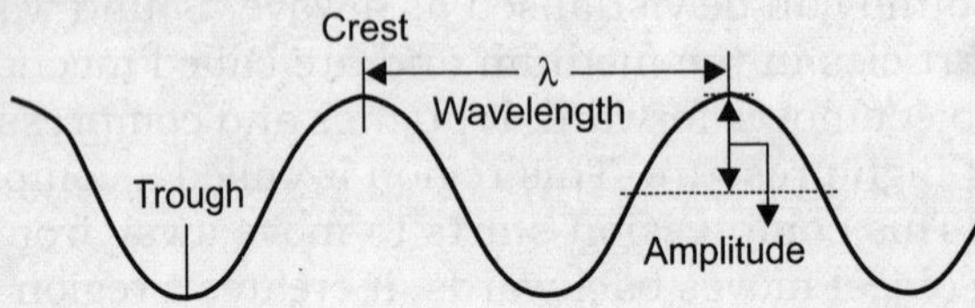

- **Wavelength:** Distance between two consecutive peaks (crest) or and troughs is called wavelength. Wavelength is represented by λ (lambda) and its SI unit is metre.
- **Frequency:** Number of oscillations of sound waves per unit time is called its frequency. Number of peak or troughs per unit of time will give frequency. It is represented by ν (nu) and its SI unit is Hertz (Hz).
- **Time Period:** The time taken to complete one oscillation is called its time period. Its unit is second and is represented by T.
- **Relation of frequency and time period:**

  $\nu = \frac{1}{T}$
- **Amplitude:** The magnitude of the maximum disturbance in the medium on either side of the mean value is called the amplitude of the wave. It is usually represented by the letter A. Its unit is metre.
- **Softness or Loudness of Sound:** If the amplitude is smaller then the sound will be softer and if it is larger then sound will be louder. Higher amplitude helps the sound wave in traveling faster.
- **Speed of sound:** It is the distance which a compression or a rarefaction travels per unit of time.

  $\text{Speed of sound} = \nu = \frac{\lambda}{T} = \frac{\text{Wavelength}}{\text{Time}}$

Or, $v = \nu\lambda$ (because $\frac{1}{T} = \nu$)

So, Speed = Wavelength × Frequency

The speed of the sound remains almost the same for all frequencies in a given medium under the same physical condition.

Speed of Sound in Different Media at 25° C.

State	*Substance*	*Speed in m/s*
Solids	Aluminium	6420
	Nickel	6040
	Steel	5960
	Iron	5950
	Brass	4700
	Glass (flint)	3980
Liquids	Water (sea)	1531
	Water (distilled)	1498
	Ethanol	1207
	Methanol	1103
Gases	Hydrogen	1284
	Helium	965
	Air	346
	Oxygen	316
	Sulphur dioxide	213

- **Reflection of Sound:** Sound reflects off a surface in the same way as light reflects and follows the same rules of reflection. The incident sound and the reflected sound make equal angles with the normal and all three are in the same plane.
- **Echo:** In bigger monuments and in large empty halls you can hear reflections of your sound after you speak something. This effect is known as echo. The sensation of sound persists in our brain for 0.1 seconds, so to hear echo the time difference between original sound and reflected sound should be more than that.
  As you know speed of sound in air = 344 m/s
  And 344 × 0.1 = 34.4 metre
  So, the minimum distance required to hear an echo from a reflecting wall or surface should be half of 34.4, means it should be 17.2 metres.
- **Reverberation:** Repeated reflections of sound results in persistence of sound and is called reverberation.
- **Use of Reverberation of Sound:** Following instruments use this property of sound:
  1. Megaphones, *Shehanais*, Trumpets
  2. Stethoscope
  3. Curved dome of concert halls
- **Range of Hearing in humans:**
  From 20 Hz to 20000 Hz
  Sounds below 20 Hz are called infrasonic.
  Sounds above 20000 Hz are called ultrasonic.

NCERT IN-TEXT QUESTIONS SOLVED

Q1. How does the sound produced by a vibrating object in a medium reach your ear?

Ans. When a disturbance is created in an object, it starts vibrating and sets the particles of the medium to vibrate. The particle of the medium is displaced from its mean position and exerts a force in the adjacent particle. As a result, the adjacent particle is disturbed from its mean position and the original particle comes back to rest. This process continues till the disturbance reaches our ear.

Q2. Explain how sound is produced by your school bell.

Ans. When the bell is hit manually with a rod, the object, *i.e.* the bell starts vibrating causing disturbance in the medium, *i.e.* air. Here the air particles do not travel, they oscillate back and forth to transmit the disturbance till it reaches our ears.

Q3. Why are sound waves called mechanical waves?

Ans. Mechanical waves are those which needs a medium for propagation. Sound waves are mechanical waves because they need a medium for propagation. If there is no medium, then sound cannot be propagated because it is the particle in the medium which oscillates back and forth and the disturbance is carried forward.

Q4. Suppose you and your friend are on the moon. Will you be able to hear any sound produced by your friend?

Ans. No. We'll not be able to hear the sound because sound requires a medium for its propagation. On the moon there is no atmosphere, *i.e.* there is vacuum. Sound can't travel through vacuum, it needs a medium for its propagation.

Q5. Which wave property determines
(*a*) loudness (*b*) pitch?

Ans. (*a*) Loudness is determined by amplitude. If larger is the amplitude, louder will be the sound produced.
(*b*) Pitch is determined by its frequency. Higher the frequency, higher will be the pitch.

Q6. Guess which sound has a higher pitch: guitar or car horn?

Ans. Car horn has the higher pitch.

Q7. What are wavelength, frequency, time period and amplitude of a sound wave?

Ans. **Wavelength:** The distance between two consecutive compressions (Ω) or two consecutive rarefactions (*R*) is called the wavelength and its SI unit is metre.

Frequency: The number of oscillations per unit time is called frequency and its unit is Hertz (*Hz*).

Time period: The time taken by two consecutive compressions or rarefactions to cross a fixed point is called the time period.

Amplitude: The magnitude of the maximum disturbance in the medium on either side of the mean value is called the amplitude of the wave.

Q8. How are the wavelength and frequency of a sound wave related to its speed?

Ans. The speed is defined as the distance travelled by a wave per unit time.

$$\text{Speed} = \frac{\text{distance}}{\text{time}} = \frac{\lambda}{T}$$

λ is the wavelength, T is the time period

$$v = \nu\lambda \quad \because \quad \boxed{\nu = \frac{1}{T}}$$

$$\therefore \quad \text{Speed} = \text{Wavelength} \times \text{Frequency}$$

Q9. Calculate the wavelength of a sound wave whose frequency is 220 Hz and speed is 440 m/s in a given medium.

Ans.

$$\text{Speed} = \text{Wavelength} \times \text{Frequency}$$

$$\nu = 220 \text{ Hz}$$

$$v = 440 \text{ m/sec}$$

$$\lambda = \frac{v}{\nu} = \frac{440}{220} = 2 \text{ metre.}$$

Q10. A person is listening to a tone of 500 Hz sitting at a distance of 450 m from the source of the sound. What is the time interval between successive compressions from the source?

Ans.

$$\nu = 500 \text{ Hz}$$
$$\lambda = 450 \text{ m}$$
$$\nu = \frac{1}{T}$$
$$\therefore \quad T = \frac{1}{\nu} = \frac{1}{500} = 0.002 \text{ second.}$$

Q11. Distinguish between loudness and intensity of sound.

Ans.

Intensity	***Loudness***
1. The amount of sound energy passing each second per unit area.	1. It is the measure of response of the ear to the sound.
2. Intensity is a physical quantity and its magnitude does not depend on the senstivity of the ear.	2. Loudness depends upon the senstivity of ear.

Q12. In which of the three media, air, water or iron, does sound travel the fastest at a particular temperature?

Ans. The speed of sound in air = 346 m/s.
The speed of sound in water = 1531 m/s.
The speed of sound in iron = 5950 m/s.
∴ The speed of sound in iron is greater and sound travels faster in iron.

Q13. An echo returned in 3 s. What is the distance of the reflecting surface from the source, given that the speed of sound is 342 ms^{-1}?

Ans. Speed of sound = 342 m/s.
Time taken for hearing an echo = 3 s.
Distance travelled $2d = v \times t$

$$2 \times d = 342 \times 3$$
$$d = \frac{342 \times 3}{2} = 513 \text{ m.}$$

Q14. Why are the ceilings of concert halls curved?

Ans. Ceilings of the concert halls are curved because sound after reflection reaches all corners of the hall.

Q15. What is the audible range of the average human ear?

Ans. The audible range of the average human ear is 20 Hz to 20000 Hz.

Q16. What is the range of frequencies associated with

(*a*) Infrasound? (*b*) Ultrasound?

Ans. (*a*) Sound of frequencies below 20 Hz are called infrasound.
(*b*) Sound of frequencies above 20 KHz are called ultrasound.

Q17. A submarine emits a sonar pulse which returns from an underwater cliff in 1.02 s. If the speed of sound in salt water is 1531 m/s, how far away is the cliff?

Ans. Speed of sound in salt water = 1531 m/sec.

$$\text{Time period} = 1.02 \text{ sec.}$$
$$\text{Distance travelled } 2 \times d = \text{speed} \times \text{time}$$
$$2 \times d = 1531 \times 1.02$$
$$\therefore \quad d = \frac{1531 \times 1.02}{2}$$
$$d = 780.9 \text{ m.}$$

NCERT TEXTBOOK QUESTIONS SOLVED

Q1. What is sound and how is it produced?

Ans. Sound is a form of energy. It is produced when the object starts vibrating.

Q2. Describe with the help of a diagram, how compressions and rarefactions are produced in air near a source of sound.

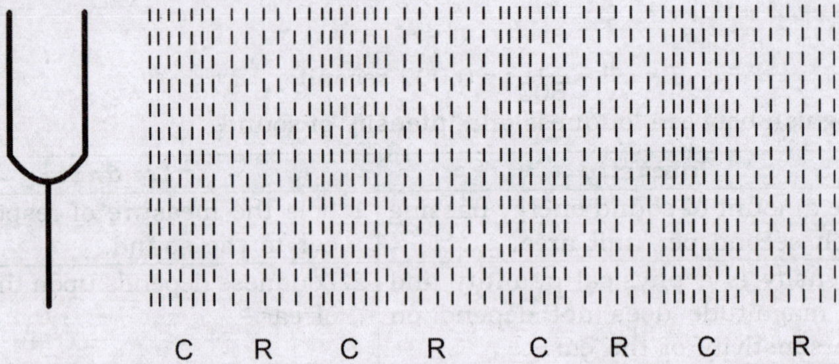

Ans. (*i*) When a vibrating object moves forward, it pushes the air in front of it and compresses the air creating a region of high pressure called compression (*C*).

(*ii*) It starts moving away from the surface of the vibrating object.

(*iii*) As this occurs the surface moves backward creating a region of low pressure called rarefaction (*R*).

Q3. Cite an experiment to show that sound needs a material medium for its propagation.

Ans. **Description:**

Take an electric bell and an air tight glass bell jar. The electric bell is suspended inside an air tight glass jar which is connected to a vacuum pump.

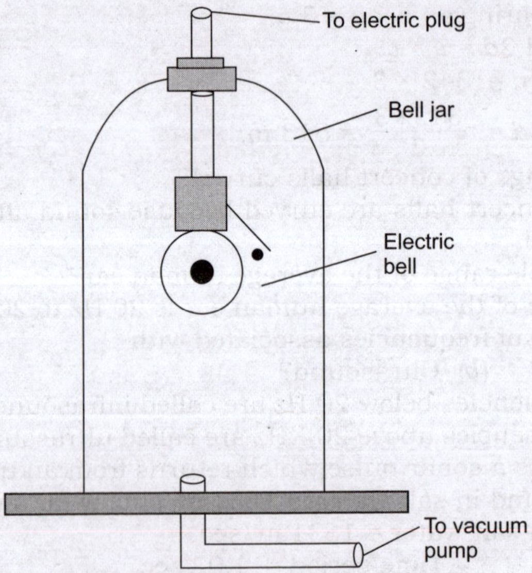

Bell experiment

Working:

(*i*) When we press the switch, we'll be able to hear the bell.

(*ii*) When the air in the jar is pumped out gradually, the sound becomes feeble although the same amount of current is flowing through the bell.

(iii) When the air is removed completely, we'll not be able to hear the sound of the bell.

Conclusion:

This experiment shows that sound requires a medium for its propagation.

Q4. Why is sound wave called a longitudinal wave?

Ans. When the sound wave travels, the air molecules oscillate in the same direction as that of propagation of sound waves. Hence they are called longitudinal waves.

Q5. Which characteristic of the sound helps you to identify your friend by his voice while sitting with others in a dark room?

Ans. The characteristic 'Quality' help us to identify our friend by his voice, although we are not actually seeing him.

Q6. Flash and thunder are produced simultaneously. But thunder is heard a few seconds after the flash is seen, why?

Ans. Speed of sound is 330 m/sec in air medium at 0°C. Whereas speed of light is 3×10^8 m/sec. When we compare the speed of light with that of speed of sound, speed of light is greater than that of speed of sound. Therefore thunder is heard a few seconds after the flash is seen.

Q7. A person has a hearing range from 20 Hz to 20 kHz. What are the typical wavelengths of sound waves in air corresponding to these two frequencies? Take the speed of sound in air as 344 ms^{-1}.

Ans. When $\nu = 20$ Hz

Speed of sound in air = 344 m/s.

wavelength, $\lambda = ?$

$$\text{Speed} = \text{Wavelength} \times \text{Frequency}$$

$$\therefore \quad \text{Wavelength} = \frac{\text{speed}}{\text{Frequency}} = \frac{344}{20} = 17.2 \text{ m.}$$

when $\nu = 20$ kHz

Speed of sound in air = 344 m/s.

$\lambda = ?$

(speed), $\upsilon = \nu \times \lambda$

$$\lambda = \frac{\upsilon}{\nu} = \frac{344}{20000} = 0.0172 \text{ m.}$$

Thus, the wavelength of sound corresponding to 20 Hz and 20 kHz is 17.2 m and 0.0172 m respectively.

Q8. Two children are at opposite ends of an aluminium rod. One strikes the end of the rod with a stone. Find the ratio of times taken by the sound wave in air and in aluminium to reach the second child.

Ans. Speed of sound in air, $V_1 = 346$ m/sec.

Speed of sound in aluminium, $V_2 = 6420$ m/sec.

Let the length of the aluminium rod = x m.

$$\text{We know that speed} = \frac{\text{distance}}{\text{time}}$$

$$\therefore \quad \text{Time} = \frac{\text{distance}}{\text{speed}}$$

$$\text{Time taken in air} = \frac{x}{346} \text{ sec.} \qquad (\because \text{distance} = x \text{ m})$$

$$\text{Time taken in aluminium} = \frac{x}{6420} \text{ sec.}$$

$$\text{Required ratio} = \frac{\frac{x}{346}}{\frac{x}{6420}} = \frac{x}{346} \times \frac{6420}{x}$$
$$= 18.55$$

Q9. The frequency of a source of sound is 100 Hz. How many times does it vibrate in a minute?

Ans. Frequency of sound = 100 Hz.

Time taken = 1 minute = 60 sec

We know, $\text{Frequency} = \frac{\text{No. of oscillations}}{\text{Time taken}}$

$\therefore$ No. of oscillations $= \nu \times t$

$= 100 \times 60 = 6000$ times.

Q10. Does sound follow the same laws of reflection as light does? Explain.

Ans. Yes, Sound follows the same laws of reflection as that of light because

(*i*) Angle of incidence of sound is always equal to that of angle of reflection of sound waves.

(*ii*) The direction in which sound is incident, the direction in which it is reflected and normal all lie in the same plane.

Q11. When a sound is reflected from a distant object, an echo is produced. Let the distance between the reflecting surface and the source of sound production remains the same. Do you hear echo sound on a hotter day?

Ans. $\text{Time} = \frac{\text{distance}}{\text{speed}}$

Time is inversely proportional to the speed. As the temperature increases, the speed increases. Thus on a hot day due to high temperature the speed of sound increases. Hence the time will decrease and we can hear the echo sooner.

Q12. Give two practical applications of reflection of sound waves.

Ans. Reflection of sound is used in megaphones, horns and musical instruments such as trumpets and shehnais. It is used in stethoscope for hearing patient's heartbeat. Ceilings of the concert halls are curved, so that sound after reflection reaches all corners of the hall. (Any two practical applications can be written).

Q13. A stone dropped from the top of a tower 500 m high into a pond of water at the base of the tower. When is the splash heard at the top? Giving, $g = 10 \text{ ms}^{-2}$ and speed of sound $= 340 \text{ ms}^{-1}$.

Ans. Distance covered by the stone = 500 m.

Initial velocity = 0 m/sec.

Acceleration due to gravity = 10 m/sec^2.

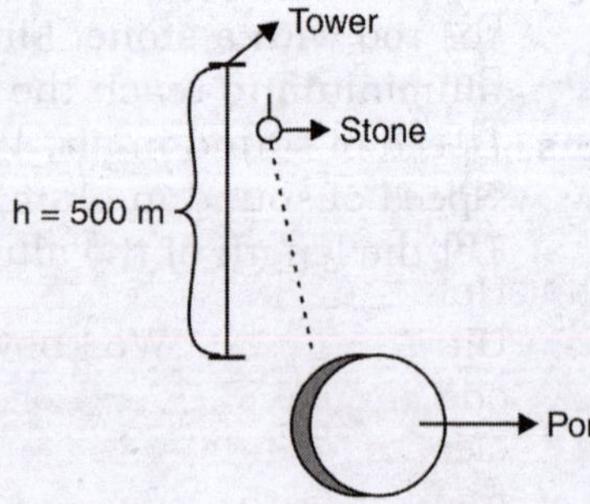

$$s = ut + \frac{1}{2} gt^2.$$
$$500 = (0 \times t) + \frac{1}{2} \times 10 \times t^2$$
$$\frac{500}{5} = t^2 \Rightarrow t = 10 \text{ sec.}$$

Thus in 10 sec. the stone reaches the pond.

Speed of sound = 340 m/sec.

Time taken by sound to cover a distance of

$$500 \text{ m} = \frac{500}{340} = 1.47 \text{ sec}$$

$\therefore$ Total time taken = 10 + 1.47 = 11.47 sec.

In 11.47 sec the splash will be heard on the top.

Q14. A sound wave travels at a speed of 339 ms^{-1}. If its wavelength is 1.5 cm, what is the frequency of the wave? Will it be audible?

Ans. Speed of sound = 339 m/sec.

Wavelength λ = 1.5 cm = 0.015 m.

$$\text{Frequency} = \frac{\text{Speed}}{\text{Wavelength}} = \frac{339}{0.015} = 22600 \text{ Hz.}$$

It will not be audible.

Q15. What is reverberation? How can it be reduced?

Ans. The persistence of sound in an auditorium is the result of repeated reflections of sound and is called reverberation.

To reduce the undesirable effects due to reverberation, roofs and walls of the auditorium are generally covered with sound absorbent materials like compressed fiberboard, rough plaster or draperies. The seat materials are also selected having sound absorption properties.

Q16. What is loudness of sound? What factors does it depend on?

Ans. The loudness of sound is determined by its amplitude. The amplitude of the sound wave depends upon the force with which an object is made to vibrate. Loud sound can travel a larger distance as it is associated with higher energy. A sound waves spreads out from its source. As it moves away from the source its amplitude as well as its loudness decreases.

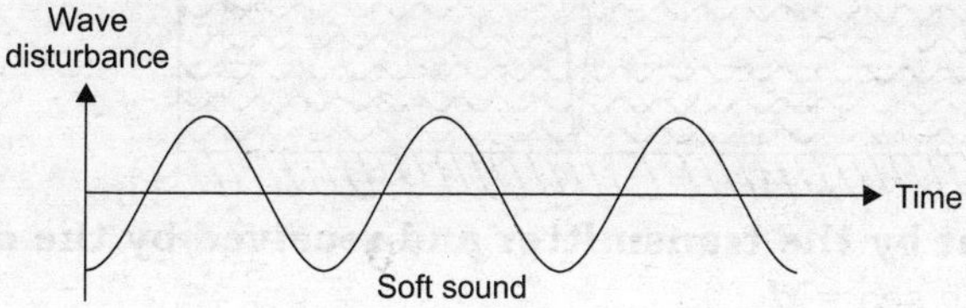

Soft sound

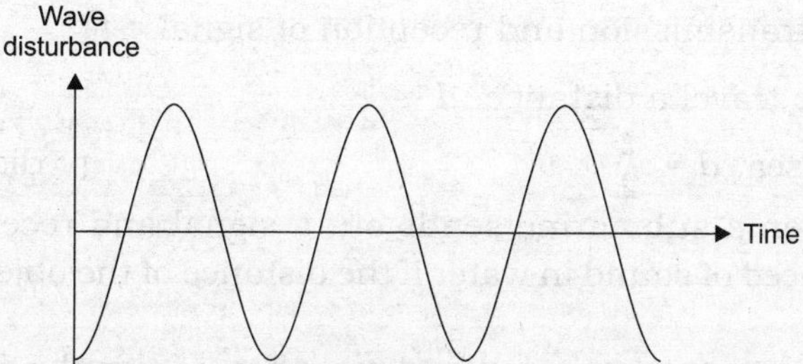

Louder sound

Q17. Explain how bats use ultrasound to catch a prey.

Ans. Bats search out its prey by emitting and detecting reflections of ultrasonic waves. The high-pitched ultrasonic squeaks of bat are reflected from the obstacles or prey and return to bat's ear. The nature of reflection tells the bat where the obstacle or prey is and what it is like.

Q18. How is ultrasound used for cleaning?

Ans. Ultrasound is used to clean parts located in hard-to-reach places (*i.e.*) spiral tube, odd shaped parts, electronic components etc. Objects to be cleaned are placed in a cleaning solution and ultrasonic waves are sent into the solution. Due to the high frequency, the dust particles, grease get detached and drop out. Thc objccts thus get thoroughly cleaned.

Q19. Explain the working and application of a sonar.

Ans. **Working:** SONAR consists of a transmitter and a detector and is installed in a boat or or a ship as shown in the figure. The transmitter produces and transmits ultrasonic waves. These waves travel through water and after striking the object on the seabed, get reflected back and are sensed by the detector. The detector converts the ultrasonic waves into electrical signals which are appropriately interpreted. The distance of the object that reflected the sound wave can be calculated by knowing the speed of sound in water and the time interval between the transmission and reception of the ultrasound.

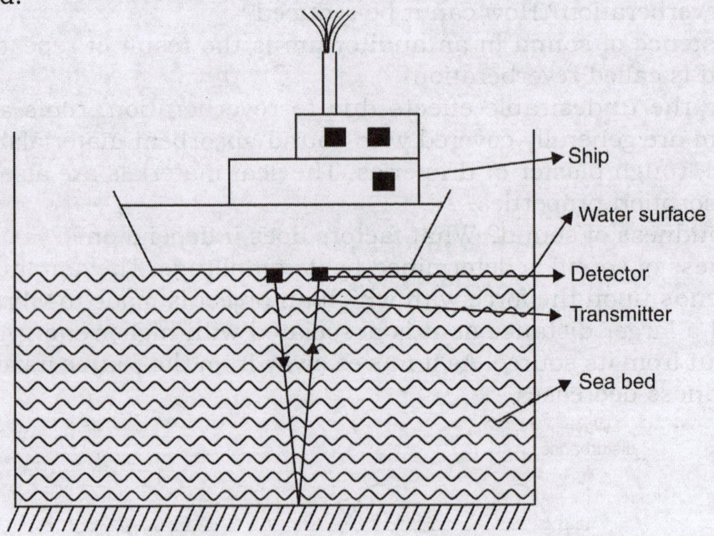

Ultrasound sent by the transmitter and received by the detector

Let, Depth of the sea = d

Speed of sound in sea water = v

Time taken for transmission and reception of signal = t

$\therefore$ Time taken to travel a distance, $d = \frac{t}{2}$

$\therefore$ Depth of the sea, $d = \frac{t}{2} \times v$ ($\because$ distance = speed × time)

Q20. A sonar device on a submarine sends out a signal and receives an echo 5 s later. Calculate the speed of sound in water if the distance of the object from the submarine is 3625 m.

Ans. Time taken between transmission and reception of signal = 5 sec.

Distance of the object from the submarine = 3625 m.

Distance travelled by the ultrasound = 3625 × 2 = 7250 m.

Speed of sound in water = $\frac{\text{distance travelled}}{\text{Time taken}} = \frac{7250}{5}$ = 1450 m/sec

Q21. Explain how defects in a metal block can be detected using ultrasound.

Ans. Ultrasounds can be used to detect cracks and flaws in metal blocks. Metallic components are used in the construction of big structures like buildings, bridges, machines and scientific equipments. The cracks or holes inside the metal blocks, which are invisible from outside reduces the strength of the structure. Ultrasonic waves are allowed to pass through the metallic block and detectors are used to detect the transmitted waves. If there is even a small defect, the ultrasound gets reflected back indicating the presence of the flaw or defect.

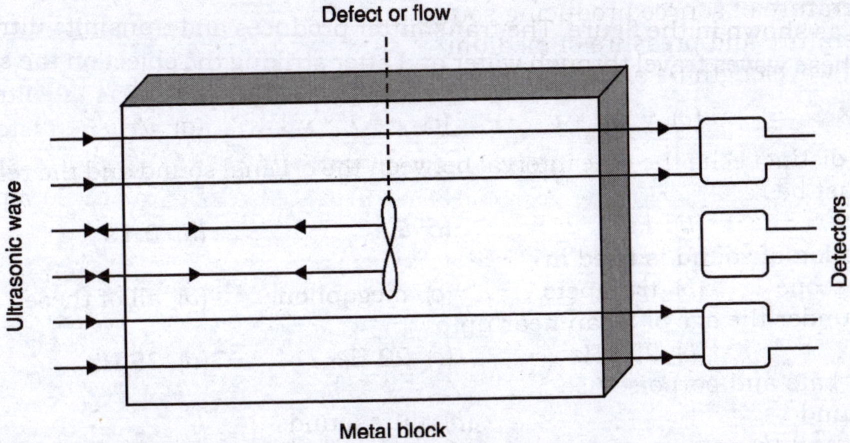

Ultrasound is reflected back from the defective locations inside a metal block

Q22. Explain how the human ear works.

Ans. The outer ear is called 'pinna. It collects the sound from the surroundings. The collected sound passes through the auditory canal. At the end of the auditory canal there is a thin membrane called the ear drum or the tympanic membrane. When a compression of the medium reaches the eardrum the pressure on the outside of the membrane increases and forces the eardrum inward. Similarly, the eardrum moves outward when a rarefaction reaches it. In this way the eardrum vibrates. The vibrations are amplified several times by three bones (the hammer, anvil and stirrup) in the middle ear. The middle ear transmits the amplified pressure variations received from the sound wave to the inner ear. In the inner ear, the pressure variations are turned into electrical signals by the cochlea. These electrical signals are sent to the brain via the auditory nerve and the brain interprets them as sound.

ADDITIONAL QUESTIONS SOLVED

I. Multiple Choice Questions

Choose the correct option:

1. A wave in slinky travelled to and fro in 5 sec the length of the slinky is 5 m. The velocity of wave is

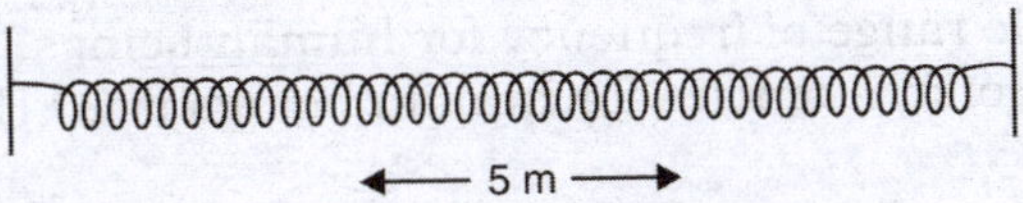

(*a*) 10 m/s (*b*) 5 m/s (*c*) 2 m/s (*d*) 25 m/s

2. Loud sound can travel a larger distance, due to
(*a*) higher amplitude (*b*) higher energy
(*c*) high frequency (*d*) high speed

3. We can distinguish between sound having same pitch and loudness, this characteristic of sound is
(*a*) tone (*b*) note (*c*) pitch (*d*) timber

4. Speed of sound depends upon
(*a*) temperature of medium
(*b*) pressure of medium

(c) temperature of source producing sound
(d) temperature and pressure of medium

5. Speed (υ), wavelength (λ) and frequency (ν) of sound are related as
(a) $\lambda = \upsilon \times \nu$ (b) $\nu = \lambda \times \upsilon$ (c) $\upsilon = \lambda \times \nu$ (d) $\upsilon = \frac{\lambda}{\nu}$

6. To hear a distinct echo the time interval between the original sound and the reflected sound must be
(a) 0.2 s (b) 1 s (c) 2 s (d) 0.1 s

7. Reverberation of sound is used in
(a) stethoscope (b) trumpets (c) megaphone (d) all of these

8. Children under the age of 5 can hear upto
(a) 20 kHz (b) 25 kHz (c) 20 Hz (d) 25 Hz

9. Dolphins, bats and porpoise use
(a) ultrasound (b) infrasound
(c) both (a) and (b) (d) none of these

10. The part of human ear that converts sound vibrations into electrical signals are
(a) Tympanic membrane (b) Hammer
(c) Stirrup (d) Cochlea

Ans. 1—(c), 2—(b), 3—(d), 4—(a), 5—(c), 6—(d), 7—(d), 8—(b), 9—(a), 10—(d).

II. Very Short Answer Type Questions

Q1. Is sound wave longitudinal or transverse?
Ans. Sound wave is longitudinal in nature.

Q2. *What is the relation between frequency (ν) and time period of a sound wave?*
Ans. $\nu = \frac{1}{T}$
Frequency is inversely proportional to time period.

Q3. In which of the three media air, water or steel does sound travel the fastest?
Ans. Sound travels fastest in steel.

Q4. Which has a higher pitch—the sound of a whistle or that of a drum?
Ans. The sound of whistle has higher pitch.

Q5. What is pitch?
Ans. The way our brain interprets the frequency of an emitted sound is called the pitch.

Q6. How can we distinguish one sound from another having the same pitch and loudness?
Ans. The quality or timber of sound helps us to distinguish one sound from another having the same pitch and loudness.

Q7. What is the audible range of frequency for human beings?
Ans. The audible range of frequencies for human beings is 20 Hz to 20,000 Hz.

Q8. What is one Hz?
Ans. Hz is the unit of frequency, called as Hertz. One Hertz is equal to one cycle per second.

Q9. Define speed of sound.
Ans. The speed of sound is defined as the distance travelled per unit time by compression or rarefaction.

Q10. What is 'note' of sound?
Ans. The sound produced due to a mixture of several frequencies is called a note, it is pleasant to listen to.

Q11. What is the time period of sound wave?
Ans. The time taken by two consecutive compressions or rarefactions to cross a fixed points is called the time period of the wave.

Q12. Find the frequency of a wave whose time period is 0.002 second.

Ans. $$\text{Frequency} = \frac{1}{\text{Time period}}$$

$$\text{Frequency} = \frac{1}{0.002} = 500 \text{ Hz}$$

Q13. What is the minimum distance required to hear distinct echo?

Ans. The minimum distance of the obstacle from the source of sound should be 17.2 m.

Q14. What is reverberation?

Ans. The repeated reflection that results in the persistence of sound is called reverberation.

Q15. What is SONAR?

Ans. SONAR means Sound Navigation and Ranging. It is a device that uses ultrasonic waves to measure the distance, direction and speed of underwater objects by getting the reflection of sound.

Q16. What is 'ultrasonic' and 'infrasonic' sound wave?

Ans. Sound waves with frequencies below the audible range (less than 20 Hz) are termed as "infrasonic" and those sound waves with frequencies above the audible range (more than 20000 Hz) are termed as "ultrasonic".

Q17. What should be the time interval between the originated sound and the reflected sound to be heard distinctly?

Ans. To hear a distinct sound the time interval between the originated sound and the reflected sound must be at least 0.1 second.

Q18. What is the function of middle ear?

Ans. It amplifies the sound received by the external ear and passes it to the internal ear.

Q19. Why does sound become faint with distance?

Ans. As sound scatters when it travels with the longer distance its wavelength is unable to reach it becomes faint.

Q20. Give two applications of echo.

Ans. Sound is used in SONAR and in Ultrasonology.

III. Short Answer Type Questions

Q1. What is a medium? Give two examples.

Ans. The matter or substance through which sound is transmitted is called a medium. It can be solid, liquid or gas. Example, air, water, metal.

Q2. Define wave-motion.

Ans. A wave is a disturbance that moves through a medium when the particles of the medium set neighbouring particles into motion. The particles of the medium do not move forward but the disturbance is carried forward.

Q3. What is 'sonic boom'?

Ans. When an object just attains a supersonic speed, it causes shock waves in air. As a result there is large change in air pressure. This results in sonic boom.

Q3. Why does sound become faint with distance?

Ans. Sound is a form of energy. As it moves away from the source its amplitude as well as its loudness decreases. The energy also get transformed in vibration of the particles of the medium.

Q5. Why do we say that sound waves are longitudinal?

Ans. Longitudinal waves need medium for propagation. The sound energy travel in the same line as the particles oscillate.

⟶ Sound energy

⟷ Particles oscillation

It forms compression and rarefaction for the longitudinal wave motion.

Sound wave shows all the characteristics of longitudinal wave so it is called as longitudinal wave.

Q6. Differentiate between longitudinal wave and transverse wave.

Ans.

Longitudinal Wave	*Transverse Wave*
1. It needs medium for propagation.	1. It may or may not need medium for propagation.
2. Particles of the medium move in a direction parallel to the direction of propagation of the disturbance. *Example*, sound wave.	2. Particles of the medium move in perpendicular direction of propagation of the disturbance. *Example*, light wave, seismic wave.

Q7. What is crest and trough?

Ans. When a wave is propagated as represented below. A peak is called the crest and a valley is called the trough of a wave.

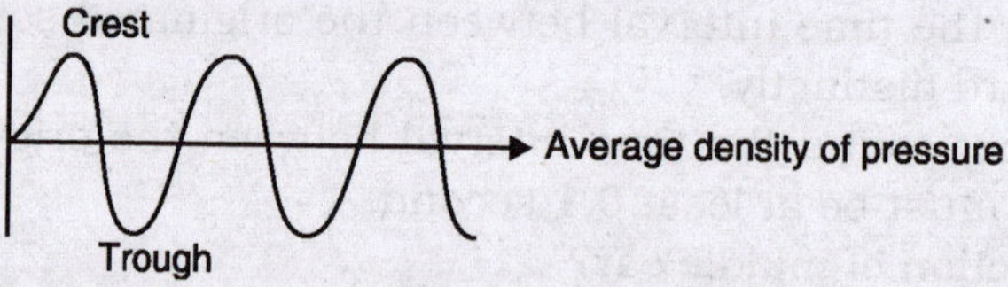

The maximum oscillation disturbance of particles of air forms crest and trough.

Q8. What is echo? Why don't we get echo in small room?

Ans. The distinct sound heard after reflection of sound from the source is called echo. For echo, the distance of reflecting surface from the source should be more than 17.2 m.

Q9. What is velocity of sound? Why does sound travel faster in the summer season than in winter?

Ans. Velocity of sound is the speed of sound in a given medium at a given temperature. As the temperature increases the speed of sound also increases, hence in summer the sound travels faster than in winter.

Q10. Draw a graphical representation of the wave shape for (a) low pitched sound and (b) a high pitched sound.

Ans. (*a*) 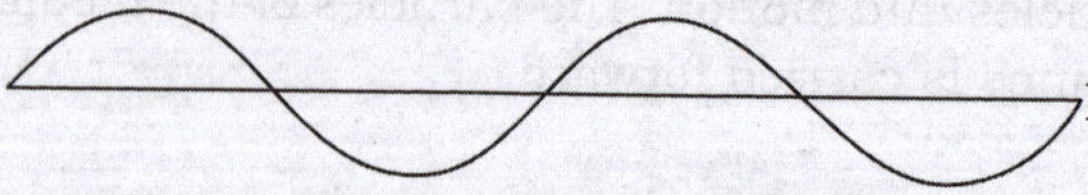 Low pitched sound

(*b*) 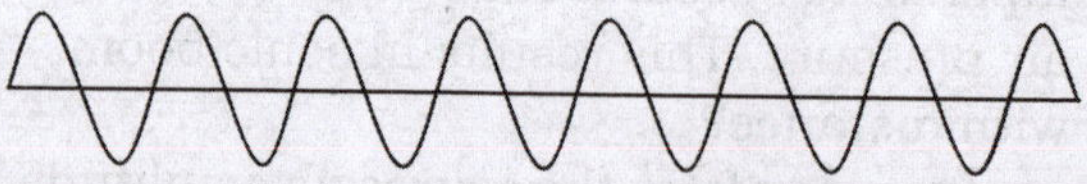 High pitched sound.

Q11. Give two applications of echo/reflection of sound.

Ans. (*i*) Ships use reflection of sound technique "SONAR" which helps in locating the depth, distance, direction and speed of underwater objects.

(*ii*) Ceilings of concert halls are curved so that sound after reflection reaches all corners of the hall.

Q12. Define amplitude, time period and frequency of sound wave.

Ans. **Amplitude:** The magnitude of the maximum disturbance in the medium on either side of the mean value is called amplitude of the wave. Its unit is metre.

Time Period: The time taken by two consecutive compressions or rarefactions to cross a fixed point is called the time period of the wave.

Frequency: The number of oscillations, occurring per unit time is called the frequency of sound wave.

Q13. A sound wave causes the density of air at a place to oscillate 1200 times in 2 minutes. Find the time period and frequency of the wave.

Ans.
$$\text{Frequency} = \frac{1200}{2 \times 60} = 10 \text{ Hz.}$$

$$\text{Time period} = ? \quad \text{Frequency} = \frac{1}{T}$$

$$\therefore \quad T = \frac{1}{\text{Frequency}} = \frac{1}{10} = 0.1 \text{ s.}$$

Q14. Give 3 uses of ultrasound.

Ans. **Uses of ultrasound:**

1. Ultrasound is used to detect cracks and flaws in metal blocks.
2. It is used in 'echo-cardiography', the ultrasonic waves are made to reflect from various parts of the heart and form the image of the heart.
3. It is used in 'ultrasonography', to detect the image of organs or to detect the abnormalities in the organs. It is also used to examine the foetus during pregnancy to detect congenital defects.

Q15. What is the function of middle ear?

Ans. Middle ear consists of three small bones called hammer, anvil and stirrup. These three bones receive the sound vibrations and increase the strength of these vibrations to amplify the vibrations received by ear-drum. These amplified vibrations are further passed to the inner ear.

Q16. A ship sends out ultrasound that return from the seabed and is detected after 3.42 s. If the speed of ultrasound through seawater is 1531 m/s. What is the distance of the seabed from the ship?

Ans. Time between transmission and detection $t = 3.42$ s.

Speed of ultrasound in seawater = 1531 m/s.

Distance travelled by the ultrasound = 2 × depth of sea = $2d$.

$$2d = \text{speed of sound} \times \text{time}$$
$$= 1531 \times 3.42 = 5236 \text{ m}$$
$$\therefore \quad 2d = 5236 \text{ m}$$
$$\therefore \quad d = \frac{5236}{2} = 2618 \text{ m.}$$

The distance of the seabed from the ship is 2618 m.

Q17. Distinguish between tone, note and noise.

Ans. **Tone:** A sound of single frequency is called a tone.

Note: The sound which is produced due to a mixture of several frequencies is called a note.

Noise: The sound which is produced due to a mixture of several frequencies but is unpleasant to the ear is called noise.

Q18. *Establish the relationship between speed, wavelength and frequency of sound.*

Ans. Speed of sound → The distance travelled by a wave or a point on a wave (compression or rarefaction) per unit time.

$$\text{Speed, } v = \frac{\text{Distance}}{\text{Time}}$$

$$v = \frac{\lambda}{T}$$

Distance = wavelength of the sound wave, it is the distance travelled by the sound wave in one time period (T) of the wave.

$$\therefore \quad v = \frac{\lambda}{T} \qquad \left(as\ \nu = \frac{1}{T}\right)$$

$$\therefore \quad v = \lambda \nu, \quad \text{Frequency} = \frac{1}{\text{Time period}}$$

$$\text{Speed} = \text{Wavelength} \times \text{Frequency.}$$

Q19. Which wave property determines

(*a*) loudness? (*b*) pitch?

Name the characteristic of the sound which help you to distinguish your friend's voice while talking in a dark room.

Ans. (*a*) Loudness is determined by amplitude.

(*b*) Pitch is determined by frequency.

The quality or timber of sound helps us to distinguish our friend's voice while talking in a dark room.

Q20. A sound produces 13 crests and 15 troughs in 3 seconds. When the second crest is produced the first is 2 cm away from the source? Calculate.

(*a*) the wavelength (*b*) the frequency (*c*) the wave speed.

Ans.

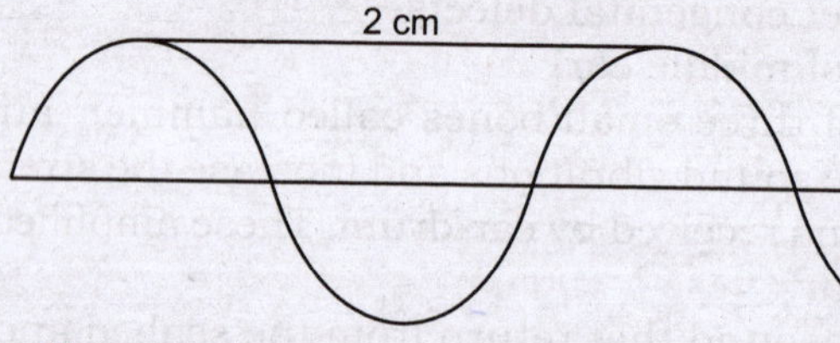

(*a*) Wavelength = distance between two consecutive crests or troughs is 2 cm.

(*b*) $\text{Frequency} = \frac{\text{Number of troughs}}{\text{Time}} = \frac{15}{3} = 5\text{Hz}$

(*c*) $\text{Wave speed} = \frac{\text{Distance}}{\text{Time}}$

Distance travelled by wave = $15 \times 2 = 30$ cm

Time = 3 seconds

$\therefore$ Wave speed = $\frac{30}{3} = 10$ cm/s.

Q21. A construction site near school is bringing lot of behavioral changes in the students. Explain

Ans. The constant work on the construction site makes loud sound and this leads to irritation, high blood pressure, loss in concentration, hearing loss and sick feeling. All these changes affect a lot on students' performance and behavior.

Q22. Lot of houses are located just next to the railway tracks. The train honks every 20 minutes when it passes from the locality. What could be the measure taken by the families to prevent them from loud sound effects of the train?

Ans. The loud sound can be avoided from entering into the house to some extent by using sound proof windows and doors. One can use the insulators to prevent the sound waves enter into the rooms.

Q23. What is Doppler effect?

Ans. As the train approaches, the sound of its horn is heard at a high pitch and as the train moved away, the sound of its horn is heard at a low pitch. This is the Doppler effect.

Q24. Sound reflects like light. How is this property of sound useful?

Ans. The reflection of sound is used in all the musical instruments which has a long tube like flute to produce a peculiar sound. It is also used in the construction. If the hard material is used it would absorb the sound and in cinema halls the soft materials are used like fiber glass and acoustic tiles which will reflect the sound.

Q25. A sound wave is described as: Mechanical wave, longitudinal in nature and is a pressure wave. Discuss.

Ans. Sound is a wave that is created by vibrating objects and propagated through a medium from one location to another. Since a sound wave is a disturbance that is transported through a medium via the mechanism of particle-to-particle interaction, a sound wave is characterized as a mechanical wave.

Longitudinal waves are waves in which the motion of the individual particles of the medium is in a direction that is parallel to the direction of energy transport. This is seen in sound waves.

Pressure wave: Since a sound wave consists of a repeating pattern of high-pressure and low-pressure regions moving through a medium, it is sometimes referred to as a pressure wave. The continuous crests and trough in the sound wave causes the pressure in sound wave.

IV. Long Answer Type Questions

Q1. Sound cannot travel in vacuum. Describe an experiment to demonstrate this.

Ans. Sound is a mechanical wave and needs a material medium to propagate. It cannot travel in vacuum and can be shown by the following experiment.

- Take an electric bell and an airtight glass bell jar. The electric bell is suspended inside the airtight bell jar. Switch 'ON' the electric bell.
- Now, connect the bell jar to vacuum pump.
- Pump out the air from the jar, the sound becomes fainter, although the same current passes through the bell.
- Pump out some more air from the jar, a very feeble sound is heard.
- When the air is completely removed from the jar, no sound is heard.

Bell jar experiment showing sound cannot travel in vacuum.

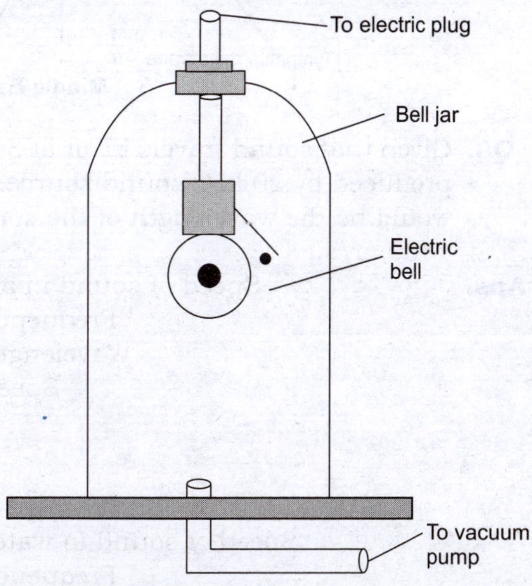

Bell experiment

Q2. Explain the structure of the human ear with the help of a diagram.

Ans. (*a*) **Outer Ear:** Pinna, auditory canal and tympanic membrane.

Pinna: It collects the sound from the surroundings.

Auditory Canal: The sound waves collected pass through this canal.

Tympanic Membrane: It is a thin membrane which receives the vibrations of sound. A compression reaches the eardrum, the pressure on the outside of the membrane increases and pushes the eardrum inward, and moves out when the rarefaction reaches.

(*b*) **Middle Ear:** Consists of three small bones called hammer, anvil and stirrup. The vibrations are received by these three bones and the strength of vibrations is increased *i.e.,* the sound is amplified and passed to inner ear.

(*c*) **Inner Ear:** It consist of cochlea and auditory nerve. Cochlea receives the amplified vibrations and convert them into electrical signals. These electrical signals are sent to the brain via the auditory nerve and the brain interprets the signals as sound.

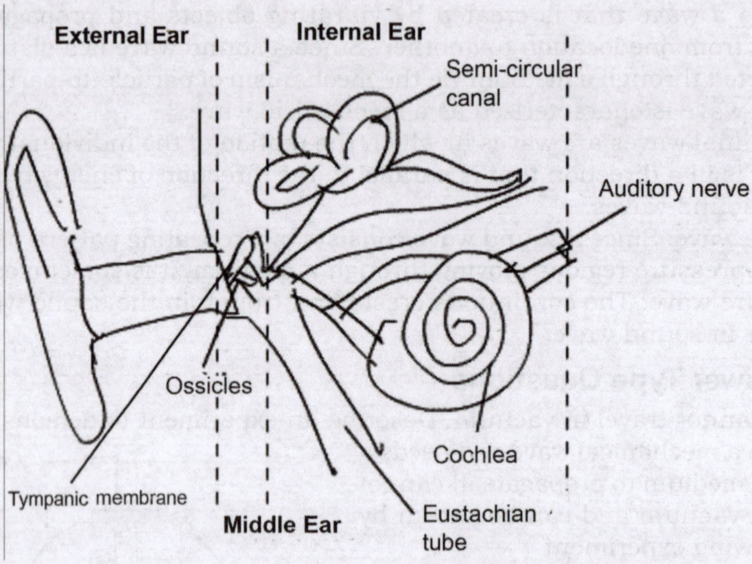

Q3. Given that sound travels in air at 340 m/sec, find the wavelength of the waves in air produced by 20 kHz sound source. If the same source is put in a water tank, what would be the wavelength of the sound waves in water? (Speed of sound in water = 1480 m/s.)

Ans. Speed of sound in air = 340 m/s.

Frequency = 20 kHz = 20×10^3 Hz

Wavelength = ?

$\therefore$ Speed = Wavelength × Frequency

$$v = \lambda \nu$$

$$\therefore \quad \lambda = \frac{v}{\nu} = \frac{\text{Speed}}{\text{Frequencey}} = \frac{340}{20 \times 10^3} = 0.017 \text{ m.}$$

Speed of sound in water = 1480 m/s

Frequency = 20×10^3 Hz

Wavelength = ?

$\therefore$ Speed = Wavelength × Frequency

$$\text{Wavelength} = \frac{\text{Speed}}{\text{Frequency}}$$

$$= \frac{1480}{20 \times 10^3} = 0.074 \text{ m.}$$

Q4. A child watching Dussehra celebration from a distance sees the effigy of Ravana burst into flames and hears the explosion associated with it 2 sec after that. How far was he from the effigy if the speed of sound in air that night was 335 m/sec?

Ans. Speed of sound in air = 335 m/s.

time required to reach the sound = 2 sec

distance of the source of sound =?

$$\therefore \quad \text{Speed} = \frac{\text{Distance}}{\text{Time}}$$

$$\therefore \quad \text{Distance} = \text{Speed} \times \text{Time}$$

$$= 335 \times 2 \text{ sec}$$

$$= 670 \text{ m.}$$

A child was 670 m away from the spot where effigy burnt.

V. Activity-Based Questions

1.
- Take a tuning fork and set it vibrating by striking its prong on a rubber pad. Bring it near your ear.
- Do you hear any sound?
- Touch one of the prongs of the vibrating tuning fork with your finger and share your experience with your friends.
- Now, suspend a table tennis ball or a small plastic ball by a thread from a support. Touch the ball gently with the prong of a vibrating tuning fork.
- Observe what happens and discuss with your friends.

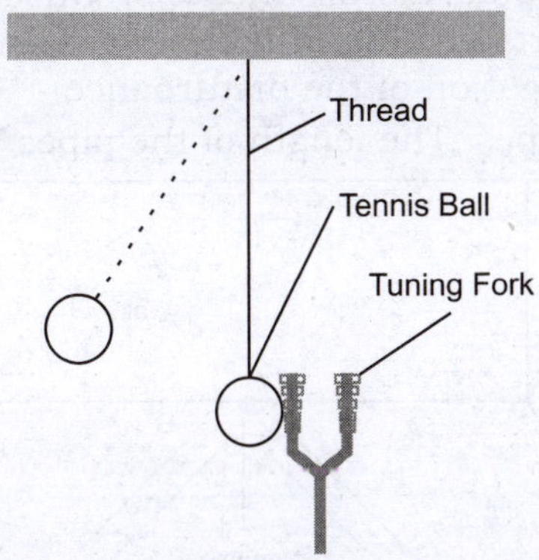

Ans.
- Yes, we heard sound.
- If we touch the ball with tuning fork set into vibration, the ball gets displaced from its mean position and starts moving.

2.
- Fill water in a beaker or a glass up to the brim. Gently touch the water surface with one of the prongs of the vibrating tuning fork.

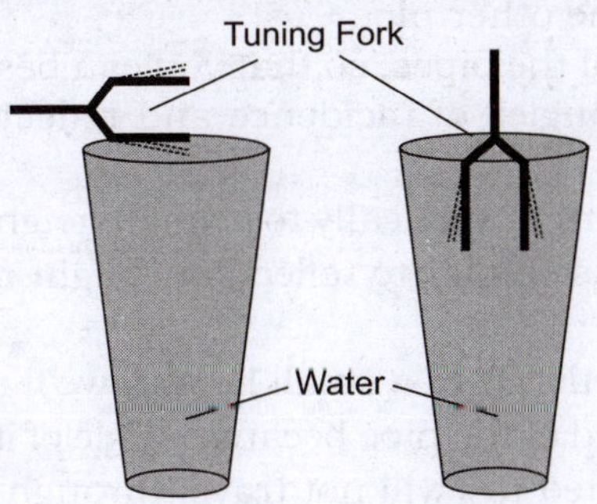

- Next dip the prongs of the vibrating tuning fork in water.
- Observe what happens in both the cases.
- Discuss with your friends why this happens.

Ans. In both the cases, sound will be produced by the tuning fork which produces ripples. But in case (1) ripples are produced which will move up and down and in case (2) ripples are produced which will move in sideways.

3.
- Take a slinky. Ask your friend to hold one end. You hold the other end. Now stretch the slinky and give it a sharp push towards your friend.
- What do you notice? If you move your hand pushing and pulling the slinky alternatively, what will you observe?
- If you mark a dot on the slinky, you'll observe that the dot on the slinky will move back and forth parallel to the direction of propagation of the disturbance.

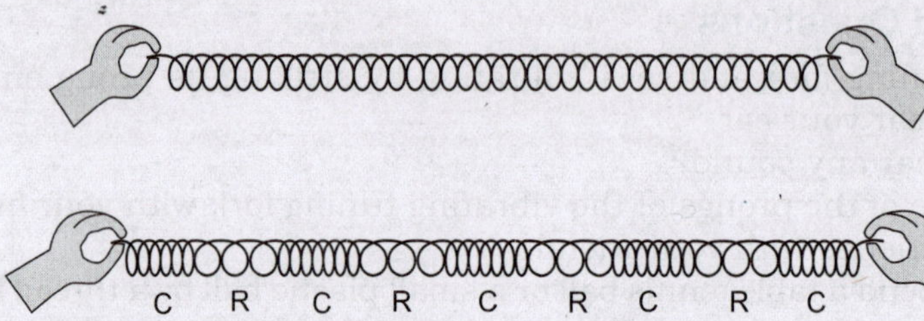

Ans. When we give a small jerk a hump is produced and this travels forward. When we give a sharp push continuous disturbance is produced. When we give a push or pull to the slinky, slinky starts moving in the forward and backward direction parallel to the direction of propagation of the disturbance.

4.
- Take two identical pipes. The length of the pipes should be sufficiently long.

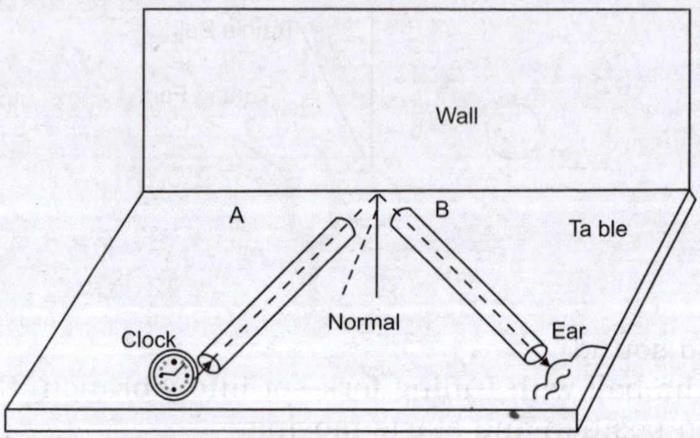

- Arrange them on a table near a wall.
- Keep a clock near the open end of one of the pipes and try to hear the sound of the clock through the other pipe.
- Adjust the position of the pipes, so that you can best hear the sound of the clock.
- Now, measure the angles of incidence and reflection and see the relationship between the angles.
- Lift the pipes on the right vertically to a small height and observe what happens.

Ans. (*i*) Reflection of sound is similar to reflection of light *i.e.* Angle of incidence = Angle of reflection.

(*ii*) If we lift the pipe vertically to a small height, we'll not be able to hear the sound through the other end of the pipe because Angle of incidence ≠ Angle of reflection. Therefore, the reflected ray will not travel through the pipe *B*.

VI. Value-Based Questions

Q1. Raj noticed that his pet dog was frightened and trying to hide in safe place in his house when some crackers were burst in the neighbourhood. He realized the problem and he decided not to burst crackers during diwali or for any other celebrations.

(a) What must be the range of crackers sound?

(b) Name two diseases that can be caused due to noise pollution.

(c) Name the values of Raj reflected in above act.

Ans. (a) The range of crackers sound must be between 20 Hz to 20 kHz.

(b) Two diseases that can occur due to noise pollution are heart attack and high blood pressure.

(c) Raj reflects the value of respecting sensitivity for animals and caring for animals.

Q2. It is not advisable to construct houses near airports, in spite of that many new residential apartments are constructed near airports. Sumit files RTI and also complains the municipal office about the same.

(a) Why one should not reside near airport?

(b) Name other two places where there is noise-pollution.

(c) What value of Sumit is reflected in this act?

Ans. (a) The landing and taking off of the air-planes causes lot of noise pollution which may lead to deafness, high blood pressure and other health problems.

(b) The other two places where there is noise-pollution are residing near the heavy traffic routes and railway stations or lines.

(c) Sumit shows participating citizen and moral responsibility values.

VII. Practical-Based Questions

Q1. The sound wave is given below. Label A-D and explain the nature of the wave.

Ans.

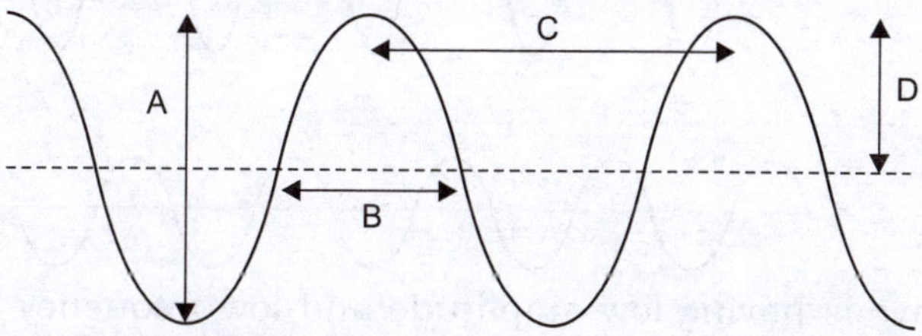

A = Elevation
B = resting position/equilibrium
C = wavelength
D = amplitude

The sound waves are mechanical and longitudinal these waves show alternate compression and rarefaction. It travels only through a medium.

Q2. The four waves are shown below: Compare and describe each wave.

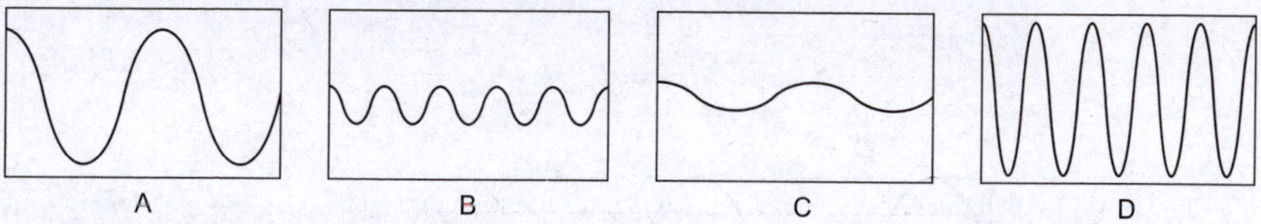

A = This wave has high amplitude and is loud

B = amplitude is very small and is not loud, it has higher frequency and hence has high pitch.

C = the wave has low amplitude and very small frequency. Hence it is soft sound and has low pitch.

D = This wave has high amplitude and hence loud, it also has high frequency and has high pitch.

Q3.

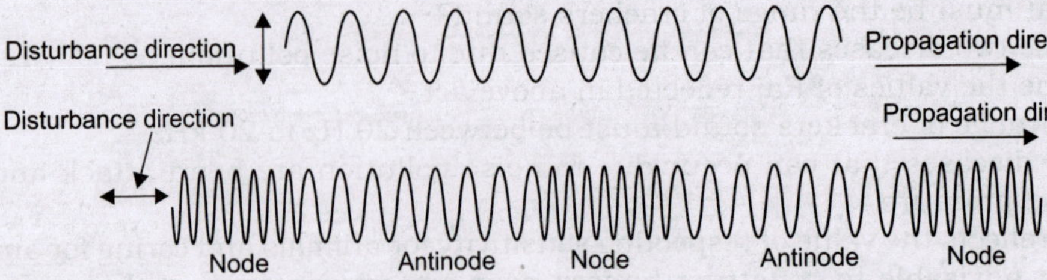

Label the two types of waves given above and explain how you can classify it.

Ans. The wave in which the propagation direction is perpendicular to the disturbance direction is a transverse wave. It does not need any medium to travel. E.g. Light wave

The second wave in which the propagation direction is same in the direction of the disturbance is called longitudinal wave. It needs medium to travel. E.g. Sound wave

Q4. Which wave is of a soothing musical note and why?

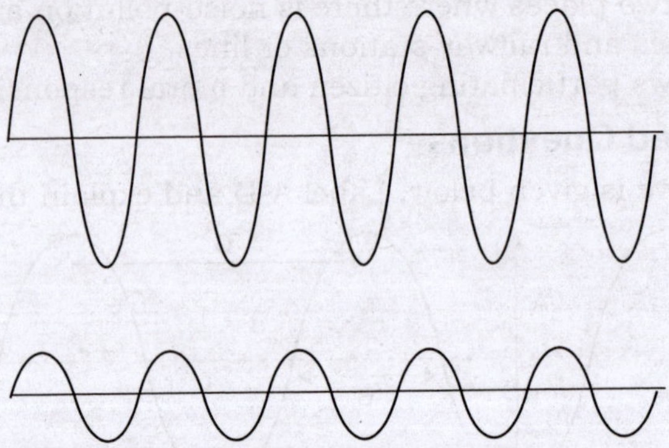

Ans. The second wave is having low amplitude and low frequency hence it is soothing music sound as it is not loud sound and has low pitch.

The wave above is having high amplitude and is very loud.

Q5. Draw the sketches of two waves A and B such that wave A has twice the wavelength and half the amplitude of wave B.

Ans.

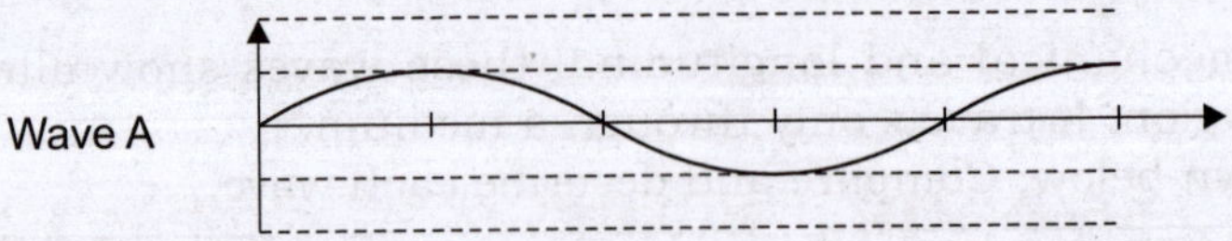

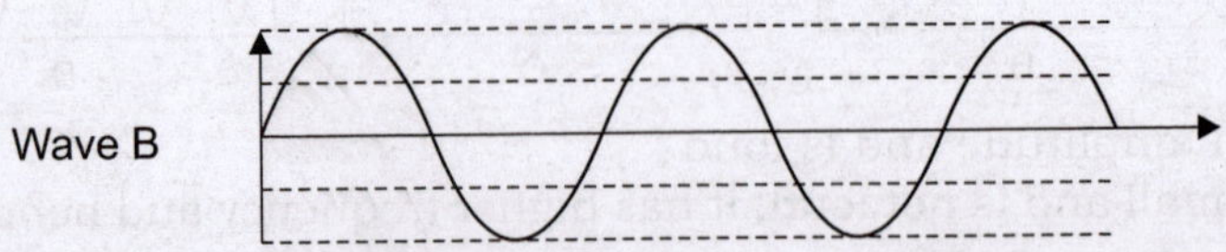

TEST YOUR SKILLS

Q1. Define wavelength.
Q2. What is the audible range of frequency for human beings?
Q3. What is the minimum distance required to hear distinct echo?
Q4. What is pitch?
Q5. What should be the time interval between the originated sound and the reflected sound to be heard distinctly?
Q6. Differentiate between longitudinal wave and transverse wave.
Q7. A ship sends out ultrasound waves that returns from the seabed and is detected after 3.42 s. If the speed of ultrasound waves through seawater is 1531 m/s. What is the distance of the seabed from the ship?
Q8. What is ultrasonic and infrasonic sound wave?
Q9. Define amplitude, time period and frequency of sound waves.
Q10. With the help of an activity show that sound cannot travel in vacuum.
Q11. (*a*) Give three uses of ultrasound. (*b*) What is SONAR?

❑❑❑

13 Why Do We Fall Ill

Syllabus

Health, Diseases, Causes of disease, Principles of treatment.

Facts that Matter

- **Introduction**
  Health is a state of complete physical, mental and social well-being.
- **Basic conditions for good health:**
  (1) Proper balanced and nutritious diet.
  (2) Personal hygiene.
  (3) Clean environment and surroundings.
  (4) Healthy air, no pollution in the surrounding.
  (5) Regular exercise.
  (6) Proper rest.
  (7) Good standard of living and economic status.
- **Disease:** When the body is not at ease *i.e.,* comfortable then it is said to have a disease. When there is a disease, the functioning or appearance of one or more systems of the body changes.
  Depending on the duration—disease is classified as acute or chronic.
- **Acute disease:** Diseases that last for only short period of time, *e.g.,* headache, common cold etc.
- **Chronic disease:** Diseases that last for long time, are called chronic diseases, *e.g.,* elephantiasis, tuberculosis, etc.
- **Causes of diseases:** Immediate cause and contributory cause.
  Immediate cause: The organisms that enter our body and causes disease is called immediate cause. For example, virus, bacteria, protozoa etc.
  Contributory cause: The secondary factors which led these organisms enter our body are called as contributory cause. For example, dirty water, unhealthy surroundings, contaminated food, improper nourishment, poverty, poor standard of living etc.
- Diseases may be due to infectious and non-infectious causes.
  (*a*) **Infectious causes:** Diseases where microbes are the immediate causes are called infections diseases. The infection spreads from one person to another. For example: malaria, cholera, food poisoning etc.
  (*b*) **Non-infectious causes:** Some diseases that do not spread in the community, but remains internal are called non-infectious diseases. For example: cancer, genetic abnormalities, high blood pressure etc.
- **Infectious diseases (Communicable diseases):** When a disease causing organism enters our body it causes **infection,** it multiplies and grows in the body of host.

Causes of Infections	***Diseases***
Bacteria	Tuberculosis, tetanus, typhoid, cholera
Virus	AIDS, polio, chickenpox, rabies, measles
Fungi	Skin diseases, food poisoning
Protozoan	Malaria, amoebiasis, kala-azar
Worm	Filariasis

- **Infectious diseases spread through:**
  (*a*) **Air:** Causes air-borne diseases due to bacteria, virus *e.g.*, common cold, influenza, measles, tuberculosis.
  (*b*) **Food and water:** Is caused due to contaminated food and water that contains bacteria, virus, worm etc. Example, cholera, typhoid and hepatitis.
  (*c*) **Contact:** Many diseases spread by contact of infected person with the healthy person. Examples, fungal infection, scabies etc.
  AIDS and syphilis spread due to sexual contact.
  (*d*) **Body fluids:** Body fluids like blood, semen, mother milk when infected can also cause disease. Example, AIDS.
- **Antibiotics:** These are the chemicals (medicine, drugs) that block biochemical pathways important for bacteria. They are used for diseases caused by bacteria.
- **Inflammation:** When an active immune system releases many cells to the affected tissue to kill-off the disease-causing microbes it is called inflammation. Local effects caused on body due to inflammation are—swelling, pain, fever and redness.
- **Principles of treatment**
  (1) To reduce the effects of the diseases.
  (2) To kill the cause of the disease *i.e.,* to kill the microbes like bacteria, fungi, protozoa.
- **Principles of Prevention**
  (1) General method (2) Specific method
- **General ways** of preventing infections relate to preventing exposure.
- Prevention of exposure can be done in following ways:
  (1) **For air-borne infections**—avoid visiting public place, cover your nose and mouth while coughing.
  (2) **For water-borne infections:** Drink, clean and boiled drinking water.
  (3) **For vector-borne infections:** Keep the surroundings clean, do not keep any puddle of water open in the surrounding as it allows the breeding of mosquitoes.
  (4) Sclf immune system that can fight off and kill microbes when it enters our body.
  (5) Availability of proper and sufficient food for everyone.
- **Specific ways:** By giving vaccines, childhood immunisation that is given to the children for preventing infectious diseases.

NCERT IN-TEXT QUESTIONS SOLVED

Q1. State any two conditions essential for good health.

Ans. Two conditions essential for good health are:
(*i*) State of physical, mental and social well-being.
(*ii*) Better surroundings or environment.

Q2. State any two conditions essential for being free of disease.

Ans. The two conditions essential for being free of disease are:
(1) Personal and domestic hygiene.
(2) Clean environment and surroundings.

Q3. Are the answers to the above questions necessarily the same or different? Why?

Ans. The answer to the above questions are different because a person may be free of disease but his mental, social or economical health may not be good.

Q4. List any three reasons why you would think that you are sick and ought to see a doctor. If only one of these symptoms were present, would you still go to the doctor? Why or why not?

Ans. The three reasons why one would think that he is sick are—(1) headache (2) cold and cough (3) loose-motions.

This indicates that there may be a disease but does not indicate what the disease is. So one would still visit the doctor for the treatment and to know the cause of above symptom.

Even in case of single symptom one needs to go to the doctor to get proper treatment.

Q5. In which of the following case do you think the long-term effects on your health are likely to be most unpleasant?

- If you get jaundice
- If you get lice
- If you get acne.

Why?

Ans. In the above cases, lice and acne are acute problems of our health which can be cured in short duration. But jaundice is the disease that can have most unpleasant effect on our health as it affects the most important organ of our body *i.e.*, liver. This disease is a chronic one.

Q6. Why are we normally advised to take bland and nourishing food when we are sick?

Ans. We are advised to take bland and nourishing food when we are sick because our body needs energy to release cells to overcome the infection, the wear and tear of body organ. The nourishing food provides nutrients to our body that will further provide energy and make new cells. No spices in the food makes its digestion process faster, does not release acids in the body that can interfere in the treatment and cure.

Q7. What are the different means by which infectious diseases are spread?

Ans. The different means by which infectious diseases spread are:

(*a*) **Through air:** They are also called air-borne diseases. The air carries bacteria, virus and the diseases that can be caused are common cold, influenza, tuberculosis etc.

(*b*) **Through food and water:** When one eats/drinks contaminated food/water, that contains bacteria, virus, worm etc. it can cause diseases like cholera typhoid, hepatitis.

(*c*) **Through contact:** Many diseases spread by contact of infected person with the healthy person. Example, fungal infections, skin diseases, scabies etc.

(*d*) **By sexual contact:** Many diseases can be transmitted through sexual contact. Example, syphilis, AIDS.

(*e*) **By body fluids:** Fluids like blood, semen, mother's milk, when infected, can also cause diseases. Example, AIDS.

(*f*) **Vectors:** The organism that spreads a disease by carrying pathogens from one place to another is called vector. Example, mosquitoes are vectors that carry pathogens like protozoa.

Q8. What precautions can you take in your school to reduce the incidence of infectious diseases?

Ans. The precautions that we can take in school to reduce the incidence of infectious diseases are given below.

(*a*) By using handkerchief while coughing or sneezing.

(*b*) Washing hands before eating tiffins.

(c) Staying at home if anyone suffers from infectious diseases.

(d) Getting vaccinated before the infection affects.

(e) Keeping the school surroundings clean, checking for stagnant water.

Q9. What is immunisation?

Ans. When the body attains immunity against any disease, due to vaccination. This process is called immunisation.

Q10. What are the immunisation programmes available at the nearest health centre in your locality? Which of these diseases are the major health problems in your area?

Ans. The immunization programmes available at the nearest health care centres are:

(1) Child immunization programme starts from 0 to 12 years.

(2) Polio eradication programme

(3) H_1N_1 screening programme

Age	*Immunisation*
Infant	Polio, B.C.G
6 weeks—9 weeks	D.P.T, tetanus
9–12 months	booster doses, chickenpox, hepatitis A, B etc.

In major areas tuberculosis cases are reported in a large number which is a major concern.

NCERT TEXTUAL QUESTIONS SOLVED

Q1. How many times did you fall ill in the last one year? What were the illnesses?

(a) Think of one change you could make in your habits in order to avoid any of/most of the above illnesses.

(b) Think of one change you would wish for in your surroundings in order to avoid any of/most of the above illness.

Ans. The illness was common cold which occurred 2-3 times in a year.

(a) One change I would make in my habits in order to avoid the above illness is that I would take proper diet rich in vitamin C and would avoid too cold food.

(b) The surroundings should be neat and clean,

Q2. A doctor/nurse/health worker is exposed to more sick people than others in the community. Find out how she/he avoids getting sick herself/himself?

Ans. A doctor/nurse/health worker when exposed to sick people they keep their nose and mouth covered, take care of hygiene, wash hands with soap before drinking water or eating food. They use mask, gloves, etc to avoid the direct contact with the person suffering from infectious diseases.

Q3. Conduct a survey in your neighbourhood to find out what the three most common diseases are. Suggest three steps that could be taken by your local authorities to bring down the incidence of these diseases.

Ans.

Common-diseases in neighbourhood	*Steps to bring down the diseases spread*
1. Malaria	1. Clean surrounding
2. Diarrhoea	2. Clean drinking water
3. Typhoid	3. Childhood immunisation

Q4. A baby is not able to tell his/her caretakers that she/he is sick. What would help us to find out

(a) that the baby is sick? (a) what is the sickness?

Ans. (*a*) The symptoms like body temperature, fever, cough, cold, loose-motions, non-stop crying, improper or no food intake etc. would help up to find that the baby is sick.

(*b*) The symptoms could help us to find out the sickness of the baby.

Q5. Under which of the following conditions is a person most likely to fall sick?

(*a*) When she is recovering from malaria.

(*b*) When she has recovered from malaria and is taking care of someone suffering from chicken-pox.

(*c*) When she is on a four-day fast after recovering from malaria and is taking care of someone suffering from chicken-pox.

Why?

Ans. (*c*) When she is on a four-day fast after recovering from malaria and is taking care of someone suffering from chicken-pox.

As the person is not taking proper diet which is required for her proper health and healing of body.

Her chances of getting chicken-pox are also high as her body's immunity has lowered.

Q6. Under which of the following conditions are you most likely to fall sick?

(*a*) When you are taking examinations.

(*b*) When you have travelled by bus and train for two days.

(*c*) When your friend is suffering from measles.

Why?

Ans. (*c*) When your friend is suffering from measles, as it is an infectious disease.

ADDITIONAL QUESTIONS SOLVED

I. Multiple Choice Questions

Choose the correct option:

1. The disease that affects our lungs is

(*a*) AIDS (*b*) rabies (*c*) polio (*d*) tuberculosis

2. The BCG vaccine is given for the immunity against

(*a*) hepatitis (*b*) jaundice (*c*) tuberculosis (*d*) malaria

3. Malaria is caused due to

(*a*) protozoa (*b*) *Anopheles* mosquito

(*c*) both (*a*) and (*b*) (*d*) none of the above

4. *Trypanosoma*, *Leishmania* and *Plasmodium* are the examples of

(*a*) virus (*b*) bacteria (*c*) protozoa (*d*) worm

5. Diarrhoea, cholera, typhoid are the diseases that have one thing in common, that is:

(*a*) All of them are caused by bacteria.

(*b*) All of them are transmitted by contaminated food and water.

(*c*) All of them are cured by antibiotics.

(*d*) All of the above.

6. The bacteria among the following is

(*a*) *Plasmodium* (*b*) *Trypanosoma* (*c*) Rabies virus (*d*) *Salmonella typhi*

7. HIV virus attacks one of the following cells in our body

(*a*) Red blood cell (*b*) White blood cell (*c*) Liver cell (*d*) Long cell

8. The pathogens of disease are

(*a*) bacteria (*b*) virus (*c*) protozoa (*d*) all of the above

9. Penicillin is a drug that can
(*a*) interfere in the biological pathway of bacteria
(*b*) an antibiotic that can kill bacteria
(*c*) both (*a*) and (*b*) (*d*) none of the above

10. The disease caused due to worm is
(*a*) tetanus (*b*) rabies
(*c*) sleeping sickness (*d*) filariasis

Ans. 1—(*d*), 2—(*c*), 3—(*c*), 4—(*c*), 5—(*d*), 6—(*d*), 7—(*b*), 8—(*d*), 9—(*c*), 10—(*d*).

II. Very Short Answer Type Questions

Q1. Define health.
Ans. Health means a state of physical, mental and social well-being.

Q2. Define disease.
Ans. Disease means being uncomfortable.

Q3. What do you mean by symptoms of disease?
Ans. Symptoms of disease are the signs of a disease which indicates the presence of a particular disease.

Q4. What are acute diseases?
Ans. Those diseases which last for very short period of time are called acute diseases. Example, headache and cold.

Q5. What are chronic diseases?
Ans. The diseases which last for very long period of time are called chronic diseases Example, tuberculosis and jaundice.

Q6. What are pathogens?
Ans. The disease causing microbes are called pathogens. Example, bacteria, virus, fungi, worms.

Q7. What are vectors?
Ans. The organisms that spread or carry pathogens from one place to another, from infected person to healthy person is called vector.
Example, mosquito, housefly etc.

Q8. What are infectious diseases?
Ans. Diseases which can spread from one person to another and microbes are the immediate cause for these diseases are called infectious diseases. Example, typhoid.

Q9. What are non-infectious diseases?
Ans. Diseases which do not spread from one person to another and remain internal are called non-infectious diseases. Example, cancer.

Q10. Name any one disease caused due to genetic abnormality.
Ans. Haemophilia.

Q11. Name two diseases caused by protozoa.
Ans. Malaria and amoebiasis.

Q12. Name two diseases caused due to bacteria.
Ans. Tuberculosis, typhoid.

Q13. Name two disease caused due to virus.
Ans. Polio, chickenpox.

Q14. Name two disease caused by fungi.
Ans. Scabies and skin infection.

Q15. What are antibiotics?
Ans. Antibiotics are drugs that block the biochemical pathways important for bacteria. These are used to cure diseases caused due to bacteria.

Q16. Give the full form of AIDS.

Ans. AIDS–Acquired Immuno Deficiency Syndrome (Syndrome means collection of symptoms).

Q17. Name the pathogen that causes sleeping sickness.

Ans. The protozoan → *Trypanosoma*.

Q18. Name the organism that causes kala-azar.

Ans. *Leishmania*.

Q19. Name two air-borne diseases.

Ans. Common cold, cough, tuberculosis.

Q20. Name two diseases that are organ specific.

Ans. Jaundice – liver.
Tuberculosis – lungs.

Q21. Which virus causes AIDS?

Ans. HIV virus causes AIDS.

Q22. Define vaccination.

Ans. Vaccination is the administration of antigenic material to stimulate an individual's immune system to develop adaptive immunity to a pathogen (infection).

Q23. What are pathogens?

Ans. A pathogen is a microorganism that causes diseases.

Q24. State four kinds of microorganisms that can act as pathogens.

Ans. Virus, bacteria, fungi and protista.

Q25. State the temperature at which the food when kept can help the bacteria grow the most.

Ans. The temperature range is 10 to 45 degree C/°C.

Q26. Name three diseases caused by pathogens.

Ans. Tetanus, Tuberculosis and malaria.

Q27. Name the type of body cell that can ingest and digest bacteria.

Ans. White blood cell lymphocyte.

Q28. Why do salads have more tendency for the growth of bacteria in it?

Ans. The salad generally consists of raw vegetables and are not cooked and hence the temperature is favourable for the optimal growth of bacteria.

III. Short Answer Type Questions

Q1. Give the difference between acute disease and chronic disease.

Ans.

Acute disease	*Chronic disease*
1. It may last for few days.	1. It lasts for longer period.
2. It does not have major effect on body.	2. It affects the body drastically.

Q2. State two main causes of disease.

Ans. Two main causes of disease are immediate cause and contributory cause. **Immediate cause:** This is due to the organisms that enter our body and cause disease. Example, virus, protozoa, bacteria.

Contributory cause: These are the secondary factors which lead these organisms to enter our body. Example, dirty water, unclean surrounding, contaminated food etc.

Q3. Define vaccine and name two vaccines.

Ans. Vaccine is a chemical/drug given in advance to a body to give immunity against certain diseases.

Vaccines given to children are:

(*a*) BCG—for tuberculosis prevention (*b*) Polio drops—for polio prevention

Q4. What is penicillin antibiotic? Give its function.

Ans. Penicillin antibiotic blocks the bacterial processes that build the cell wall. Due to this drug, the bacteria is unable to make a protective cell wall and dies easily. It is used to cure the diseases and infections caused by bacteria.

Q5. Bacteria is a cell, antibiotics can kill these bacteria (cell), Human body is also made of cells how does it affect our body?

Ans. Antibiotics block the biochemical pathway of bacteria by which it makes a protective cell wall around it. Antibiotic does not allow the bacteria to make this cell wall because of which they die.

Human body cell don't make any cell wall so antibiotics cannot have any such effect on our body.

Q6. How does cholera becomes an epidemic in a locality?

Ans. Cholera is an infectious disease that spreads due to unsafe water. It can spread in a locality; if a person suffering from cholera lives in the locality and the excreta of this person get mixed with the drinking water used by people living nearby. The cholera-causing microbe enters the new hosts through the water they drink and cause disease in them.

Q7. Name the organs affected due to the following diseases:

Malaria, jaundice, Japanese encephalitis, typhoid.

Ans. (*i*) Malaria: Infects liver and red blood cells

(*ii*) Jaundice: Infects the liver.

(*iii*) Japanese encephalitis: Infects the brain

(*iv*) Typhoid: Infects blood.

Q8. Why are sick patients advised to take bed rest?

Ans. Doctors advise to take bed rest for sick patients so that they can conserve their energy which can be used for healing of their body organs which were affected due to certain disease.

Q9. How do we kill microbes that enter our body and cause diseases?

Ans. Microbes can be killed by using medicines. These microbes are of different categories—virus, bacteria, fungi or protozoa. Each of these groups of organisms have some essential biochemical life processes which is peculiar to a particular group and is not shared by others. These pathways are not used by us. By using drugs that blocks the microbial synthesis pathway without affecting us can kill the microbes.

Q10. What are disease specific means of prevention?

Ans. The disease specific means of prevention are the use of vaccines. The vaccines, are used against tetanus, diphtheria, whooping cough, measles, polio and many others.

Q11. Why can't we make antiviral medicines/drugs?

Ans. The viruses lie on the border line of living and non-living organisms. The viruses can live, grow and multiply only inside the host body. They cannot be grown or cultured and their biological pathways cannot be affected. Hence, the antiviral medicines/drugs is difficult to make.

Q12. Write a short note on malaria as a disease, its symptoms and control.

Ans. Malaria is caused by protozoa that lives in blood. This parasite enters our body through a female *Anopheles* mosquito bite which is the vector, visits water to lay eggs, the protozoa enters our blood stream when female mosquito bites us. This protozoa affects our liver and red blood cells.

Symptoms: Very high fever with periodic shivering, headache and muscular pain.

Control: Use of quinine drug, keeping the surroundings clean with no stagnant water, use of mosquito repellent creams, nets, can control the spread of this disease.

Q13. What is AIDS? How does a person get affected with HIV?

Ans. AIDS means Acquired Immuno Deficiency Syndrome, which is caused due to HIV—human immuno deficiency virus. This virus reduces the immunity of human body. Therefore if any microbe enters the body of a person it causes disease killing the person.

The virus is transmitted from infected person to other person by any of the following way:

(a) Blood transfusion.
(b) From mother (infected) to baby in the womb.
(c) From mother's milk to lactating baby.
(d) By sexual contact.
(e) Sharing of needle with an infected person.

Q14. Becoming exposed to or infected with an infectious microbe does not necessarily mean developing noticeable disease. Explain.

Ans. This is because the immune system of our body normally fights off microbes. Our body have cells that are specialised in killing infecting microbes. Whenever any microbes or foreign body enters our system, these cells become active and kill the microbes that could cause any damage to the body. These immune cells manage to kill off the infection and a person does not get disease.

Q15. What are three limitations for the approach to deal with infectious diseases?

Ans. The three limitations are:

(1) If someone has a disease, their body functions are damaged and may never recover completely.

(2) As the treatment will take time, the person suffering from a disease is likely to be bedridden for some time.

(3) The infectious person can serve as the source from where the infection may spread to other people.

Q16. Give the common methods of transmission of diseases.

Ans.

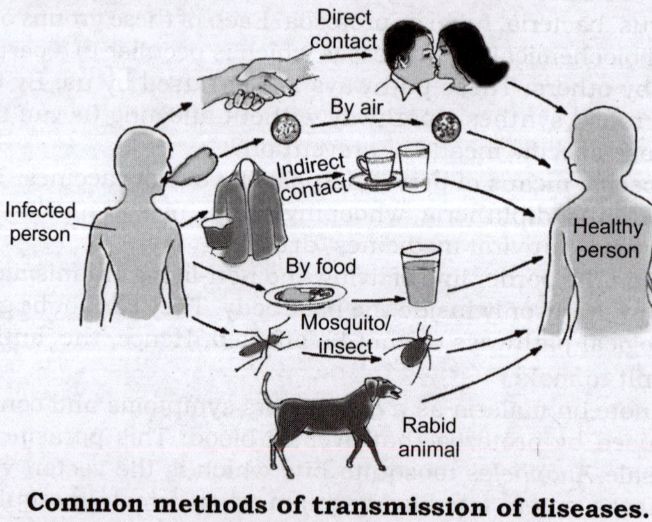

Common methods of transmission of diseases.

The common methods of transmission of diseases are:

(1) By air – cough, cold, tuberculosis
(2) By food and water – typhoid, jaundice
(3) By mosquito bite – malaria

(4) By rabid animal – rabies
(5) By direct contact – skin infection, small pox, AIDS
(6) By indirect contact – typhoid, chickenpox

Q17. What are the basic conditions for good health?

Ans. The basic conditions for good health are:
(1) Proper balanced and nutritious diet
(2) Personal hygiene
(3) Clean surroundings and clean environment
(4) Regular rest
(5) Proper rest
(6) Good economic status.

Q18. (*a*) Give two examples of diseases which can be spread by contaminated drinking water.
(*b*) How can the spread of such diseases be prevented?

Ans. (*a*) Typhoid and cholera can be spread by contaminated water.
(*b*) The spread of such diseases can be prevented by (*i*) effective disposal of sewage, (*ii*) purification of drinking water.

Q19. What sources of water are (*a*) most likely, (*b*) least likely to contain pathogenic bacteria?

Ans. (*a*) Water most likely to contain pathogenic bacteria will be that which is received from untreated or partially treated sewage.
(*b*) Water least likely to be contaminated will be that which comes from unpopulated areas or has filtered through rock layers into underground aquifers.

Q20. Which body cells are attacked by the malarial parasite? How can malarial parasites be transmitted from an infected person to a healthy person?

Ans. The malarial parasite attacks red blood cells. The malarial parasite is transmitted when a healthy person is bitten by a mosquito which has fed on an infected person

Q21. (*a*) What kind of food is most likely to contain Salmonella bacteria?
(*b*) What illness is caused by Salmonella typhimurium?
(*c*) What is the usual method of killing Salmonella bacteria in food?

Ans. (*a*) Salmonella bacteria are most likely to be present in poultry (chicken, duck, turkey), eggs, beef or pork, and unpasteurised milk.
(b) Salmonella typhimurium causes food poisoning.
(c) High temperature kills bacteria or deactivates them. Cooking usually kills Salmonella bacteria in food.

Q22. Match each disease with its correct type of vaccine.

(a) Tuberculosis	(*i*) Harmless forms of virus
(b) whooping cough	(*ii*) Inactivated toxin
(c) Diphtheria	(*iii*) Killed bacteria
(d) Polio	(*iv*) Harmless form of bacteria.

Ans.

(*a*) Tuberculosis	(*iv*) Harmless form of bacteria
(b) Whooping cough	(*iii*) Killed bacteria
(c) Diphtheria	(*ii*) Inactivated toxin
(*d*) Polio	(*i*) Harmless form of virus

Q23. What is the purpose of the mask worn by doctors during an operation?

Ans. The masks worn by doctors prevent reaching of infected droplets from the patient to the doctor. Any infection causing germs can be prevented from entering into the system of the doctor.

Q24. Classify human diseases.

Ans.

Diseases

- Congenital diseases (present since birth)
- Acquired diseases (Develop after birth)
  - Communicable diseases (Spread from infected person to healthy person)
  - non-communicable diseases (Do not spread from one person to another)
    - Degenerative disease (caused due to malfunctioning of vital body organ)
    - Deficiency diseases (caused due to lack of nutrients in diet)
    - Allergies (caused due to hypersensitivity of the body to certain foreign substances)
    - Cancer (caused due to uncontrolled growth of cells/ tissues)
    - Other diseases (caused due to various physical agents or any other reason)

Q25. What is congenital disease? Give one example.

Ans. Congenital disease is present from birth (e.g. hole in the heart in infants). They are caused by some genetic abnormality or metabolic disorder or malfunctioning of an organ.

Q26. What are acquired disease and how are they classified?

Ans. **Acquired disease:** The disease which may occur after birth during one's lifetime. Acquired diseases may generally be classified into:

(*i*) **Infections diseases:** The diseases which can be transmitted from one person to another person. e.g. measles.

(*ii*) **Degenerative diseases:** The diseases caused due to the malfunction of some vital organs of the body e.g. heart failure.

IV. Long Answer Type Questions

Q1. If someone in the family gets infectious disease, what precautions will you advice to the other family members?

Ans. For an infectious diseased person in the family following precautions should be taken:

(1) The surroundings and the house should be clean.
(2) The infected person should be kept isolated in a separate room.
(3) The clothes and utensils of patient should be sanitized regularly.
(4) Separate towels and handkerchief should be used by the patient.
(5) Children should not be allowed to visit the infected person.
(6) Clean and boiled drinking water should be given to the patient.
(7) A balanced and nutritious diet which will provide lot of energy should be given.
(8) There should be silence and the patient should be given lot of bed rest to overcome the infection.

Q2. What is a disease? Classify disease based on duration and infection cause.

Ans. **Disease** can be defined as the state of human health which is not at ease i.e. not comfortable. During disease, the functioning or appearance of one or more systems of the body changes.

Classification:

(*a*) **Based on duration**

Acute diseases: Diseases that last for only short period of time. Example, headache, common cold etc.

Chronic diseases: Diseases that last for long time is called chronic disease Example, tuberculosis.

(*b*) **Based on cause:** Disease can be grouped as infectious/communicable disease and non-infectious or non-communicable disease.

Infectious diseases: These diseases are caused due to microbes and can spread from one person to another.

Non-infectious diseases: These type of diseases do not spread in the community, but remains internal. Example, cancer, genetic abnormalities.

Q3. What are the different ways used for the treatment and prevention of diseases?

Ans. **Principles of treatment for diseases are:**

(1) To reduce the effect of the diseases.

(2) To kill the cause of the disease *i.e.,* to kill the microbes like bacteria, fungi, protozoa.

Principles of prevention are:

(*a*) **General ways:** It is related to preventing exposure to the microbes. This can be done in following ways:

(*i*) **For avoiding air-borne infections**—Avoid visiting public place, cover your nose and mouth while sneezing or coughing

(*ii*) **For water-borne infection**—Drink safe, clean and boiled water.

(*iii*) **For vector-borne diseases**—Keep the surroundings clean, keep food and water covered and clean. Do not allow any water to stand as it becomes a breeding ground for mosquitoes.

(*iv*) **Self immunity**—It is self-defence mechanism in our system that can fight off and kill microbes that enter our body.

(*b*) **Specific ways**—By giving vaccines, childhood immunisation that is given to children for preventing infections and diseases.

Q4. State the mode of transmission for the following diseases:
Malaria, AIDS, jaundice, typhoid, cholera, Rabies, Tuberculosis, Diarrhoea, Hepatitis, Influenza.

Ans.

Acute disease	*Chronic disease*
1. It may last for few days.	1. It lasts for longer period.
2. It does not have major effect on body.	2. It affects the body drastically.

Ans.

Sl. No.	*Disease*	*Mode of transmission*
1.	Malaria	Mosquito bite (female Anopheles mosquito carries protozoa)
2.	AIDS	Infected blood, semen, mother's milk, from mother to foetus.
3.	Jaundice	Contaminated water.
4.	Typhoid	Contaminated food and water.
5.	Cholera	Contaminated food and water.
6.	Rabies	Bite of rabid animal.
7.	Tuberculosis	Cough and sneeze droplets.
8.	Diarrhoea	Contaminated food and water.
9.	Hepatitis	Contaminated food and water
10.	Influenza	Cough and sneeze droplets.

Q5. Name all the micro-organisms that causes infectious disease and name few diseases caused by each micro-organism.

Ans.

Infections Causing Micro-organism	***Disease***
Bacteria	Tuberculosis, typhoid, diarrhoea, cholera
Virus	Polio, AIDS, chickenpox
Protozoa	Malaria, amoebiasis, kala-azar, sleeping sickness
Fungi	Food poisoning, skin diseases

V. Value-Based Questions

Q1. AIDS is spreading globally at very fast rate, a group of class-IX students made a module on its prevention and posted it on social networking site.

(*a*) What is the cause of AIDS? (*b*) Give any two preventions for it.

(*c*) What value of these students is reflected in this act?

Ans. (*a*) HIV virus.

(*b*) Two preventive measures of AIDS are use of disposable injections, scanning of blood before transfusion for HIV.

(*c*) Students showed moral responsibility and general awareness.

Q2. There is a ban on sale of junk food items in school canteens. A student notices that in his school canteen cold drink, chips and cup noodles were sold. He reports this matter to his teachers and school office. Thereafter the sale of junk food in canteen was stopped and monitored.

(*a*) Why is balanced diet necessary for maintaining healthy body?

(*b*) Name two diseases caused due to junk food.

(*c*) What values of this student is reflected?

Ans. (*a*) Balanced diet provides all the nutrients to our body in appropriate amount and keeps our body healthy.

(*b*) Heart diseases and obesity.

(*c*) The student showed general awareness and responsible citizen.

Q3. Sudha's brother who is 5 years old had high fever for two days, doctor prescribes him antibiotics. Sudha hesitantly asks for the name of the disease his brother had and why was he advised to take antibiotics without any diagnosis?

(*a*) Is fever a disease?

(*b*) What is the role of antibiotics?

(*c*) What value of Sudha is reflected in the above act?

Ans. (*a*) Fever is not a disease it is a symptom.

(*b*) Antibiotics are medicines advised to be taken only when the immune system of a patient is unable to fight against the microbes.

(*c*) Sudha showed moral responsibility and general awareness.

Q4. Malaria was on the outbreak in a locality of a town. People thought that the bite of mosquitoes cause malaria and started killing mosquitoes. Anita told the masses to clean the breeding grounds of mosquitoes, to add oil on the water bodies and clean all the areas, where stagnant water was present.

(*a*) What is the cause of malaria?

(*b*) Give two ways to prevent it.

(*c*) What value of Anita is reflected in this act?

Ans. (*a*) Malaria is caused due to the protozoa named *Plasmodium*.

(*b*) Two ways to prevent malaria are—

(*i*) Clear all breeding grounds of mosquitoes *i.e.*, stagnant water.

(*ii*) Use mosquito repellents.

(*c*) Anita showed the values of social responsibility and self-awareness.

Q5. Latika was suffering with chickenpox and was advised to stay at home by her doctor. Latika's friend persuades her to go for class picnic alongwith her and have fun. But Latika refuses and stays at home.

(*a*) What is the cause of chickenpox?

(*b*) Give one precaution for it.

(*c*) What value of Latika is reflected in not going for picnic.

Ans. (*a*) Virus causes chickenpox.

(*b*) One precaution of avoiding spread of chickenpox is to stay away from public places when one is suffering from it. Take vaccination.

(*c*) Latika showed moral responsibility and self awareness.

TEST YOUR SKILLS

Q1. Name one disease that affects our lungs.

Q2. Name the vector and pathogen of malaria.

Q3. What are antibiotics?

Q4. Name two air-borne diseases.

Q5. Give the difference between acute disease and chronic disease.

Q6. Define vaccine and name two vaccines.

Q7. What is AIDS? How does a person get defected with HIV?

Q8. Name the organs affected due to the following diseases:

(*a*) Jaundice (*b*) Japanese encephalitis

Q9. Name all the micro-organisms that causes infectious disease and name atleast one disease caused due to each micro-organism.

Q10. What are the different ways used for the treatment and prevention of diseases?

Q11. Write a short note on malaria as a disease, its symptoms and control.

❑❑❑

14 Natural Resources

Syllabus

Natural resources, Water cycle, Carbon cycle, Nitrogen cycle.

Facts that Matter

- Life exists on the earth due to its ambient temperature, water, food and energy from the sun.
- **Lithosphere:** The outer crust of the earth is called the lithosphere.
- **Hydrosphere:** Sum of all water bodies is called hydrosphere.
- **Atmosphere:** Air that covers the earth is called atmosphere.
  Acts as a protective blanket around the earth. Maintains the temperature on the surface of earth. Winds are caused due to uneven heating of atmosphere, these winds maintains the pressure difference and causes cold and hot air, sea and land breeze, brings rain etc.
- **Biosphere:** The life-supporting zone of the earth where the atmosphere, hydrosphere and lithosphere interact and make life possible is called biosphere.
  It consists of biotic components–living things and abiotic components–non living things like air, water and soil.
- **Air:** It is a mixture of many gases like oxygen, nitrogen, carbon dioxide, water vapour and other gases.
- **Nitrogen** is used by plants for protein synthesis.
- **Oxygen** sustains life used for respiration and combustion.
- **Carbon dioxide** used by plants for preparing food by photosynthesis.
- **Water vapour:** provides moisture.
- **Rain:** The clouds formed due to the evaporation of water condense and precipitate as rain.
- **Water:** Various sources of water are available *i.e.,* surface water, underground water, snow, ice-bergs, water vapour in atmosphere.
  Use of Water
  — Water is used for transportation.
  — Sustain life
  — Used by plants and animals for life-processes. Water available for drinking should be conserved and used wisely.
- **Soil:** Soil is formed by a very slow process *i.e.,* by weathering of rocks. It consists of various nutrients for the growth of the plants. It is also a home of many microbes.
  Varieties of soil are:
  1. Sandy soil 2. Loamy soil 3. Clayey soil 4. Black soil
  5. Red soil 6. Alluvial soil 7. Laterite soil.
- **Temperature:** Temperature and light is also required for all biotic components.
- **Pollution:** Contamination of natural sources with unwanted substances.
  —**Air Pollution:** Air contaminated with smoke, fumes, dust, pollen grain, etc.

— **Water Pollution:** Water contaminated by sewage, industrial waste, excreta, chemicals, fertilizers, etc.

— **Soil Pollution:** Soil gets contaminated with fertilizers, pesticides, garbage, chemicals, etc.

- **Biogeochemical Cycles:** A constant interaction between biotic and abiotic components of the biosphere makes a system and these flow of components form a cycle called biogeo chemical cycle.
- **Water Cycle:** Water from various sources evaporates, condenses and again precipitates as rain, falls on the land, flows back in the sea and river. This is known as water cycle.

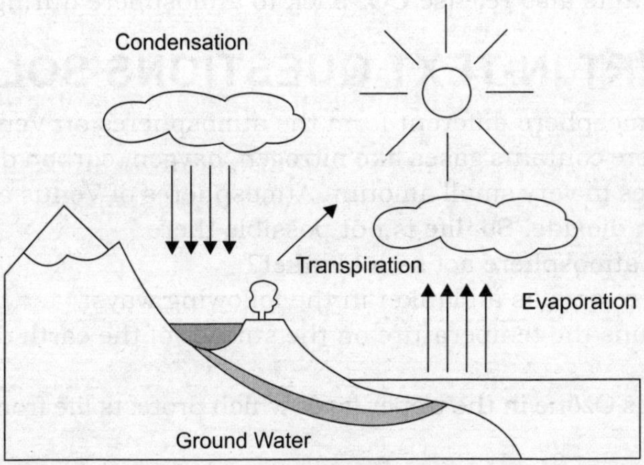

Water Cycle

- **Nitrogen Cycle:**

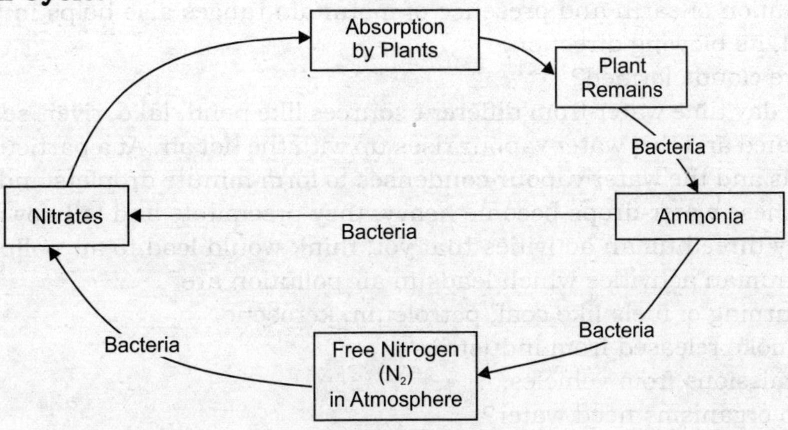

Nitrogen Cycle

Nitrogen from the atmosphere is fixed by the process of nitrification. Nitrification is done by nitrogen fixing bacteria e.g. *Rhizobium* present in soil, these compounds of nitrogen are absorbed by plants. The fixation is also done by atmosphere or industries. In atmosphere, during lightning, high temperatures and pressures created in air convert nitrogen into oxides of nitrogen, which dissolves in water forming nitric and nitrous acids and is then used by life forms.

Plants contain nitrogen in the form of proteins or other complex compounds. Plants are eaten by animals. When dead bacteria present in soil act on and convert plants and animals of various compounds of nitrogen into nitrates and nitrities. Another group of bacteria convert these nitrates and nitrites into free, elemental nitrogen, this process is called denitrification.

- **Carbon Cycle:** Carbon is present in the compound form in atmosphere *i.e.*, CO_2, carbonates in water which forms limestone.

  CO_2 is taken by plants during photosynthesis to form organic compounds like glucose, carbohydrates. These plants are further eaten by animals and decomposition gives CO_2 back to atmosphere. Plants and animals which get buried under the earth and does not decompose form coal and petroleum respectively.

  Animals and plants also release CO_2 back to atmosphere during respiration.

NCERT IN-TEXT QUESTIONS SOLVED

Q1. How is our atmosphere different form the atmospheres on Venus and Mars?

Ans. Our atmosphere contains gases like nitrogen, oxygen, carbon dioxide, water vapour and other gases in very small amount. Atmospheres of Venus and Mars have about 95% of carbon dioxide. So, life is not possible there.

Q2. How does the atmosphere act as a blanket?

Ans. The atmosphere acts as a blanket in the following ways:

(1) It maintains the temperature on the surface of the earth during day and night time.

(2) It contains Ozone in the upper layer which protects life from harmful ultraviolet radiation.

Q3. What causes winds?

Ans. The uneven heating of the atmosphere in different regions of the earth causes wind. The rotation of earth and presence of mountain ranges also helps in the formation of wind, its blowing direction.

Q4. How are clouds formed?

Ans. During day time water from different sources like pond, lake, river, sea, well etc get evaporated and this water vapour rises up with the hot air. At a particular height the air cools and the water vapour condenses to form minute droplets and form clouds. When these water-drops become heavy, they precipitate and fall down as rain.

Q5. List any three human activities that you think would lead to air pollution.

Ans. Three human activities which leads to air pollution are

(1) Burning of fuels like coal, petroleum, kerosene.

(2) Smoke released from industries

(3) Emissions from vehicles.

Q6. Why do organisms need water?

Ans. Organisms need water for the following activities:

(1) All cellular processes occur due to water.

(2) Transportation of substances in our body takes place by dissolving in water.

(3) Terrestrial animals require fresh water for transportation of minerals and for getting rid of waste from their body.

(4) Plants require water for photosynthesis.

Q7. What is the major source of fresh water in the city/town/village where you live?

Ans. The major sources of water are

(*a*) Water in the form of snow, ice-covered mountains.

(*b*) Underground water well.
(*c*) Surface water like in lakes, rivers, ponds.
(*d*) Rainfall.
(*e*) Stored rain water in tanks, dams.

Q8. Do you know of any activity which may be polluting this water source?

Ans. Yes, the water is polluted by (*a*) sewage (*b*) dumping waste in river (*c*) factory waste etc.

Q9. How is soil formed?

Ans. Factors that helps in the formation of soil and the process of formation are:

(1) **Sun:** The sun heats up rocks during the day so that they expand. At night these rocks cool down and contract, this causes cracks in the rocks.

(2) **Water:** Water during rainfall enter these cracks, if this water freezes, it exerts pressure on the cracks and the rocks break. When water flows, it wears the hard rock and carries small particles of rock down stream.

(3) **Wind:** Strong winds erode rocks down, which rub with each other and small particles are carried away by wind.

(4) **Living Organisms:** Like lichen grows on the surface of the rock, they release certain substances that causes the rock surface to powder down and form a thin layer of soil.

Q10. What is soil erosion?

Ans. The removal of top soil by air, wind, water is called soil erosion.

Q11. What are the methods of preventing or reducing soil erosion?

Ans. Methods to reduce soil erosion:

(1) Soil should have some vegetations like grass growing on it, so that it does not get carried away by rain water or wind.

(2) Afforestation or planting of trees, so that roots hold the soil and prevent soil erosion.

Q12. What are the different states in which water is found during the water cycle?

Ans. Various states in which water is found during the water cycle are

(1) Water in liquid state present in various sources- lakes, rivers, underground water.

(2) Water vapour–gaseous state, water evaporates from water bodies and due to transpiration by plants.

(3) Clouds–condensed water vapour is present in clouds.

(4) Water as rain or snowfall.

Q13. Name two biologically important compounds that contain both oxygen and nitrogen?

Ans. Two biologically important compounds that contain both oxygen and nitrogen are DNA, protein, carbohydrates.

Q14. List any three human activities which would lead to an increase in the carbon-dioxide content for air?

Ans. (1) Burning of fuels like coal, petrol, diesel.

(2) Breathing releases CO_2, exercises, which increases the breathing rate.

(3) Using air conditioner, releases CO_2 in air.

Q15. What is the greenhouse effect?

Ans. Gases like CO_2 and methane trap sun's radiation and don't allow it to go back. This causes warming of atmosphere. This effect is called greenhouse effect.

Q16. What are the two forms of oxygen found in the atmosphere?

Ans. Oxygen is present in free form like O_2 (oxygen molecule), Ozone (O_3) and combined form like oxides of metals and non-metals e.g. CO_2, NO_2, SO_2, H_2O.

NCERT TEXTUAL QUESTIONS SOLVED

Q1. Why is the atmosphere essential for life?

Ans. Atmosphere is very important for sustaining life because

(1) It contains various gases like O_2, CO_2, N_2 which are required for various life processes by plants and animals.

(2) CO_2 gas is used by plants to prepare food by the process called photosynthesis.

(3) Oxygen is required for burning, combustion and respiration.

(4) Ozone layer is acting as a protective layer, which avoids/prevents harmful U.V rays to enter the earth's atmosphere.

(5) CO_2 dissolved in water forms carbonates which is required by marine animals to form shells.

Q2. Why is water essential for life?

Ans. (1) About 70% weight of human being is due to water.

(2) All cellular processes takes place in water as medium.

(3) All reactions take place within our body and within the cells occur between substances that are dissolved in water.

(4) Transportation of substances from one form to another takes place due to water.

(5) Terrestrial life-forms require fresh water for the transportation of substances and also to get rid of high amounts of wastes.

Q3. How are living organisms dependent on the soil? Are organisms that live in water totally independent of soil as a resource?

Ans. All living organisms are directly or indirectly dependent on soil. Plants obtain water and minerals from the soil and prepare food for themselves and animals.

Other organisms that live in water are not totally independent of soil because the microbes growing on the soil in water are the primary producers in the soil which start the food chain and even other microbes that live in soil help in the decomposition of dead plants and animals in water to return the nutrients, elements back to the water.

Q4. You have seen weather reports on television and in newspapers. How do you think we are able to predict the weather?

Ans. Historical data on weather is stored in computers. These help in creating a model for weather pattern. Based on temperature humidity and wind speed of a given time frame, these data help meteorologists forecast the weather.

Q5. We know that many human activities lead to increasing levels of pollution of the air, water-bodies and soil. Do you think that isolating these activities to specific and limited areas would help in reducing pollutions?

Ans. If the human activities which leads to increasing level of air, water and soil pollution is spread in wider area then the pollutants will spread more, but yes, if it is limited and confined to a place then the soil and water pollution can be controlled to some extent and air pollution can also be minimised.

Q6. Write a note on how forests influence the quality of our air, soil and water resources.

Ans. Role of forest:

Air:

(*a*) It helps in purifying the air by absorbing pollutants.

(*b*) It adds oxygen to the air and takes carbon-dioxide gas during photosynthesis. Therefore greenhouse effect is controlled.

(*c*) Transpiration helps in the formation of clouds, maintains the temperature of surrounding area and gives cooling effect.

Soil:

(*a*) Plants in forest hold the soil thereby preventing soil erosion.

(*b*) It holds the soil which helps in increasing the underground water level.

(*c*) Adds nutrients to the soil as lot of vegetation present in forest gets decomposed.

Water: Forest helps in bringing rain and increasing the level of water in underground levels.

ADDITIONAL QUESTIONS SOLVED

I. Multiple Choice Questions

Choose the correct option:

1. The micro-organisms which helps in the formation of soil is
(*a*) bacteria (*b*) moss (*c*) lichen (*d*) (*b*) and (*c*)

2. Burning of fossil fuels add
(*a*) CO_2, SO_2, NO_2 gases in air (*b*) C, SO_2, N_2 gases in air
(*c*) CO, SO_3, NO_3 gases in air (*d*) CH_4, CO_2, NO_2 gases in air

3. Greenhouse gases is/are
(*a*) CO_2 (*b*) CH_4 (*c*) CFC (*d*) all of these

4. Nitrogen fixation can be done by
(*a*) industries (*b*) *Rhizobium* (*c*) lightning (*d*) all of the above

5. Atmosphere maintain the temperature on the surface of the earth because
(*a*) It contains water vapour in it
(*b*) It holds air, which is bad conductor of heat
(*c*) It reflects the heat rays (*d*) It absorbs the heat rays

6. Molecules of proteins contain
(*a*) carbon (*b*) nitrogen (*c*) oxygen (*d*) all of these

7. Life cannot sustain on Mars and Venus because major component in atmosphere is
(*a*) oxygen (*b*) carbon dioxide (*c*) nitrogen (*d*) ozone

8. On the moon the temperature ranges from – 190°C to 110°C. This is due to
(*a*) No water bodies present (*b*) Water bodies present
(*c*) No bio-geo-chemical cycle (*d*) No atmosphere

9. Depletion of ozone molecules in the stratosphere is due to
(*a*) chlorine compound (*b*) fluorine compound
(*c*) halogen compound (*d*) none of these

10. The life-supporting zone of earth is
(*a*) lithosphere (*b*) hydrosphere (*c*) atmosphere (*d*) biosphere

Ans. 1—(*c*), 2—(*a*), 3—(*d*), 4—(*d*), 5—(*b*), 6—(*d*), 7—(*b*), 8—(*d*), 9—(*c*), 10—(*d*).

II. Very Short Answer Type Questions

Q1. Name two greenhouse gases.

Ans. Methane and CO_2.

Q2. Name two chemicals that are depleting ozone layer?

Ans. Chlorofluorocarbons and compounds of chlorine and fluorine or halogen gases.

Q3. Name two gases released by fossil fuels and cause acid rain.

Ans. SO_2 and NO_2 which forms sulphurous acid and nitric acid.

Q4. Name types of soil?

Ans. Soil based on size of particles—sandy, clay.
Soil based on nutrient and nature—laterite soil, black soil, red soil, alluvial soil.

Q5. What is nitrification?

Ans. Conversion of free nitrogen present in atmosphere into compound of nitrogen i.e. nitrite and then nitrite to nitrates is called nitrification.

Q6. Name a nitrogen fixing bacteria.

Ans. *Rhizobium* bacteria.

Q7. State three methods by which free nitrogen can be converted into nitrates.

Ans. Biological fixation, lightning and industrial fixation.

Q8. Name four factors which lead to soil formation.

Ans. Sun, water, wind and living organisms.

Q9. What is humus?

Ans. The top most part of the soil which contains dead remains of plants and animal wastes like excreta, that adds nutrients to the soil.

Q10. What is soil erosion?

Ans. The topmost layer of soil that is loose, fertile and helps in the growth of vegetation gets carried away by wind and rain water is called soil erosion.

Q11. What is denitrification?

Ans. Conversion of nitrates into free nitrogen is called denitrification.

Q12. How does carbon exist in all life forms?

Ans. Carbon is present in all life forms in the form of proteins, carbohydrates, fats, nucleic acids and vitamins.

Q13. Name two biological important compounds of nitrogen.

Ans. Alkaloid, urea, DNA, RNA and proteins.

Q14. Name two elemental form of carbon.

Ans. Graphite and Diamond.

Q15. Name two combined forms of carbon.

Ans. CO_2, carbonate and hydrogen carbonate.

Q16. Give two biotic components of the biosphere.

Ans. Plants and animals.

Q17. Name the free living nitrogen fixing bacteria.

Ans. Rhizopus bacteria

Q18. What is the role of photosynthesis in carbon cycle?

Ans. Photosynthesis helps in the intake of carbon dioxide and thereby reduces the percentage of carbon dioxide in the environment.

Q19. Name a chemical responsible for the depletion of ozone layer in the atmosphere.

Ans. CFC also known as chloró-fluro carbon.

Q20. What would happen if ozone layer in the atmosphere disappears?

Ans. The harmful radiations of UV light from sun will enter the earth's biosphere and kill many living organisms.

III. Short Answer Type Questions

Q1. What is bad ozone and good ozone?

Ans. Ozone when present in the earth's surface is very poisonous gas hence called bad ozone. Ozone when present in stratosphere, is very protective in nature as it does not allow the harmful ultraviolet radiations to enter the earth's atmosphere.

Q2. State two harmful effects of ozone hole or ozone layer depletion.

Ans. (1) Ozone layer depletion allows harmful ultra violet radiations to reach the earth surface that may cause skin cancer, cataract etc.

(2) U.V. rays also ionize the cells, change the gene structure in animals and plants.

Q3. What make the quality and type of soils?

Ans. Type of soil is decided by the average size of particles found in it and the quality of soil is decided by the amount of humus and the microscopic organisms found in it.

Q4. What is top soil?

Ans. The top most layer of the soil that contains humus and living organisms in additions to the soil particles is called the top soil.

Q5. What is global warming?

Ans. An increase in the carbon dioxide content in the atmosphere would cause more heat to be trapped and retained by the atmosphere which leads to increase in the temperature of earth's surface and is called global warming.

Q6. What is biogeochemical cycle?

Ans. A constant interaction between the biotic and abiotic components of the biosphere makes it a dynamic but stable system. This flow of components is in cycle form and is called biogeochemical cycle.

Q7. How do fossil fuel cause air pollution?

Ans. The fossil fuels, like coal and petroleum, contain small amounts of nitrogen and sulphur. When these fuels are burnt, nitrogen and sulphur are also burnt and produce the oxides of nitrogen and sulphur, which pollutes air. The combustion of fossil fuels also increase the amount of suspended particles in air which leads to air pollution.

Q8. What is smog?

Ans. Presence of high levels of all the pollutants like unburnt carbon particles, smoke, oxides of nitrogen, sulphur, carbon etc. lowers the visibility in cold weather when water also condenses in air. This is known as smog.

Q9. What are the diseases caused by air pollution?

Ans. The pollutants present in air cause many breathing problems like asthma, it increases the allergy, cancer, heart diseases and respiratory problems.

Q10. How can lichen help in indicating the pollutants in air?

Ans. Lichens are very sensitive to the levels of contaminants like sulphur dioxide in the air. Lichens generally grow on the barks of the trees. The trees on the road-side do not show this lichen growth, if in any area the growth of lichens decreases or vanishes the air will be polluted.

Q11. Inspite of breathing out carbon-dioxide in a large amount and released by combustion, the atmosphere has a mere fraction of CO_2 only. Why?

Ans. The percentage of carbon-dioxide in our atmosphere is just a mere fraction because carbon-dioxide is fixed in two ways:

(*i*) Green plants convert carbon-dioxide into glucose in the presence of sunlight.

(*ii*) Many marine animals use carbonates dissolved in sea-water to make their shells.

Q12. Why is Earth a unique planet on which life exists?

Ans. Life exists only on Earth because many factors responsible for the life to sustain on it are

(1) Comfortable temperature (2) Atmosphere (3) Water

Q13. What is biosphere?

Ans. The life-supporting zone of the Earth where the atmosphere, the hydrosphere and the lithosphere interact and make life possible, is known as the biosphere.

Q14. How does atmosphere helps in climate control?

Ans. (*a*) The atmosphere keeps the average temperature of the Earth fairly steady during the day and night.

(*b*) It prevents the sudden increase in temperature during the day light hours.

(*c*) During night, it does not allow the heat to escape out into space.

Q15. How are winds caused and what decides the breeze to be gentle, strong wind or a terrible storm?

Ans. Heated air rises creating a low pressure area. This low pressure area is filled by air from cooler areas. The cycle creates flow of air causing wind.
The other factors that influence the wind flow is the rotation of the Earth and the presence of mountain ranges in the paths of the wind.

Q16. What is air pollution? How is it caused? Give its two harmful effects?

Ans. The contamination of air with unwanted gases, particles like dust etc which makes it unfit for inhalation is called air pollution.

Causes:

(*a*) Burning of fossil fuels release SO_2, CO_2 and NO_2 gases.
(*b*) Burning of fuels release unburnt carbon particles and smoke.
(*c*) Smoke from industries.

Harmful effects:

(*a*) It causes respiratory problems.
(*b*) It causes allergies, asthma, cancer and heart diseases.

Q17. What is water pollution? Give its causes and harmful effects?

Ans. Water when contaminated with unwanted substances, chemicals which makes it unfit for use and causes diseases is called water pollution.

Causes:

(1) Sewage from towns, cities is dumped in the water.
(2) Fertilizers, pesticides, insecticides get washed away by water from farm lands.
(3) Effluent from industries.

Harmful effects:

(1) Polluted water when consumed cause many diseases which are water-borne like cholera, typhoid, etc.
(2) Mercury in salts dumped by industries causes brain disorder—Minamata disease.
(3) Many life-forms which are susceptible to temperature changes die.

Q18. Explain the physical, chemical and biological factors which lead to the formation of soil.

Ans. Physical factors

Wind: When the wind blows it erodes big rocks which rub and hit with the other rocks breaking into smaller pieces which are further carried by wind to form soil.

Sun: The heat of sun causes expansion of the rocks due to heating during day time and it contracts at night. This expansion and contraction causes cracks in the rocks, which breaks slowly to form soil.

Water: When it rains the force of rain water erodes the rocks which breaks to form soil.

At times this water enters the cracks present in the rocks and freezes when temperature falls which breaks the rocks to forms soil.

Chemical factor

Water: Water when reacts with carbonates and phosphates present in the rocks, it form soluble compounds which make the rock hollow from inside.

Biological factor: Living organisms also help in the formation of soil. The lichen that grows on moist surface of rocks releases certain substances that causes the rock surface to powder down and form thin layer of soil. Other small plant like moss, are able to grow on this surface now.

The roots of big trees sometimes go into cracks in the rocks and when the tree grows bigger the crack in the rocks is forced bigger.

Q19. Explain water cycle with diagram.

Ans. 1. Water from different water bodies gets evaporated due to sun's heat. Plants also loose water during transpiration.

2. The hot air rises up with this water vapour.
3. Water vapour condenses to form big water droplets and clouds.
4. Rain water fall from clouds.
5. The rain water re-enters the water-bodies. This process in which water evaporates, falls on the land as rain and later flows back into the sea, rivers is known as water cycle.

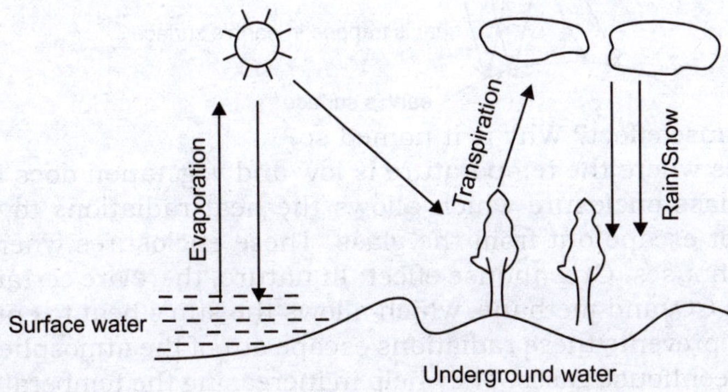

Water Cycle

Q20. What is acid rain? Give its harmful effects.

Ans. The gases released due to combustion of fossil fuels are SO_2, NO_2, CO_2, these gases remain suspended in the air. When it rains the rain water mixes with these gases to form sulphuric acid, nitrous acid, carbonic acid and comes down on the surface of the earth in the form of acid rain.

Harmful effects of acid-rain:
1. It corrodes statues, monuments of marble, building etc.
2. It makes the soil acidic.
3. It damages crops, plantations.

Q21. State in brief the role of photosynthesis and respiration in carbon cycle in nature.

Ans. Photosynthesis: Plants take in carbon-dioxide to prepare food and give out oxygen. Respiration: Plants/animals take in oxygen and give out carbon-dioxide. Both these processes are involved in balancing the carbon dioxide gas in nature.

Q22. What is the difference in fog and smog? Give two harmful effects of smog.

Ans. The water-vapour present in air when condenses due to very low temperature is called fog. The smoke released in the air due to burning of fuels mixes with the fog and forms smog. (smoke + fog = smog)

Harmful effects of smog:
1. It decreases the visibility and cause adverse effect on aeroplane landing, railways and road transport.

Q23. Explain the importance of ozone to mankind.

Ans. Ozone is a molecule of oxygen with three atoms of oxygen O_3.

It covers the Earth's atmosphere and is present in stratosphere. It does not allow the harmful ultra-violet radiation coming from the sun to enter our Earth.

These ultra-violet radiations cause ionizing effect, can cause cancer and genetic disorder in any life-forms.

The ozone is getting depleted at the south pole near Antartica. The ozone depletion is due to the halogens like CFC (chlorofluorocarbon) released in the air. Chlorine, fluorine reacts with the ozone and splits it, thereby leading to formation of a big hole called ozone hole.

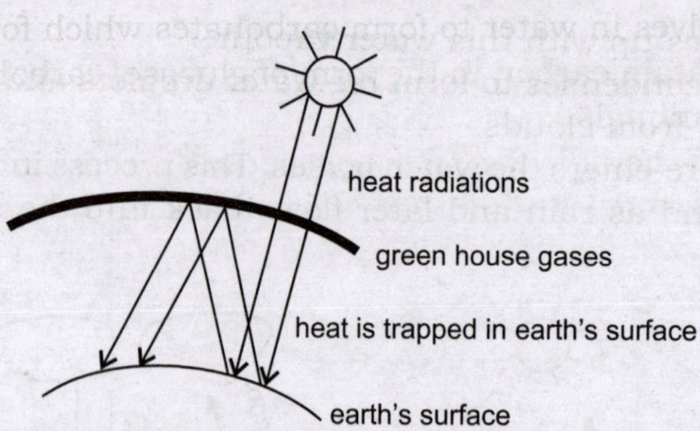

Q24. What is greenhouse effect? Why is it named so?

Ans. In cold countries where the temperature is low and vegetation does not grow, heat is trapped by glass enclosure which allows the heat radiations to enter into the glass but cannot escape out from the glass. These enclosures where plants grow are called greenhouses. Greenhouse effect: In nature, there are certain gases in the atmosphere like CO_2 and methane, which allows the sun's heat to enter the Earth's atmosphere but prevents these radiations escape out of the atmosphere these gases are known as greenhouse gases. They help in increasing the temperature and hence this effect is called as greenhouse effect.

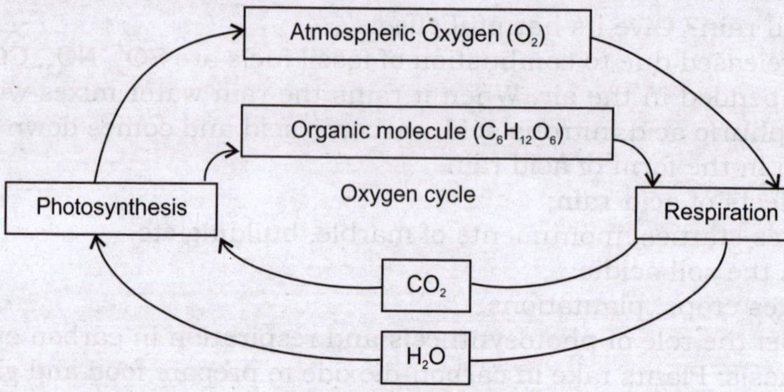

Green House Effect

Q25. How does oxygen occur in nature? Explain oxygen-cycle in nature.

Ans. Oxygen exist in two different forms in nature.

Free form: 21% as oxygen gas.

Combined form: In the form of oxides of metals and non-metals in the earth's crust, atmosphere and water. It is also present in carbohydrates, fats and proteins.

Oxygen cycle: Oxygen from the atmosphere is used up in three processes, namely combustion, respiration and in the formation of oxides of nitrogen.

Oxygen is returned to atmosphere by the process called photosynthesis.

Q26. (*a*) Give the existence of carbon.

(*b*) Explain the carbon-cycle in nature.

Ans. (*a*) Carbon exist in two different forms in nature-free and combined form.

Free form: It occurs in the elemental form as diamond and graphite.

Combined form: It occurs as carbon-dioxide, carbonates and hydrogen carbonate, salts in various minerals. It is also present in proteins, carbohydrates fats, nucleic acids and vitamins.

(*b*) **Carbon cycle:**

(i) Carbon-dioxide present in nature is used by plants during photosynthesis to form glucose and carbohydrate.

(ii) CO_2 dissolves in water to form carbonates which forms limestone.

(iii) Plants contain carbon in the form of glucose, carbohydrate which is eaten by other animals.

(iv) Plants and animals can form petroleum if submerged under the Earth and plants form coal. But if get decomposed after dying they release carbon back to the atmosphere by decomposition (dead) and respiration (living).

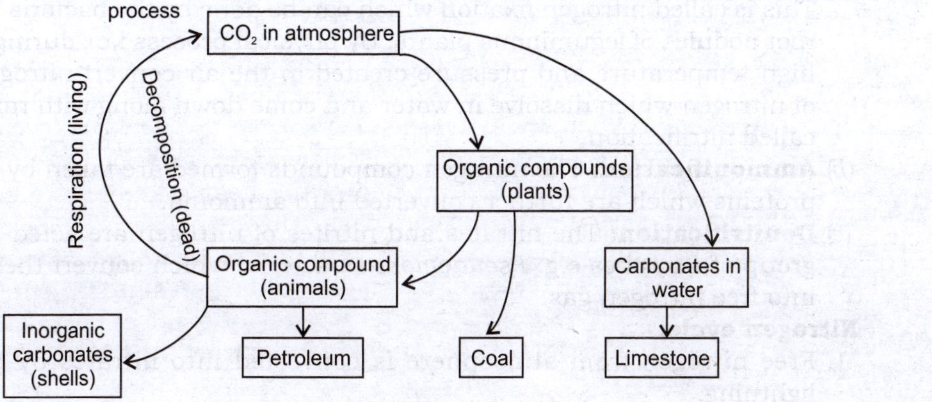

Carbon Cycle

Q27. Discuss the uses of nitrogen.

Ans. Nitrogen is crucially important component for all life. It is an important part of many cells and processes such as amino acids, proteins and even our DNA. It is also needed to make chlorophyll in plants, which is used in photosynthesis to make their food.

Q28. What is meant by water cycle? How are nutrients from the land made available to marine organisms by this cycle?

Ans. Water cycle is a continuous process by which water is circulated throughout the earth by the atmosphere through evaporation, condensation, precipitation, and the transpiration of plants and animals. The rain water washes the top soil with minerals and nutrients in it and the nutrients are carried away and discharged to the water bodies and this is how these are made available to aquatic bodies.

Q29. State the role of respiration in oxygen cycle.

Ans. Respiration uses oxygen and releases carbon dioxide. From the oxygen cycle the oxygen is utilized and all animals undergoing aerobic respiration uses the oxygen for breaking down of food to release energy.

Q30. How is carbon dioxide fixed in the atmosphere?

Ans. The carbon dioxide gas is released in the atmosphere by the activities like respiration and combustion. This gas is used by all the autotrophs containing chlorophyll for the photosynthesis and some amount of this gas also gets dissolved in the water and very little amount of gas gets dissolved in the rain water to form carbonic acid and is brought down from the atmosphere to land.

Q31. Name two biologically important compounds that contain both oxygen and nitrogen. What is the role of nitrogen fixing bacteria?

Ans. Nitrites and nitrate contains both oxygen and nitrogen. The plants need nitrogen for their growth and they cannot absorb the free nitrogen available in the air. Hence the nitrogen fixing bacteria available in the soil converts this nitrogen into compounds like nitrates which dissolves in water and is taken by plants through roots. Nitrogen fixing bacteria like rhizobium is commonly found in the root nodules of leguminous plants like peas and ground nuts.

IV. Long Answer Type Questions

Q1. Explain nitrogen-cycle in nature and define all the terms involved in it.

Ans. Terms involved in nitrogen-cycle are

(*a*) **Nitrogen fixation:** Plants cannot use free nitrogen present in the air. This nitrogen molecule is converted into nitrates and nitrites which can be taken up and used to make the required molecule.
This is called nitrogen fixation which can be done by the bacteria that live in the root nodules of leguminous plants. By physical process i.e., during lightning, the high temperature and pressure created in the air convert nitrogen into oxides of nitrogen which dissolve in water and come down along with rain. This is also called nitrification.

(*b*) **Ammonification:** The nitrogen compounds formed are taken by plants to form proteins which are further converted into ammonia.

(*c*) **Denitrification:** The nitrates and nitrites of nitrogen are acted upon by other group of microbes e.g. *Pseudomonas* bacteria, which convert these compounds into free nitrogen gas.

Nitrogen cycle:

1. Free nitrogen from atmosphere is converted into nitrates by bacteria or by lightning.
2. Nitrates mix with soil, is absorbed by the plants to make proteins.
3. The proteins in plants and animals are converted into amino acids and ammonia.
4. Ammonia is converted into nitrates and then these nitrates and nitrites present in soil is acted upon by other group of bacteria called denitrifying bacteria. This process is called denitrification, nitrates are converted into free nitrogen and is released back to the atmosphere.

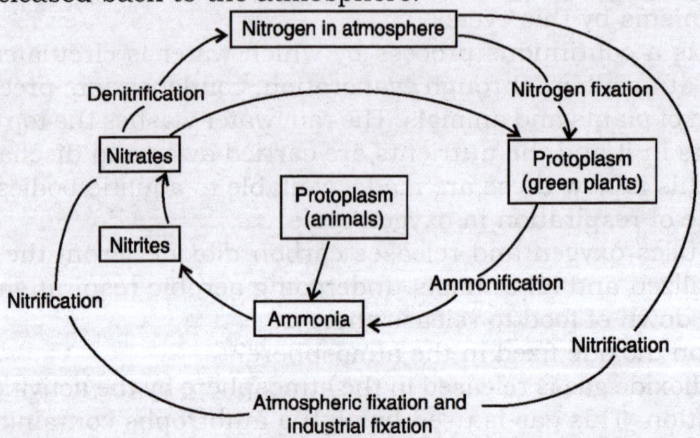

Nitrogen Cycle

Q2. Explain biosphere.

Ans. Biosphere: It consists of the sphere where life exist. Life can exist if all the spheres given below are present.

(*a*) **Lithosphere:** The crust of the earth also called as land which forms the upper layer of the earth *i.e.* soil. The soil provides all the nutrients for all organisms.

(*b*) **Hydrosphere:** Water available in various forms on the earth is called hydrosphere. Water exists in solid—(ice), liquid—(water and gaseous)—(water vapour). It is used by all life forms for their survival.
Water helps in the transportation of nutrients, dissolves nutrients and minerals in it, make it available for the plants.

(c) **Atmosphere:** Atmosphere consist of air with different gases present in it like O_2, N_2, CO_2 and other gases. Ozone present in stratosphere helps the life-forms from harmful ultraviolet radiations of the sunlight.

Various gases present in the atmosphere are useful for combustion (O_2), respiration (O_2), photosynthesis (CO_2) etc.

Q3. What is biogeochemical cycles? Explain the pathway of carbon cycle with the help of a labelled diagram.

Ans. A biogeochemical cycle is defined as the movement of elements through organisms and the environment. The geological activities add the elements present in them into the easily accessible environment from which all living (bio) organisms can use them. This happens due to the chemical processes, such as the formation of molecules.

The Carbon cycle is usually thought of as four major reservoirs of carbon; the atmosphere, the terrestrial biosphere (freshwater systems and non-living organic material, e.g. soil, carbon), the oceans (that has dissolved inorganic carbon, living and non-living marine biotic factors) and the sediments (which includes fossil fuels) interconnected by pathways of exchange.

The movement of carbon occur because of various chemical, physical, geological, and biological processes. The ocean contains the largest active pool of carbon near the surface of the Earth, but the deep ocean does not rapidly exchange with the atmosphere.

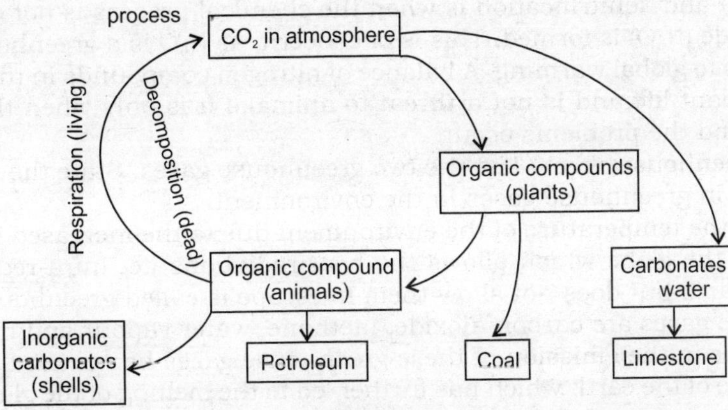

Carbon Cycle

Q4. What is nitrogen fixation? Mention two differences between nitrification and denitrification processes. Name the organisms involved in this processes.

Ans. As part of these life processes, nitrogen is transformed from one chemical form to another. The transformations that nitrogen undergoes as it moves between the atmosphere, the land and living things make up the nitrogen cycle.

Nitrogen in its gaseous form can't be used by most of the living organisms. It needs to be converted(or 'fixed')to a more usable form through a process called fixation. There are three ways by which nitrogen can be fixed to be useful for living things:

(i) **Biologically:** Nitrogen gas diffuses into the soil from the atmosphere, and species of bacteria convert this nitrogen to ammonium ions (NH_4^+), which can be used by plants. Legumes (such as rhizobium) are often grown by farmers because they have nodules on their roots that contain nitrogen-fixing bacteria.

(ii) **Through lightning:** Lightning converts atmospheric nitrogen into ammonia and nitrate (NO_3) that enter soil with rainfall.

(iii) **Industries:** In industries nitrogen gas is converted into ammonia (NH_3^-) and nitrogen-rich fertilizers to supplement the amount of nitrogen fixed naturally.

Nitrification: Nitrifying bacteria in the soil convert ammonia into nitrite (NO_2^-) and then into nitrate (NO_3^-). This process is called nitrification. Compounds such as nitrate, nitrite, ammonia and ammonium can be taken up from soils by plants and then used in the formation of plant and animal proteins. For examples:

- The bacteria that convert ammonia to nitrite—Nitrosomonas, Nitrosococcus, Nitrosospira.
- Bacteria that convert nitrite to nitrate—Nitrobacter, Nitrospina, Nitrococcus, Nitrospira.

Denitrification: Denitrification completes the nitrogen cycle by converting nitrate (NO_3^-) back to gaseous nitrogen (N_2). Denitrifying bacteria are the agents of this process. These bacteria use nitrate instead of oxygen when obtaining energy, releasing nitrogen gas to the atmosphere. For examples: Thiobacillus denitrificans, Micrococcus denitrificans, Paracoccus denitrificans, Pseudomonas.

Q5. Explain how nitrogen compounds adds to the environment and what are the impacts of it?

Ans. Increased nitrogen inputs (into the soil) has helped in the production of food which can feed more people. The agricultural practices are responsible for the nitrogen fixation on Earth through fertilizers and the cultivation of nitrogen-fixing crops. The nitrogen in excess can reach from soils into waterways. The nitrogen that collects in water contributes to eutrophication. The other problem that can occur during nitrification and denitrification is when the chemical process is not completed and nitrous oxide (N_2O) is formed. This is of concern, as N_2O is a greenhouse gas and it contributes to global warming. A balance of nitrogen compounds in the environment supports plant life and is not a threat to animals. It is only when the cycle is not balanced and the problems occur.

Q6. What is greenhouse effect? List the two greenhouse gases. State the ultimate effect of increase in greenhouse gases in the environment.

Ans. The rise in the temperature of the environment due to the increased layers of gases enveloping the globe which allows the heat radiations i.e. Infra-red radiations to enter the earth but does not allow them to escape is called greenhouse effect.
Greenhouse gases are carbon dioxide, methane, water vapour and nitrous oxide.
The increase in the emission of these greenhouse gases has caused the rise in the temperature of the earth which has further led to the melting of the glaciers resulting in rise of the sea level. It is predicted that in coming years the coral reefs will be destroyed and most of the coastal areas will be submerged under water.

V. Value-Based Questions

Q1. Simran saw a child sleeping in a car parked with closed doors and glass rolled up in the open area on a sunny day near the market. She immediately raised an alarm and with the help of police she got the window glass rolled down.

(*a*) Why was it not safe to keep the doors with window glass rolled-up for a child inside the car?

(*b*) Name two gases that can lead to above effect.

(*c*) What value of Simran is reflected in the above act?

Ans. (*a*) It was not safe for the child in the car with locked doors and windows rolled up, the sunlight would result in the greenhouse effect in the car. This would increase the temperature in the car and also result in the increase in CO_2 level which would lead to suffocation.

(*b*) Carbon-dioxide gas and methane gas can lead to greenhouse effect.

(*c*) Simran reflects the aware citizen value and responsible behaviour.

Q2. After doing a project on "Save water", Amit realised the problem of shortage of drinking water on Earth. Amit started regulating the misuse of water in his vicinity.

(*a*) What is the percentage of drinking water available on the Earth?

(*b*) Give any two practices that one should follow to save water.

(*c*) What value of Amit is reflected in this act?

Ans. (*a*) 1.7% of drinking water is available on the Earth.

(*b*) To save water

(*i*) Do not use shower to take bath everyday instead use bucket of water.

(*ii*) Avoid using washing machine for fewer clothes.

(*c*) Amit showed the value of responsible behaviour and participating citizen.

Q3. Few villages in Punjab were upset as canals that brought water to their village were full of chemical and froth in it. They could not use this water for farming. The Panchayat found that it was a chemical factory nearby that dumped the waste in canal. After lot of hue and cry the company stopped dumping the waste in canals.

(*a*) State two causes of water pollution.

(*b*) Name any two harmful effects of polluted water.

(*c*) State the value of both the factory man and the Panchayat reflected in this act.

Ans. (*a*) Two causes of water pollution are sewage and effluent from industries dumped in water.

(*b*) Two harmful effects of water pollution are:

(*i*) It may cause diseases like cholera, typhoid etc.

(*ii*) Many life-forms/water creatures die due to pollutants in water.

(*c*) Factory man showed irresponsible behaviour and Panchayat reflected the moral responsibility.

Q4. Rashi lived near an industrial area in Delhi. During winters she saw that the smoke had reduced the visibility in the area. Rashi requested the industries to fit in chimney in the precipitators so that it would not release smoke particulates in air.

(*a*) What is smog?

(*b*) Name two diseases caused due to air pollution.

(*c*) What value of Rashi is reflected in this act?

Ans. (*a*) When smoke is added to fog, smog is formed.

(*b*) Air pollution causes respiratory problems and allergies.

(*c*) Rashi showed the value of self-awareness, responsible behaviour.

TEST YOUR SKILLS

Q1. Name two greenhouse gases.

Q2. Name two chemicals that are depleting ozone layer.

Q3. What is soil erosion?

Q4. What is humus?

Q5. What is nitrification?

Q6. What is smog?

Q7. How does atmosphere help in climate control?

Q8. What is acid rain? Give its harmful effects.

Q9. Explain nitrogen cycle in nature.

Q10. What is the importance of ozone to mankind?

Q11. Explain the physical, chemical and biological factors which lead to the formation of soil.

15 Improvement in Food Resources

Syllabus

Plant and animal breeding and selection for quality improvement and management, Use of fertilizers, Manures, Protection from pests and diseases, Organic farming.

Facts that Matter

- Food supplies proteins, carbohydrates, fats, vitamins and minerals, all of which we require for body development, growth and health.
- Different crops require different climatic conditions, temperature and photoperiods for their growth and completion of their life cycle. Photoperiods are related to the duration of sunlight. Growth of plants and flowers are dependent on sunlight.
- **Successful crop production depends upon many factors such as:**
  (*i*) Understanding how crops grow and develop.
  (*ii*) Effect of various nutrients, climate, water on the growth of the plant.
  (*iii*) Modification and management of each factor for increasing the yield of the crop.
- The crops which are grown in rainy season (the kharif season, from June to October) are called as kharif crops.
  Example: Paddy, soyabean, pigeon pea, maize, cotton, green gram and black gram are kharif crops.
- The crops which are grown in winter season (the rabi season, from November to April) are called rabi crops.
  Example: Wheat, gram, peas, mustard and linseed are rabi crops.
- **Crop variety improvement:** It can be done either by hybridisation or by introducing a gene.
  (*i*) **Crop improvement by hybridisation:** Hybridisation refers to crossing between genetically dissimilar plants. This crossing may be intervarietal (between different varieties), interspecific (between two different species of the same genus) or intergeneric (between different genera).
  (*ii*) **Crop improvement by introducing a gene:** This provides the desired characteristics and results in genetically modified crops.
- Cultivation practices and crop yield are related to weather, soil quality and availability of water. Since weather conditions such as drought and flood situations are unpredictable, varieties that can be grown in diverse climatic conditions are useful.
- **The factors for which variety improvement is done are:**
  (*i*) **Higher yield:** To increase productivity of the crop per acre.
  (*ii*) **Improved quality:** The quality of crop products vary from crop to crop. *E.g.*, protein quality is important in pulses, oil quality in oilseeds and preserving quality in fruits and vegetables.
  (*iii*) **Biotic and abiotic resistance:** Biotic factors are the diseases, insects and nematodes while abiotic factors are the drought, salinity, water logging, heat, cold and frost which affect the crop productivity. Varieties resistant to these

factors (stresses) can be improved to increase crop production.

(*iv*) **Change in maturity duration:** Shorter maturity period of crop reduces the cost of crop production and makes the variety economical. Uniform maturity makes the harvesting process easy and reduces losses during harvesting.

(*v*) **Wider adaptability:** It allows the crops to be grown under different climatic conditions in different areas.

(*vi*) **Desirable agronomic characteristics:** It increases productivity, for example, tallness and profuse branching are desirable characters for fodder crops; while dwarfness is desired in cereals, so that less nutrients are consumed by these crops.

- **Plant nutrients:** Nutrients are supplied to plants by air, water and soil. There are sixteen nutrients which are essential for plants. Air supplies carbon and oxygen; hydrogen comes from water and soil supplies the other thirteen nutrients to plants. Amongst these thirteen nutrients, six are required in large quantities and are therefore called macro-nutrients. The other seven nutrients are used by plants in small quantities and are therefore called micro-nutrients.
- **Nutrients supplied by air, water and soil**

Source	Nutrients
Air	Carbon, Oxygen
Water	Hydrogen, Oxygen
Soil	(*i*) **Macro-nutrients:** Nitrogen, phosphorus, potassium, calcium, magnesium and sulphur. (*ii*) **Micro-nutrients:** Iron, manganese, boron, zinc, copper, molybdenum and chlorine.

- **Manure:** Manure contains large quantities of organic matter and also supplies small quantities of nutrients to the soil. Manure is prepared by the decomposition of animal excreta and plant waste. Manure helps in enriching soil with nutrients and organic matter and increasing soil fertility. On the basis of the kind of biological waste used to make manure, it can be classified into three types: (*i*) Compost (*ii*) Vermi-compost (*iii*) Green manure.

(*i*) **Compost:** It can be prepared by farm waste material such as livestock excreta (cow dung etc.), vegetables waste, animal refuse, domestic waste, sewage waste, straw, eradicated weeds, etc. These materials are decomposed in pits and this process of decomposition is also called composting. This compost is rich in organic matter and nutrients.

(*ii*) **Vermi-compost:** The compost which is made by the decomposition of plant and animal refuse with the help of redworm is called vermi-compost.

(*iii*) **Green manure:** Prior to the sowing of the crop seeds, some plants like sun hemp or guar are grown and then mulched by ploughing them into the soil. These green plants thus turn into green manure which helps in enriching the soil in nitrogen and phosphorus.

- **Fertilizers:** Fertilizers are commercially produced plant nutrients. Fertilizers supply nitrogen, phosphorus and potassium. They are used to ensure good vegetative growth (leaves, branches and flowers), giving rise to healthy plants. Fertilizers are an important factor in the higher yields of high-cost farming.
- **Organic farming:** It is a farming system with minimal or no use of chemicals as fertilizers, herbicides, pesticides, etc. and with a maximum input of organic manures, recycled farm-wastes (straw and livestock excreta), use of bio-agents such as culture

of blue-green algae in preparation of biofertilizers, neem leaves or turmeric specifically in grain storage as bio-pesticides with healthy cropping systems [mixed cropping inter-cropping and crop rotation]. These cropping systems are beneficial in insect, pest and weed control besides providing nutrients.

- **Irrigation:** Proper irrigation is very important for the success of crops. Ensuring that the crop gets water at the right stages during their growing season, can increase the expected yield of a crop. Different kinds of irrigation systems include wells, canals, rivers and tanks.
  - (*i*) **Wells:** These are of two types namely dug wells and tube wells. In a dug well, water is collected from water bearing strata. Tube wells can tap water from the deeper strata. From these wells, water is lifted by pumps for irrigation.
  - (*ii*) **River lift system:** In areas where canal flow is insufficient or irregular due to inadequate reservoir release, the lift system is more rational. Water is directly drawn from the rivers for supplementing irrigation in areas close to rivers.
  - (*iii*) **Tanks:** These are small storage reservoirs, which intercept and store the run-off of smaller catchment areas.
- **Cropping patterns:** It includes different ways of growing crops so as to get the maximum benefit. These different ways include the following:
  - (*i*) **Mixed cropping:** Mixed cropping is growing two or more crops simultaneously on the same piece of land, for example, wheat + gram, or wheat + mustard, or groundnut + sunflower. This reduces disease risk and gives some insurance against failure of one of the crops.
  - (*ii*) **Inter-cropping:** It involves growing two or more crops simultaneously on the same field in definite pattern. A few rows of one crop alternate with a few rows of a second crop, for example, soyabean + maize, or finger millet (bajra) + cowpea (lobia). The crops are selected such that their nutrient requirements are different. This ensures maximum utilisation of the nutrients supplied, and also prevents pests and diseases from spreading to all the plants belonging to one crop in a field. This way, both crops can give better returns.
  - (*iii*) **Crop rotation:** The growing of different crops on a piece of land in a pre-planned succession is known as crop rotation. Depending upon the duration, crop rotation is done for different crop combinations. The availability of moisture and irrigation facilities decide the choice of the crop to be cultivated after one harvest. If crop rotation is done properly then two or three crops can be grown in a year with good harvest.
- **The food requirements of dairy animals are of two types:** (*a*) maintenance requirement which is the food required to support the animals to live a healthy life, and (*b*) milk producing requirement, which is the type of food required during the lactation period.
- **Weeds:** Weeds are unwanted plants in the cultivated field, for example, *Xanthium* (gokhroo), *Parthenium* (gazar ghas) and *Cyperinus rotundus* (motha). They compete for food, space and light. Weeds take up nutrients and reduce the growth of the crop. Therefore, removal of weeds from cultivated fields during the early stages of crop growth is essential for a good harvest.
- **Methods of weed control:** The most effective method is the mechanical removal. Preventive methods such as proper seed bed preparation, timely sowing of crops, inter-cropping and crop-rotation also help in weed control.
- **Insect pests:** Generally insect pests attack the plants in three ways: (*i*) They cut the

root, stem and leaf, (*ii*) they suck the cell sap from various parts of the plant, and (*iii*) They bore into stem and fruits. They thus affect the health of the crop and reduce yields.

- **Preventive measures against pest include:**
  - (*i*) The use of disease resistant varieties.
  - (*ii*) Growing two or more crops simultaneously on the same field.
  - (*iii*) **Summer ploughing:** In this method, fields are ploughed deep in summers to destroy both pests as well as weeds.
- Animal husbandry is the scientific management of animal livestock. It includes various aspects such as feeding, breeding and disease control. Animal-based farming includes cattle, goat, sheep, poultry and fish farming.
- Milk producing females are called milch animals (dairy animals), while the one used for farm labour are called draught animals.
- **Animal feed includes:** (*a*) Roughage, which is largely, fibre and (*b*) Concentrates which are low in fibre and contain relatively high levels of protein and other nutrients.
- **The improved poultry breeds are developed for the following desirable traits:**
  - (*i*) Number and quality of chicks.
  - (*ii*) Dwarf broiler parent for commercial chick production.
  - (*iii*) Summer adaptation capacity.
  - (*iv*) Low maintenance requirements.
  - (*v*) Reduction in the size of the egg-laying bird with ability to utilise more fibrous cheaper diets formulated using agricultural by-products.
- **Production of poultry birds:** For good production of poultry birds, good management practices are important. These include maintenance of temperature and hygenic conditions in housing and poultry feed, as well as prevention and control of diseases and pests.

  The housing, nutritional and environmental requirements of broilers are somewhere different from those of egg layers. The ration (daily food requirement) for broilers is protein rich with adequate fat. The level of vitamins A and K is kept high in the poultry feeds.
- **Fish Production:** There are two ways of obtaining fish. One is from natural resources, which is called capture fishing. The other way is by fish farming, which is called culture fishery.
- **Popular marine fish varieties include:** Pomphret, mackerel, tuna, sardines and Bombay duck. Marine fish of high economic value includes mullets, bhetki pearl spots, prawns, mussels and oysters.
- As marine fish stocks get further depleted, the demand for more fish can only be met by culture fisheries, a practice called mariculture.
- **Fish resources are of two types:**
  - (*a*) **Fresh water resources** such as canals, ponds, reservoirs and rivers.
  - (*b*) **Brackish water resources** (where sea water and fresh water mix together) such as estuaries and lagoons.
- More extensive fish farming can be done in composite fish culture systems. Both local and imported fish species are used in such systems.

  In such a system, a combination of five or six species is used in a single fish pond. These species are selected so that they do not compete for food among them having different types of food habits. As a result, the food available in all parts of the pond is used.

NCERT IN-TEXT QUESTIONS SOLVED

Q1. What do we get from cereals, pulses, fruits and vegetables?

Ans. Cereals give carbohydrates which provide energy.

Pulses give proteins which build our body.

Vegetables and fruits provide vitamins and minerals.

Q2. How do biotic and abiotic factors affect crop production?

Ans. Factors responsible for loss of grains, during storage and production are:

(*a*) Biotic factors like rodents, pests, insects, etc.

(*b*) Abiotic factors like temperature, humidity, moisture, etc.

Combination of both biotic and abiotic factors causes :

(*i*) infestation of insects	(*ii*) weight loss
(*iii*) poor germination ability	(*iv*) degradation in quality
(*v*) discolouration	(*vi*) poor market price

Q3. What are the desirable agronomic characteristics for crop improvements?

Ans. Desirable agronomic characteristics for crop improvements are:

(*a*) Tallness and profuse branching are desirable characters for fodder crops.

(*b*) Dwarfness is desired in cereals, so that less nutrients are consumed by these crops.

Q4. *What are macro-nutrients and why are they called macro-nutrients?*

Ans. Macro-nutrients are the essential elements which are utilised by plants in large quantities. Many macro-nutrients are required by the plants for the following functions:

- As the constituent of protoplasm
- N, P, S are present in proteins
- Ca is present in cell wall
- Mg is important constituent of chlorophyll

Q5. How do plants get nutrients?

Ans. Plants get nutrients from air, water and soil. There are sixteen nutrients essential for the growth of plants. Carbon and Oxygen are supplied by air and hydrogen is supplied by water. The remaining thirteen nutrients are supplied by soil.

Q6. Compare the use of manure and fertilizers in maintaining soil fertility.

Ans. **Effects of using manures on soil quality:**

(*i*) The manures enrich the soil with nutrients.

(*ii*) They provide a lot of organic matter (humus) to the soil and thus restores water retention capacity of sandy soils and drainage in clayey soil.

(*iii*) The addition of manures reduces soil erosion.

(*iv*) They provide food for soil organisms, like soil friendly bacteria.

Effects of using fertilizers on soil quality:

(*i*) By the continuous use of fertilizers, the soil becomes powdery, dry and rate of soil erosion increases.

(*ii*) By the use of fertilizers, the organic matter decreases which further decreases the porosity of soil and the plant roots do not get oxygen properly.

(*iii*) The nature of soil changes to acidic or basic.

Q7. Which of the following conditions will give the most benefits? Why?

(*a*) Farmers use high-quality seeds, do not adopt irrigation or use fertilizers.

(*b*) Farmers use ordinary seeds, adopt irrigation and use fertilizer.

(*c*) Farmers use quality seeds, adopt irrigation, use fertilizer and use crop protection measures.

Ans. In this, (*c*) Farmers use quality seeds, adopt irrigation, use fertilizer and use crop protection measures.

Use of any quality seeds is not sufficient until they are properly irrigated, enriched with fertilizers and protected from biotic factors. Hence, option (*c*) will give the most benefits.

Q8. Why should preventive measures and biological control methods be preferred for protecting crops?

Ans. Diseases in plants are caused by pathogens. To get rid of pathogens, some preventive measures and biological control methods are used as they are simple, economic and minimise pollution without affecting the soil quality.

Q9. What factors may be responsible for losses of grains during storage?

Ans. The factors responsible for losses of grains during storage are:

(*i*) Abiotic factors like moisture (present in food grains), humidity (of air) and temperature.

(*ii*) Biotic factors like insects, rodents, birds, mites, bacteria and fungi.

Q10. Which method is commonly used for improving cattle breeds and why?

Ans. Cross breeding is a process in which indigenous varities of cattle are crossed by exotic breeds to get a breed which is high yielding. During cross breeding, the desired characters are taken into consideration. The offspring should be high yielding, should have early maturity and should be resistant to climatic conditions.

Q11. Discuss the implications of the following statement:

"It is interesting to note that poultry is India's most efficient converter of low fibre food stuff (which is unfit for human consumption) into highly nutritious animal protein food".

Ans. The basic aim of poultry farming is to raise domestic fowl for egg production and chicken meat. These poultry birds are not only the efficient converters of agricultural by-products, particularly cheaper fibrous wastes (which is unfit for human consumption but can be formulated into cheaper diets for poultry birds) into high quality meat and also help in providing egg, feathers and nutrient rich manure. For this reasons, it is said that, "poultry is India's most efficient converter of low fibre food stuff into highly nutritious animal protein food".

Q12. What management practices are common in dairy and poultry farming?

Ans.

1. **Shelter:** Dairy animals and poultry birds require proper shelter, *i.e.*, well designed dairy and hygienic shelter.
2. **Feeding:** To get good yield of food product, proper feed is provided to dairy animals and poultry birds.
3. **Caring for animal health:** Animal and birds must be protected from diseases caused by virus, bacteria or fungi.

Q13. What are the differences between broilers and layers and in their management?

Ans. The poultry bird groomed for obtaining meat is called broiler. The egg laying poultry bird is called layer.

The housing, nutritional and environmental requirements of broilers are somewhat different from those of egg layers.

The ration (daily food requirement) for broilers is protein rich with adequate fat. The level of vitamins A and K is kept high in the poultry feeds while layers require enough space and proper lightning. Layers require restricted feed with vitamins and minerals.

Q14. How are fish obtained?

Ans. There are two ways of obtaining fish. One is from natural resources, which is called capture fishing. The other way is by fish farming, which is called culture fishery.

Q15. What are the advantages of composite fish culture?

Ans. In composite fish culture, a combination of five or six fish species is used in a single fishpond. These species are selected so that they do not compete for food among them and are having different types of food habits. As a result, the food available in all the parts of the pond is used. For example, Catlas are surface feeders, Rohus feed in the middle-zone of the pond, Mrigals and Common Carps are bottom feeders and Grass Carps feed on the weeds, together these species can use all the food in the pond without competing with each other. This increases the fish yield from pond.

Q16. What are the desirable characters of bee varieties suitable for honey production?

Ans. (*i*) The variety of bee should be able to collect a large amount of honey.

(*ii*) The bees should stay in a given beehive for a longer period.

(*iii*) The bees should have capacity of breeding well.

(*iv*) The variety of bee should be disease resistant.

Q17. What is pasturage and how is it related to honey production?

Ans. The pasturage means the flowers available to the bees for nectar and pollen collection. In addition to adequate quantities of pasturage, the kind of flowers available will determine the taste of the honey.

NCERT TEXTUAL QUESTIONS SOLVED

Q1. Explain any one method of crop production which ensures high yield.

Ans. One method used for crop production which ensures high yield is **plant breeding**. It is the science involved in improving the varieties of crops by breeding plants. The plants from different areas/places is picked up with desired traits and then hybridisation or cross-breeding of these varieties is done to obtain a plant/crop of desired characteristic.

The high yielding crop variety shows the following characteristics:

High yield, early maturation, less water for irrigation, better quality seeds are produced, less fertilizers required, adapts itself to the environmental conditions.

Q2. Why are manure and fertilizers used in fields?

Ans. They are used to ensure good vegetative growth (leaves, branches and flowers), giving rise to healthy plants, that results in high crop production.

Q3. What are the advantages of inter-cropping and crop rotation?

Ans. **Advantages of using inter-cropping:**

(*i*) It helps to maintain soil fertility. (*ii*) It increases productivity per unit area.

(*iii*) Save labour and time.

(*iv*) Both crops can be easily harvested and processed separately.

Advantages of using crop rotation:

(*i*) It improves the soil fertility.

(*ii*) It avoids depletion of a particular nutrient from soil.

(*iii*) It minimise pest infestation and diseases.

(*iv*) It helps in weed control.

(*v*) It prevents change in the chemical nature of the soil.

Q4. What is genetic manipulation? How is it useful in agricultural practices?

Ans. Genetic manipulation is a process of incorporating desirable (genes) characters into crop varieties by hybridisation. Hybridisation involves crossing between genetically dissimilar plants. This is done for production of varieties with desirable characteristics like profuse branching in fodder crops, high yielding varieties in maize, wheat, etc.

Genetic manipulation is useful in developing varieties which shows:

- Increased yield
- Better quality
- Shorter and early maturity period
- Better adaptability to adverse environmental conditions
- Desirable characteristics

Q5. How do storage grain losses occur?

Ans. The factors responsible for loss of grains during storage are:

(*i*) Abiotic factors like moisture (present in foodgrains), humidity (of air) and temperature.

(*ii*) Biotic factors like insects, rodents, birds, mites and bacteria.

Q6. How do good animal husbandry practices benefit farmers?

Ans. Good animal husbandry practices are beneficial to the farmers in the following ways:

(*i*) Improvement of breeds of the domesticated animals.

(*ii*) Increasing the yield of foodstuffs such as milk, eggs and meat.

(*iii*) Proper management of domestic animals in terms of shelter, feeding, care and protection against diseases.

Which ultimately helps the farmers to improve their economic condition.

Q7. What are the benefits of cattle farming?

Ans. Cattle farming is beneficial in the following ways:

(*i*) Milk production is increased by high yielding animals.

(*ii*) Good quality of meat, fibre and skin can be obtained.

(*iii*) Good breed of draught animals can be obtained.

Q8. For increasing production, what is common in poultry, fisheries and bee-keeping?

Ans. Through cross breeding, the production of poultry, fisheries and bee-keeping can be increased.

Q9. How do you differentiate between capture fishing, mariculture, and aquaculture?

Ans. **Capture fishing:** It is the fishing in which fishes are captured from natural resources like pond, sea water and estuaries.

Mariculture: It is the culture of fish in marine water. Varieties like prawns, oysters, bhetki and mullets are cultured for fishing.

Aquaculture: It is done both in fresh water and in marine water.

ADDITIONAL QUESTIONS SOLVED

I. Multiple Choice Questions

Choose the correct option:

1. The use of fertilizers in farming is an example of
   (*a*) No cost production (*b*) Low cost production
   (*c*) High cost production (*d*) None of these
2. Nitrogen, phosphorus, potassium are examples of
   (*a*) micro-nutrients (*b*) macro-nutrients
   (*c*) fertilizer (*d*) both (*a*) and (*b*)
3. *Xanthium*, *Parthenium*, *Cyperinus* are the examples of
   (*a*) diseases (*b*) pesticides (*c*) weeds (*d*) pathogens
4. Mullets, bhetki, pearl spots, prawns, mussels are the example of
   (*a*) marine fishes (*b*) fresh-water fishes
   (*c*) finned fishes (*d*) shell fish
5. *Apis cerana indica* is commonly known as
   (*a*) Indian cow (*b*) Indian buffalo (*c*) Indian bee (*d*) None of these
6. The production and management of fish is called
   (*a*) pisciculture (*b*) apiculture (*c*) sericulture (*d*) aquaculture
7. Catla and Rohu are examples of
   (*a*) freshwater fish (*b*) marine water fish
   (*c*) both (*a*) and (*b*) (*d*) none of these
8. Pasturage is related to
   (*a*) cattle (*b*) fishery (*c*) apiculture (*d*) poultry
9. Growing two or more crops in definite patterns is known as
   (*a*) crop rotation (*b*) inter-cropping (*c*) mixed cropping (*d*) organic cropping
10. Leghorn and Aseel are related to
    (*a*) apiculture (*b*) dairy farming (*c*) pisciculture (*d*) poultry

Ans. 1—(*c*), 2—(*b*), 3—(*c*), 4—(*a*), 5—(*c*), 6—(*a*), 7—(*a*), 8—(*c*), 9—(*b*), 10—(*d*).

II. Very Short Answer Type Questions

Q1. Name any two fodder crops.

Ans. Berseem, oats or sudan grass are raised as food for the livestock, called fodder crops.

Q2. What do you understand by photoperiod of sunlight?

Ans. Photoperiod are related to the duration of sunlight required for plant growth.

Q3. Name two kharif crops.

Ans. Paddy and soyabean.

Q4. Name two rabi crops.

Ans. Wheat and gram.

Q5. Define hybridisation.

Ans. Hybridisation refers to crossing between genetically dissimilar plants, to obtain, better variety of crops.

Q6. What are genetically modified crops?

Ans. By introducing a gene with required characters into a crop for its improvement is called genetically modified crop.

Q7. "Shorter the duration of the crop from sowing to harvesting, the more economical is the variety". Give reason for this.

Ans. Due to short duration of crop growth, farmers can grow more crops in a year, and reduce the cost of crop production.

Q8. Name different types of crop production practices involved in India.
Ans. They are (*a*) no cost production, (*b*) low cost production and (c) high cost production.
Q9. Who provides nutrients to plants?
Ans. Nutrients to plants are provided by air, water and soil.
Q10. What are macro-nutrients?
Ans. The nutrients required by plants in larger quantity is called macro-nutrients. They are nitrogen, phosphorus, potassium, calcium, magnesium and sulphur.
Q11. Name the nutrients that plant obtain from air and water.
Ans. Air — Carbon and oxygen
Water — Hydrogen and oxygen
Q12. State the difference between compost and vermi-compost.
Ans. The **compost** is obtained by decomposition of organic waste like animal excreta, plant waste etc. naturally due to decomposition by bacteria.
Vermi-compost: To hasten the process of decomposition redworms are added to this organic matter to obtain compost.
Q13. Name any two weeds.
Ans. *Parthenium* and *Xanthium*.
Q14. What causes disease in plants?
Ans. It is caused by pathogens such as bacteria, fungi and viruses.
Q15. Name two Indian cattle.
Ans. *Bos indicus* – cows
Bos bubalis – buffaloes
Q16. Name two exotic breeds of cattle.
Ans. Jersey and Brown Swiss
Q17. Name two variety of food required for milch animals.
Ans. (*a*) Maintenance requirement – food required to keep animal healthy
(*b*) Milk producing requirement – food required for increased lactation
Animal food includes roughage and concentrate also.
Q18. State the meaning of capture fishing and culture fishing.
Ans. **Capture fishing:** It is done from natural resources.
Culture fishing: It is done by fish farming.
Q19. Name four marine fish varieties.
Ans. Pomphret, mackerel, tuna and sardines.
Q20. What is apiculture?
Ans. Keeping bee for obtaining honey commercially is called apiculture.
Q21. Name the products obtained from apiculture.
Ans. Honey and wax both are obtained from apiculture.
Q22. Explain why organisms need food?
Ans. All living organisms need food to sustain and maintain their life processes.
Q23. What are the contents provided by food?
Ans. Food is the source of energy for all living non-producers. It has contents like carbohydrates, fats and proteins.
Q24. Do you know what are the major sources of food?
Ans. The major sources of food are food grains, pulses, vegetables, fruits and other animal products.
Q25. Name the organism used in the preparation of vermicomposting.
Ans. The red worms are used for vermicomposting.
Q26. Name the chemicals required for the growth of plants.
Ans. Plants need chemicals like nitrogen, phosphorus and potassium.

Q27. What is the role of fertilizers in crop production?

Ans. The fertilizers are important chemicals which are used as supplements for the plants to fulfill the requirements for proper growth and production of food grains and pulses.

Q28. It is advised to use the fertilizers in limited amount. Why?

Ans. The extra use of fertilizers are not absorbed by the plants and remain in the soil, which later flow with the rain water and thereby causes soil and water pollution.

III. Short Answer Type Questions

Q1. What are the major group of activities involved for improving of crop yields?

Ans. (*a*) Crop variety improvement

(*b*) Crop production improvement

(*c*) Crop protection improvement

Q2. What are the different ways/methods of hybridisation?

Ans. Hybridisation can be

(*a*) Intervarietal – between different varieties of crops

(*b*) Interspecific – between two species of same genus

(*c*) Intergeneric – between two different genera

Q3. What are the main characters required in a crop during its improvement practices?

Ans. The useful characters that are required in a crop during its improvement:

(*a*) Disease resistance (*b*) Response to fertilizer

(*c*) Product quality and (*d*) High yield

Q4. State the difference between macro-nutrients and micro-nutrients.

Ans.

Macro-nutrients	***Micro-nutrients***
1. These are required by crops in larger quantity.	1. These are required by crops in very small quantity.
2. ***Six*** macro-nutrients are: Nitrogen, phosphorus, potassium, calcium, magnesium and sulphur.	2. **Seven** micro-nutrients are : Iron, manganese, boron, zinc, copper, molybdenum and chlorine.

Q5. How do deficiency of nutrients affect the crop?

Ans. Deficiency of any nutrient affects physiological processes in plants including reproduction, growth and susceptibility to diseases.

Q6. State the difference between manure and fertilizer.

Ans.

Manure	***Fertilizer***
1. It consists of organic matter.	1. It consists of inorganic matter.
2. Prepared from animal excreta and plant waste.	2. It is prepared commercially from chemicals.
3. Its use causes no pollution.	3. It causes pollution in soil and water.

Q7. What are the harmful effects of fertilizer?

Ans. It causes soil and water pollution. Continuous use can also destroy soil fertility.

Q8. What is organic farming?

Ans. It is the farming in which no chemical fertilizers, pesticides or herbicides are used. But uses all organic matter for its growth like manure, neem leaves as pesticides and for grain storage.

Q9. State the preventive and control measures used before grains are stored.

Ans. (*a*) Cleaning of the grains

(*b*) Proper drying of the produce in sunlight, there should be no moisture.

(*c*) Fumigation of produce using chemicals that kills pest.

Q10. Name few varieties of bees used for commercial honey production.

Ans. *Apis cerana indica* – Indian bee

A. *dorsata* – rock bee (local varieties)

A. *florae* – the little bee

A. *mellifera* – Italian bee variety

Q11. What decide the quantity and quality of honey production in apiary?

Ans. **For quality of honey:** The pasturage, *i.e.,* the kind of flowers available to the bees for nectar and pollen collection will determine the taste of the honey.

For quantity of honey: Variety of bee used for the collection of honey. For example, A. *mellifera* is used to increase yield of honey.

Q12. How are crops useful to us? What do they provide?

Ans. Crops provide us food for our daily body nutrient. Carbohydrate for energy requirement – Cereals such as wheat, rice, maize.

Protein for body building — Pulses like gram, lentil

Fats for energy — Oil seed like mustard, sunflower

Vitamins and minerals — From vegetables, spices and fruits

Fodder crops — For livestocks

Q13. What are the factors for which variety improvement of crop is done?

Ans. (*a*) **Higher yield:** It increases production of crop.

(*b*) **Biotic and abiotic resistance:** Crop should be resistant to biotic factors like diseases, insects, pests and abiotic factor like drought, salinity, heat, cold, frost and water logging.

(*c*) **Change in maturity duration:** Short-duration maturity allows farmer to grow more crops in a year and reduces the cost of crop production.

(*d*) **Wider adaptability:** Crop should be able to adapt to changing environmental conditions.

(*e*) **Desirable agronomic characteristics:** The tallness and dwarfness of crop. Dwarfness is required for cereals, so that less nutrients are consumed.

Q14. Name the sources and the nutrients supplied by them to the plants.

Ans.

Source	**Nutrients**
Air	Carbon, oxygen
Water	Hydrogen, oxygen
Soil	**Macro-nutrients** (six)
	Nitrogen, phosphorus, potassium, calcium, magnesium, sulphur
	Micro-nutrients (seven)
	Iron, manganese, boron, zinc, copper, molybdenum, chlorine

Q15. What are manures? Give its classification.

Ans. Manures contain large quantities of organic matter and supplies small quantities of nutrients to the soil. It is prepared naturally by the decomposition of animal waste, excreta and plant waste.

- It helps in the soil enrichment with nutrients.
- It helps in improving the soil structure.
- It helps in increasing the water holding capacity in sandy soils.
- In clayey soils it helps in the water drainage and prevent water logging.

Manure is classified based on the kind of biological material used to make it as: (*i*) Compost (*ii*) Vermi-compost (*iii*) Green manure

(i) **Compost:** The farm waste and livestock excreta, along with vegetable waste, sewage waste, weeds, straws etc. are allowed to decompose in a pit is called compost. The compost is rich in nutrients.

(ii) **Vermi-compost:** When the above given matter is allowed to decompose in the pit along with some earthworms, the decomposition speeds up and is called vermi-composting.

(iii) **Green manure:** Some plants like sun-hemp or guar are grown and then mulched by ploughing them into the soil. This is done before the sowing of crop seeds into the field.

These green plants present in the soil acts as green manure which enriches the soil in nitrogen and phosphorus.

Q16. What are fertilizers? Excess use of fertilizers is not advisable, explain?

Ans. Fertilizers are obtained artificially on commercial basis. It is a chemical which contains the nutrients required for the crop to grow. Fertilizers supply various nutrients as they are nutrient specific e.g.–urea provides nitrogen. Mixed fertilizer provides any two mixture of nutrients. They are expensive but their use yield large production hence are a factor of **high cost farming**.

Excessive use of fertilizers are not advisable as:

(a) It leads to soil and water pollution.

(b) It can destroy the fertility of soil. As the soil is not replenished, micro-organisms in the soil are harmed by fertilizers.

Q17. What are the different patterns of cropping?

Or

What are the different cropping systems?

Ans. Different ways/patterns/systems of growing crops are:

(a) Mixed cropping (b) Inter-cropping (c) Crop rotation.

Mixed cropping: It is a method in which two or more crops grow simultaneously on the same piece of land.

Example, Wheat + grain, wheat + mustard or groundnut + sunflower.

This helps in the reduction of risk factor and provides insurance against failure of one of the crops.

Inter-cropping: It is a method of growing two or more crops simultaneously on the same field in a definite patterns. A few row of one crop alternate with a few rows of second crop.

Example, soyabean + maize or bajra + lobia

Crop rotation: The growing of different crops on a piece of land in a pre-planned succession is known as crop rotation.

The availability of moisture and irrigation facility decides the choice of crop to be cultivated after one harvest.

Q18. How does insect pests attack the plant and affect it?

Ans. Insect pests attack the plants in three ways:

(i) They cut the root, stem and leaf.

(ii) They suck the cell sap from various parts of the plant.

(iii) They bore into stem and fruits.

This way they affect the health of the crop and reduces yield.

Q19. Give different methods of weed control.

Ans. Weeds can be controlled by different methods:

(a) **Weedicides:** These are the chemicals sprayed on the weeds to kill them. Excessive use is poisonous and causes environmental pollution.

(*b*) **Mechanical removal:** In this method weeds are uprooted by removing manually or by machines.

(*c*) **Preventive methods:** Proper seed bed preparation, timely sowing of crops, intercropping and crop rotation helps in weed control.

Q20. What are the new variety/traits obtained by cross breeding of Indian and exotic breeds of poultry?

Ans. The new variety/traits obtained by cross breeding of Indian and exotic breeds of poultry are:

(*i*) Number and quality of chicks
(*ii*) Dwarf broiler parent for commercial chick production
(*iii*) Summer adaptation capacity/tolerance to high temperature
(*iv*) Low maintenance requirements
(*v*) Reduction in the size of the egg-laying bird with ability to utilise more fibrous and cheaper diet, formulated using agricultural by-products

Q21. *State the difference between egg-layers and broiler.*

Ans.

Egg-layers	*Broiler*
1. They are fed on protein-rich feed.	1. They are fed on protein and vitamin-rich supplementary feed for good growth rate.
2. Used for laying eggs.	2. Used for meat purposes. Lot of protein included in the diet.

Q22. What are the different types of fisheries?

Ans. The capture fishing, culture fishing, mariculture and aquaculture.

Q23. What is 'apiculture'? Name a few products obtained from apiculture.

Ans. The rearing of honey bees is called apiculture. The products obtained from apiculture are honey and wax.

Q24. What are weeds and fertilizers?

Ans. Weeds are unwanted plants that grow in the competition of crops and compete for minerals, water and sunlight with the crops.

Fertilizers: The chemicals which are used to add minerals in the water /soil for the plants to uptake for better and fast growth is called fertilizer.

Q25. How is excess use of fertilizers affecting the environment?

Ans. The excess use of fertilizers affects the environment by causing soil and water pollution, It also causes eutrophication leading to the death of many marine animals.

Q26. What are the different ways of hybridization used for food development?

Ans. The hybridization of plants, for crops, vegetables, fruits to increase the yield and size. The hybridization of cattle for producing the breed that could give more milk and/ or meat can help in the growth of food.

Q27. What do you understand by organic farming?

Ans. The farming which includes only the biomass, organic matter obtained from the living organisms waste like crop waste and animal waste to enrich the soil is called organic farming. This does not include the chemical fertilizers which are produced in the labs.

Q28. Define one method of crop production ensuring high yield.

Ans. The rotation of crop with the organic manure will certainly grow much richer crop without affecting the health and the nature of the soil in the long run.

Q29. Give points of difference between egg producing chicken and broiler producing chicken.

Ans. Egg-layers	Broiler
1. They are fed on protein-rich feed.	1. They are fed on protein and vitamin-rich supplementary feed for good growth rate.
2. Used for laying eggs.	2. Used for meat purposes. Lot of protein included in the diet.

IV. Long Answer Type Questions

Q1. What are the various methods of irrigation in India?

Ans. Most of agriculture in India is rain-fed, several different kinds of irrigation system are adopted to supply water to agricultural lands. The resources are–wells, canals, rivers and tanks.

- **Wells:** Dug wells and tube wells. In dug wells water is collected from water—bearing strata.
- **Tubewells:** Can tap water from deeper strata.
- **Canals:** Most extensive irrigation system. Canals receive water from reservoirs or rivers. The main canal is divided into branch canals having further distributaries to irrigate fields.
- **River lift system:** Water is directly drawn from the river for supplementing irrigation in areas close to rivers.
- **Tanks:** These are small storage reservoirs, which intercept and store the run-off of smaller catchment areas.

Q2. Large amount of food grains get spoiled every year in India due to improper storage of food grains. How can this be avoided?

Ans. Food grains get spoiled by insects, fungi, rodents, bacteria, moisture, temperature in the place of storage.

Storage losses can be minimised by following preventive and control measures.

(*i*) The seeds/grains that are to be stored should be dry, with no moisture in it.
(*ii*) The grains should be cleaned.
(*iii*) The grains should be fumigated using chemicals that kills pest.
(*iv*) The storage houses should be water proof.
(*v*) The grains should be stored in sealed gunny bags or metal containers.
(*vi*) The bags should be stacked in order *i.e.* in pile for proper fumigation, and should be kept few centimetres away from the wall.
(*vii*) The ventilators if any should be closed tightly, to avoid birds visiting the storage house and destroying the grains.
(*viii*) The walls and the floor should be water-proof with no holes in it, to avoid rodents, pests.

Q3. Explain different types of fisheries.

Ans. The different types of fisheries are marine fisheries, inland fisheries, capture fishing, mariculture and aquaculture.

- **Marine fisheries:** Marine fishes are caught using fishing nets. Large schools of fishes is located by satellites. Some are farmed in sea water.
- **Mariculture:** Marine fishes are cultured in seawater this culture of fisheries is called mariculture.
- **Inland fisheries:** The fisheries done in fresh water resources like canals, ponds, reservoirs and rivers is called inland fisheries.
- **Capture fishing:** It is done in sea-water, estuaries and lagoons.
- **Aquaculture:** Culture of fish done in different water bodies is called aquaculture.

Q4. What are the practices used for dairy industry?

Ans. The practices required for raising dairy animals to get the optimum yield are: (*i*) Shelter, (*ii*) feeding, (*iii*) rearing of animals, (*iv*) breeding.

(*i*) **Shelter:** The shelter should be clean, spacious and airy.

(*ii*) **Feeding:** Proper food is essential for dairy animals, two types of food are roughage and concentrates. Proper feed at proper time is required for dairy animals.

(*iii*) **Rearing of animals:** Providing them proper health care and protection from pathogens, diseases and proper vaccination.

(*iv*) **Breeding:** The crossing of different variety of milch animals to obtain a breed that can produce more yield of milk.

V. Value-Based Questions

Q1. A group of Eco Club students made a compost pit in the school, they collected all bio-degradable waste from the school canteen and used it to prepare the compost.

(*a*) Name two waste that can be used for the compost and two wastes obtained from canteen which cannot be used for the compost making?

(*b*) What is the other important component required for making the compost?

(*c*) What values of Eco Club students are reflected in this act?

Ans. (*a*) Two waste used for compost are vegetable peels and fruit peels. Two waste material that cannot be used as compost are polythene bags and plastic items.

(*b*) Bacteria and fungi present in soil are the other important component for making compost.

(*c*) Eco Club students reflect the value of group work, responsible citizens.

Q2. Surjeet read an article in the newspaper that prolonged and excess use of pesticides and fertilizers leads to cancer in human beings. He also saw the increased number of cancer patients in his town. He started educating the farmers in his town to minimize or stop the use of chemicals in farming and adopt the organic farming.

(*a*) What is the most common pesticide used in our country?

(*b*) Give one difference in organic farming and chemical farming.

(*c*) What value of Surjeet is seen in the above act?

Ans. (*a*) The common pesticide is DDT.

(*b*) **Organic farming:** It is a farming system with minimal or no use of chemicals as fertilizers, herbicides, pesticides etc.

Chemical farming: Generally, chemicals are used as fertilizers, herbicides, pesticides etc. to increase crop yield.

(*c*) Surjeet showed the value of responsible person, leadership quality, initiative taker and a concerned citizen

Q3. Large number of Bhetki fish died and got crushed in the turbines of hydroelectric power stations while they migrated from river to sea. The environmentalist gave power plant the solution to this problem. Now all Bhetki fish is removed with the help of special technique and hence do not enter the turbines to crush and die.

(*a*) What is pisciculture?

(*b*) Suggest two different varieties of fish.

(*c*) What value of environmentalist is reflected in the above case?

Ans. (*a*) The rearing of fish on large scale is called pisciculture.

(*b*) Two varieties of fish are bony and cartilaginous.

(*c*) Environmentalist showed the value of concerned and caring individuals.

Q4. A group of gardening club students prepared a kitchen garden in the school campus and did organic farming to grow the vegetables. Then the students presented their group work in the assembly to spread the awareness and make students understand the importance of organic products.

(*a*) What is horticulture?

(*b*) What is green manure?

(*c*) State the values of gardening club students.

Ans. (*a*) Production of vegetables and fruits commercially is called horticulture.

(*b*) The green plants like guar or sun hemp are turned into the soil which enriches the soil with nitrogen and phosphorus and is called green manure.

(*c*) Values of gardening club students are aware individuals and responsible behaviour.

TEST YOUR SKILLS

Q1. Name two weeds.

Q2. Define hybridisation.

Q3. What are macro-nutrients?

Q4. What is apiculture?

Q5. What is "green manure"?

Q6. How do good animal husbandry practices benefit farmers?

Q7. What decides the quantity and quality of honey production in apiculture?

Q8. What are the new variety traits obtained by cross breeding of Indian and exotic breeds of poultry?

Q9. Explain different types of fisheries.

Q10. State the difference between egg producing chicken and broiler producing chicken. Name one exotic breed and one indigenous breed of chicken.

Q11. Large amount of food grains get spoiled every year in India due to improper storage of food grain. How can this be avoided?

❑❑❑